Muhammad Ali: By the Numbers

Bob Canobbio & Lee Groves

ISBN 978-0-692-97979-2
CompuBox, Inc –Manorville, NY
Library of Congress Card Control Number (Pending)
Muhammad Ali: By the Numbers
Authors: Canobbio, Bob., Groves, Lee.
Available Formats:
eBook | Paperback distribution

Publisher: New Book Authors | *http://Newbookauthors.com*

Table of Contents

ABOUT THE AUTHORS

Bob Canobbio is the co-founder of CompuBox Inc. and has served as the company's owner and president since September 2002. Before that he worked as a researcher for HBO and Sports Illustrated and worked as a boxing editor at Sports Information Database with Logan Hobson, with whom he founded CompuBox in 1985. Beginning with the second Livingstone Bramble-Ray Mancini fight, CompuBox operators have been ringside at shows in more than 40 U.S. states as well as Canada, England, Wales, Germany, Japan, Puerto Rico, South Korea and Argentina. Among the thousands of fights Canobbio counted include Buster Douglas-Mike Tyson, Lennox Lewis-Mike Tyson, Marvelous Marvin Hagler-Thomas Hearns, Ray Leonard-Marvelous Marvin Hagler and the 1988 Seoul Olympics. Canobbio currently resides in Manorville, N.Y. with his wife Ceil and they are the parents of five -- Rebekah, Jamie, Nicolas, Dan and Roby.

Lee Groves is a boxing writer and historian based in Friendly, West Virginia. He is a full member of the Boxing Writers Association of America, from which, as of 2017, he has won 15 awards, including two first-place honors in 2011 and 2013. He has been an elector for the International Boxing Hall of Fame since 2001 and has been a full-time writer, researcher and punch-counter for CompuBox, Inc. since 2007. He is the author of "Tales from the Vault: A Celebration of 100 Boxing Closet Classics" and possesses one of the world's largest and deepest private sports video collections, a collection that includes more than 50,000 boxing matches.

FOREWORD

By Jonathan Eig

I never saw Muhammad Ali fight in person. I did see him on television, though, sometimes live and sometimes in tape-delayed broadcasts. Even now, when I watch replays of Muhammad Ali's bouts, I find it difficult to take my eyes off him. His opponents disappear for long stretches. I'm too busy concentrating on Ali's feet, his hands, his eyes, his mouth. There's too much going on to think about the man he's fighting. Ali's like a magnet -- the most powerful magnet in the history of boxing; he draws us in, closer and closer, and we are helpless to resist. The pull must have been even greater on those who watched him fight in person, in Madison Square Garden, in Manila, in Zaire, in Las Vegas, or anywhere else that crowds rose to their feet and chanted his name.

Even when Ali was at his most *unpopular* -- when he was thrashing Floyd Patterson or Ernie Terrell, for example -- the crowds never chanted "Go, Floyd!" or "Let him have it, Ernie!" They merely booed Ali and hollered with blood lust when Ali was hit. Almost all eyes and all feelings of fury were on Ali, the wittiest, cleverest, prettiest, slickest, most dazzling heavyweight boxer…of *alllll tiiiimes.* People wanted to see him dead, or at least badly hurt. Only in the latter phase of his career did that change.

A case could be made that Ali's prettiness and his magnetism helped him win fights. After all, a ringside judge has only one set of eyes. If he's prone, same as the rest of us, to watch Ali, how can he objectively evaluate the work of Ali *and* his opponent? He can't! That's one reason I turned to the experts at CompuBox Inc. when I wrote my biography of Ali. I wanted to see if we could come up with reliable statistics to judge Ali the boxer and to separate him as much as possible from Muhammad Ali the superstar and charisma machine. I also wanted to see if we could calculate how many punches Ali took in the course of his career to better understand the kind of punishment he endured.

Numbers alone are not enough to judge a boxing match. Numbers don't reveal how much a punch hurts. Numbers don't measure a fighter's determination, or the strength of his chin. When you go to a fight, or even watch one on television, you would never think of keeping a detailed score sheet, as you might at a baseball game. It would take the fun out of it.

But statistics can help us tell stories. In Ali's life, the numbers helped tell stories big and small.

Here's a small example: On March 13, 1963, when Cassius Clay fought Doug Jones in Madison

Square Garden, the crowd heavily favored the hometown fighter Jones. Clay was seen as a loudmouth, and fans wanted Jones to shut that loud mouth and also blacken both of Clay's eyes if possible. Jones made Clay look bad at times. In many ways, this was a preview of the Ali-Frazier fights to come. Jones kept surging, getting inside, and Clay seemed unable to stop the surge. By the end of the fight, most spectators, including many of the reporters on hand, thought Jones had beaten Clay. But the decision went to Clay, and the punch stats compiled by CompuBox and printed in these pages indicate that the judges got it right: Clay had thrown and landed far more punches than Jones, especially in the final round.

In other fights, the numbers suggest the judges might have erred, seduced perhaps by Ali's charm. Did Ali deserve the win against Ken Norton at Yankee Stadium? After reviewing the numbers and watching the fight several times, I would say he did not. Feel free to argue with me.

The numbers help tell a bigger story, too; they help tell the toll boxing took on Ali. Boxing punishes almost every fighter. Ali believed he would be one of the rare exceptions. He believed he was quick and slick enough to avoid punishing blows and emerge from the sport fully intact, physically and mentally. He was wrong, of course, and the numbers help us understand why.

In the early stages of Ali's career, he was indeed quick and slick. But he never entirely avoided damage. And the longer he fought, the slower he got, and the more he got hit.

I can remember watching some of Ali's final fights on television. I can remember the 38-year-old Ali screaming in pain at body blows landed by Larry Holmes. I can remember Ali sagging on his stool between rounds. Those are the images seared most deeply in my memory. But then there's this new, equally searing fact: Holmes landed 340 punches that night to Ali's 42.

Damn.

The numbers aren't everything, but, man, do they have power. Man, do they tell a story.

-- Jonathan Eig, July 21, 2017

ACKNOWLEDGEMENTS

I'd like to thank my awesome wife Ceil and my children Rebekah, Jamie, Nicolas (now VP of Operations for CompuBox and a veteran punch-counter who worked his first CompuBox fight at age 19), Dan (host of CompuBox TV's Inside Boxing Live, Social Media Director for CompuBox and also a punch counter) and Roby (analytics consultant) for all their love and support over the years. For the first 15 years, Ceil held down the fort at home while I traveled weekly from city to city, building the CompuBox brand. I am forever grateful to Ceil for her constant encouragement and understanding over the years, both in business and life in general.

I'd also like to thank Logan Hobson, the co-founder of CompuBox and my partner for 17 years. We had lots of laughs along the way which made the grind of weekly travel much more bearable.

I'd also like to thank Ross Greenberg, who in 1985 while a producer at HBO Sports, believed in Logan and me enough to employ CompuBox and our original punch-counting program on the network's boxing telecasts beginning with the rematch between Ray Mancini and Livingstone Bramble.

I'd like to thank the late Joe Carnicelli and Dennis Allen for 20-plus years of punch-counting service to CompuBox. Joe holds the CompuBox record for shows worked in one year: 60. Also, thanks to Saul Avelar, a CompuBox workhorse in the early years, and to the late Genaro Hernandez, a true gentleman who accepted any/all punch counting assignments thrown his way. Thanks also to Andy Kasprzak, Aris Pina, Ben Chan, Shaun Glover and Jason Griggs for their contributions to CompuBox.

A special thanks goes out to Lee Groves -- a tireless professional. He's not only a punch counter (live and historical counts), he's also a driven and talented writer who has elevated the prose associated with CompuBox's analytics to another level. Every company should have a Lee Groves on their staff and I'm very grateful to have the opportunity to work with him on a daily basis.

Last but not least I'd like to thank Bob Foster for throwing that picture-perfect left hook that KO'd Dick Tiger on May 24, 1968. I watched that fight on my Dad's black-and-white TV and have been hooked on "the sweet science" ever since. It's been a great and sometimes surreal ride.

-- Bob Canobbio

*

As is the case with most books, the names on the cover represent only a small percentage of the people who had a part in making "Muhammad Ali: By the Numbers" a reality.

I would first like to thank God for the gifts He granted me as well as the path by which I eventually achieved my dream jobs with CompuBox and RingTV.com, RING magazine's web site. I would like to thank the men who gave me those dream jobs, my co-author Bob Canobbio and the trio of Doug Fischer of RingTV.com and onetime RING editors-in-chief Nigel Collins and Steve Farhood (both of whom took a chance on me in the late-1980s). Fischer and recent RING editor Michael Rosenthal graciously allowed me to use material from past articles I wrote about Ali to serve as the framework for three of the fights you'll read about here: The first Liston fight, the "Thrilla in Manila" (Ali-Frazier III) and "The Rumble in the Jungle" (Ali-Foreman).

Others who deserve special mention include Farhood -- a 2017 International Boxing Hall of Fame inductee -- onetime light-heavyweight champion and outstanding trainer Eddie Mustafa Muhammad, CompuBox co-founder Logan Hobson, and Florida/Nevada Boxing Hall of Fame member as well as "In This Corner" host James "Smitty" Smith, all of whom were interviewed for this book. Your unique insights only enhanced the quality of this project.

This past spring, veteran punch-counter and onetime UPI scribe Joe Carnicelli mailed me his original copy rolls that contained previews and fight reports for Holmes-Ali while also including an article that ran in the Ottawa Journal that detailed the cancellation of their proposed fight in Rio de Janeiro. His generosity and willingness to help was truly appreciated. Unfortunately, on September 15, 2017, Joe passed away at age 75. While his physical body is now stilled, his spirit and contributions will forever be remembered.

I am also very thankful for the help provided by Colleen Patchin of the Nevada State Athletic Commission, who provided us with the complete Holmes-Ali scorecards just one day after I made the request. I also would like to thank IBHOF inductee Marc Ratner, a former Nevada State Athletic Commission director (and friend), for providing contact information.

I would also like to thank "Mr. Magazine" owner Kevin Bandel and his son Tyler, from whom I purchased 113 back issues of THE RING during the 2017 IBHOF induction weekend. When I subsequently discovered that the July 1963 issue had several missing pages, Kevin sent me a replacement issue free of charge. Plus, he also filled two subsequent orders that helped close significant gaps in my magazine collection. As a result, I now have every issue of THE RING dating back to January 1960. Those magazines yielded an extraordinary amount of background material that added considerable context and depth to this narrative. Thank you for your help in making this book the best it can be.

Thanks also to the many writers and authors who produced such detailed and textured works in the magazines and books from which I conducted research for this book. Their writing produced valuable insight in terms of the back stories rendered (and footnoted) here.

Nic Canobbio merits high praise for his work on the postcards Bob and I used as pre-publicity for the book. He beautifully brought to life the concept I envisioned when the idea was hatched, and for that I am grateful. He also provided valuable assistance in formatting the scorecards as well as the punch-count charts that appear throughout the book. (A note about the charts:

Although Ali will be referred to as Cassius Clay in the first section of the book, the name Ali will be featured on all punch-count charts, primarily because keeping all stats under the same name in the database simplified the process of compiling averages for all 47 fights profiled).

The good folks who run and maintain Boxrec.com deserve a huge round of applause and appreciation, for their web site provided indispensable information that appears throughout.

Kudos are extended to the good folks at Newbookauthors.com, and specifically Erica Hughes, the president of Author Relations and Book Services. She personally replied to my initial e-mail just 90 minutes after I sent it, and from there offered excellent advice and help throughout the book-making process, especially when it became extremely complicated. I also would like to thank CreateSpace, to whom Erica sent the camera-ready PDFs and who published my first book "Tales From the Vault" nearly eight years ago.

Bob Yalen not only is one of boxing's best archivists, he's an even better person. He took time out of his extremely busy schedule to dig through his vault and access numerous sources to extract all available information regarding the round-by-round scoring of Ali's fights. The results of his hard work, which will be presented here for the first time, provides a valuable statistical dimension to this book. Had it not been for him, we would have had only six scorecards, and not all of them had complete information. Now, because of him, we will present scorecards from 47 of his fights, of which 29 have complete information from all three judges. Of the other 18 scorecards, 13 have partial information with final totals and five have totals only. That is as comprehensive a rendering as can be achieved and it couldn't have been done without Bob.

I would like to say thank you to my mother Linda and my older sister Cindy for their everlasting love and support. A special mention should be given to my father Gary, who passed away in June 2017 following a short bout with liver cancer. I told Dad about this book project shortly before we watched our final fight together -- Anthony Joshua-Wladimir Klitschko on April 29 -- and I know for a fact that he dearly wanted this project to succeed. This book is dedicated to you.

Finally, I would like to thank you, the reader, for purchasing this book. We all are given a certain amount of time to spend on this earth and as I get older I realize just how valuable one's time can be. Bob and I invested a good chunk of our time in preparing this book and we hope that our efforts will be pleasing enough to you that you'll walk away feeling that your time with our work was time well spent.

-- Lee Groves

INTRODUCTION

Ever since Cassius Clay vaulted onto the world stage by winning gold at the 1960 Summer Olympics in Rome, his fusion of leading-man looks, majestic athleticism and overflowing charisma made him a media magnet. Once he became Muhammad Ali, he extended his sphere of influence far beyond the athletic arena, so much so that he became the subject of numerous books, movies, television shows, plays, songs, advertisements and even comic books. The story of Ali was so rich and so textured that he became the most chronicled athlete the world has ever known.

Despite the trillions of words that have been written and spoken about Ali in the nearly six decades since the Rome games, virtually none of them addressed one vital part of his boxing life -- the numerical part. "Muhammad Ali: By the Numbers" publishes, for the first time ever, complete round-by-round punch stats for 47 of Ali's 61 professional fights, including 43 of his final 44. As much as CompuBox wanted to access complete footage of every Ali fight, the video simply doesn't exist. Because most of the gaps occur in his first 15 fights, this book still offers a representative sample of Ali's legendary 21-year pro career.

We all know how beautifully the young Ali floated around the ring, but just how effective was the bee's sting? We all know how tough the older Ali was during his second reign as he curled himself against the ropes and unflinchingly absorbed his opponents' most powerful bombs, but how often did those bombs penetrate Ali's shell? The numbers during the second half of Ali's career -- especially in his final nine fights -- are not only stunning they are also explanatory. Those figures, at least in part, reveal why Ali's motor skills started to decline at such an alarmingly early age and why that erosion ended up being so profound.

While CompuBox had a few of Ali's fights in its master database, the genesis for this book occurred when author Jonathan Eig approached the company about quantifying how much punishment he dished out -- and how much he took -- so that a hard number could be reached for his book "Ali: A Life." The lack of three-minutes-per-round footage for all 61 fights prevented that objective from being entirely executed, but Eig believed the data was so enlightening and provocative that he suggested a separate book be done to more fully examine this part of his ring life.

"Muhammad Ali: By the Numbers" accomplishes that mission in two ways. First, award-winning boxing writer Lee Groves, who has worked full-time with the company since 2007, compiled the numbers and wrote the manuscript by reviewing all the available video footage, consulting hundreds of back issues of various boxing magazines and referencing other sources such as Ali biographies, books written by Ali opponents and, in a nod to the modern age, YouTube videos and other online resources. The result is a richly researched book that offers invaluable at-the-time insight as well as other factoids and back stories that couldn't have been gleaned from web searches alone.

One particularly vivid result of the research can be found in the retelling of the Ali-Liston rematch, one of the most controversial fights in boxing history. The political and social machinations surrounding the fight are chronicled from several angles, as are the personal recollections from referee Jersey Joe Walcott, RING publisher Nat Fleischer (who was seated beside timekeeper Francis McDonough and had played a role in the fight being stopped) and, at least briefly, from Liston himself.

Second, Bob Canobbio -- who, with Logan Hobson, created CompuBox Inc. in 1985 -- applied his gift for deep analysis to compile the "Inside the Numbers" nuggets that appear throughout this book as well as assemble the various charts that spotlight other statistical aspects of his career. Some of the more illuminating information Canobbio unearthed is the comparison reports for each of the four phases of Ali's career that make up the dividing lines in this book -- the Young Clay, the Prime Ali, the Ali of the "comeback years" and the Past-Prime Ali.

Another fascinating set of numbers grouped for the first time in this book are all available round-by-round judges' scorecards for his fights, which will be printed in close proximity with the CompuBox statistics at the end of each bout. These come courtesy of master researcher (and boxing lifer) Bob Yalen, who assembled this vital information years earlier and graciously allowed it to appear here. The association between the scorecards and the statistics should yield interesting comparisons as well as eye-opening contrasts.

For the reasons stated here, "Muhammad Ali: By the Numbers" represents the final frontier in terms of examining the life and career of the man known as "The Greatest." Interestingly, the statistics both confirm long-held beliefs while also unearthing trends that are sure to surprise and maybe even shock. It is our hope that this book will fulfill its mission of providing a one-of-a-kind perspective in an entertaining and informative fashion.

Without further delay, let the statistical storytelling begin.

-- Bob Canobbio and Lee Groves
July 22, 2017

THE YOUNG CLAY: JOHNSON THROUGH COOPER I

As explained in the introduction, the opening act of this fistic symphony is missing a few pages because complete footage for 13 of the 19 fights in this phase are not available. That said, the six contests that are profiled here -- Alonzo Johnson, Alex Miteff, Sonny Banks, Archie Moore, Doug Jones and the first Henry Cooper fight -- represent significant touchstones in the early ring life of Cassius Clay.

The Johnson fight, his eighth outing as a pro -- was Clay's national television debut in the paid ranks. The Miteff bout saw Clay handle an unexpectedly stiff challenge thanks to the Argentine's prodigious body attack while the Banks bout marked Clay's first appearance at Madison Square Garden (as well as the first knockdown of his pro career). Clay's fight with Moore represented a passing of the torch from the grand old master to his (briefly) onetime apprentice. Clay's encounter with Jones was the most polarizing and controversial fight of his path to a championship opportunity. The importance of the Cooper bout was twofold: His first outing beyond America's shores and his brush with disaster at the end of round four thanks to the lethal left hook known as " 'Enry's 'Ammer."

One note: Although the world knows him as Muhammad Ali, that name did not exist until a few days after he won the heavyweight championship from Sonny Liston. Therefore, his birth name will be used in this section of the book.

One would have thought that the lithe racehorse that raced through his competition would have racked up more dominant numbers given his youthful energy and massive advantages in hand and foot speed. Maybe that would have been the case had complete footage of every fight been available but against these foes -- probably the best of the lot -- Clay actually absorbed a higher percentage of overall punches than his six profiled opponents (29.2% given versus 32.4% received). This stat confirms the criticisms of veteran ring observers that decried his dangling arms and his tendency to pull away from punches instead of using proper defensive techniques.

Clay compensated in several ways. First, he maintained a high work rate -- his 64.8 punches per round was exactly 20 more than the 44.8 heavyweight average -- and his mobility was such that he limited his opponents to just 38 punches per round. That yawning gap in activity allowed Clay to land far more total punches each round (18.9 versus 12.3) while also amassing a smaller but significant edge in landed power shots per round (12.5 versus 9.4). Clay's command of distance was also confirmed by his ability to limit his opponents' jab (10.4 thrown/2.9 connects per round) as well as his ability to connect with a slightly higher percentage of power punches than his foes (36.1% to 34.1%).

One potential reason for his lower-than-expected overall marksmanship is his enthusiastic but still-developing jab. During this phase Clay fired 30.2 jabs each round -- significantly higher than the 20.4 heavyweight average -- and while his 6.4 connects per round exceeds the 5.3 division norm, his precision (21.2%) wasn't what it would become in later years. One piece of proof: In 39 rounds of action Clay landed 10 or more jabs in a given round just three times (twice against Miteff, once against Johnson), while in the other phases of his career he achieved that threshold 148 times.

That said, Clay's raw numbers were impressive. He led 739-481 overall, 250-115 jabs and 489-366 power because, unlike the other phases, his opponents never out-landed him in total punches and he was never out-jabbed. In fact, Ali absorbed fewer than 10 jabs in his fights with Miteff (2), Banks (0) and Moore (6) while in those fights Ali landed 80 (39 versus Miteff, 16 against Banks and 25 versus Moore). The only sniffs of statistical success came from Miteff, who prevailed 114-106 in power connects, and from Cooper, who led 30-17 in that same category.

It is surprising that Clay rated a minus-3.2 in the CompuBox plus-minus rating that compares the overall percentage of punches landed with the overall percentage of punches taken. Despite his defensive issues, Clay was still excellent enough to stop most of his opponents in the appointed round while also appearing to be the alpha fighter at virtually all times. Such are the gifts of youth, talent and overflowing self-belief, assets that would take the young Clay to heights even he couldn't have fully envisioned.

1.

Once a touted prospect is signed, the management team and the head trainer assume the awesome responsibility of maximizing the fighter's potential in terms of money-making prowess, in-ring accomplishments and emotional development in the heat of competition. A primary part of that task is choosing the right opponents at the right time from the prospect's perspective, and, at least so far, the Louisville Sponsoring Group and chief second Angelo Dundee, who joined the team in fight number two, (1) had done a masterful job of introducing Cassius Clay to the pro game.

As Dundee would repeat countless times, a trainer is only as good as the fighter with whom he works and in Clay he had a bona fide blue-chipper. The teen-aged Clay stood 6-foot-2 and possessed dazzling hand and foot speed as well as a hunger for training and expanding his knowledge of the game. His deep amateur pedigree was also a huge plus, although his precise amateur record is unknown (he is credited with marks of 99-8, 100-5, 100-8, 118-5, 127-5 and 137-7). What could be confirmed was that Clay was a six-time Kentucky Golden Gloves champion who earned his place on the 1960 U.S. Olympic team by outpointing Jimmy Jones to win the Chicago Golden Gloves Tournament of Champions in March, stopping Jeff Davis at 1:25 of round two to win his second consecutive National AAU light heavyweight title in Toledo in April, knocking out Gary Jawish at 1:46 of round three to capture the Inter City Golden Gloves heavyweight championship six weeks later, (2) and beating Henry Hooper (KO 3), Fred Lewis (W3) and Allen Hudson (KO 3) to win the Olympic Trials in San Francisco. (3)

In Rome, Clay impressively stopped Belgium's Yvon Because in round two and scored 5-0 shutouts over the Soviet Union's Gennadiy Shatkov and Australia's Anthony Madigan to reach the final against 26-year-old Polish southpaw Zbigniew Pietrzykowski, a six-time national champion who won bronze in the 1956 Melbourne games as a middleweight and who would win another bronze at light heavyweight at the Tokyo games four years later. Pietrzykowski advanced to the 1960 final by sweeping the judges' scorecards against Guyana's Carl Crawford, West Germany's Emil Willer and Bulgaria's Petar Spassov before earning a 4-1 nod against Italy's Giulio Saraudi in the semifinal. (4).

Pietrzykowski's left-handed stance presented considerable trouble to Clay in the first round, for the Pole prevailed 16-11 despite being out-thrown 70-52. He even managed to out-jab the youngster 7-4 because he was much more accurate (32%-10%). Clay evened the contest in the second by out-throwing the veteran 68-52 and out-landing him 15-11 overall as well as 13-10 in power punches. After two rounds, the fight, and the gold medal, was still up for grabs.

According to ringside reporter and RING publisher Nat Fleischer, Clay's U.S. teammates Humberto Barrera (flyweight), Jerry Armstrong (bantamweight) and Quincy Daniels (light welterweight) were victims of biased officiating and this fight certainly was close enough to steal. (5) While Wilbert "Skeeter" McClure had won light middleweight gold against Italy's Carmelo Bossi and Edward Crook won the middleweight tournament against Poland's Tadeusz Walasek earlier in the day, (6) the setbacks by his other teammates surely had to be weighing on Clay's mind. He knew he had to leave no doubt.

Stepping up and seizing the moment, Clay left no doubt. In the most important three minutes of his boxing life thus far, Clay unleashed 98 punches to Pietrzykowski's 48, nearly doubled the Pole's power punch attempts (66-34) and, most importantly, out-landed him 28-9 overall and 23-8 power. The surge left Pietrzykowski a bloody mess while allowing Clay to secure connect leads of 54-36 overall, 11-9 jabs and 43-27 power as well as the Olympic championship by a 5-0 decision. Given the raucous support the crowd of 16,200 inside the Palazzetto dello Sport gave the six Italians in the boxing finals, it is a tribute to the American squad that they were able to tie the home nation with three gold medals. (7)

"Clay and Crook deserve high honors for their spirited fighting and hard hitting, though each had a close call for two rounds," Fleischer wrote. "Clay's last round assault on Pietrzykowski was the outstanding hitting of the tournament. The exhibition of perfect hitting by the 18-year-old Kentucky schoolboy Clay featured the tourney. Had he not gone all out in the final round he would have lost the verdict since the bout was about even and it's a cinch that if Pietrzykowski had won the last round, Clay would have been declared the loser. But Cassius was fully prepared after a talk by his coach Jules Menendez, manager Harry Becker and me. Having seen the Pole in action several times, I told him that if the fight went beyond two rounds, he had to go all out to win.

"*'I'll do that,'* he told Becker and he stuck to his promise. He attacked so viciously that he had his opponent out on his feet, resting against the ropes, blood streaming from nose and mouth, arms hanging at his sides. He was a helpless boxer when the bell came to his rescue.

"Uncle Sam may well feel proud of the newly risen heavyweight whose idol is Floyd Patterson," Fleischer concluded. "Clay may have a bright future as a professional. Clay was a delighted young kid when, the following morning, Floyd visited him in the (Olympic) Village." (8)

Clay turned professional 55 days later with a shutout decision over 26-fight veteran Tunney Hunsaker, who came into the fight off a ninth-round TKO loss against future heavyweight title challenger Tom McNeeley, his sixth defeat in a row. While Clay fulfilled expectations by romping to a six-round decision win, his form in doing so disappointed observers who wanted to see signs of potential greatness.

"Afterwards, Clay remarked that he was a bit nervous and that he had trouble with the style of

Hunsaker, which was far different than anything he had encountered as an amateur," read a photo caption in the January 1961 issue of THE RING. (9)

Two months later Clay scored his first victory under Dundee's charge -- a fourth-round TKO over Herb Siler -- then received a nice 19th birthday present in the form of Tony Esperti, who came into the ring scaling a flabby 197 and coated with nearly six years' worth of ring rust. The only surprise was that Esperti, who was on a three-fight losing streak, lasted until the 1:30 mark of round three.

Clay raised eyebrows when, on February 6, 1961, the night before he would face his fourth pro opponent, he sparred with former heavyweight champion Ingemar Johansson at Miami's Fifth Street Gym. Johansson was preparing for his rubber match with Floyd Patterson that was to take place March 13 at Miami Beach. While Clay wasn't on the original list of sparring partners, his gift of gab enabled him to secure a spot in the day's rotation.

"The ex-champ was concerned only with sharpening his jabs and practicing how to punch down, since Patterson was sure to fight him out of a crouch," a writer for International Boxing recalled. "There was this time in the first round when Clay sent Johansson back into the ropes with a two-fisted body attack and Ingo rebounded and nailed Cassius on the temple with a swishing right. Clay appeared hurt as he immediately stepped in and grabbed Ingemar's arms. Johansson didn't try to shake him off. He merely stood still, with arms outstretched -- the signal to break clean."

Clay released Johansson and spent the rest of the sparring session pumping jabs and staying out of danger. (10) Although Johansson clearly held back during the workout, Clay got a first-hand idea of what it was like to be in the ring with a top-flight professional. Better yet, Clay impressed that top-flight professional. "He's good, this fellow," Johansson said. "He did a lot of jumping around, and isn't a bit like Patterson as he changes around too much. I hope I can get him for more sparring as he sharpens me up." (11)

The next evening, Clay, fighting on the undercard of Harold Johnson-Jesse Bowdry (which was for the vacant NBA light heavyweight title) in Miami, crushed Jimmy Robinson in just 94 seconds. Robinson was a late sub for the 8-4-2 Miami heavyweight Willie Gulatt, (12) who, like Esperti, was on a three-fight slide.

Two weeks later, again in Miami, Clay attempted two significant leaps: His first main event and an opponent that boasted far more professional experience than either he or his previous opponents. Although the 35-11-1 Donnie Fleeman had lost four of his last five, his accumulated wisdom still concerned Clay. He need not have worried so much, for Clay controlled the action throughout and dished out enough punishment to persuade Fleeman to retire on the stool between rounds six and seven.

"I was scared to death before I got in the ring," Clay said. "Fighting a pro who has had 45 (sic) fights is quite different than what I faced before. This fellow had been 24 rounds with (title challenger) Roy Harris and beat (former heavyweight champion) Ezzard Charles. Now that I whipped him, I guess I'm a little greater than average." (13)

Fleeman, to his credit, was honest about his performance. "I was nothing else but a human speed bag for him to punch as he pleased," he said. "I had nothing going for me. I was a sitting duck." (14)

When Clay returned to Louisville to fight the 43-2 LaMar Clark, the 5,441 fans that packed Freedom Hall represented the city's largest fight crowd in more than two years. (15) Clark had assembled one of history's longest knockout strings as he stretched opponents in 41 straight fights between January 1958 and January 1960, but he came into the Clay fight a loser of two of his last three -- both by knockout. Clay made it three out of four as he scored a clean knockout in just four minutes and 27 seconds.

Clay's five-fight knockout streak ended against six-foot-six Hawaiian journeyman Duke Sabedong in the prospect's Las Vegas debut on June 26, 1961. Twenty-six days after schooling Sabedong, Clay was ready to take the next step: A nationally televised fight.

*

The circumstances appeared ideal from Clay's standpoint. The fight was to be held at Freedom Hall (also known as the Kentucky Fair and Exposition Center) in Clay's hometown of Louisville, and the opponent was to be 26-year-old Alonzo Johnson, who once scored back-to-back 10-round decisions over Nino Valdes and future light heavyweight champion Willie Pastrano but was now a 18-7 (6 KO) journeyman who had lost six of his last eight to Alex Miteff (twice), Tony Anthony, Zora Folley, Pastrano and Eddie Machen. Tellingly, each loss was by decision, so if the objective for Clay's team was to test their man's stamina and composure under increased scrutiny, Johnson appeared to be the perfect foil: Good enough to push the prospect but not good enough to push him over the cliff.

A hot night in Louisville was made even hotter by the 5,160 paying customers who filled the arena and the TV lights installed by ABC for its "Fight of the Week" series. The internal psychological heat for both men was even more intense: Clay wanted to impress a nationwide audience while Johnson was hoping to score a signature win.

The first round illustrated the vast difference in speed between the whippet-like Clay, who bounced lightly on his toes, and the thicker Johnson, who pressed forward and targeted the body. Clay set the pace by throwing 52 punches, landing seven of his 34 jabs, and connecting with a light, quick right that caused Johnson to briefly back away. Still, Johnson got in enough punches (10 of 32 overall and 6 of 16 power shots) to make it a competitive round.

Clay asserted his superiority in the second by landing lead right hands over Johnson's jab -- a tactic that would be a staple of his offense in future years -- while firing jabs and exuding youthful energy. But while he established daylight in that round by out-landing Johnson 19-11 overall, Johnson fulfilled his role by bouncing back and producing his best round of the fight in round three, mostly on the strength of a second-half surge. That rally was highlighted by a four-punch salvo capped by a hook that caused Clay to clinch.

Interestingly, Johnson's successes sparked loud cheers from Clay's hometown crowd. Perhaps that was a product of the natural urge to root for the underdog but it might also be that Clay's persona wasn't universally popular, even among those who knew him best.

In the third, Johnson achieved fight highs of 54 punches, 22 total connects and 14 landed power shots, and he even out-jabbed Clay 8-7. No, Johnson would not be a pushover; if Clay was to win he would have to work for it. And work Clay did, for with 37 seconds left in the fourth Clay landed a right to the side of the head that caused Johnson to pitch forward. The fall appeared to be a genuine knockdown and referee Don Asbury, a former fighter who had officiated Johnson's rematch loss to Pastrano and Clay's stoppage of Clark, initially pointed Clay toward a corner (he errantly directed Clay to his own corner instead of a neutral one), but then, for whatever reason, stopped his count at two, wiped Johnson's gloves and allowed the fight to continue. Johnson did enough to make it back to his corner, but Clay had nevertheless amplified his command of the bout.

Clay continued to roll in the fifth as he enjoyed his best statistical round of the fight: 68 punches and 20 total connects that included 15 of 32 power shots (47%). Much of that success was achieved shortly before the two-minute mark when Clay fired a five-punch flurry capped by a hook followed by another four-punch combination that brought loud cheers from his partisans. Despite the tumult, Johnson still managed to out-jab Clay 7-5, the second time in three rounds that Johnson did a better job of jabbing than the man who would be regarded as one of history's best jabbers.

The pace slowed markedly in the sixth, but Clay successfully controlled distance by landing a fight-high nine jabs. With less than 30 seconds remaining in the seventh, Clay landed a stinging lead right to the face, a one-two, a hook and a right to the side of the head that caused Johnson to land heavily on his behind. But for the second time in the fight, referee Asbury overlooked an apparent knockdown and authorized the fight to continue.

The eighth was fairly even, but it also was clear the heat was starting to get to both men. According to the Weather Underground's web site, Louisville had experienced a sweltering 91-degree day and even during mid-evening the outside temperature was still in the low 80s. But when one added the TV lights, the heat generated by the crowd and the exertion of 24 minutes of fight action, the toll on both athletes was significant. Between rounds eight and nine, Clay, though still a teen-ager, slumped forward on his stool and appeared terribly fatigued. Yes, he was winning the fight, but he still had to fight six more minutes to earn the victory.

The ninth saw both men try to push through their physical duress but the action wasn't enough to satisfy the crowd, who tried to prod the fighters by booing and stomping their feet. Clay and Johnson tried their best to comply, and, at least in the ninth, Johnson did the slightly better job as he out-landed Clay for the second straight round (14-11 overall and 12-10 power).

Although the outcome was hardly in doubt, Clay still needed to up his game in the 10th to prevent questions about his stamina from being raised. That he did -- with emphasis.

A slashing right caused Johnson to stumble forward, and while the veteran desperately lunged to secure a balance-saving clinch, Clay landed a left to the ear that felled Johnson for the third time in the fight. And, for the third time in the fight, Asbury waved off a potential knockdown. The throng urged Clay to gun for the knockout but Johnson fought out of the fog well enough to last until the final bell.

Statistically speaking, Clay performed well enough to win but he wasn't overwhelming. Though he was the far busier man (56.7 punches per round to Johnson's 44.2), he led by only 139-125 overall, 45-38 jabs and 94-87 power because Johnson was more accurate overall (28%-25%) and in jabs (27%-16%). Johnson also scored heavily to the body as 61 of his 87 power connects hit the flanks while only nine of Clay's 94 targeted that area. But Clay was more precise where he needed to be -- in power shots (33%-29%) -- and thus earned the unanimous decision. Despite his three errant knockdown calls, Asbury still gave Clay every round (50-44 under the five-point must system) while Walter Beck saw Clay a razor-thin 48-47 winner. Judge Harlow Edwards' 48-45 score appeared closest to reality, for Johnson did out-land Clay in three rounds.

All in all, it was a highly successful night for Clay and his team. Not only did Clay run his record to 8-0, he responded well to the mild adversities that occurred. He didn't complain when his knockdowns weren't counted and he didn't get frustrated when Johnson fought back. He did his job, did it well and earned the privilege of proceeding to the next assignment with his prospect designation intact.

INSIDE THE NUMBERS: In his eighth pro fight, Clay landed only 16.1% of his jabs (he landed 29.4% in all his fights counted) and showed ability to absorb a body punch, as 61 of Johnson's 125 landed punches (49%) struck the flanks. Johnson out-landed Clay in three of ten rounds.

Date:	July 22, 1961				City: Louisville, KY					Venue: Freedom Hall					
Opponent:	Alonzo Johnson															
Result:	Clay by unanimous decision															

Referee: Don Asbury

Round	1	2	3	4	5	6	7	8	9	10	11	12	13	14	15	Total
Clay	5	5	5	5	5	5	5	5	5	5						50
Johnson																44

Judge: Harlow Edwards

Round	1	2	3	4	5	6	7	8	9	10	11	12	13	14	15	Total
Clay																48
Johnson																45

Judge: Walter Beck

Round	1	2	3	4	5	6	7	8	9	10	11	12	13	14	15	Total
Clay																48
Johnson																47

MUHAMMAD ALI UD 10 ALONZO JOHNSON
07/22/61 - LOUISVILLE

Total Punches Landed / Thrown										
	1	2	3	4	5	6	7	8	9	10
ALI	11/52	19/59	14/60	16/58	20/68	14/53	12/63	10/49	11/55	12/50
	21.2%	32.2%	23.3%	27.6%	29.4%	26.4%	19%	20.4%	20%	24%
JOHNSON	10/32	11/41	22/54	12/48	16/53	12/44	9/39	11/46	14/46	8/39
	31.3%	26.8%	40.7%	25%	30.2%	27.3%	23.1%	23.9%	30.4%	20.5%

Jab Landed / Thrown										
	1	2	3	4	5	6	7	8	9	10
ALI	7/34	5/27	7/36	6/29	5/36	9/33	2/31	3/24	1/17	0/13
	20.6%	18.5%	19.4%	20.7%	13.9%	27.3%	6.5%	12.5%	5.9%	0%
JOHNSON	4/16	1/14	8/26	6/12	7/23	4/14	4/14	2/11	2/9	0/4
	25%	7.1%	30.8%	50%	30.4%	28.6%	28.6%	18.2%	22.2%	0%

Power Punches Landed / Thrown										
	1	2	3	4	5	6	7	8	9	10
ALI	4/18	14/32	7/24	10/29	15/32	5/20	10/32	7/25	10/38	12/37
	22.2%	43.8%	29.2%	34.5%	46.9%	25%	31.3%	28%	26.3%	32.4%
JOHNSON	6/16	10/27	14/28	6/36	9/30	8/30	5/25	9/35	12/37	8/35
	37.5%	37%	50%	16.7%	30%	26.7%	20%	25.7%	32.4%	22.9%

Final Punch Stat Report		
Total Punches (Body Landed)	Total Jabs (Body Landed)	Power Punches (Body Landed)
ALI		
139 (0)/567	45 (0)/280	94 (0)/287
24.5%	16.1%	32.8%
JOHNSON		
125 (0)/442	38 (0)/143	87 (0)/299
28.3%	26.6%	29.1%

10

2.

Less than three months after making his national TV debut against Alonzo Johnson, Clay was back on the small screen. The network and series carrying the fight was the same (ABC's "Fight of the Week"), the referee was the same (Don Asbury) and the venue was the same (Freedom Hall, also known as the Kentucky Fair and Exposition Center, in Louisville). While the identity of the opponent was different -- Argentina's Alex Miteff -- his career position was nearly as the same as that of Johnson: A 26-year-old once good enough to be rated fourth in the world at heavyweight -- and seventh as recently as the June 1961 issue of THE RING (1) -- beating Nino Valdes (as Johnson had) and drawing with George Chuvalo in the first of their two fights (Chuvalo won the rematch nearly three years later by 10-round split decision) but whose stock had fallen off dramatically as he had lost two of his last seven and three of his last four, with cuts being a major issue in consecutive defeats to Chuvalo, Cleveland Williams (KO by 5) and Bob Cleroux (KO by 7).

A plus: Miteff (24-10-1, 14 KO) was coming off a two-round KO win over Jimmy McCarter just 37 days earlier. Another: Miteff had beaten Johnson twice, the first by 10-round decision at Madison Square Garden two years earlier, and the other by 10-round decision at St. Nicholas Arena in New York City seven months before meeting Clay. For these reasons, Miteff was viewed as a slight step up for the prospect.

That opinion was reflected in the 2-to-1 odds favoring Clay but the attendance (3,509 paid) was markedly smaller than the 5,160 who saw the Johnson fight. (2) Clay scaled a spidery 188, which was to be the lowest weight of his pro career, while the stocky Miteff was a solid 210.

Clay, usually known for his constant movement and elusiveness, opted to switch up his strategy by becoming the aggressor. He tried to push Miteff back by firing slashing combinations but the Argentine responded by weaving inside, shooting the occasional hook and targeting Clay's spindly body. Midway through the round Clay got a rise out of the crowd by planting his feet and unleashing an extended volley to Miteff's head but Miteff remained unmoved. At round's end it was clear Clay had gotten off to a good start and the numbers backed up that contention as he landed 23 of his 72 punches while Miteff went 14 of 42 -- all of which were power shots.

Clay continued to pursue Miteff in the second, and while he popped back the South American's head with lead rights and right uppercuts to the jaw, Clay also absorbed plenty of return fire. ABC's microphones illustrated the force of Miteff's body shots, some of which forced Clay to clinch. Miteff may well have won the round as he landed 33 of his 56 punches (59%) to Clay's 22 of 71 (31%). Once again, Miteff didn't throw a single jab.

Miteff's success prompted Clay to change gears in the third as he danced on his toes, pumped stiff jabs and followed them with whistling combinations. A jolting right sent Miteff retreating toward the ropes and a left-right to the body -- something rarely seen from Clay -- forced him to pause for a split-second. Because Clay's pace slowed in the final two minutes, Miteff was able to work his way back into the round, a round that saw Clay land 25 of his 82 total punches to Miteff's 19 of 49. And yes, Miteff threw two jabs, one of which landed.

Miteff continued his dogged pursuit in the fourth and Clay held him off with his lightning-quick punches, some of which, as had been the case in the third, targeted the body. Unlike most of his previous fights as an amateur and a pro where his head shots were enough to get the job done, Clay was forced to expand his target zone and his repertoire of punches -- especially the right uppercut at close range -- to keep the bull-strong Argentine at bay. In statistical terms the fourth was Clay's best yet as he landed 28 total punches and 24 power shots but Miteff hung in strong by being accurate (20 of 44, 46% overall, 19 of 39, 49% power).

Clay started the fifth with both fists blazing as a hook-right to the face drove Miteff to the ropes and a right to the body-left hook to the face burst sustained the momentum. Once again, Miteff rode out the early storm, regained his equilibrium and resumed his steady, draining attack highlighted by looping rights and rugged body shots. Clay's jab was in excellent working order as three flush ones popped back Miteff's head while the other six he landed in the round helped create puffiness around the left eye and a trickle of blood below it. In the round Clay had landed a fight-high 30 punches to Miteff's 19, but, more importantly, he had finally seized full control of the contest.

Miteff, perhaps in a display of bravado, began the sixth by suddenly dropping his hands and inviting Clay to hit him. Of course, Clay accepted the challenge and drove him across the ring with a pair of jabs and a right cross. Miteff got the message and promptly maintained a high guard for the remainder of the contest.

The good news for Miteff in round six was that he landed 11 of his 18 punches (61%). The bad news was that Clay was to score one of the few one-punch TKOs of his career. Before the fight, Clay said his fight plan was to land "two fast left jabs, a rapid right cross and a left hook." (3)

That's exactly how the end of the fight unfolded, except that the hook was completely unnecessary. With Miteff's left eye swelling rapidly, Clay flicked out two jabs and followed it with a hard right to the cheek that floored Miteff hard. The woozy South American arose at Asbury's count of five but his wobbly legs and dazed expression prompted the local official to wave off the fight at the 1:45 mark. As trainer Gil Clancy wiped the blood from Miteff's eye, Clay walked over and briefly commiserated with his victim, the ninth of his career overall and the sixth by stoppage.

After the fight, Clay called the final right hand the best he ever threw since taking up boxing at age 12. (4)

Somewhat surprisingly, judge Walter Beck had Miteff ahead 24-23 on the five-point must system, no doubt giving weight to the robust body attack that accounted for 70 of his 114 power connects. Beck was overruled by referee Asbury (24-22) and judge Bill Cook (25-21), who had given Clay every round.

Clay out-landed Miteff 145-116 overall and 39-2 in jabs but Miteff prevailed 114-106 in landed power shots and was the more accurate hitter overall (44%-34%) and in power punches (44%-39%). Of Clay's 145 total connects, 16 were to the body, an unusually high number for him.

Ringside commentator Don Dunphy opined that Miteff was undoubtedly the toughest of Clay's young career, and, at least thus far, he was correct.

Less than a year after their meeting on television Clay and Miteff would be paired once again -- this time on the big screen. They each had small parts in the 1962 film "Requiem for a Heavyweight": Clay as the younger fighter that explosively ends the career of Anthony Quinn's Louis "Mountain" Rivera and Miteff as Quinn's body double. (5)

Needless to say, Miteff's experience with Clay on the movie set was much less painful.

INSIDE THE NUMBERS: In his ninth pro fight, Clay again absorbed a heavy dose of body punches, as 70 of Miteff's 116 landed punches (60.3%) struck the flanks. Miteff landed 44.4% of his power shots in the fight. Clay improved his jab accuracy from the Johnson fight, landing 24.8%.

Date:	October 7, 1961				City: Louisville, KY				Venue: Freedom Hall							
Opponent:	Alex Miteff															
Result:	Clay by TKO at 1:45 of the 6th round															
Referee:	**Don Asbury**															
Round	1	2	3	4	5	6	7	8	9	10	11	12	13	14	15	Total
Clay																24
Miteff																22
Judge:	**Walter Beck**															
Round	1	2	3	4	5	6	7	8	9	10	11	12	13	14	15	Total
Clay																23
Miteff																24
Judge:	**Bill Cook**															
Round	1	2	3	4	5	6	7	8	9	10	11	12	13	14	15	Total
Clay																25
Miteff																21

MUHAMMAD ALI KO 6 ALEX MITEFF
10/07/61 - LOUISVILLE

Total Punches Landed / Thrown	1	2	3	4	5	6	7	8	9	10
ALI	23/72	22/71	25/82	28/75	30/81	17/50	-/-	-/-	-/-	-/-
	31.9%	31%	30.5%	37.3%	37%	34%	-	-	-	-
MITEFF	14/42	33/56	19/49	20/44	19/57	11/18	-/-	-/-	-/-	-/-
	33.3%	58.9%	38.8%	45.5%	33.3%	61.1%	-	-	-	-

Jab Landed / Thrown	1	2	3	4	5	6	7	8	9	10
ALI	5/20	5/25	9/39	4/22	9/27	7/24	-/-	-/-	-/-	-/-
	25%	20%	23.1%	18.2%	33.3%	29.2%	-	-	-	-
MITEFF	0/0	0/0	1/2	1/5	0/2	0/0	-/-	-/-	-/-	-/-
	0%	0%	50%	20%	0%	0%	-	-	-	-

Power Punches Landed / Thrown	1	2	3	4	5	6	7	8	9	10
ALI	18/52	17/46	16/43	24/53	21/54	10/26	-/-	-/-	-/-	-/-
	34.6%	37%	37.2%	45.3%	38.9%	38.5%	-	-	-	-
MITEFF	14/42	33/56	18/47	19/39	19/55	11/18	-/-	-/-	-/-	-/-
	33.3%	58.9%	38.3%	48.7%	34.5%	61.1%	-	-	-	-

Final Punch Stat Report	Total Punches	Total Jabs	Power Punches
ALI	145/431	39/157	106/274
	33.6%	24.8%	38.7%
MITEFF	116/266	2/9	114/257
	43.6%	22.2%	44.4%

3.

In years gone by, a prospect sparked instant curiosity -- if not outright credibility -- when he was invited to fight in New York City for the first time. But if a prospect's "Big Apple" debut took place inside Madison Square Garden or even Yankee Stadium, it was a sure sign that those in the know thought the youngster could be something special.

Such was the case with Cassius Clay, 1960 Olympic gold medalist, lightning-quick heavyweight and matchless motor-mouth. If any fighter was made for the media capital of the world it was Clay, whose never-ending chatter inspired nicknames such as "Gaseous Cassius" and "The Louisville Lip." His precociousness in terms of marketing was further illustrated in two ways: First, he was engaging in just his 11th professional fight, and second, his bout was moved up to the main event spot after a training injury to Eddie Machen postponed his featured contest against Cleveland Williams. (1)

To Clay, this dynamic move toward the big-time was a long time coming. His long-stated goal was to replace Floyd Patterson as the youngest heavyweight champion in history, so, even at the tender age of 20, the passage of time was exerting an unusual amount of pressure. Shortly after out-pointing German veteran Willi Besmanoff in Louisville the previous November, Clay vented about his management's choice of opponents.

"Why do they have to get me unrated bums?" he asked the press. "I'm tired of being fed on set-ups. I can't get a title shot by knocking out a bunch of has-beens or novices, mostly fighters who are over the hill. I'm tired of fighting such men. How can I hope to get the ranking I believe I deserve if I am going to continue to fight men I know I can easily whip? The public expects more from me and I think it is time that I receive some recognition, the kind I deserve, and obtain matches with rated heavyweights." (2)

"All I hear is 'get more experience,' " he complained later. "Why? I'm good enough to take (champion) Floyd Patterson any night right now!" (3)

But instead of Eddie Machen, Zora Folley, or Sonny Liston, Clay -- who debuted in THE RING rankings at number nine in the March 1962 issue (4) -- was paired with Lucien "Sonny" Banks, a 21-year-old native of Birmingham Ridge, Miss. who, two fights earlier, had flattened Tunney Hunsaker (Ali's pro debut opponent) in two rounds. Despite Clay's protestations, Banks was perceived to be a dangerous puncher because all but one of his 10 victories were scored inside the distance. Going into the fight with Clay, Banks was riding a five-fight knockout streak, four of which ended in two rounds or less.

Though Banks was largely unknown to the general sporting public, Angelo Dundee, the man who picked the opponents, saw him as a potential danger to his man.

"Very tough fight, a nothing-to-win kind of a fight," he said years later. "The media didn't know him (but) I knew the guy was a great left hooker. I warned him about being a converted southpaw but he didn't listen too good." (5)

As was his custom at the time, Clay, the 5-to-1 favorite, (6) issued a prediction: A fourth-round knockout. The fight began with Clay flitting about and gauging distance with his jab while the heavier-footed Banks moderately pursued him. Although Banks landed his vaunted left several times, Clay absorbed the blows fairly well and continued to work his plan.

The dynamic instantly changed with 75 seconds remaining. After Clay maneuvered Banks to a neutral corner and prepared to fire a hook to the chest, the upstart cranked a scorching counter hook over the top that left Clay flat on his back. The crowd, well aware of his prediction, cheered the loquacious upstart's comeuppance.

Embarrassed more than hurt, Clay scrambled to his feet within three seconds and waited for referee Ruby Goldstein to complete his mandatory eight count. Once the action resumed, Clay dodged a wild follow-up hook, then convinced Banks he wasn't in any danger by continuing to fight as if nothing bad had happened. In fact, it was Clay who finished the round more strongly.

Though Banks clearly earned the round, Clay threw more than twice as many punches (44-21) while edging Banks 12-9 in total connects.

The definitive question asked of every hopeful is "how does he react to adversity?" In Clay's case, the answer was "beautifully."

The second round saw Clay take the fight to Banks, keeping him at arm's length with his lashing jab and uncorking well-coordinated combinations. While Banks' hooks continued to land from time to time, Clay showed no more ill effects. A right to the chin caused Banks to lurch forward and get caught between the middle strands but Goldstein didn't deem it a knockdown. That would come 40 seconds later as Clay won an exchange of hooks and floored Banks in nearly the same spot of the ring Clay's backside had struck a few minutes earlier. Like Clay, Banks regained his feet with dispatch and lasted out the rest of the round, a round that saw Clay prevail 25-9 in total connects and 21-9 in landed power shots.

Clay erased all doubts about his superiority in the third as he bounced combinations off Banks' skull before hurting him with a hook to the jaw late in the session. Another left-right nearly knocked Banks through the strands and a second hook almost produced a second knockdown. Banks was fortunate to end the round on his feet, for Clay out-landed him 42-3 in total punches,

8-0 in jabs and 34-3 in power shots. Worse yet for Banks, Clay connected on 60% of his hooks and crosses (34 of 57).

The one-minute rest did nothing to relieve Banks' duress and Clay smartly pounced. A compact hook to the temple caused Banks to reel backward while a final hook to the ear sent him tottering back toward the ropes. That prompted Goldstein to step in and stop the fight, a move that drew scattered boos borne more of disappointment than a sense of injustice. After all, the garrulous amateur soothsayer had just proven himself correct and he finished the job just 26 seconds into the predicted round.

Clay's third-round surge not only broke open a close fight but also created vast statistical gulfs as he prevailed 84-21 overall, 16-0 jabs and 68-21 power. He also was the more precise puncher as he landed 41% of his total punches and 52% of his power shots compared to Banks' 30% and 34% respectively.

"I knew that night there was greatness in Muhammad Ali," Dundee declared several decades later. "Because he got nailed with a perfect left hook, coming in, got knocked down, he was out on the way down, he woke up. Once his backside hit the canvas he woke up bright-eyed and bushy-tailed. (It was) remarkable how he survived that one punch." (7)

Clay, though still hungering to fight the best, was shown he wasn't quite ready for them -- at least, not now.

"That was my first time knocked down as a professional and I had to get up to take care of things after that because it was rather embarrassing, me on the floor," a somewhat chastened Clay said in his dressing room. "As you know, I think that I'm the greatest and I'm not supposed to be on the floor, so I had to get up and put him on out, in four, as I predicted."

Shortly after dispatching Archie Moore nine months later, Clay saw the Banks fight as a vital psychological turning point.

"Only once in my boxing experience have I been low. That was in the first round against Sonny Banks," Clay told THE RING's Nat Loubet. "Things failed to go right. I said, 'now, Cassius, don't panic. Be calm. Just keep fighting like you were. Things happen.'

"That was a very important fight for me," he continued. "For one thing, I found out I could take a punch and come back strong. After I got up, I moved fast, stuck him with my left and, after a while, annihilated him." (8)

> *INSIDE THE NUMBERS: Clay rebounded from a first round knockdown to outland Banks 67-12 in total punches in rounds two and three. Clay put on a dazzling power punch display in round three, landing 34 of 57 (59.6%).*

17

MUHAMMAD ALI KO 4 SONNY BANKS
02/10/62 - NEW YORK

Total Punches Landed / Thrown										
	1	2	3	4	5	6	7	8	9	10
ALI	12/44	25/70	42/82	5/8	-/-	-/-	-/-	-/-	-/-	-/-
	27.3%	35.7%	51.2%	62.5%	-	-	-	-	-	-
BANKS	9/21	9/26	3/19	0/3	-/-	-/-	-/-	-/-	-/-	-/-
	42.9%	34.6%	15.8%	0%	-	-	-	-	-	-

Jab Landed / Thrown										
	1	2	3	4	5	6	7	8	9	10
ALI	3/20	4/24	8/25	1/3	-/-	-/-	-/-	-/-	-/-	-/-
	15%	16.7%	32%	33.3%	-	-	-	-	-	-
BANKS	0/2	0/1	0/5	0/0	-/-	-/-	-/-	-/-	-/-	-/-
	0%	0%	0%	0%	-	-	-	-	-	-

Power Punches Landed / Thrown										
	1	2	3	4	5	6	7	8	9	10
ALI	9/24	21/46	34/57	4/5	-/-	-/-	-/-	-/-	-/-	-/-
	37.5%	45.7%	59.6%	80%	-	-	-	-	-	-
BANKS	9/19	9/25	3/14	0/3	-/-	-/-	-/-	-/-	-/-	-/-
	47.4%	36%	21.4%	0%	-	-	-	-	-	-

Final Punch Stat Report			
	Total Punches	Total Jabs	Power Punches
ALI	84/204	16/72	68/132
	41.2%	22.2%	51.5%
BANKS	21/69	0/8	21/61
	30.4%	0%	34.4%

4.

After scoring his off-the-floor stoppage of Sonny Banks, Clay continued to rack up the wins --
and the knockouts. Eighteen days after halting Banks, he toppled Don Warner at Miami Beach in
four rounds. Then, a little less than two months later, Clay, now rated 10th by THE RING, (1) did
the same against George Logan in the Los Angeles Sports Arena (though it took him exactly a
minute longer to finish the job). Twenty-six days later at St. Nicholas Arena in New York City, he
stopped the 16-0 Billy Daniels on cuts in round seven.

Two months and a day after the Daniels bout, Clay returned to the Sports Arena to meet
Argentina's Alejandro Lavorante, who had been ranked as high as third in the world until
Archie Moore stopped him in 10 rounds in March 1962. The Moore defeat was his second in his
last three fights after starting his career 17-1. Before a crowd of 12,000, Clay staggered Lavorante
in the second, opened a cut in the corner of the left eye in the fourth and ended the fight by
scoring two knockdowns in the fifth to make good on his prediction. (2) When Clay signed to
meet Archie Moore, again at the Sports Arena, he brazenly boasted "don't block the aisle and
don't block the door/you will all go home after round four." (3)

Moore, never one to allow himself to be topped, chimed in: "The only way I'll fall in four is by
toppling over Clay's prostrate form." While Clay vowed to stop Moore with a "pension punch,"
Moore responded he was working on "the lip-buttoner," a reference to one nickname for Clay:
"The Louisville Lip." (4)

Coming into the fight -- a scheduled 12-round title eliminator with the winner in line to meet
newly crowned heavyweight champion Sonny Liston -- Moore was the grand old man of
boxing. Turning pro more than six years before the 20-year-old Clay was born, "Ancient Archie"
had traveled the globe and suffered more than his share of ups and downs and myriad career
roadblocks before finally securing a crack at light heavyweight champion Joey Maxim in his
162nd professional fight. Fighting before his adopted hometown fans in St. Louis, Mo., Moore,
who had celebrated his 36th birthday four days earlier, out-boxed and out-foxed Maxim to win
an overwhelming 15-round decision. Incredibly, Moore would hold the undisputed
championship for nearly eight years, then, after the National Boxing Association stripped him of
its belt in October 1960 for inactivity -- a move that prompted Moore to appeal to the United
Nations (5) --Moore notched a final defense of the New York State Athletic Commission's
version of the title by out-pointing Giulio Rinaldi over 15 rounds in June 1961.

Now campaigning as a heavyweight, Moore, still recognized as a light heavyweight champion
in some quarters, stopped Pete Rademacher in six rounds, halted Lavorante in 10, scorched
Howard King in 75 seconds and fought a 10-round draw with future light heavyweight

champion Willie Pastrano while weighing an unsightly 201 1/2 pounds.

The numbers associated with Moore were beyond staggering: Not only was Moore closing in on his 46th birthday and was beginning his 28th year as a professional, he had amassed a record of 185-22-10 with 131 knockouts, the latter figure being an all-time, all-divisions record he still holds nearly 20 years after his death in 1998. Given the glacial scheduling of today's fighters, he'll probably own the mark until the end of time.

By signing to face Clay, Moore would be fighting someone who was more than a quarter-century younger, had more than 200 fewer professional fights and 119 less knockouts. That said, Clay owned equally cavernous advantages in hand speed, mobility and manic energy.

Another striking contrast was their public personas, personas that paralleled their styles inside the ring. While Clay was loud, child-like and overflowing with magnetism and confidence, Moore was calm, calculating, cerebral, whimsical and quirky. From time to time he spoke with a faux British accent and he liked to shroud himself in mystery. He spoke often of "escapology" and "breathology" as well as an Aboriginal diet he said helped him shed excess poundage. His look amplified his reputation: Graying temples, a round and friendly face highlighted by a megawatt smile, and a goatee that that made him appear more like a jazz musician than a professional pugilist (although, according to Moore, the facial hair was grown in honor of "Murderer's Row," the octet of forgotten African-American fighters denied rightful title opportunities in the 1930s and 1940s). (6)

For many years no one knew his exact age or place of birth. His mother said he was born in 1913 in Benoit, Miss., while Moore cited 1916 and Collinsville, Ill. When asked about the discrepancy, Moore joked, "I guess my mother should know, since she was there. But I have given it a lot of thought and have decided that I must have been three when I was born." (7)

The Louisville Sponsoring Group was so impressed with Moore that it recommended "The Old Mongoose" as Clay's first trainer. Soon after beating Tunney Hunsaker in his pro debut, Clay traveled to Moore's training camp -- nicknamed "The Salt Mine" -- in Ramona, Calif. While Clay was eager to learn boxing techniques from Moore, he detested the chores that went with being in the camp: Washing dishes, cooking meals and sweeping floors among them. Though the arrangement was terminated within weeks (8) -- Angelo Dundee was hired to replace Moore -- Clay was impressed by one aspect of Moore's camp: The boulders bearing the names of past great fighters. Years later, as Muhammad Ali, Clay copied Moore's decor at his Deer Lake, Pa. training camp, and to prove there were no hard feelings, Moore's name was painted on one of the rocks.

Clay was a solid 3-to-1 favorite over the aging icon, who was now living in San Diego. While Moore represented a step up for Clay, the most compelling story line was whether the youngster would make good on his prediction of a fourth-round KO. Of his 12 previous KOs, Clay had correctly called the result and the round 10 times.

Though looking somewhat fitter than was the case for the Pastrano fight, Moore still scaled a bulky 197 1/2. Meanwhile, Clay topped the 200-pound mark for the first time in his career as he weighed 204.

Despite the boos that Clay heard as he walked toward the ring, he must have been satisfied with the results of his pre-fight salesmanship because it drew a capacity crowd of 16,200 that generated a gate of $182,599.76, the second largest take of 1963 behind the $370,000 recorded by Ingemar Johansson-Dick Richardson in Gothenburg, Sweden nearly five months earlier. (9) For the record, Moore was paid $75,000 while Clay made $40,000. (10)

Moore entered the arena to thunderous cheers, and after stepping through the ropes he executed a quick twirl, approached Clay and offered his right glove, which Clay shook without looking at his antagonist.

After ring announcer Jimmy Lennon Sr.'s excellent rendition of the National Anthem -- no surprise since he was the uncle of the singing Lennon Sisters -- Lennon introduced various boxing dignitaries, the last of which was a beaming Liston, no doubt heartened by the overwhelming applause his name and his presence generated.

The fight started as expected with the fleet-footed Clay circling energetically and Moore operating behind his trademark cross-armed "armadillo" defense. Moore's constantly rolling upper body forced Clay to punch down at him, a tactic that negatively affected the youngster's accuracy. Clay peppered Moore's guard with an almost ceaseless stream of combinations but, at least early on, Moore skillfully picked off most of the blows. At times, Moore dipped so low that his head was below Clay's belt line but the Kentuckian, both arms dangling at his side, continued to blast away at will.

After Clay missed with a right, Moore connected with a flush counter right to the jaw that brought a roar from the pro-Moore crowd. Clay, unhurt by what may have been the "lip-buttoner," continued to fire away with dazzling up-and-down combinations for the remainder of the round.

Aesthetically and statistically, round one was Clay's by a wide margin. He threw 86 punches to Moore's 21 and led 20-8 overall, 5-1 in jabs and 15-7 in power shots. But when Moore threw, he landed. The evidence: Moore landed 38% of his total punches to Clay's 23% and 47% of his hooks and crosses to Clay's 25%.

Clay's start to round two was even better than that of the first as his jab found the mark more often and he accelerated his output, actions surely designed to soften up Moore for what he hoped would happen in round four. Clay's frenetic pace kept Moore so focused on defense that he barely had time to punch back, but, again, when he did, he hit pay dirt. A soft lead right tickled Clay's chin while the second of two jabs and a hook to the body bounced off his frame. Still, the difference in speed and flexibility was graphic; Clay's punches cut through the air swiftly and fluidly while Moore's, though blindingly quick for a man his age, were stiffer, less frequent and more forced.

A right to the top of the head caused Moore's legs to dip with a little more than a minute left in the round, but Moore shook it off and responded with two hooks to the stomach, the first of which Clay indicated was below the belt. Moore then produced his best rally of the fight as several jabs found the mark and his power shots forced Clay to retreat to the ropes and slap on a clinch. Once Clay escaped to ring center he ended the round with a solid right to the forehead and a 10-punch salvo capped by a left uppercut to the face.

While the second was more competitive than the first, the numbers still heavily favored Clay as he out-threw Moore 96 to 35, out-landed him 28-14 overall, led 7-4 in landed jabs and prevailed 21-10 in power connects. But again, Moore was the more precise hitter as he landed 40% of his total punches and 48% of his power punches to Clay's 29% overall and 31% power.

The start of round three looked much like the previous two as Clay fearlessly whaled away and Moore responded with singular shots that landed with a diamond cutter's precision.

One particularly heavy right to the chin caused Clay to clinch but whatever dizziness was produced in the moment was gone in a flash. When Clay landed a lead right to the jaw seconds later, Moore's shuddering legs prompted the younger man to follow with a flush one-two to the face and two more rights that drove Moore across the ring. Now, Moore's weaving had the look of a survival tactic rather than a strategic gambit and the succession of left uppercuts that crashed off his chin indicated the end might be near.

The groggy Moore tried to stave off the avalanche with a pair of hooks, but Clay easily leaned away from both before retreating to ring center.

As the clock wound down, some ringsiders wondered if Clay had purposely throttled down to wait for round four and make his prediction come true. Maybe so, but Clay still finished the round with a final volley that seemed to tee up Moore for what the prospect hoped would be the final wave.

In round three Clay landed 26 of his 97 overall punches, 9 of his 34 jabs and 17 of his 63 power shots while Moore slipped to 10 of 29 overall, 0 of 6 jabs and 10 of 23 power. Once again, Moore's percentages were superior (35%-27% overall and 44%-27% power) but the overarching action suggested those numbers would soon be rendered moot.

Between rounds, Moore pulled out a familiar psychological card by refusing to sit on the stool.

Clay, however, would not be fooled; he knew he had stunned the "Ol' Mongoose" and was now ready to bag him. Once the bell sounded to start round four, Clay assumed the role of unapologetic aggressor. There would be no more dancing or backward steps for him. Instead, it was Moore who was on the retreat, and, as he did so, the weight and wear of more than 200 ring wars appeared that much heavier. The deep upper-body rolls that marked the first two rounds were no longer evident, for Clay's punches had drained him of the fuel he needed to sustain his unique "escapology."

Moments after Moore landed a lead right to the chin, Clay responded with a right cross-left uppercut to the face that staggered Moore, then an uppercut-hook-cross that dropped him heavily to the canvas. To add insult to injury, Clay stood over his fallen opponent, raised his arms over his head and broke into a rhythmic celebratory shuffle. Referee Tommy Hart pointed Clay toward a neutral corner, but, unbeknownst to Hart, Clay stayed where he was and waited for Hart to wipe off Moore's gloves and complete the mandatory eight count. When he turned around and saw Clay, he said nothing and allowed the assault to continue unabated.

A right followed by three quick lefts dropped the dizzied Moore to a knee, making clear the end was at hand. Moore arose at six, then braced for the final attack.

It only lasted seven punches. The next-to-last blow, a right to the face, floored Moore for the third time. This time, no count was necessary. With a wave of Hart's arms, the generational torch had been passed.

As soon as the combat was officially declared over, Clay rushed over to Moore, embraced him, leaned in and spent several seconds talking into Moore's left ear. The time: 1:35 of round four. The stats: 92-35 overall, 25-6 jabs and 67-29 power, including gaps of 18-3 overall, 4-1 jabs and 14-2 power in the final round, a round which THE RING deemed the second best of 1962 behind Round One of Liston-Patterson. (11)

While there were boasts after the fight, there also was praise. "Archie Moore's a great fighter and he did the best he could," Clay told broadcaster Jim Healy. "As I have predicted, he must fall in four. And if you have witnessed it, you've seen he done fell in four. Now I want Sonny Liston and he must fall in eight."

While Clay was looking forward to future glories, Moore was forced to confront his fistic mortality.

"Did the sun go down tonight?" one reporter asked Moore in his dressing room.

"Maybe no, but it was covered by a cloud," Moore replied with tears in his eyes. "It might blow away, the cloud might. Every morning brings a new ray of sunshine, a new ray of hope. I've had cloudy nights before." (12)

There would be one more night for Moore. Exactly four months later he faced Mike DiBiase, a wrestler who was making his professional boxing debut -- a foreshadowing of the Floyd Mayweather-Conor McGregor clash more than a half-century later. The fight took place in Madison Square Garden, but the one located in Phoenix, not New York. Moore-DiBiase was as big a mismatch as Clay-Moore had been, for after taking a lopsided beating a cut eye caused the fight to be stopped in Moore's favor at the 20-second mark of round three. With that, the great career of Archie Moore ended. As for Clay, the great nights were just beginning.

INSIDE THE NUMBERS: Clay came out blazing against The Ol' Mongoose, averaging 93 punches thrown per round in the opening nine minutes after averaging 60 thrown per round in his previous three fights. Again, Clay was touched, as Moore landed 37.6% of his 30 punches thrown per round and 45% of his power punches (20 thrown per round). Clay landed 24.8% of his jabs, throwing nearly 30 per round -- 10 more than the heavyweight average.

Date:	November 15, 1962				City: Los Angeles, CA				Venue: Sports Arena							
Opponent:	Archie Moore															
Result:	Clay by TKO at 1:35 of the 4th round															
Referee:	Tommy Hart															
	Round	1	2	3	4	5	6	7	8	9	10	11	12	13	14	15	Total
	Clay	10	10	10													30
	Moore	9	9	9													27
Judge:	George Latka															
	Round	1	2	3	4	5	6	7	8	9	10	11	12	13	14	15	Total
	Clay	10	10	10													30
	Moore	9	9	9													27
Judge:	Lee Grossman															
	Round	1	2	3	4	5	6	7	8	9	10	11	12	13	14	15	Total
	Clay	10	10	10													30
	Moore	9	9	9													27

MUHAMMAD ALI KO 4 ARCHIE MOORE
11/15/62 - LOS ANGELES

Total Punches Landed / Thrown												
	1	2	3	4	5	6	7	8	9	10	11	12
ALI	20/86	28/96	26/97	18/46	-/-	-/-	-/-	-/-	-/-	-/-	-/-	-/-
	23.3%	29.2%	26.8%	39.1%	-	-	-	-	-	-	-	-
MOORE	8/21	14/35	10/29	3/8	-/-	-/-	-/-	-/-	-/-	-/-	-/-	-/-
	38.1%	40%	34.5%	37.5%	-	-	-	-	-	-	-	-

Jab Landed / Thrown												
	1	2	3	4	5	6	7	8	9	10	11	12
ALI	5/26	7/28	9/34	4/13	-/-	-/-	-/-	-/-	-/-	-/-	-/-	-/-
	19.2%	25%	26.5%	30.8%	-	-	-	-	-	-	-	-
MOORE	1/6	4/14	0/6	1/3	-/-	-/-	-/-	-/-	-/-	-/-	-/-	-/-
	16.7%	28.6%	0%	33.3%	-	-	-	-	-	-	-	-

Power Punches Landed / Thrown												
	1	2	3	4	5	6	7	8	9	10	11	12
ALI	15/60	21/68	17/63	14/33	-/-	-/-	-/-	-/-	-/-	-/-	-/-	-/-
	25%	30.9%	27%	42.4%	-	-	-	-	-	-	-	-
MOORE	7/15	10/21	10/23	2/5	-/-	-/-	-/-	-/-	-/-	-/-	-/-	-/-
	46.7%	47.6%	43.5%	40%	-	-	-	-	-	-	-	-

Final Punch Stat Report			
	Total Punches (Body Landed)	Total Jabs (Body Landed)	Power Punches (Body Landed)
ALI	92 (0)/325	25 (0)/101	67 (0)/224
	28.3%	24.8%	29.9%
MOORE	35 (0)/93	6 (0)/29	29 (0)/64
	37.6%	20.7%	45.3%

5.

MARCH 13, 1963 - MADISON SQUARE GARDEN, NEW YORK, NY
CASSIUS CLAY W 10 DOUG JONES

The knockout of Moore vaulted Clay up to second in THE RING's rankings behind former champion Floyd Patterson (1) and a little less than two months later he justified his standing by traveling to Pittsburgh and stopping former NFL player Charlie Powell in the third, which, of course, was the predicted round. That said, Powell gave Clay a rugged scrap for the first two rounds as a hook to the body and a right to the chin gained the youngster's respect. But in the third, Clay's blinding speed and whipping combinations bloodied Powell's mouth and left eye, then drove him to the floor. (2)

"I would like to fight Jones (ranked sixth) and Billy Daniels (ranked seventh) on the same night," Clay asserted. "In this way, I can make greater progress." (3) In regard to that progress, Madison Square Garden matchmaker Teddy Brenner announced immediately after the Powell victory that he had signed Clay to fight Doug Jones on March 13 in Jones' hometown of New York City. (4)

Jones represented yet another step up the ladder for Clay in terms of opposition. The 26-year-old was at his physical peak and was coming off his most important victory to date, a seventh round knockout over Zora Folley that had avenged a previous 10-round decision defeat in Denver that was widely criticized. In what was called one of the best televised fights of 1962, Jones was floored by a right in round one but began to take charge in the third. The comeback built steam in rounds four through six, then, in round seven, a one-two to the chin caused Folley to collapse. Folley did his best to rise but, at referee Arthur Mercante's count of eight, his legs gave out, his body pitched forward and he was counted out. (5)

Jones began his career by winning his first 19 fights, with his victims including former middleweight champion Carl "Bobo" Olson, Von Clay (three times) and Pete Rademacher before suffering consecutive losses on points to Eddie Machen, Harold Johnson (for the vacant world light heavyweight championship) and Folley, who edged Jones over 10 rounds. The slide continued less than two months later when he traveled to Germany and drew over 10 rounds with 33-0-3 local Erich Schoppner, a verdict some say was decided more by geography than what happened inside the ring.

But Jones resurrected his career with back-to-back knockouts over future Hall of Famer Bob Foster and the man for whom Foster was a late substitute, Folley. Jones' off-the-floor rematch win over Folley was considered a major upset given that Folley, the 12-to-5 favorite, was next in line to challenge heavyweight champion Sonny Liston. Now, Jones, who entered the first Folley fight as the second-ranked contender for the light heavyweight crown, was one fight away from meeting Liston himself. Though Jones described himself as "quiet and peaceful," he was confident he had what it took to beat Clay and get to Liston.

"What's my impression of Cassius? Oh, alright." the Harlem native told THE RING's Dan Daniel. "You say, 'just alright? Nothing more?' Well, you never know about a fighter until he is in the ring with you. Clay throws a lot of punches. Is he a power hitter? From the looks of it, he punches pretty good. Will I say that I can beat him? Yes, I will say that, and back it up if we meet. I am not a braggart. But I will say this: I will beat any man with whom I get into a ring. I can beat Clay, just like I beat the other Clay, name of Von." (6)

Of course, Clay — the one named Cassius — had other plans. He originally predicted a sixth-round stoppage only to cut it to four after seeing a picture of Jones reading a book with an obviously makeshift handwritten cover bearing the title "The Rise and Fall of Cassius Clay." (7)

The Folley victory vaulted Jones to third in the rankings while also lifting Clay, who had been below Folley, to second. The importance of the contest, Jones' status as hometown hero and Clay's talent for self-promotion resulted in a house numbering 18,732 -- the first boxing sellout at Madison Square Garden in six years -- a gross gate of $104,943 and additional revenue from 40 closed-circuit locations in 38 cities. (8) It was obvious that big-time heavyweight boxing had returned to the Big Apple, and the numbers were even more amazing considering that New York City was in the midst of a newspaper strike. The magnitude of the occasion was further illustrated moments before the introductions when former heavyweight champions Jack Dempsey and Gene Tunney jointly climbed through the ropes and shook hands. At the morning weigh-in Clay scaled 202 1/2 to Jones' 188. Despite their close proximity in the rankings, Clay was a 3-to-1 betting favorite. (9)

As usual, Clay began the fight on the move and pulled straight back from Jones' blows instead of moving his head to one side or the other. That bad habit bit Clay hard 45 seconds into the fight when the off-balance youngster was nailed with a looping right that sent him tottering back into the ropes. As the partisans gleefully roared, Clay hung on tightly for several seconds to clear his head. Once referee Joe LoScalzo separated them, Clay went back to basics: Jabs, one-twos and occasional counter rights that jolted Jones' head but garnered scant reaction from the audience. While Clay appeared to have an edge for the remainder of the round, Jones' harder punches created the far stronger impression.

Clay fared slightly better statistically as he out-landed Jones 16-13 overall and 11-6 in power punches. But Jones out-jabbed Clay 7-5 and won the round on two scorecards with a single right hand bomb. That bomb, however, proved Jones was talented enough to stun Clay, and if he could do it once, many thought, he could do it again...and again...and again. If he did it enough times, he could pull off a gargantuan upset.

Jones pursued Clay heavily in the second and each time he launched a lunging punch at Clay --

no matter if it hit or if it missed -- the patrons unleashed loud and hopeful cheers. Meanwhile, Clay picked up his game by landing double jab-right hand combinations, right leads and other slashing punches that kept Jones at bay. His efforts were greeted either by stony silence or disappointed groans. The second round was a clear statistical win for Clay as he threw more (59-40), landed more (21-13 overall, 7-3 jabs, 14-10 power) and did so more accurately (36%-33% overall, 23%-19% jabs, 48%-42% power).

Clay's third-round performance was even more commanding as his combinations, especially in the final minute, clearly rattled Jones. In terms of statistics, Clay out-threw Jones 64-25 and led 18-7 overall and 13-3 power. But the most intriguing segment of the bout was at hand; would Clay fulfill his prediction of a fourth round knockout?

About a minute into the session Clay let loose a lightning-like flurry but the unhurt Jones responded with a counter right and a left jab that jolted Clay's head back. As the clock continued to tick, Clay dramatically increased his work rate but most of his punches were either blocked or dodged by the skillful -- and fundamentally sound -- Jones. With one minute to go, a clearly winded Clay drew in a deep breath and for the remainder of the round his punches carried considerably less snap. At the 15-second mark it became clear Clay would not fulfill his prophecy and the observers let him have it verbally by loosing ear-splitting boos. Clay's failure to stop Jones wasn't because he didn't try. He threw 84 punches and 44 power shots -- both highs for the fight to this point -- but Jones, who trailed by just 15-14 in total connects, did a good job of evading Clay's punches as Clay landed just 18% of his total blows while landing 42% of his.

Freed from the burden of his final prediction, Clay returned to his customary stick-and-move tactics in the fifth while Jones doggedly pursued. Clay's jab sliced through Jones' defense with far more frequency (he would land 10 in this round compared to the 19 connects he logged in the previous four rounds) and his flashy combinations kept Jones from closing the distance and launching any consistent attack, though two rights landed in the final minute brought the only roars of the round. They were only two of the 10 connects Jones recorded in the round while Clay, who out-threw Jones 70-36, landed 15. At the midway mark Clay achieved statistical leads of 85-57 overall, 29-21 jabs and 56-36 power, but the bout was still perceived to be close because the audience's cheers magnified each one of Jones' successes.

As round six arrived Clay still had a chance to make good on his original prediction. Once again, he turned on the offense as he unleashed 72 punches and kept the plodding Jones to 43. While he prevailed 19-10 in total connects Clay didn't come close to upending his smaller but more solidly built opponent. At round's end, the audience emitted a rousing cheer as their man successfully thwarted the braggart's attempt at soothsaying for the second time.

The seventh was much like the sixth as Clay began and ended most exchanges, used his jab (9 of 54) to keep Jones at arm's length and used his vast edge in activity (80 punches to 35) to control the distance between them and pile up points. Through it all, the audience buzzed quietly and awaited the next chance to let out the next roar. Aside from a single right hand at the midway point, however, the gathering remained largely silent.

For the second consecutive round Clay out-landed Jones 19-10 overall but despite Clay's growing statistical dominance, blow-by-blow man Chris Schenkel, as well as ringside reporters, still characterized the fight as one whose result was still in the balance. The judges' scorecards bore out that belief, for while Clay was well ahead on referee LoScalzo's card (5-1-1), judges Frank Forbes and Artie Aidala had Jones ahead 4-2-1 and 4-3 respectively.

That school of thought probably extended to chief second Angelo Dundee and Clay himself, because after an eighth round that saw Clay continue to widen his statistical gaps (79-48 in punches thrown, 21-13 in total connects and 13-8 in landed power shots) Clay accelerated his pace even more and staged a garrison finish. Clay's blows created a bruise around Jones' left eye and the smaller man was reduced to a desperate swinger while Clay peppered him with light but scoring punches. By the end of round nine Clay had thrown 98 punches to Jones' 52 and out-landed him 22-14 overall and 11-3 jabs. However, both landed 11 power shots, which may have been persuasive enough to make the round close in some minds.

Clay sought to squelch all debate in the 10th by starting fast and rattling Jones' head with clean combinations. Following a lull in the middle minute, Clay staged a final sprint toward the finish line with a dizzying series of multi-punch salvos that served to affix a final exclamation point. The gaps in production were staggering; Clay out-threw Jones 101-51, out-landed him 42-19 overall (including 34-16 in power connects) and was more accurate overall (42%-37%) as well as in power punches (49%-40%). Still, because of the dynamics previously described, an air of suspense hung over the arena as everyone awaited the final verdict.

Ring announcer Johnny Addie announced that the two judges, Forbes and Aidala, each scored 5-4-1 under the rounds system then in effect in New York. The moment he uttered the words "for Clay," vociferous boos and cries of "fix" rained down upon the ring and debris was thrown from all directions. The reaction drowned out the announcement of referee LoScalzo's score, which was 8-1-1 for Clay. Clay's surges in rounds 8-10 proved decisive on the scorecards as LoScalzo and Forbes gave Clay all three rounds while Aidala scored the eighth even and awarded Clay rounds nine and 10.

It has been written that the referee usually knows best as far as scoring a fight because he's closest to the action. In this case, the statistics proved the saying correct. Clay out-landed Jones by wide margins in every category -- 208-123 overall, 71-38 jabs and 137-85 power -- and the round-by-round breakdowns revealed that not only did Clay out-land Jones in all 10 rounds, he out-jabbed him in eight rounds and recorded an enormous 8-1-1 gulf in power connects.

While Clay-Jones was not a competitive fight statistically, the high stakes drama and the misplaced squabbling surrounding the verdict may have contributed to the bout being declared

THE RING's 1963's Fight of the Year.

"In picking the Fight of the Year it is wise to give consideration not only to action but to relevance and significance," wrote THE RING's Nat Loubet. "In designating the Clay-Jones affair as The Fight of the Year, THE RING magazine did not pick it as the most sanguinary scrap of the 12 months. However, it was a splendid fight and it caused a lot of controversy, many of the fans who packed the Garden in a no-television test coming away with the impression that the winner had been declared the loser. THE RING magazine's staff supported the decision strongly. Clay did not maul Jones. But Clay did drive Doug out of his path to a heavyweight championship shot. The victory over Jones gave The Lip more predominant importance, for the time being, than that accorded to champion Sonny Liston, whose second fast victory over Floyd Patterson hardly rated Fight of the Year rating." (10)

Clay, for his part, agreed he had endured a tough night at the office. "Well, this fellow surprised me," Clay told Schenkel. "I predicted four and I thought I had him going in four but he's just tougher than I thought he was. Can't call them all. But I understand Sonny Liston is watching this fight and as soon as I get to Miami, I want that bum and he will fall in eight."

When Schenkel asked about giving Jones a rematch, Clay said he wouldn't because he felt Jones was now out of the way and that a rematch would torpedo his ultimate objective: Beating Floyd Patterson's record of becoming the youngest heavyweight champion in history. As for his failed prediction, Clay later squared it up by declaring, "First, I called it in six. Then I called it in four. Four and six, that's 10, right?" (11)

Because "Gaseous Cassius" failed to live up to the self-inflicted high expectations and because Jones performed better than his status as a 3-to-1 underdog would have suggested, Clay was roasted by the New York media once the newspapers resumed rolling off the presses. It also wrecked the timeline established by Clay's management team, which, according to THE RING's Loubet, called for a May 24 fight with George Chuvalo in Las Vegas and a September fight with heavyweight champion Sonny Liston. (12)

Loubet, however, was an exception in terms of how the press digested the Clay-Jones fight. "In the first two rounds Clay was rocked but he came back strong to use his long reach and mobility to outpunch Jones. In the ninth and 10th Clay sensed that time was running out not only on his chances of delivering a kayo. The fight was sufficiently close so that he had to make an all-out effort. This he did. He outpunched Jones in those two heats and even managed to stagger Doug in both rounds, but none of his blows carried the magical soporific. Those two rounds saved Clay.

"Let's not take Clay too cheaply on the basis of this showing," he concluded. "He is a fine prospect for the future and, with proper training and seasoning, could make a strong bid for the title." (13)

However one chooses to perceive the result, the win still placed Clay in prime position to meet the winner of the rematch between Liston and Patterson, which would take place a little more than four months later. As the champ and the ex-champ prepared to complete their business, Clay and his team decided to take yet another step in his progression: His first fight beyond America's shores.

INSIDE THE NUMBERS: Clay nearly doubled Jones in punches landed (208-123) and thrown (762-416). Clay threw nearly as many jabs per round (39, landing just 18.3%) as Jones did total punches (42). Clay had just a 52-punch edge in power landed (5.2 per round). Jones had a strong second round, landing 41.7% of his power punches, but never connected on more than 38% of his power shots in any other round. Clay closed the show in style, landing fight highs in total punches (42 of 101, 42%) and power punches (34 of 70 power shots, 48.6%) in round ten.

Date:	March 13, 1963					City: New York, NY				Venue: Madison Square Garden						
Opponent:	Doug Jones															
Result:	Clay by unanimous decision															

Referee:	Joe LoScalzo															
	Round	1	2	3	4	5	6	7	8	9	10	11	12	13	14	15	Total
	Clay	E	X	X	X	X	X		X	X	X						8 (1E)
	Jones	E						X									1 (1E)

Judge:	Frank Forbes															
	Round	1	2	3	4	5	6	7	8	9	10	11	12	13	14	15	Total
	Clay		X	X	E				X	X	X						5 (1E)
	Jones	X	X			E	X	X									4 (1E)

Judge:	Artie Aidala															
	Round	1	2	3	4	5	6	7	8	9	10	11	12	13	14	15	Total
	Clay		X	X				X	E	X	X						5 (1E)
	Jones	X			X	X	X		E								4 (1E)

MUHAMMAD ALI UD 10 DOUG JONES
03/13/63 - NEW YORK

Total Punches Landed / Thrown										
	1	2	3	4	5	6	7	8	9	10
ALI	16/55	21/59	18/64	15/84	15/70	19/72	19/80	21/79	22/98	42/101
	29.1%	35.6%	28.1%	17.9%	21.4%	26.4%	23.8%	26.6%	22.4%	41.6%
JONES	13/53	13/40	7/25	14/33	10/36	10/43	10/35	13/48	14/52	19/51
	24.5%	32.5%	28%	42.4%	27.8%	23.3%	28.6%	27.1%	26.9%	37.3%

Jab Landed / Thrown										
	1	2	3	4	5	6	7	8	9	10
ALI	5/23	7/30	5/37	2/40	10/48	6/40	9/54	8/38	11/47	8/31
	21.7%	23.3%	13.5%	5%	20.8%	15%	16.7%	21.1%	23.4%	25.8%
JONES	7/16	3/16	4/10	6/12	1/12	5/19	1/8	5/15	3/12	3/11
	43.8%	18.8%	40%	50%	8.3%	26.3%	12.5%	33.3%	25%	27.3%

Power Punches Landed / Thrown										
	1	2	3	4	5	6	7	8	9	10
ALI	11/32	14/29	13/27	13/44	5/22	13/32	10/26	13/41	11/51	34/70
	34.4%	48.3%	48.1%	29.5%	22.7%	40.6%	38.5%	31.7%	21.6%	48.6%
JONES	6/37	10/24	3/15	8/21	9/24	5/24	9/27	8/33	11/40	16/40
	16.2%	41.7%	20%	38.1%	37.5%	20.8%	33.3%	24.2%	27.5%	40%

Final Punch Stat Report			
Total	Total Punches	Total Jabs	Power Punches
ALI	208/762	71/388	137/374
	27.3%	18.3%	36.6%
JONES	123/416	38/131	85/285
	29.6%	29%	29.8%

6.

JUNE 18, 1963 - WEMBLEY STADIUM, LONDON, U.K.
CASSIUS CLAY KO 5 HENRY COOPER I

From the moment his plane touched down on the eastern side of the Atlantic, Cassius Clay was in full marketing mode. As he walked down the steps of the aircraft that carried him to his destination, he held up his right hand and flashed the number five, the round he thought he would finish his next opponent, longtime British and Commonwealth heavyweight champion Henry Cooper. It was something he would do from his arrival in late May until the fight on June 18 at London's Wembley Stadium.

Yes, he was already a known sporting figure beyond the U.S. thanks to his gold medal at the 1960 Olympics in Rome, but if he was to create an indelible imprint on the global scene he knew he needed to spend as much time selling himself (and his fights) as he would preparing his body for battle. This was especially true for Clay coming off the Jones fight, a fight many mistakenly thought he deserved to lose because his work in the ring didn't square up with his robust pre-fight rhetoric. In other words, although Clay remained undefeated and highly ranked -- he retained his number-two spot with THE RING (1) -- he had work to do as far as restoring his positive career trajectory.

While the U.S. sportswriters demanded that Clay tone down his boasting, the rebellious Clay chose to intensify it.

"I'm not even worried about this big bum (Cooper)," Clay said while conducting an interview from the driver's seat of his car. "Cooper will only be a warm-up until I get to that big, ugly bear Sonny Liston." He later said that if he didn't stop Cooper in five he wouldn't return to the U.S. for 30 days. (2)

Clay took every opportunity to antagonize Cooper and the British public. For example, when asked about his impressions of England, he said, "Great Britain is a nice place, but I'm from America and I'm not used to it. The cars are too small, the streets are too narrow -- I like open spaces -- and I haven't seen as many pretty girls like I do at home." (3)

Ali's words ignited a furor that translated to a decent turnout -- approximately 35,000 instead of the hoped-for 50,000 (4) -- but the majority of his barbs were targeted at his challenger.

"Henry Cooper is nothing but a tramp. He's a bum," Clay opined at a press conference. "I'm the world's greatest. He must fall in five rounds but if he talks about me, I'll cut it to three."

Along the way, he called Cooper a cripple and declared himself "the prettiest fighter in the ring today."

"This will be no contest," Clay yelled at the weigh-in conducted at the Palladium Theatre, where he scaled a career-high 207 to Cooper's 185 1/2. The event drew approximately 2,000 people, a number the Daily Mail characterized as a record. "This will be a total annihilation. Just be at the fight. I'm ready to back up everything I'm saying."

The final twist of the knife in terms of stoking the public's fury was the ostentatious crown he wore at the weigh-in as well as inside the ring. Clay got the idea from Louisville attorney Gordon Davidson, who convinced Clay to ask costumers at the Palladium to find him a crown to go along with his ankle-length robe. That they did, and it served its purpose to a tee. (5)

"You got a Queen, you need a King," Clay said as the jeers rained down on him. "I am King!" While Clay embodied the "ugly American," Cooper was the quintessential British sporting hero: Humble, understated and classy in victory as well as in defeat. The ex-plasterer affectionately known as "Our 'Enry" didn't bite on Clay's verbal bait, and, as Sports Illustrated's Huston Horn brilliantly wrote, he absorbed the whole scene "with the patient, unrewarding optimism of an English sundial." He understood that Clay's antics not only would help the promotion but also enhance Cooper's own bottom line.

"He's building up the gate," he surmised. "And I'm on a percentage just like he is." (6)

The 29-year-old Cooper entered the Clay fight with a modest 27-8-1 record that included 18 knockouts, most of which were produced by a mighty left hook dubbed " 'Enry's 'Ammer." The blow generated so much power because Cooper was a natural southpaw who fought out of the orthodox stance. Conversely, most of his losses were blamed on the scar tissue that hooded his eyes and by now it was so tender that even the most modest contact opened the floodgates. Despite this handicap, Cooper was a highly accomplished fighter on the continental level; he had held the British and Commonwealth titles for more than seven years and added the vacant European title the day before Clay dethroned Sonny Liston by outpointing Brian London, who Cooper had previously defeated to win his other titles. Other victims include Joe Bygraves (who also stopped Cooper in nine), Joe Erskine thrice (after Erskine twice decisioned Cooper), Alex Miteff, Roy Harris and Zora Folley (who halted Cooper in their rematch).

Cooper's most recent outing was a fifth round knockout against Dick Richardson to successfully defend his British and Commonwealth titles. It was a typical Cooper fight: With blood flowing from both eyes, Cooper unleashed a massive hook that put Richardson on his back and ended the fight with only two seconds to spare. (7)

Cooper had been a notoriously slow starter in previous fights but here he roared out of the corner and instantly took the fight to Clay behind his terrifying hook, which connected on Clay's chin the second time he tried it and produced blood from the American's nose as the round wore on. Meanwhile, Clay was content to circle clockwise and fire plenty of jabs. In fact, the jab accounted for 10 of his 11 first-round connects and 36 of his 44 attempted punches. But Cooper carried round one with his powerful left, which resulted in 14 total connects (four jabs and 10 power punches). Cooper couldn't have dreamed of a better start, and that start brightened the spirits of the Cooper partisans who braved the rainy weather. That enthusiasm extended to ringside commentator Harry Carpenter.

"That first round has done wonders for British professional boxing," he declared. "People are on their feet at the ringside now cheering Cooper. A fantastic start by the British champion, completely overthrowing all his old nervousness at the start and come out there a fighting man. This is quite the most extraordinary fight night I've ever experienced in Britain."

The battle of left hands continued in the second as Cooper nearly matched Clay jab-for-jab (Ali was 16 of 49 to Cooper's 14 of 30) but one of Clay's jabs opened a cut under Cooper's left eye. The relief over the location of the first cut vanished seconds into the third when Clay's left ripped open a cut *over* Cooper's left eye. The spurting crimson forced Cooper to fight more desperately because he knew better than anyone that he no longer had the luxury of breaking Clay down over 12 rounds. If the job was to be done, it had to be done soon.

Even as Cooper wiped away the blood with the thumb of his left glove, Clay continued to work methodically. He didn't allow the sight of Cooper's crimson to make him fight faster than necessary. However, he did taunt Cooper by lowering his gloves to hip level while yanking his head away from Cooper's bombs and making faces at him. Because he postured more than punched, Clay was out-landed 14-11 overall in the third. Through three rounds, Clay trailed 47-41 overall and 24-6 in power connects.

Danny Holland did his best to control Cooper's bleeding but it only took a few jabs from Clay to spoil his quality handiwork. Almost every jab Clay threw targeted the left eye and the stats indicated he did so effectively (14 of 39, 36%). But while Clay came out ahead 18-13 overall, the fourth round will best be remembered for what happened in its final seconds.

A moment after Cooper slipped under Clay's flinging hook, Cooper turned the American toward the ropes, set his feet and whipped a compact hook that struck the point of Clay's chin. It was " 'Enry's 'Ammer" at its most destructive, and its fearsome force caused Clay's back to land between the two lowest strands before bouncing off and hitting the floor.

The aftermath of Cooper's missile ignited a sonic roar from the Wembley crowd. In that moment, a seemingly impossible dream was within reach, and for the British public it would have been sweet justice for the barbs Clay spewed about Cooper, the nation and its monarchy. But, alas for Cooper and the crowd, the round-ending bell sounded even before Clay arose. Walking to his corner under his own power, he was met by chief second Angelo Dundee, whose actions may well have saved Clay from a disastrous defeat. In doing so, however, he and his seconds bent and broke the rules. In terms of the former, Dundee admitted to widening a tiny tear in the glove that he initially spotted following round one. (8) As far as the latter, the video clearly showed an assistant stuffing a capsule of smelling salts under Clay's nose, a violation that, had it been spotted, could have resulted in disqualification.

Dundee informed referee Tommy Little of the tear but contrary to popular belief that Clay was given five minutes to recuperate the between-rounds break, at least according to the video, was only seconds beyond the regulation one minute.

However, a November 1975 story by THE RING's Ron Olver indicated that the rest period indeed was extended, but not to the extremes that had been alleged.

"Clay got up at four. He seemed OK and was hustled to his corner by his seconds," timekeeper Stan Courtney told Olver, who noted that Courtney kept written notes of every fight he had officiated. "Board secretary Teddy Waltham, sitting at the ringside, had a pair of gloves by his side, and took them up into Clay's corner. As far as I remember he stayed there while the job of fitting on the new pair was completed. At no time was I instructed to stop my watch to allow for the re-fitting of the gloves; therefore, I waited until I got the signal from referee Little to ring the bell. When I did so, my watch showed that the interval between rounds had, in fact, been one minute 40 seconds." (9)

Realizing his entire career path was at grave risk, Clay rocketed out of the corner and nailed Cooper with a right hand that connected flush with Cooper's cut and caused the Englishman's legs to buckle. A second right to the gash moments later turned what had been a steady but manageable flow of blood into an uncontrollable cascade.

With some ringsiders shouting for the fight to be stopped while others desperately yelling for Cooper to land another haymaker, Little had seen enough and waved off the fight. Cooper, while chagrined, accepted Little's action with his typical grace.

"He said he would (stop me in five rounds) and he did it," Cooper said. "That's how it goes. It can't be helped. But we didn't do so bad for a bum and a cripple, did we?" (10)

Clay, who out-landed Cooper by just 71-61 overall and was outdone 30-17 in power connects, had much kinder words for Cooper.

"He is not a bum, I admit," Clay said. "I really underestimated the fellow. My nose has never bled until I fought him and his left hook was as good or better than the people had predicted. And I must say he had me on the floor at the end of the fourth round. I've been on the floor once but I wasn't really shook like I was (here). and I have to say he really should be the number-two contender next to me. After all, I'm still the greatest." (11)

THE RING agreed, for it awarded Clay his first Fighter of the Year award, not only for his tumultuous wins over Jones and Cooper but also for the positive impact he had on boxing as a whole.

"Cassius is not the greatest title contender we have had in this generation of heavyweight competition," wrote THE RING's Dan Daniel. "But everything considered, he is the Most Valuable Boxer since Rocky Marciano retired from the ring undefeated." (12)

Clay, too, was undefeated, for the Cooper win advanced his record to 19-0 and 15 knockouts. More importantly, however, Clay had made his mark as an athlete/international celebrity while also sweeping away the final roadblock between himself and the man he called "The Big Ugly Bear": Sonny Liston.

> *INSIDE THE NUMBERS: A jab-fest for Clay in that 54 of his 71 landed punches (76%) were jabs (CompuBox average: 28%) and 178 of his 238 thrown punches (75%) were jabs (CompuBox average: 42%).*

MUHAMMAD ALI TKO 5 HENRY COOPER
06/18/63 - LONDON

Total Punches Landed / Thrown										
	1	2	3	4	5	6	7	8	9	10
ALI	11/44	19/60	11/43	18/54	12/37	-/-	-/-	-/-	-/-	-/-
	25%	31.7%	25.6%	33.3%	32.4%	-	-	-	-	-
COOPER	14/41	19/47	14/51	13/47	1/11	-/-	-/-	-/-	-/-	-/-
	34.1%	40.4%	27.5%	27.7%	9.1%	-	-	-	-	-

Jab Landed / Thrown										
	1	2	3	4	5	6	7	8	9	10
ALI	10/36	16/49	9/33	14/39	5/21	-/-	-/-	-/-	-/-	-/-
	27.8%	32.7%	27.3%	35.9%	23.8%	-	-	-	-	-
COOPER	4/7	14/30	5/30	7/16	1/4	-/-	-/-	-/-	-/-	-/-
	57.1%	46.7%	16.7%	43.8%	25%	-	-	-	-	-

Power Punches Landed / Thrown										
	1	2	3	4	5	6	7	8	9	10
ALI	1/8	3/11	2/10	4/15	7/16	-/-	-/-	-/-	-/-	-/-
	12.5%	27.3%	20%	26.7%	43.8%	-	-	-	-	-
COOPER	10/34	5/17	9/21	6/31	0/7	-/-	-/-	-/-	-/-	-/-
	29.4%	29.4%	42.9%	19.4%	0%	-	-	-	-	-

Final Punch Stat Report			
	Total Punches	Total Jabs	Power Punches
ALI	71/238	54/178	17/60
	29.8%	30.3%	28.3%
COOPER	61/197	31/87	30/110
	31%	35.6%	27.3%

PRIME ALI: LISTON I THROUGH FOLLEY

Before we at CompuBox began running the numbers for this part of Ali's career, it was expected that the stats would confirm the dominance we long had perceived when viewing the footage in a more casual manner. After all, the Ali that defeated Sonny Liston a second time as well as Floyd Patterson, George Chuvalo, Henry Cooper (in fight two), Brian London, Karl Mildenberger, Cleveland Williams, Ernie Terrell and Zora Folley rarely lost rounds and left the ring looking just as handsome as he did entering it. The numbers, however, tell a different story.

Yes, the Prime Ali generated plenty of excellent numbers. He out-landed his 10 opponents by nearly 600 punches (1,508-933) while also leading 840-333 in jabs and 668-600 in power punches. His jab was at its breathtaking peak as he averaged 10.5 connects per round, landed it 33% of the time and recorded double-digit connects 43 times during this phase -- including 23 in a row from round eight of the first Patterson fight through the 15 rounds of the first Chuvalo match. He amassed his career high in punches landed against Chuvalo (474) and the numbers for the Cleveland Williams fight were as spectacular as one might think they would be. Moreover, his 18.9 connects per round -- the same average he produced in his six "Young Clay" bouts -- was achieved with far fewer punches (51.6 per round in this phase as opposed to 64.8) and his 42.4% power precision was the highest of his career. Finally, Ali's 7.2 punch-per-round difference between he and his opponents was the widest of the four phases and he still enjoyed a 16.8-punch-per-round gap in terms of activity (51.6 versus 34.8).

But while his offense was in fine form, the Prime Ali's defense was surprisingly leaky, at least in terms of how accurate his opponents were in comparison. Three antagonists -- Chuvalo, Mildenberger and Folley -- recorded a higher percentage of power connects and on 25 occasions his counterparts connected on 50% or more of their hooks, crosses and uppercuts (Liston twice in fight one, Patterson twice, Chuvalo 11 times, Mildenberger six times, Terrell two times and Folley twice). Collectively they landed 43.1% of their power punches to Ali's 42.4%, which meant that during those rare times they were in range to reach him, they reached him -- often.

Yet it is this version of Ali that most fans and historians envision when they pick him to win virtually every mythical matchup. That's because, as author Jonathan Eig said in the foreword, our eyes tend to watch only Ali and ignore the efforts of his opponents. Who could blame us? After all, the Prime Ali possessed balletic movement, comet-quick combinations, unprecedented athletic ability for a boxer his size and a physical presence that explodes from video screens while his opponents, by comparison, are bland, colorless and ordinary.

In his later years Ali fancied himself an amateur magician and it is during this part of his career that he pulled off his greatest illusion. One significant part of that illusion is that he left the ring with virtually no proof that he had just been in a boxing match. The other is that whenever he took a heavy punch he maintained the same facial expression so as to not betray any pain he might have been feeling, then made sure to strike back immediately so that any memory of his being hit would be wiped out. Ali did this round after round, fight after fight, year after year, and, in the end, he exited this phase of his career with a record of 29-0 with 23 knockouts.

Ali's out-of-the-ring troubles forced him to accelerate his schedule to a level not seen since Joe Louis and his "Bum of the Month" club in the late 1930s and early 1940s. This allowed Ali's fans to have even more opportunities to savor his talent while enabling Ali's foes more occasions to express their fury. The common denominator: Both groups paid to see him fight and, to Ali, that was *the* bottom line.

Of all the statistics revealed in this book, the ones printed in this section may well be the most shocking because they shatter the myth that the Prime Ali was an expert defender. In light of this information, some experts may have to reconsider not only how they perceive the best version of Ali but also how he might fare against the best of the best. That's because any man who can be hit can be hurt, and any man who can be hurt can be knocked out. Ali's chin held up well against the murderer's row of Liston, Frazier, Norton, Shavers, Lyle and Foreman but how would he fare against today's supersized hitters, much less the power wielded by Dempsey, Tunney, Louis, Marciano, Holmes, Lewis, Tyson, Holyfield and the Klitschko brothers?

Let the new debates begin.

INSIDE THE NUMBERS: Prime Ali amassed a +3 plus/minus rating, the highest rating from the four phases of his career outlined in this book. When he was good, he was very good in his prime: Patterson landed just 65 punches in 12 rounds (5.4 per round). As a point of comparison, Juan Manuel Marquez landed 69 punches in his one-sided 12-round loss to Floyd Mayweather. Brian London landed seven punches in a 7:40 span versus Ali, while Cleveland Williams landed just 10 punches in 7:08 of ring time. Prime Ali averaged 31.8 jabs thrown per round, 30% more than the heavyweight average. Ali landed 33% of his jabs, an exceptional figure given that only three fighters active in 2017 (Mayweather, Gennady Golovkin and Andre Ward) landed 30% or more of their jabs.

7.

Up until this point in his career, the public at large perceived Cassius Marcellus Clay to be a walking amusement park. His over-the-top boasting, predictive poetry, and in-ring showmanship breathed new life into a sport struggling with recent ring deaths, disappearing TV outlets, and souring press coverage. In Clay, however, "The Sweet Science" had a fresh-faced and vibrant counterpoint to the argument that boxing was a dying sport. Clay attracted reporters like money attracted mobsters and his ability to fill every notebook with quotable quotes kept him, and boxing, in the spotlight.

By the time the 22-year-old number-one contender met world heavyweight champion Charles "Sonny" Liston on February 25, 1964 at the Miami Beach Convention Center, many believed the youngster's carnival show was about to get the hook. Nat Fleischer, publisher of THE RING, reflected conventional thought when he wrote the following in the September 1963 issue:

"I shudder to think about what could happen to Clay," he wrote. "Cassius is two years away. He is a very valuable property. He is very important to boxing. He has stirred up a lot of latent interest. He was important even as pre-fight Vegas dressing. Boxing needs Clay. It would be highly deplorable if The Lip were belted out, as he would be if in 1963 instead of 1965 he accepted the title shot. He hasn't been around enough. He hasn't fought enough. He hasn't seen enough opposition of class. He could no more stop Liston than the old red barn could impede a tornado." (1)

Despite his short reign, Liston's standing as a champion -- even among hard-to-please old-timers -- approached that of the legends. After witnessing Liston stop Mike DeJohn in February 1959, former heavyweight champion Rocky Marciano declared, "his left jab is like a bludgeon" while British trainer Teddy Bentham, the chief second of featherweight king Davey "Springfield Rifle" Moore, said "I wouldn't bet on a grizzly bear against Liston." When considering Liston's ability, Madison Square Garden matchmaker Teddy Brenner simply shook his head and asked, "who would you pick to lick him?" (2)

In a story entitled "How Good is Liston?" by Ted Carroll in the October 1963 RING, longtime observers such as 75-year-old Jack "Doc Moore," legendary trainer Charley Goldman, septuagenarian expert Charlie Rose and longtime Joe Louis sparring partner George Nicholson had high praise for Liston.

"As for Liston, I have seen every heavyweight champion for 63 years since Jeffries, and I want to go on record as saying that Liston would have been tough for the best of them," Rose declared.

(3)

"Let's not kid ourselves about this Liston: This is a fellow who has licked the clever fellows, Machen and Folley, the puncher Cleveland Williams, and the fast guy, Patterson," Goldman added. "Results are what count and Sonny has given us results." (4) Comedian Joe E. Lewis, a frequent presence at ringside, succinctly expressed his admiration by stating, "I wish he'd fight Russia." (5) Not only were insiders impressed with Liston, so were those paid to observe from ringside. Of 58 sportswriters polled before the fight, 55 picked Liston to win, and the vast majority thought he would finish the job in short order. In hindsight it is almost inconceivable to think of Clay as being such a huge underdog, but at the time several factors strongly pointed toward a Liston victory.

While Liston was a textbook fighter with enormous power in each fist, Clay was long on physical gifts -- supersonic movement, tremendous hand speed, and lightning reflexes -- but short on technique and weaponry. Yes, Clay's jab and right cross were first-rate, but his left hook flailed, his uppercut sailed, he rarely targeted the body, and he knew nothing about nor had any taste for infighting. Worse yet, Clay pulled straight back from punches instead of slipping to one side or the other and didn't use his arms and elbows to pick off blows. One could fairly say that Clay was a one-dimensional fighter. While that dimension was eye-catching and occasionally wondrous, there was good reason to believe Liston's fists would send Clay straight to the fifth dimension.

Clay, of course, had an explanation for his seemingly loose-limbed and careless approach. "The critics say, 'Cassius, you stand up straight too much. You back into the ropes too much.' " he told THE RING's Nat Loubet. "And I say, 'If I do those things, they have a purpose, and I always want to be myself, not a copy, not somebody's second duplicate.' You have to realize that my speed enables me to overcome certain things which you may call faults." (6) Nonetheless, there were legitimate questions about Clay's ability to take a punch, a laughable notion today but a logical concern in 1964. He suffered a flash knockdown against Sonny Banks and was nearly knocked senseless by Henry Cooper in his most recent fight eight months earlier. Clay was felled both times by left hooks -- and Liston's best punch was the left hook. One first-hand witness to the potency of Liston's hook was Roy Harris -- a native of the colorfully named Cut and Shoot, Texas -- who was stopped by Liston in just 155 seconds.

"I started easily enough, and poked three of four left jabs into Sonny's face. He was an open target and I couldn't miss him," Harris told THE RING's Jersey Jones. "I guess that's where I made my big mistake. I became careless. Next thing I know I was under the lower rope, half-in, half-out of the ring, and referee Jimmy Webb was counting over me. I was told later that Liston had clipped me with a left hook. I wasn't hurt, but the punch affected my legs. They felt rubbery as I pulled myself to my feet. My head was clear, and I knew what I wanted to do, but the legs wouldn't cooperate. I couldn't move away from Liston's ponderous rush. Next time I went down it was more from pushing than punching and the third time I slipped and skidded to the canvas.

When I went down for the fourth time, I was wrestled, not punched, and could have gotten up again, but I guess the referee figured I'd only run into more trouble and maybe serious injury, and he didn't want anything like that to happen."

Though stopped by Liston, Harris proved prescient when he wrote the following:

"Sonny is the most powerful heavyweight in the ring today, as well as a pulverizing puncher. He's certain to hurt anybody he hits. But a puncher must have a target to shoot at, and if he has trouble reaching that target, what happens to his punch?" (7)

Harris was speaking about then-champion Floyd Patterson, who was about to meet Liston for the first of their two fights, but those words could have applied to Clay as well. That said, there were several more reasons to doubt Clay's chances.

Besides his technique and chin, Clay's ability to deliver a hurtful blow was questioned. Clay's knockout record was glittery enough -- he had stopped 10 of his last 11 opponents, including five in four rounds or less -- but his shot-for-shot power was nowhere near that of Liston, a bone-breaking hitter of the highest order. In his three fights since March 8, 1961, Liston was in the ring for only six minutes 14 seconds. Two of those fights were against Patterson, who lost the belt in 126 seconds in fight one and was rendered horizontal in 130 seconds in the rematch. Even more stunning: After the rematch Liston revealed that he had injured his left elbow in training and that there had been talk of postponing the fight a second time (in March 1963 the rematch was pushed back because of problems in Liston's knee). However, a Detroit doctor who was a friend of Liston's manager Jack Nilon treated Liston in secret and the story never leaked out. (8)

Finally, Clay was thought to be too immature to handle the likes of Liston, a hardened ex-con who intimidated opponents by stuffing towels underneath his robe and fixing a withering stare during instructions. That criticism seemingly was confirmed beyond doubt the morning of the fight when Clay instigated one of boxing history's most chaotic weigh-ins.

"Float like a butterfly, sting like a bee...aaaaaahhhhhhh! Rumble, young man, rumble... aaaaaahhhhhhh!" he and court jester Drew "Bundini" Brown shouted. Chief second Angelo Dundee and legendary middleweight Sugar Ray Robinson looked on as Clay banged his walking stick on the floor and screamed at Liston like a madman. With widened eyes blazing with either confidence or with fear, Clay was held back as he lunged at the champion. He was so worked up that his blood pressure registered 200-over-100 and his pulse was 120 beats per minute. The weights -- 210 1/2 for Clay, 218 for Liston -- were incidental.

Clay's antics drew a $2,500 fine from the boxing commission, and the assembled sportswriters wondered if Clay would even show up for the fight. (9)

But it was all an act -- a perfectly conceived and beautifully executed act. A second examination revealed that Clay's blood pressure had returned to normal and that his heart rate was an athletic 54 beats per minute. (10) All thoughts of canceling the fight were put to rest. The weigh-in was the penultimate step in what had been a masterful psychological campaign that had lasted more than a year. It was the ultimate irony: By convincing Liston he was out of control emotionally, Clay won complete control of the war between the ears. The final act of his campaign took place at ring center when the 6-foot-3 inch Clay stood at full attention, looked down at his 6-foot-1 opponent and reportedly whispered, "Now I got you, chump!"

From the opening bell, the fun-loving Clay vanished. He carved wide circles around the charging champion, lashed him with jabs and befuddled him with slippery upper body movement. This was expected; even the most partisan Liston backer knew Clay was the much quicker man. What happened with 45 seconds remaining in the round wasn't expected, though: A lead right-left hook combination drove Liston backward and brought cheers from the surprised crowd. The emboldened Clay continued to rake Liston's face for the remainder of the round, which unquestionably belonged to the challenger.

In the first three minutes, Clay epitomized the ideal of hit and don't get hit; he out-landed Liston 21-6 overall, 12-3 jabs and 9-3 power while leading 45%-13% in total connects, 41%-10% in jabs and 50%-21% in power punches. Liston performed better in round two as he upped his work rate to 62 punches and out-landed Clay 19-12, including 12-0 in power connects. Amazingly, Clay didn't attempt a single power shot in the round.

The first inkling that something special was in the air occurred early in the third when Clay's double jab set up a right to the side of the head that wobbled Liston, then did so again with a hook to the ear. Moments later, a flush one-two opened a cut under Liston's left eye. The wounded champion stormed after Clay with dozens of winging punches that Clay dipped, slipped and sidestepped with the well-grooved grace of Gene Kelly. Another Liston wave in the final minute was more effective, especially a right uppercut that crashed through Clay's guard.

"Hold the phone," Theater Network Television's blow-by-blow man Steve Ellis said. "Cassius is a bit hurt." He was indeed, but the young challenger neutralized the threat by settling down and re-establishing his jab by round's end. While Liston out-landed Clay 20-18, it was mostly because he threw so many more punches (84-60).

Clay continued his hit-and-run tactics in the fourth and his accurate jabbing (15 of 28, 54%) aggravated the cut under Liston's eye. A hurtful lead right-left jab drove Clay backward, but otherwise it was another round for the upstart as he out-landed Liston 18-13 overall.

But as soon as Clay sat on the stool he started to blink furiously. Clay impulsively ordered Dundee to cut off the gloves but the veteran corner man, who, for the second consecutive fight, was called upon to save his charge from a potential loss, kept his cool and reassured his panicking charge that everything would be OK.

"I didn't know what the heck was going on," Dundee recalled in 1989. "He said, 'cut the gloves off. I want to prove to the world there's dirty work afoot.' And I said, 'whoa, whoa, back up, baby. C'mon now, this is for the title, this is the big apple. What are you doing? Sit down!' So I get him down, I get the sponge and I pour the water into his eyes trying to cleanse whatever's there, but before I did that I put my pinkie in his eye and I put in into my eye. It burned like hell. There was something caustic in both eyes.

"Joe Polino (one of Liston's trainers) had used Monsell's Solution on that cut," Dundee continued. "Now what had happened was that probably (Clay) put his forehead leaning in on the guy -- because Liston was starting to wear in with those body shots -- and my kid, sweating profusely, it went into both eyes. Let's face it, biggest fight of his life and he's blind. He can't see and he's hitting the panic button." (11)

Referee Barney Felix said he started to notice Clay's duress even before round four was over. "Toward the end of the fourth round Liston hit Clay with a terrific left hook to the body," he wrote in the January 1966 RING. "This blow hurt, but big. It was responsible for the hernia Clay suffered. The blow took all the fight out of Clay and he may have been ready to quit. That he wanted out was my impression.

"As the bell ended the fourth round he began complaining that Liston had rubbed liniment on his gloves and into Clay's eyes," he continued. "He complained to Angelo Dundee, his second, who, in turn, advised me of the situation. I walked to Liston's corner during this rest period, smelled his gloves and even tasted them. There was nothing but sweat on his gloves and I so notified Dundee. When the bell for the fifth round sounded, Clay remained seated on his stool. I walked toward his corner yelling, 'get out here and fight, Clay, or I'll count you out!' At this moment, Angelo pushed him off the stool and yelled, 'get out there and fight!' " (12)

While the remarks of Dundee and Felix are subject to debate, the video revealed that the frazzled challenger held his arms high in surrender as Felix began to walk toward Clay's corner. Soon after the bell rang, it was evident that Liston, too, had seen Clay's duress and, for the first time in the fight, began to take charge.

At one point Liston ripped 16 unanswered punches to Clay's body before the challenger finally broke free and motored away. Clay used every survival tactic at his disposal to keep himself upright -- and to keep Liston at bay. As the round wore on, Clay's eyes started to clear while Liston's gas tank emptied to a dangerous level. When the bell sounded, Liston's last best chance at victory had disappeared. Yes, he out-landed Clay 37-1 overall and 30-0 in power shots -- figures that greatly skewed the final numbers -- but by surviving this trial by fire Clay had cleared a vital, and, perhaps the final, hurdle to achieving his lifelong dream.

His vision fully restored, Clay began the sixth by nailing Liston with a flush right to the jaw, after which he shredded the champion with stiletto-sharp jabs (21 of 42, 50%) and opportunistic power punching. Liston had no answers for Clay's splendid display and by round's end he had been out-thrown 57-27 and out-landed 25-8.

Between rounds six and seven an extraordinary scene unfolded. One corner man rubbed Liston's left shoulder while another held a small ice pack on the back of the fighter's neck. Still another, Polino, worked on the cut, while a bigger ice pack was applied to a mouse under the right eye. But the real action was taking place within Liston's mind.

Liston had faced plenty of adversity in and out of the ring, but now, against this unheralded kid, he had reached his breaking point. Liston told his corner he couldn't lift his left arm anymore, an arm he used to throw 21 jabs in round six and 171 jabs for the fight.

As the 10-second whistle cut through the air, Clay rose from his stool and looked across the ring. Moments before the bell sounded Clay knew exactly what had happened: Sonny Liston, the supposedly unbeatable monster who was placed alongside Jack Dempsey, Joe Louis, and Rocky Marciano as the heavyweight division's most impressive punchers, became the first man since Jess Willard in 1919 to surrender the heavyweight championship of the world while sitting on the stool. The scope of Clay's accomplishment couldn't be overstated: Not only did he beat the "Big Ugly Bear," he made him quit.

Because of Liston's gigantic fifth round, a round that was achieved only because Clay couldn't see him clearly, Liston actually out-landed Clay 103-95 overall while also forging a big lead in landed power shots (63-25). But Clay led 70-40 in jabs and he was the more precise hitter in all phases (40%-31% overall, 40%-23% jabs, 40.3%-39.6% power).

Nilon, Liston's manager, said the champion had suffered a shoulder injury during training and, due to the injury, Liston did no sparring on February 3, 4, 5 and 14.

"When Nilon was asked why he had not demanded a postponement until he could produce a fit, thoroughly able champion in the ring, Jack indicated that Sonny figured to win anyway," Nat Loubet wrote in the April 1964 issue of THE RING. Liston, for his part, charged his shoulder had been injured by a punch "after the bell had ended the first round, and Clay kept punching at me." He reported he had no feeling from the left side of his neck down to his elbow. (13)

Given how Liston fought inside the ring, however, that story is impossible to believe."The fact is, of course, he did raise his left arm after that, and threw many hooks and jabs, the majority of which whistled harmlessly through the air," a RING writer without a byline opined in a March 1971 feature. (14)

Incredibly, at the time of the stoppage, Liston was still very much in the fight. Judge Gus Jacobsen had Clay ahead 59-56 but colleague Bernie Lovett had Liston up 58-56 while referee Barney Felix saw it 57-57.

In the wake of Clay's earthquake victory, a victory that established the 22-year-old as the youngest man ever to dethrone a defending champion to that point in time (21-year-old Floyd Patterson had beaten Archie Moore for the title left vacant by Rocky Marciano), Clay made it a point to scold his doubters in the press.

"What are you gonna say now, huh?" Clay asked during the post-fight press conference. " 'He can't go one round.' 'He might go two.' 'He holds his head back.' 'He holds his hands too low.' Well, I'm still pretty. All you reporters made it hard on Liston. Never write about me like that. Never make me six-to-one; it just makes me angry. Never make me no underdog, and never talk about who's gonna stop me. Ain't nobody gonna stop me. Not a heavyweight in the world fast enough to stop me. Liston's one of the most powerfulest in the world, and he looked like a baby. I held my hands down. I just played with him. I shook all of you up." (15)

The following morning, Ali shook up the world again as he confirmed reports he had joined the Nation of Islam. Eight days later, on a Chicago radio show, Nation of Islam leader Elijah Muhammad announced that the new heavyweight champion would also have a new name -- Muhammad Ali.

INSIDE THE NUMBERS: The evolution of the Clay jab continued here as 70 of his 95 landed punches were jabs. He landed 11.7 jabs per round -- double the heavyweight average (throwing 29.5 per round). He landed 39.5% of his jabs (heavyweight average: 26%). Clay landed 21 of 42 jabs in round six, while Liston managed just 8 of 27 total punches after going 37 of 70 in round five. An under-duress Clay went just 1 of 7 in total punches in round five. Liston jabbed with Clay, averaging 28.5 per round, but landed just 23.4% over six rounds.

Date:	February 25, 1964				City: Miami Beach, FL			Venue: Miami Beach Convention Center								
Opponent:	Sonny Liston															
Result:	Clay by TKO after the 6th round (corner retirement) -- Won World Heavyweight Title															

Referee:	Barney Felix															
Round	1	2	3	4	5	6	7	8	9	10	11	12	13	14	15	Total
Clay	10	9	10	9	9	10										57
Liston	9	10	9	10	10	9										57

Judge:	Bernie Lovett															
Round	1	2	3	4	5	6	7	8	9	10	11	12	13	14	15	Total
Clay	10	9	10	9	8	10										56
Liston	9	10	10	10	10	9										58

Judge:	Gus Jacobsen															
Round	1	2	3	4	5	6	7	8	9	10	11	12	13	14	15	Total
Clay	10	10	10	10	9	10										59
Liston	9	10	9	9	10	9										56

MUHAMMAD ALI TKO 6 SONNY LISTON
02/25/64 - MIAMI BEACH

Total Punches Landed / Thrown												
	1	2	3	4	5	6	7	8	9	10	11	12
ALI	21/47	12/35	18/60	18/33	1/7	25/57	-/-	-/-	-/-	-/-	-/-	-/-
	44.7%	34.3%	30%	54.5%	14.3%	43.9%	-	-	-	-	-	-
LISTON	6/45	19/62	20/84	13/42	37/70	8/27	-/-	-/-	-/-	-/-	-/-	-/-
	13.3%	30.6%	23.8%	31%	52.9%	29.6%	-	-	-	-	-	-

Jab Landed / Thrown												
	1	2	3	4	5	6	7	8	9	10	11	12
ALI	12/29	12/35	9/36	15/28	1/7	21/42	-/-	-/-	-/-	-/-	-/-	-/-
	41.4%	34.3%	25%	53.6%	14.3%	50%	-	-	-	-	-	-
LISTON	3/31	7/31	10/38	9/30	7/20	4/21	-/-	-/-	-/-	-/-	-/-	-/-
	9.7%	22.6%	26.3%	30%	35%	19%	-	-	-	-	-	-

Power Punches Landed / Thrown												
	1	2	3	4	5	6	7	8	9	10	11	12
ALI	9/18	0/0	9/24	3/5	0/0	4/15	-/-	-/-	-/-	-/-	-/-	-/-
	50%	0%	37.5%	60%	0%	26.7%	-	-	-	-	-	-
LISTON	3/14	12/31	10/46	4/12	30/50	4/6	-/-	-/-	-/-	-/-	-/-	-/-
	21.4%	38.7%	21.7%	33.3%	60%	66.7%	-	-	-	-	-	-

Final Punch Stat Report			
	Total Punches	Total Jabs	Power Punches
ALI	95/239	70/177	25/62
	39.7%	39.5%	40.3%
LISTON	103/330	40/171	63/159
	31.2%	23.4%	39.6%

8.

MAY 25, 1965 - ST. DOMINIC'S HALL, LEWISTON, MAINE
MUHAMMAD ALI KO 1 SONNY LISTON II

As is the case with all weight classes, the heavyweight division has seen its share of controversial matches. Many believed Jack Dempsey was robbed of a knockout victory over Gene Tunney in their 1927 rematch thanks to referee Dave Barry's "long count." In reality, Barry correctly followed the neutral-corner rule -- a rule Dempsey representatives Leo P. Flynn and Bill Duffy insisted be used during negotiations -- that authorized him to stop the count if the standing fighter doesn't go to the appointed corner, which Dempsey failed to do. More recent observers still can't believe Lennox Lewis only got a draw in his first fight with Evander Holyfield, a bout he dominated in every conceivable way.

But no other fight in heavyweight championship history has been debated more than the shocking end of Muhammad Ali's rematch against Sonny Liston. In terms of appearance, presentation and execution, everything had a shady, "under the table" feel, and the final result stretched all bounds of credulity.

The implications of Cassius Clay's transformation to Muhammad Ali were enormous. For many years, the heavyweight championship was one of the few possessions that bestowed a special brand of majesty upon its owner. His public regard was favorably compared to that of religious figures and world leaders, and if he was a particularly special athlete and man -- like Joe Louis -- he could become a catalyst for positive societal change.

While Ali eventually became a universally beloved icon, the Ali of 1964 was the willing epicenter of intense sociopolitical turmoil. No longer was he just the jovial jester that engaged in playful trash talk to sell tickets; his religious conversion added a layer of substance that supporters perceived as maturity and that detractors saw as in-your-face hostility. His standing on the scene directly contributed to the chaos that would be Ali-Liston II.

"If the sad state of boxing wasn't dolorous enough, this latest episode in the ill-starred serial between these two reluctant dragons has plunged it to a new low," wrote New York Times columnist Arthur Daley two weeks before the bout. "The clock has been turned back half a century or more to the era when pugilists were scrambling to keep at least one step in front of the law. Clay could have saved it. When he was winning his Olympic championship at Rome in 1960, he was a likeable young man of infinite charm and attractive personality, all the requisites for becoming as popular a heavyweight king as was Joe Louis. Then it happened. He decided he'd rather switch than fight." (1)

The World Boxing Association, who had recently adopted a ban on immediate championship

49

rematches and had removed Liston from its rankings following the loss to Clay/Ali, voted unanimously to strip Ali of its title in August 1964. (2) However, Ali's claim was still recognized by four other powerful entities: The World Boxing Council, the New York State Athletic Commission, THE RING and the general public who still thought of Ali, however grudgingly, as the "man who beat the man."

After extended wrangling concerning if, then where, the rematch would be staged -- initial interest was shown by Louisville, Tulsa, Baltimore and Philadelphia before they withdrew their bids (3) -- the rematch was set for November 16, 1964 at the Boston Garden despite the fact that the Massachusetts commission, a WBA member, had voted against the fight at the August convention.

"Although Herman Greenberg, Chairman of the Massachusetts Commission, was opposed to the return bout, when he and his co-workers returned to Boston (from the WBA convention in Norfolk, Va.), they found that sentiment among the Big Shots of the Bay State was strongly for it," Nat Fleischer wrote in his December 1964 column for THE RING. "Governor Endicott Peabody, recently defeated for re-nomination, was strongly in favor of obtaining the fight for Massachusetts." (4) In short, when big money talks, mountains can be moved.

To gain the governor's approval, wrote Fleischer, contracts were drawn that stipulated there would be no further return bouts, that neither of the contestants had any financial interests in the promotion other than the purses they would get, that Liston had severed his affiliation with the directorship of Inter-Continental Promotions Inc. -- a promotional company organized by Liston's promoter Jack Nilon, Nilon's brothers Robert and James, and Liston, the titular head of the venture -- and that each fighter will deposit $50,000 as a binder to insure the WBA's number-one challenger would get a fight with the winner for the "undisputed" title. (5)

With all parties in agreement, Boston was set to host its first heavyweight title fight since Joe Louis stopped Al McCoy in December 1940. The spurned WBA acerbically declared the bout as being for "the championship of Massachusetts." (6)

Despite the result of the first fight, Liston was still installed as a 13-to-5 favorite to join his two-time victim Floyd Patterson as the only men to regain the heavyweight title. This may have reflected the general disbelief that still surrounded the result of fight one, but it may also have been influenced by Ali's lack of focus on boxing since winning the title.

"Clay led a soft life for many months after his acquisition of the championship," wrote THE RING's Dan Daniel. "He toured Africa, he set himself up as the savior of his race. Then, when he returned to the United States, he got married (to Sonji Roi)." (7)

Meanwhile, all reports indicated that Liston had worked himself into tremendous condition -- Liston was already down to 220 pounds on September 7 (8) -- but three days before the fight Ali suffered a hernia that required immediate surgery. Just like that, the rematch was gone -- at least for the time being.

"This was a common but serious operation," said Dr. William McDermott, who performed the one-hour procedure. "Clay had been suffering from an incarcerated groin hernia, with a congenital defect in the abdominal wall. If the hernia stays in the bowel it could become dangerous. If it isn't taken care of immediately this is what happens: It obstructs the abdominal tract, and that causes the vomiting. The blood supply gets shut off and the hernia becomes strangulated. It could have gone on for several hours. It wasn't that dangerous. But, of course, it was much better to come right down to the hospital, as he did." When asked about Ali's injury, Liston's reply was typically blunt. "It could have been worse," he said. "It could have been me." (9)

The postponement resulted in a $200,000 loss for SportVision (the closed-circuit carrier) and other entities -- theaters who had committed to carrying the fight, various Boston-area hotels and surrounding businesses, newspapers that had paid for their reporters' accommodations and the fighters themselves -- also incurred significant financial damage. (10)

The fight was rescheduled for May 25, 1965 at the Garden, and the agreement that helped the fight come into being was amended so that the winner had to fight one of the top four contenders listed by THE RING, not the WBA. (11) It was a stunning admission by the WBA, for this expressed a profound lack of faith in its ratings committee and the rankings they generated.

The fight was a hard sell because both men were thought to be villainous. Rumors of underworld influence eventually caused the fight to be pulled out of Boston just 18 days before the opening bell. The event was moved 140 miles north to Lewiston, Maine, a manufacturing town whose population at the time numbered 41,000, and the site was St. Dominic's Hall, better known in town as the home rink for a successful junior hockey team. Not since 1923, when Dempsey outpointed Tommy Gibbons in Shelby, Montana, had a heavyweight championship fight taken place in such a sparsely populated town.

The assassination of Malcolm X four days before the fight cast an additional pall over the proceedings. Some thought Ali, who had sided with Nation of Islam leader Elijah Muhammad over Malcolm in the months before the killing, would be the target of pro-Malcolm assassins. Liston, who had also received death threats, feared the gunmen would miss Ali and hit him. As a result, security was extremely tight around both men and at the event itself. The negative atmosphere surrounding the combatants in terms of public regard, combined with the murderous foreshadowing, caused ticket sales to tank. On fight night, only 2,434 tickets were sold, which meant that less than half of the maximum 4,900 seats would be filled.

The weigh-in, which was conducted before a crowd of approximately 1,000 people inside the arena 10 1/2 hours before fight time, had none of the fireworks that surrounded Clay-Liston I.

Both men carried less weight into the ring; the 206-pound Clay was four-and-a-half pounds lighter while the 215 1/4-pound Liston was two-and-three-quarters pound less. In retrospect, however, Liston couldn't recapture the conditioning magic he apparently had enjoyed the previous autumn.

The same throaty boos that greeted Ali at the weigh-in earlier in the day reignited the moment he came into view of the paying audience and was even more intense when ring announcer Johnny Addie introduced him by his new name. Blow-by-blow man Steve Ellis, reflecting the conventional wisdom at the time, quickly added, "Muhammad Ali, better known as Cassius Clay."

Following a brief but hard stare-down, the rematch was finally on. Ali came right out of his corner and threw a lead right to Liston's shoulder, then tossed a light cuffing hook to the ear. After circling a bit, Ali broke out into a mini-shuffle that was stopped by a stiff Liston jab. The nonplussed Ali continued to dance with arms hanging loosely, then landed a right to the top of the head. Liston responded with a light right to the ribs, and another that was blocked by Ali's elbow.

Then, with startling suddenness, it happened.

Dancing clockwise toward the neutral corner, Ali pulled away from a lunging Liston jab, planted his feet and struck Liston with a lightning-quick counter right that jerked the ex-champion's head to the side and caused his legs to collapse underneath him. Even before Liston finished tumbling to the floor an enraged Ali stood over him, yelled invective and motioned with his right glove for Liston to get up, a moment immortalized by Hall of Fame photographer Neil Leifer. The referee, former heavyweight champion Jersey Joe Walcott, tried mightily to get Ali to retreat to a neutral corner but Ali, perhaps convinced that Liston wasn't nearly as hurt as he was letting on, circled around Walcott and continued to shout at his fallen victim. All the while, official timekeeper Francis McDonough, a retired printer from Portland, Maine, was pounding his 10-count on the ring apron.

As soon as Walcott regained control and began to lead Ali to the corner, Liston, who was initially flat on his back but had slowly rolled over onto his stomach, finally started to rise. He managed to balance himself on his right knee the moment the timekeeper hit the canvas the 10th time, but then he lost his equilibrium and again fell back-first to the canvas. Meanwhile, Clay was running a victory lap around the ring and Walcott, knowing he couldn't get Ali to comply with the neutral-corner rule, turned his attention to the downed Liston and began counting over him. But as soon as he started, someone, perhaps RING founder and publisher Nat Fleischer or timekeeper McDonough, caught his eye and momentarily distracted Walcott's attention.

Walcott was at a loss as to what he should do next because four different people demanded action from him: Ali, who was still running about the ring and was now leaping in the air, the fallen Liston, and the duo of Fleischer and McDonough.

Walcott chose to tend to Liston, who was just starting to get to his feet. Now up, a seemingly clear-eyed challenger extended both gloves so Walcott could clean them. Before he could, Fleischer called out and urgently demanded to speak to him. So, Walcott began to walk toward Fleischer, with his trailing right arm extended in a quasi-"time out" signal.

"Just before Liston got to his feet, Walcott, for the first time during this chaotic situation, turned toward the knockdown timer and (McDonough) waved him over and requested me to do likewise," Fleischer wrote in the August 1965 issue. "It was only then that Walcott had faced the knockdown timer who told him, 'I counted him out twice. I counted 12 the first time, then up to 20. He's out.' " (12)

With Walcott out of the picture -- figuratively and quite literally in terms of the TV screen -- the fighters were left to their own devices. Following a brief pause, they did what fighters do: They resumed fighting. Clay threw six punches at the cowering Liston when Walcott suddenly reappeared, stepped between the combatants and stopped the fight. Ali's handlers sprinted into the ring, one of which, Drew "Bundini" Brown, grabbed Ali's waist and lifted him into the air. The perplexed Liston stood alone.

McDonough had told Walcott that the fight should have already been declared over since Liston had been down for more than the required 10 seconds. A review of the video proved McDonough right in the strictest sense, for Liston was down 18 seconds before getting to his feet. However, since Ali had never fully retreated to the farthest neutral corner, Walcott was within his rights to suspend his count until Ali had complied. That's what Barry did with Dempsey against Tunney and Walcott should have done with Ali.

"Asked whether he had stopped the fight, (Walcott) replied, 'no, the timer counted him out.' " Fleischer wrote. "Thus, for the first time in the history of championship boxing, the timer, not the referee, who had sole charge of the ring, declared a fighter the winner by a knockout although that sole prerogative belongs to the referee.

"Several reporters declared that I, not an official, had stopped the fight," Fleischer continued. "Nothing like that took place. I merely aided in bringing Walcott over to the official knockdown timer at his request, since he couldn't get Jersey Joe's attention. The 67-year-old official was hemmed in at the ringside (area) and couldn't get up to announce to Joe that Liston had lost by a knockout. It was a bungled promotion from the outset." (13)

Walcott, of course, saw matters differently.

"The reason I stayed with Clay and kept pushing him away was because I was afraid he was going to kick Liston in the head," he told THE RING's Ed Brennan. "Clay was like a wild man.

He was running around the ring and shouting for Sonny to get up. Can you imagine what they would be saying about me if Clay had kicked Liston in the head? And you know he might have hit Sonny as he was getting up. If he did that, he might have injured Liston permanently.

"Like all referees, I was in there to protect the fighter on the floor," he continued. "Liston was a whipped man. I could see that by the glassy look in his eyes. That's why I kept running after Clay and kept pushing him away. I did everything a referee should do to protect a fallen fighter. Clay never gave me a chance to start counting. I couldn't hear the count from the knockdown timekeeper. I was trying to pick up the count but I couldn't hear it. They should have had a loudspeaker. But I think it was more important to keep that wild man Clay away from Liston than run over to get the count."

Walcott also said he had a hard time seeing the timekeeper.

"I kept pushing Clay away and looking for the timekeeper, who was a small man and hard to see," he said. "I finally saw him waving his hands in front of his face. I then ran over to him and he said, 'the fight is over. I counted to 12.' Nat Fleischer of RING magazine was next to him. Fleischer has been around boxing longer than anybody I know. I looked at him and he said, 'that's right. The fight is over, he counted to 12.' It wouldn't have made any difference if I had picked up the count at four or five as most referees do because Liston was out. I could have counted another 15 or 16 seconds over him. You add that to the 12 seconds the timekeeper counted and you know Sonny was really knocked out." (14)

Although Walcott successfully oversaw the previous month's lightweight championship bout between champion Carlos Ortiz and challenger Ismael Laguna in Panama City, he lacked the experience to properly handle the tumult swirling about him. As a result, according to Boxrec.com, more than 13 years would pass before Walcott got another refereeing assignment.

The statistics saw both men landing four punches. All of Ali's connects were power shots while Liston landed two jabs and two power punches. For once, however, the numbers didn't tell much of the story.

The faces around ringside first registered shock and disappointment, emotions that quickly turned to anger the moment Addie errantly announced the time of the knockout as one minute (a video review had the fight ending at the 1 minute 28 second mark).

"There was only one punch, a short right to the side of my face," Liston said later, pointing to his cheekbone. "I couldn't hear the count, but it was a good punch. I have been hit harder, though, by Cleveland Williams." When asked if he quit, Liston said, "no, I did not." (15)

"Did I tell the world that I had a surprise, and that if I told you the surprise you would not come to the fight?" Ali asked Ellis just before chants of "Fix! Fix! Fix!" reverberated throughout the arena. Ali later called the knockout blow the "anchor punch," which he said was taught to him by comedian/actor Stepin Fetchit, who said he learned it from Jack Johnson, one of Ali's heroes. Ali said the main principle of the punch was to time the right hand to land as the opponent came in, thus doubling the force. Skeptics, however, called it the "phantom punch," for they didn't believe it carried enough power to knock out a man who once fought several rounds with a broken jaw before losing on points to Marty Marshall in 1954. "I saw that punch and it couldn't have crushed a grape," Jimmy Cannon famously quipped. And Fleischer, who spent many hours with Johnson in THE RING's offices, said the longtime champ never mentioned anything about an "anchor punch." (16)

Just before he left the ring, Ali couldn't resist a final parting shot. Speaking as Liston, Ali said "this time I'm a bigger fool/Flat on my back, not on the stool."

For Ali the Liston case may have been closed for good but for the rest of us the debate will rage until the end of time.

INSIDE THE NUMBERS: Ali didn't need to land a jab as he connected with only 4 power punches before the end came.

MUHAMMAD ALI KO 1 SONNY LISTON
05/25/65 - LEWISTON

Total Punches Landed / Thrown												
	1	2	3	4	5	6	7	8	9	10	11	12
ALI	4/9	-/-	-/-	-/-	-/-	-/-	-/-	-/-	-/-	-/-	-/-	-/-
	44.4%	-	-	-	-	-	-	-	-	-	-	-
LISTON	4/21	-/-	-/-	-/-	-/-	-/-	-/-	-/-	-/-	-/-	-/-	-/-
	19%	-	-	-	-	-	-	-	-	-	-	-

Jab Landed / Thrown												
	1	2	3	4	5	6	7	8	9	10	11	12
ALI	0/2	-/-	-/-	-/-	-/-	-/-	-/-	-/-	-/-	-/-	-/-	-/-
	0%	-	-	-	-	-	-	-	-	-	-	-
LISTON	2/15	-/-	-/-	-/-	-/-	-/-	-/-	-/-	-/-	-/-	-/-	-/-
	13.3%	-	-	-	-	-	-	-	-	-	-	-

Power Punches Landed / Thrown												
	1	2	3	4	5	6	7	8	9	10	11	12
ALI	4/7	-/-	-/-	-/-	-/-	-/-	-/-	-/-	-/-	-/-	-/-	-/-
	57.1%	-	-	-	-	-	-	-	-	-	-	-
LISTON	2/6	-/-	-/-	-/-	-/-	-/-	-/-	-/-	-/-	-/-	-/-	-/-
	33.3%	-	-	-	-	-	-	-	-	-	-	-

Final Punch Stat Report			
	Total Punches	Total Jabs	Power Punches
ALI	4/9	0/2	4/7
	44.4%	0%	57.1%
LISTON	4/21	2/15	2/6
	19%	13.3%	33.3%

9.

NOVEMBER 22, 1965 - CONVENTION CENTER, LAS VEGAS, NV

MUHAMMAD ALI KO 12 FLOYD PATTERSON I

With each passing day, the schism between Muhammad Ali and the majority of the general public in the United States widened. His conversion to the Nation of Islam was seen as a hostile act in white Christian-majority America because of the "Black Muslims' " separatist/anti-Caucasian rhetoric. The controversy surrounding the Ali-Liston rematch only amplified the racial tensions and the conspiracy theories. While still popular abroad, many of Ali's countrymen no longer saw him as the Olympic hero he once had been. Wherever he went, loud and heartfelt boos were heard more often than not, for he was no longer just an athlete, he was a revolutionary.

Meanwhile, Ali felt he wasn't being given the proper credit for beating "The Big Ugly Bear" not once, but twice inside the distance. He was skewered by sportswriters and columnists and that disrespect extended to administrative circles. The WBA, which would be based in the U.S. until moving to Panama in 1975, had stripped Ali of its belt for accepting the Liston rematch in 1964 and had since crowned Ernie Terrell its champion by virtue of his 15-round decision over Eddie Machen in March 1965.

It had been more than two years since the general public had been comfortable with its heavyweight champion, and the man who held that distinction, Floyd Patterson, was Ali's next challenger. Their fight was set for November 22, 1965 at the Convention Center in Las Vegas.

Still just 30, Patterson was a 13-year professional who had already created plenty of history. At 17, he was one of the youngest Olympic boxing champions in history when he won middleweight gold at the 1952 Helsinki Games and, at 21 years 336 days, was the youngest man to date to win a version of the heavyweight title. He also was the first to regain the heavyweight championship thanks to his crushing fifth-round one-punch knockout over previous conqueror Ingemar Johansson in June 1960. Afflicted with profound shyness as a child, Patterson used boxing as therapy. As a result, Patterson struck a pleasing balance in life: He was bold enough to climb into a ring and compete with world-class athletes but was humble and graceful enough beyond the ropes to become a beloved figure.

Ali's public relationship with Patterson was complex and inconsistent. At times Ali was so enthusiastic upon seeing Patterson that he behaved more like the president of his fan club than an athletic peer. One such example of Ali's esteem took place in February 1965 during Patterson's thrilling decision victory over George Chuvalo when Ali, while acting as a color commentator, openly rooted for the former champion and tried his best to help him.

"I could not hear what Clay was saying," Patterson said. "But he was in full view from my corner. If he thought I had a round he made a significant signal, forming index finger and thumb into an 'O.' If Clay figured I had lost the round he showed his displeasure. And, from time to time, he told me that I was not doing enough jabbing.

"I got a lot of help from Cassius," a chuckling Patterson concluded. "A lot of help from an unlooked-for quarter." (1) But here, Ali's hostility toward Patterson was venomous. The source of that enmity was ignited when the ex-champ, a devout Roman Catholic, started to frame the match in terms that went far beyond sport.

"I detest the Black Muslims," he told THE RING's Dan Daniel. "They are a hate group and Clay is doing a terrible disservice to boxing and the heavyweight title by being associated with them. I have hated the Muslims all along. But I developed an especially strong hatred for them after Malcolm X commented on the assassination of President Kennedy with the terrible statement 'chickens must come home to roost.' Malcolm is a sharp fellow and Clay seems to be all confused by this man, by the Muslims in general." (2) Patterson ratcheted up the rhetoric even more in an article he wrote for Sports Illustrated: "I say it, and I say it flatly, that the image of a Black Muslim as the world heavyweight champion disgraces the sport and the nation. Cassius Clay must be beaten and the Black Muslims' scourge removed from boxing." (3)

To Ali, those were not just fighting words, they were words that commanded him to do more than just defeat him inside the ring. "I want to punish him. To cause him pain," Ali told Sports Illustrated's Gilbert Rogin shortly before the fight. "You find out what a person don't like, then you give it to him. He don't like to be embarrassed because he has so much pride, so I'm going to make him ashamed. He is going to suffer serious chastisement. The man picked the wrong time to start talking to the wrong man. We don't consider the Muslims have the title any more than the Baptists thought they had it when Joe Louis was champ. Does he think I'm going to be ignorant enough to attack his religion? Why I should I act the fool? He says he's going to bring the title back to America. I act like I belong to America more than he do. I represented it beautiful in Scotland. I never wink at a woman or go out of a hotel after dark. See, I'm no bogeyman, like they say. Why should I let one old Negro make a fool of me?

"Floyd would be smart to come out and make a national apology," Ali continued. "I've got an unseen power going for me. There'll be almost four billion Muslims praying for their brother in Islam. We've got sympathizers in his own camp. How is he going to buck all this? This little, old dumb pork chop eater don't have a chance." (4)

All the physical advantages belonged to Ali. At 23, he was nearly seven years younger than Patterson and he owned significant edges in height (three inches), reach (seven inches) and foot speed. Patterson was considered to be the fastest-handed heavyweight champion in history but most minds were changed the instant Cassius Clay seized the crown from Liston.

Patterson had won five straight since his back-to-back humiliations against Liston to run his record to 43-4 with 32 knockouts. Two fights earlier he won a pulsating 12-round decision over Chuvalo that would be declared THE RING's 1965 Fight of the Year and came into the Ali fight off a three-round knockout over Tod Herring in Sweden, where Patterson had become an adopted hero thanks to his three-fight series against Ingemar Johansson and the classy way with which he comported himself.

Ali opened the fight as a 14-to-5 favorite and by fight night they lengthened to 3-to-1. (5) Ali was similarly favored in a poll of 23 experts conducted by THE RING in its December 1965 issue as he was the choice of 16, Patterson of six and, because he still didn't know what happened in either Liston fight, New York Journal-American columnist Jimmy Cannon abstained. (6)

Unbeknownst to most, Patterson entered the ring with a slipped disc in his back and was still mourning the recent passing of trainer Dan Florio, who was replaced by Al Silvani. In the other corner, a seething Ali was prepared to administer a severe physical and psychological battering.

"Back it up now," Ali told Patterson during the pre-fight instructions, referencing his pre-fight statements. "I'm waiting for you."

Ali spent the first round on the move, pushing down on Patterson's neck, whispering in his ear during the clinches and executing lightning-quick hand and foot feints to force Patterson out of position. Patterson, without full range of motion in his back, had to bend his knees to duck under Ali's punches. A lunging, grazing hook by Patterson was roundly cheered while Ali tried to belittle the challenger by measuring with the left hand and suddenly throwing both hands at Patterson in a quasi-peek-a-boo move, shouting, "watch it! Watch it" as he did so.

After the bell ending round one Ali threw both arms in the air to goose the crowd of 8,106 -- of which 7,402 were paid (7) -- into even more robust booing. He ceded the round to Patterson, for he landed none of his 12 punch attempts (all but one of which were half-speed jabs) while Patterson connected on 6 of 25, most of which were body shots. It would be the only time Patterson would out-perform Ali in any aspect of the fight, statistically or otherwise.

Ali finally went to work starting in round two as he got his jab untracked (13 of 58), fired 65 punches to Patterson's 19 and out-landed him 14-4 overall and 13-3 jabs. He was still in semi-clown mode but even in first gear he showed himself to be the far superior athlete. He let out a "hoot!" on most of the punches he threw, as if he wanted to further accentuate his hand speed. Patterson doggedly pursued Ali, landing a jab to the body and whiffing on an overhand right that looked as if had been thrown underwater when compared to Ali's lightning bolts. Along with the physical punishment he inflicted, Ali made sure to pierce Patterson's psyche with verbal spears. "Come on American," he said. "Come on 'white' American." (8)

The pattern continued in rounds three through five as Ali continued to dominate range with his legs and his jab. Sixty-nine of his 77 punches in round three were jabs, as were 43 of his 49 blows in the fourth and 49 of his 57 punches in the fifth. During that stretch Ali led 34-10 in landed jabs and stretched his overall connect lead to 52-28 despite the goose-egg in round one. Neither man followed their punches with power shots; Ali because he wouldn't and Patterson because he couldn't. Ali tried just eight power shots in round three, six in the fourth and eight in the fifth, landing a scant four of them in that nine-minute stretch. Patterson actually landed eight of his hooks and crosses, but he probably felt more pain in throwing them than Ali did in receiving them.

Ali's first serious attempt at scoring a knockout began a minute into the sixth when he strung together several left-rights and unleashed follow-up volleys. The attrition caused Patterson to take a knee in the final minute but because Ali refused to remain in a neutral corner -- a chronic problem for him -- Patterson received an extra seven seconds to recuperate. Patterson appeared even stiffer that he had been upon rising and though he landed a solid left hook in the closing seconds he lacked the tools to make a serious dent.

Still, the sixth would be Patterson's best as he reached double-digit connects for the only time in the fight --14 -- and achieved his highest output (34 punches). That said, Ali also achieved his best numbers to date: 102 punches thrown, 28 total connects, 16 landed jabs and 12 landed power shots.

The surge of the sixth reverted to the previous pattern in the seventh as a comfortable Ali out-boxed Patterson as he pleased. Meanwhile, Patterson struggled with his back and at times he rolled his right shoulder in an attempt to stretch the affected muscles. Between rounds seven and eight -- as well as the interval between rounds nine and 10 -- assistant trainer Buster Watson tried to pop Patterson's back into place by lifting him in the air and bouncing him up and down.

Ali continued to peck away at Patterson in the eighth, out-throwing the challenger 91 to 20 and out-landing him 22-5 overall. The action grew even more lopsided in the ninth, as Ali threw 73 punches to Patterson's 12 and prevailed 18-1 in overall connects, and the 10th, as Ali went 27 of 95 to Patterson's 7 of 21 and connected on 20 of his 60 jabs to Patterson's 3 of 9. A healthy Patterson would have had serious problems dealing with Ali's gifts but now, with a crippling back problem, his case was hopeless.

Yet Patterson, game to his core, soldiered on. Ali landed so often and so cleanly that many thought he could end the fight at the moment of his choosing but because he continued to throw far more jabs than power punches -- and because of his stated desire to punish Patterson for his pre-fight rhetoric -- there was reason to think Ali was making good on his vow to torture the challenger before putting him away.

The aching Patterson could only throw 15 punches in the 11th, landing three, while Ali breezed to a 13 of 70 effort that included 11 of 56 jabs. Patterson cringed noticeably after a couple of winging rights that missed the target by embarrassingly wide margins and Ali, satisfied with the fact he was proving his point, coldly resumed his dissection.

Between rounds 11 and 12 Silvani took over the back-stretching duties as ringside physician Dr. Donald Romeo oversaw the activity and asked Patterson if he wanted to continue. When referee Harry Kessler visited the corner, Dr. Romeo appeared to advise him to stop the fight if the action became even more lopsided than it had already been.

Finally, Ali had had enough of the charade and in the 12th he planted his feet and cut loose with combinations. Patterson was so enfeebled than even lead left uppercuts by Ali were landing flush, but his pride would not permit him to fall at Ali's feet once again. Ali shook his head and almost begged him to quit but when Patterson refused the assault escalated.

With 42 seconds remaining in the 12th Kessler finally stepped in and stopped the slaughter. Tellingly, Ali rushed over to Patterson and said a few words with an expression that was anything but hostile. As is often the case with grudge matches, Ali had used the ring to address his ill feelings and prove his point. Once the business was done, it was done.

"I have to say one thing for Floyd: I was doing my best," Ali told blow-by-blow man Steve Ellis. "I am just so surprised that he could take so many punches. I figured the fight would go six or seven, but I wasn't taking no chances; he's a real man, he didn't fall." But then his anger resurfaced.

"I predicted that the way he was talking about me that I would give him a good whipping, and I'm so thankful that he did have the power to stand up like he did because what he got was a good whipping," he said, coughing through the interview. "It's time for the boxing public, also the American public, to give me the justice that I'm due for actually saying what I would do."

Ali had also predicted that he would make Patterson miss six times to his one. He didn't quite reach that level, but the final numbers illustrated his dominance. He out-landed Patterson 210-65 overall, 140-29 jabs and 70-36 power. Interestingly, Patterson was slightly more accurate overall (26%-25%) but Ali led 22.4%-21.5% in jab precision and 30.6%-30% power. But the crux of his success was in his vastly superior activity; Ali averaged 72.6 punches per round while Patterson could only muster 23.7. The final four rounds were particularly hard to watch; during that stretch Ali out-landed Patterson 93-13 overall, 55-5 jabs and 38-8 power and in the 12th he led 35-2 overall, 11-1 jabs and 24-1 power while out-throwing Patterson 95-14.

"I think I would have made a more interesting fight against Clay if it were not for my injured back," Patterson said. "I was beaten by a better fighter. Mr. Clay will be a great fighter when he gets more experience." (9)

The Ali-Patterson fight continued a string of heavyweight championship contests that left a sour taste. The last truly satisfying title tilt was the March 1961 rubber match between Patterson and Johansson in which three knockdowns were scored in round one (two by Johansson, one by Patterson) before Patterson scored the fourth and final one in the sixth. The next six bouts, however, failed to even approach Patterson-Johansson III in terms of two-way competitiveness. First, Patterson floored the brave but badly outclassed Tom McNeeley 11 times in less than four rounds, after which came the two disastrous one-round blowouts against Sonny Liston, then the two controversy-laden Clay/Ali-Liston fights, and, now, the Ali-Patterson skewering.

The legendary Joe Louis reflected the majority of public sentiment when he wrote that Ali had treated Patterson mercilessly. "I would have been ashamed to do it," an uncharacteristically scathing Louis said of Ali's "carrying" of Patterson. "Clay wasn't doing his best as a fighter. He was putting on a show, like the wrestlers. He could have knocked out Patterson any time he really went to work, certainly no later than the sixth, when he had Floyd on the floor. Yet he clowned around without letup and it was finally the referee, Harry Krause, who called it off without Patterson being down again. Let's face it: Clay is selfish and cruel." (10)

Ali might have resolved his issues with Patterson, but other missions still needed to be addressed. After all, Terrell held the WBA belt that was stripped from him. The fight was originally scheduled for March 29, 1966 in Terrell's native Chicago, but the fight was cancelled after Ali, reacting to being reclassified from 1-Y to 1-A, declared he had no quarrel with the Viet Cong. A new opponent -- and a new locale -- was sought. The results of the search: George Chuvalo and Toronto's Maple Leaf Gardens.

INSIDE THE NUMBERS: Talk about slow starts: Ali did not land a single punch in round one and landed just five power punches in the first five rounds. In his career Ali landed zero punches in a round on six other occasions (round one versus Jimmy Young, round two against Leon Spinks in fight one, rounds one and four against Ron Lyle, round seven against Alfredo Evangelista and round 10 against Larry Holmes). In fact, 24 of Ali's 70 landed power punches in the fight came in the last round. Damage was done with the jab, as Ali landed an average of 11.6 of his 52.1 thrown per round. Ali landed more jabs (140) than Patterson threw (135). The hobbled Patterson landed an average of 5.4 of 21.3 total punches per round, landing in single digits in terms of total connects in 11 of 12 rounds.

Date:	November 22, 1965			City: Las Vegas, NV				Venue: Las Vegas Convention Center							
Opponent:	Floyd Patterson															
Result:	Ali by TKO at 2:18 of the 12th round -- Retained World Heavyweight Title															

Referee:	Harold Krause															
	Round	1	2	3	4	5	6	7	8	9	10	11	12	13	14	15	Total
	Ali	4	5	5	5	5	5	5	5	5	5	4					53
	Patterson	5	4	4	4	5	3	4	4	4	4	5					46

Judge:	Harold Buck															
	Round	1	2	3	4	5	6	7	8	9	10	11	12	13	14	15	Total
	Ali	4	5	5	5	5	5	5	5	5	5	5					54
	Patterson	5	4	4	5	4	3	4	4	4	4	4					45

Judge:	Bill Stremmell															
	Round	1	2	3	4	5	6	7	8	9	10	11	12	13	14	15	Total
	Ali	4	5	5	5	5	5	5	5	5	5	5					54
	Patterson	5	4	4	4	4	2	4	4	4	4	4					43

MUHAMMAD ALI KO 12 FLOYD PATTERSON

11/22/65 - Las Vegas

Total Punches Landed / Thrown															
	1	2	3	4	5	6	7	8	9	10	11	12	13	14	15
ALI	0/12	14/65	13/77	10/49	15/57	28/102	15/68	22/91	18/73	27/95	13/70	35/95	-/-	-/-	-/-
	0%	21.5%	16.9%	20.4%	26.3%	27.5%	22.1%	24.2%	24.7%	28.4%	18.6%	36.8%	-	-	-
PATTERSON	6/25	4/19	5/29	6/28	7/16	14/34	5/22	5/20	1/12	7/21	3/15	2/14	-/-	-/-	-/-
	24%	21.1%	17.2%	21.4%	43.8%	41.2%	22.7%	25%	8.3%	33.3%	20%	14.3%	-	-	-

Jab Landed / Thrown															
	1	2	3	4	5	6	7	8	9	10	11	12	13	14	15
ALI	0/11	13/58	11/69	9/43	14/49	16/65	10/54	12/63	13/55	20/60	11/56	11/42	-/-	-/-	-/-
	0%	22.4%	15.9%	20.9%	28.6%	24.6%	18.5%	19%	23.6%	33.3%	19.6%	26.2%	-	-	-
PATTERSON	1/13	3/13	3/18	3/16	4/11	6/18	1/8	3/9	0/5	3/9	1/8	1/7	-/-	-/-	-/-
	7.7%	23.1%	16.7%	18.8%	36.4%	33.3%	12.5%	33.3%	0%	33.3%	12.5%	14.3%	-	-	-

Power Punches Landed / Thrown															
	1	2	3	4	5	6	7	8	9	10	11	12	13	14	15
ALI	0/1	1/7	2/8	1/6	1/8	12/37	5/14	10/28	5/18	7/35	2/14	24/53	-/-	-/-	-/-
	0%	14.3%	25%	16.7%	12.5%	32.4%	35.7%	35.7%	27.8%	20%	14.3%	45.3%	-	-	-
PATTERSON	5/12	1/6	2/11	3/12	3/5	8/16	4/14	2/11	1/7	4/12	2/7	1/7	-/-	-/-	-/-
	41.7%	16.7%	18.2%	25%	60%	50%	28.6%	18.2%	14.3%	33.3%	28.6%	14.3%	-	-	-

Final Punch Stat Report			
	Total Punches	Total Jabs	Power Punches
ALI	210/854	140/625	70/229
	24.6%	22.4%	30.6%
PATTERSON	65/255	29/135	36/120
	25.5%	21.5%	30%

64

10.

During the latter part of his career, Muhammad Ali was convinced he needed to absorb inordinate punishment during sparring to properly prepare himself for the bombardment he knew would come on fight night. Whether this theory was a byproduct of Ali's enormous self-belief or an excuse to keep the money train going as his skills decayed, the damage to his well-being was beyond dispute. It was a trade-off Ali was more than willing to make.

"After the layoff, Ali came back and his legs weren't like they've been before, and when he lost his legs, he lost his first line of defense," Dr. Ferdie Pacheco told author Thomas Hauser. "That was when he discovered something which was both very good and very bad...he discovered he could take a punch. Before the layoff, he wouldn't let anyone touch him in the gym. Workouts consisted of Ali running and saying, 'this guy can't hit me.' But afterward, when he couldn't run that way anymore, he found he could dog it. He could run for a round and rest for a round, and let himself get punched against the ropes while he thought he was toughening his body. But Ali was stubborn, he did what he wanted to do. And when he started to get lazy in the gym, which came before his greatest glories, that was the beginning of the end." (1)

While Ali put this mindset into action time and again throughout the 1970s -- when it became a necessity instead of a strategic plaything -- the seeds may have been planted in the mid-1960s, when the butterfly still had his wings and the bee still had his sting. During his training for his March 29, 1966 fight against George Chuvalo, who accepted the bout on 17 days' notice after the Terrell fight was canceled, (2) Ali ordered his sparring partners to hit him in the body so that he could be properly prepared for Chuvalo's formidable body attack.

That attack, as well as a vicious left hook, accounted for many of the 27 knockouts in Chuvalo's 34-11-2 record. Though only 28, Chuvalo had been a pro for nearly 10 years and his first foray into those ranks was unlike any other. Taking part in the Jack Dempsey Heavyweight Novice Tournament at Toronto's Maple Leaf Gardens, Chuvalo defeated four men in a single night -- all by knockout -- to win that tournament. Barely-discriminate matchmaking resulted in plenty of dents in Chuvalo's record, but victories over Mike DeJohn (W 10) and Doug Jones (KO 11), extremely competitive losses to Terrell and Floyd Patterson (the latter being THE RING's 1965 Fight of the Year) and the fact that Toronto native Chuvalo was *the* definitive late sub for a heavyweight title fight at the Maple Leaf Gardens justified this unexpected chance at boxing's ultimate prize.

Chuvalo might have sported a less-than-glittering ring record, but his combination of power and ruggedness promised a long night for the champion.

RING founder Nat Fleischer offered this descriptive summation of Chuvalo: "Chuvalo is a crude, strong, powerful, flatfooted pugilist who knows only one way to fight -- the old bare-knuckle style in which roughness and body pummeling were featured. Scientific boxing is not part of Chuvalo's equipment." (3)

Once the opening bell sounded Chuvalo gave his 13,918 hometown partisans plenty for which to cheer. Although Ali began the fight on the move, it didn't take long for Ali to plant his feet and trade with Chuvalo, for he dearly wanted to become the first man to knock Chuvalo out. With Ali hooking Chuvalo's left arm and firing plenty of verbal bullets, the challenger legally used his free right hand to blast away at Ali's side. At one point Chuvalo landed 13 consecutive rights to the ribs while on another occasion he landed eight more. That allowed Chuvalo to match Ali's 26 total connects in round one and to land 24 of his 39 power shots.

Ali's stubbornness continued in round two and that allowed Chuvalo to enjoy his best statistical round of the fight -- 40 of 63 total punches (64%) and 38 of 53 power shots (72%). Yes, Ali jabbed well (19 of 36, 53%) and connected accurately (22 of 44, 50% overall) but he was no match for Chuvalo in the trenches. In fact, he didn't even try to be, for in the round he went just 3 for 8 in power shots.

While Ali was trying to prove his toughness, Chuvalo continued to plug away -- and did so with great success. He again out-landed Ali in rounds three and four (31-24 overall and 26-12 power in the third, 23-20 overall and 19-5 power in the fourth), which swelled the challenger's connect leads to 120-92 overall and 107-30 power through four rounds. Chuvalo's early effectiveness was shocking given the gulf in fistic gifts and vast difference in preparation time.

After Ali easily won the fifth by getting on his toes and staying off the ropes -- resulting in connect leads of 26-8 overall and 17-1 jabs -- he tempted fate once more in the sixth by remaining on the inside and retreating to the ropes. With a little more than a minute to go Chuvalo unleashed a two-fisted body barrage that resulted in nearly a dozen connects and vaulted him to leads of 25-21 overall and 18-7 power. It would be the last time in the fight that Chuvalo would out-shine Ali in terms of total connects.

By now Ali had learned his lesson. The fifth round showed that when he fought his way -- circling to the left, being the first to start every skirmish and commanding range with his jab -- Chuvalo lacked the foot speed and timing to mount a sustained attack. Starting in round seven, Ali returned to being the fastest heavyweight who had yet lived and he was rewarded with unquestioned numerical dominance. Upping his work rate from 54 punches in round six to a stratospheric 99 in the seventh, Ali out-landed Chuvalo 39-18 overall, 18-0 jabs and 21-18 power to irreversibly change the tenor of the contest. The events of the seventh continued through the rest of the contest as Ali dramatically increased his average output from 51.5 punches per round to 81 while Chuvalo's pace ebbed from 49.2 over the first six to 41.7 in rounds 7-15.

Ali's jab, always a defining weapon, was superlative against Chuvalo. He achieved double-digit connects in every round and his 274 landed jabs would be the highest total Ali ever recorded in a CompuBox-tracked fight. Including the final eight rounds of the Patterson fight, Ali extended his string of double-digit jab connect rounds to a career-long 23.

Through it all, however, Chuvalo continued to pursue Ali with ceaseless energy and single-minded determination, assets no doubt amplified by his hometown crowd's ear-splitting support. His constant aggression forced Ali to fight every second of every round, which resulted in the prime Ali showcasing his full range of skill as well as his extraordinary stamina. But not only did Chuvalo chase Ali, he cashed in, albeit sporadically. During those spots when he was in punching range and let his hands go, Chuvalo connected at an alarmingly high rate. From round seven onward, Chuvalo landed more than half of his overall punches five times, topping off at 60% in the 12th. For the fight Chuvalo exceeded 50% overall accuracy nine times and 60% twice, extraordinary figures given Ali's reputation for elusiveness.

Chuvalo was even more precise with his power punches because in rounds 7-15 he exceeded 50% in all but the 13th (43%) and 15th rounds (46%), with his bests being 61.9% in the ninth and 61.5% in the 12th. In terms of power punch percentage Chuvalo topped 50% 11 times, 60% five times and 70% once.

Meanwhile, in rounds seven through 15 Ali out-landed Chuvalo 335-182 overall and 181-11 jabs to stretch his leads in the fight to 474-335 overall and 274-32 jabs. But Chuvalo's precise power shots enabled him to out-land Ali 171-154 in rounds 7-15 and 303-200 for the fight.

The challenger's body punching was his greatest success. In all, he connected 267 times to Ali's flanks, more than any other opponent ever had -- or ever would. That also resulted in his being the more accurate fighter overall (50%-46%) and in power punches (56%-49%).

Ali made fun of Chuvalo's wide-swinging body attack before the fight by dubbing him "The Washerwoman," but during and after the fight Ali learned it was no laughing matter. The proof: After the fight Ali urinated blood and visited a local hospital. Conversely, Chuvalo went dancing with his wife. (4)

"This was my toughest battle," Ali said. "I bruised my knuckles on him. I have a sore kidney from the pounding Chuvalo gave me when he cornered me. He was tougher than Patterson or Liston. He's tougher than Terrell. But I didn't like the way the referee permitted him to foul me so often."

"The low punches were of no consequence," referee Jackie Silvers replied. "They weren't hurting Clay. Chuvalo is not a low blow hitter. He's a body banger. If you're going to be watching that close for low blows, there would be no fight. I did remind him several times to keep 'em up."

To that, Fleischer shot back: "A truly strange attitude for a referee in a world title bout!" (5)

Chuvalo, a 7-to-1 underdog largely dismissed by the boxing press during the pre-fight build-up, earned accolades afterward.

"Some of us said that this Canadian should have been selling peanuts in the aisles rather than throwing punches in the ring. We were wrong," said one New York Times correspondent. "Cassius Clay has never been given a harder, more bruising fight. Chuvalo was the honest worker. He comes to fight. He wasn't scared, or cocky or overconfident. He was willing to take a lot of punishment for the opportunity to give some. And he did." (6)

Moreover, Ali learned that he was tough enough to take any man's best, not just in a single round but for the entire 15-round distance. Ali carried that nugget of knowledge with him into the next decade, and while it served him well throughout most of that era in terms of extending his career it also contributed heavily to the profound health issues that defined the second half of his life.

INSIDE THE NUMBERS: Chuvalo made Ali work for his victory. Ali threw 1,038 punches, his second highest total among fights counted (he fired 1,132 versus Mac Foster) and he landed 474 punches, the highest total among the 47 fights counted. This fight also was number-one for Ali among fights counted in terms of total connects per round (31.6 of his 69.2 thrown per round, and number of jabs landed in a fight (274), average jabs landed per round (22.8, nearly four times the heavyweight average). Ali landed 12 or more jabs in every round, including 36 in round nine -- the second highest single round total (his 37 in the seventh round against Al "Blue" Lewis was first). Note: As of January 2018, CompuBox heavyweight record for jabs landed in a round is 38 -- held amazingly by the Klitschko brothers (Wladimir vs. Hasim Rahman and Vitali vs. Ed Mahone). Chuvalo out landed Ali 303-200 in power shots, hitting on 55.5% for the fight -- the third highest percentage by an Ali opponent. Only Larry Holmes (65%) and Joe Frazier in fight one (63%) landed a higher percentage of power shots versus Ali. Ali took a terrible beating to the body, as 267 of Chuvalo's 335 connects (79.7% -- nearly triple the CompuBox average) were to Ali's flanks.

Date:	March 29, 1966						City: Toronto, Canada			Venue: Maple Leaf Gardens						
Opponent:	George Chuvalo															
Result:	Ali by unanimous decision -- Retains World Heavyweight Title															

Referee: Jackie Silvers

Round	1	2	3	4	5	6	7	8	9	10	11	12	13	14	15	Total
Ali	5	4	5	5	5	4	5	5	5	5	5	5	5	5	5	73
Chuvalo	4	5	4	5	4	5	4	5	4	4	3	4	4	5	5	65

Judge: Tony Canzano

Round	1	2	3	4	5	6	7	8	9	10	11	12	13	14	15	Total
Ali	5	4	5	5	5	5	5	5	5	5	5	5	5	5	5	74
Chuvalo	5	5	4	4	4	5	4	4	4	4	4	4	4	4	4	63

Judge: Jackie Johnstone

Round	1	2	3	4	5	6	7	8	9	10	11	12	13	14	15	Total
Ali	5	4	5	5	5	5	5	5	5	5	5	5	5	5	5	74
Chuvalo	4	5	4	5	4	4	4	4	4	4	4	4	4	4	4	62

MUHAMMAD ALI UD 15 GEORGE CHUVALO
03/29/66 - TORONTO

Total Punches Landed / Thrown

	1	2	3	4	5	6	7	8	9	10	11	12	13	14	15
ALI	26/51	22/44	24/66	20/43	26/51	21/54	39/99	31/64	47/74	25/64	43/92	41/84	42/87	30/68	37/97
	51%	50%	36.4%	46.5%	51%	38.9%	39.4%	48.4%	63.5%	39.1%	46.7%	48.8%	48.3%	44.1%	38.1%
CHUVALO	26/47	40/63	31/56	23/53	8/31	25/45	18/33	19/49	18/34	21/41	23/44	24/40	18/47	19/39	22/48
	55.3%	63.5%	55.4%	43.4%	25.8%	55.6%	54.5%	38.8%	52.9%	51.2%	52.3%	60%	38.3%	48.7%	45.8%

Jab Landed / Thrown

	1	2	3	4	5	6	7	8	9	10	11	12	13	14	15
ALI	16/31	19/36	12/45	15/35	17/33	14/33	18/49	22/48	36/57	18/46	21/44	17/41	17/40	17/46	15/48
	51.6%	52.8%	26.7%	42.9%	51.5%	42.4%	36.7%	45.8%	63.2%	39.1%	47.7%	41.5%	42.5%	37%	31.3%
CHUVALO	2/8	2/10	5/15	4/14	1/11	7/14	0/1	0/13	5/13	5/11	0/5	0/1	0/5	1/3	0/0
	25%	20%	33.3%	28.6%	9.1%	50%	0%	0%	38.5%	45.5%	0%	0%	0%	33.3%	0%

Power Punches Landed / Thrown

	1	2	3	4	5	6	7	8	9	10	11	12	13	14	15
ALI	10/20	3/8	12/21	5/8	9/18	7/21	21/50	9/16	11/17	7/18	22/48	24/43	25/47	13/22	22/49
	50%	37.5%	57.1%	62.5%	50%	33.3%	42%	56.3%	64.7%	38.9%	45.8%	55.8%	53.2%	59.1%	44.9%
CHUVALO	24/39	38/53	26/41	19/39	7/20	18/31	18/32	19/36	13/21	16/30	23/39	24/39	18/42	18/36	22/48
	61.5%	71.7%	63.4%	48.7%	35%	58.1%	56.3%	52.8%	61.9%	53.3%	59%	61.5%	42.9%	50%	45.8%

Final Punch Stat Report

	Total Punches	Total Jabs	Power Punches
ALI	474/1038	274/632	200/406
	45.7%	43.4%	49.3%
CHUVALO	335/670	32/124	303/546
	50%	25.8%	55.5%

11.

In the 35 months that elapsed since their initial encounter at Wembley Stadium, the lives of Cassius Clay and Henry Cooper stood in stark contrast. The winds of change had hit the former hardest, in good ways and bad.

First, he now was the heavyweight champion of the world and was about to make his fourth title defense.

Second, Cassius Clay no longer existed, for on the morning after winning the title from Sonny Liston he announced he had joined the Nation of Islam. He called himself "Cassius X" at first, but several days later the new champion learned that Nation of Islam leader Elijah Muhammad had officially renamed him Muhammad Ali.

Third, Ali's life away from the ring was in turmoil, for six weeks before he fought George Chuvalo Ali's local draft board reclassified him from 1-Y to 1-A, which rendered him eligible for military service. (1) After initially wondering why he would be singled out, he widened his argument to one based on morals and religion. In doing so, he uttered the most famous -- or infamous -- sentence of his public life: "I ain't got no quarrel with the Viet Cong."

With that he established himself as a prominent anti-establishment voice, and a few days later he submitted paperwork for conscientious objector status. While he waited for a reply he kept busy by beating Chuvalo, then meeting Cooper.

As a result of his achievements inside the ring and the rancor he inspired outside it, Ali had become a global sporting celebrity who could no longer move freely.

"When we first came to England for the first fight, we could walk the streets (and) nobody bothered us," Angelo Dundee said in the documentary "When Ali Came to Britain." "But when he came back, he got to be a controversial figure. We couldn't move!"

Conversely, Cooper enjoyed a stable family life outside the ropes while his fistic life was pretty much status quo. He was still the British and Empire heavyweight champion, and eight months after losing to Clay/Ali he added the vacant European title by out-pointing Brian London over 15. In all, he fought eight times between February 1964 and February 1966, winning six and losing two. His last two fights, early knockouts over the ninth-ranked Hubert Hilton (KO 2) and Alabama journeyman Jefferson Davis (KO 1), were produced by "'Enry's 'Ammer," his lethal left hook. When he lost, he did so in lopsided fashion and during the seventh round against Amos

Johnson he suffered a cut over his left eye. To the British public Cooper was forever "Our 'Enry," and that love affair remained strong no matter the final result.

The memory of Cooper decking the future champion at the end of round four raised hopes he could do it again. Not only did the British public invest their maximum best wishes emotionally, 45,973 of them dug into their pockets and crowded into the Arsenal 's Highbury Stadium to witness what they hoped would be the coronation of a new heavyweight monarch. It was the first heavyweight championship fight staged in England since Tommy Burns stopped local hope Jack Palmer in four rounds 58 years earlier, a fight in which Palmer was floored nine times according to Boxrec.

Cooper's 188 pounds was two-and-a-half pounds heavier than the 1963 fight while Ali was a stunningly light 201 1/2, his lowest poundage since he weighed 199 against Alejandro Lavorante nearly four years earlier and the lowest figure he would ever scale in a championship fight.

With the crowd at a fever pitch, the opening round saw Ali circling away from Cooper's powerful left and firing lightning quick jabs while the challenger purposefully pursued. Cooper's jab also worked well (6 of 14, 43%) and his sustained aggression allowed him to forge early leads of 11-6 overall and 5-2 power.

The second and third rounds followed a similar pattern as the much quicker Ali used hand and foot feints to keep Cooper honest and his increasingly accurate and effective jab (7 of 16, 44% in round two, 10 of 20, 50% in round three) to dictate range and to work on Cooper's notoriously brittle scar tissue. The stoic and dogged Cooper did his best to cut off Ali's escape routes and thrilled his legion of partisans with an overhand right and a shotgun jab late in round two as well as a powerful hook early in the third. Ali, on the other hand, drew loud boos -- and a caution from Scottish referee George Smith -- for pulling Cooper's head down in the third. Cooper's higher work rate (38 per round to Ali's 25.5) allowed him to expand his connect leads to 33-27 overall and 17-6 power over the first nine minutes, but, best of all, Cooper's scar tissue held up despite being struck 21 times by Ali's jab.

Ali fired a psychological dagger at Cooper between rounds three and four by refusing the stool and dancing in his corner. Cooper, as was his wont, ignored Ali and tended to his own business.

Early in the fourth Ali bitterly complained about a pair of low lefts, an act that did him no good with the Cooper partisans (who howled back at him) or with referee Smith (who ignored him). The action from both fighters intensified as each invested more power behind their blows, but it was Ali's jab that defined the round. Ali connected on 20 of his 33 jabs, which translated to a sky-high 61% connect rate, and allowed Ali to open up a 26-12 overall connect lead as well as seize a 53-45 edge in total connects. The round ended with good news for both men; not only did Ali dominate the round, he also managed to keep his feet and avoid the end-of-the-round disaster that befell him in 1963. As for Cooper, he concluded the session with a slight swelling under the left eye, but, fortunately for him, no blood. At least, not yet.

The fifth was a largely even round in terms of raw numbers (14-13 Ali overall, 12-10 Ali jabs, 3-2 Cooper power) but the 24-year-old Ali demonstrated a mature discipline that he didn't show in 1963, when he taunted Cooper by fighting with his hands at hip level and threw flailing punches that often missed the mark. Here, in round five, he landed 44% of his total punches and 41% of his jabs while limiting Cooper to 30% overall and 18% power. Better yet for him, he kept fighting within a defined blueprint, which was to keep his distance, respect Cooper's power by circling away from it and working on the challenger's eyes with his persistent jab. One of those jabs knocked out Cooper's mouthpiece, which Cooper found the time to kick away with his left foot.

As the two men readied themselves for the next round, each had a reason to feel good about his performance. Ali's reasons were stated in the previous paragraph while Cooper had to have been encouraged that, for the most, he stayed even with the champion. Through five rounds he trailed just 67-58 overall and 53-33 jabs while leading 25-14 in power connects. Not bad for someone who had turned 32 just 18 days earlier and had, up to this point, a good but spotty pro ring career. Against the fastest heavyweight who had yet lived, Cooper, nearly three inches shorter and nearly a stone lighter, was more than holding his own.

Then came round six -- the round in which the roof caved in.

Thirty seconds into the session Cooper pushed Ali toward the neutral corner pad. As he did so, Ali connected with a short right to Cooper's brow, and a split-second later the crimson began to spurt out. Cooper instantly knew what had just happened and what it meant: A fight that had been largely even and well-waged was now a race against time, and given Cooper's history that time was alarmingly short. An enraged Cooper jerked his head down in frustration, then pawed at the blood that had already flooded the area around the orbital socket and was dripping down his cheek. The crowd, too, immediately recognized Cooper's plight and let out a palpable groan. Smith stopped the action and briefly examined the gash before allowing the fight to continue, but everyone knew that, for Cooper, it was now or never.

As Cooper accelerated his pursuit, the Arsenal crowd tried to push their hero onward. A solid right to the jaw increased the volume even more but a pair of savage left-rights to the face by Ali prompted Smith to step in and stop the fight. A distraught Cooper registered his angst by jerking his arms downward, suspecting that he'd never earn another chance at his sport's ultimate prize.

In the end, Ali emerged with connect leads of 80-60 overall and 56-34 jabs but Cooper prevailed 26-24 in landed power shots. Ali's accuracy was exquisite in every way (43% overall, 44% jabs, 41% power) while his defense held up well when compared to previous efforts (28% overall, 32% jabs, 25% power).

While Ali earned his reputation as a villain with the British public by twice beating their national treasure, Ali took the first step toward reversing that perception the following day when he appeared as a guest on a talk show hosted by Eamonn Andrews. While appearing with Noel Coward, Dudley Moore and Lucille Ball, Ali showed a softer, humbler side that charmed the live audience as well as the thousands who watched it on TV.

"In this country we got to love him quickly, and we kind of saw the irony in him," said broadcaster Desmond Lynam in "When Ali Came to Britain" a few decades later. "We became huge fans of his. I really got to like the man a great deal, almost love him. He was a fantastic guy."

The British were among the first to fully embrace his new name, and with the turmoil around him at home growing by the day, Ali decided to extend his visit a while longer, for less than two months later, again in London, he would meet his next challenger, Blackpool's Brian London.

INSIDE THE NUMBERS: Again, Ali's jab was a major weapon. He landed 44.4% in rematch with Cooper (he landed 30.3% of his jabs in first fight), including 32 of 62 (51.6%) in rounds four and five. Ali had just a 151-120 edge in punches landed in the two Cooper fights and Henry landed 33.5% of his jabs in his two losses.

MUHAMMAD ALI TKO 6 HENRY COOPER

05/21/66 - LONDON

Total Punches Landed / Thrown															
	1	2	3	4	5	6	7	8	9	10	11	12	13	14	15
ALI	6/23	9/22	12/29	26/45	14/32	13/34	-/-	-/-	-/-	-/-	-/-	-/-	-/-	-/-	-/-
	26.1%	40.9%	41.4%	57.8%	43.8%	38.2%	-	-	-	-	-	-	-	-	-
COOPER	11/30	11/40	11/36	12/40	13/44	2/21	-/-	-/-	-/-	-/-	-/-	-/-	-/-	-/-	-/-
	36.7%	27.5%	30.6%	30%	29.5%	9.5%	-	-	-	-	-	-	-	-	-

Jab Landed / Thrown															
	1	2	3	4	5	6	7	8	9	10	11	12	13	14	15
ALI	4/16	7/16	10/20	20/33	12/29	3/12	-/-	-/-	-/-	-/-	-/-	-/-	-/-	-/-	-/-
	25%	43.8%	50%	60.6%	41.4%	25%	-	-	-	-	-	-	-	-	-
COOPER	6/14	6/21	4/14	7/20	10/27	1/12	-/-	-/-	-/-	-/-	-/-	-/-	-/-	-/-	-/-
	42.9%	28.6%	28.6%	35%	37%	8.3%	-	-	-	-	-	-	-	-	-

Power Punches Landed / Thrown															
	1	2	3	4	5	6	7	8	9	10	11	12	13	14	15
ALI	2/7	2/6	2/9	6/12	2/3	10/22	-/-	-/-	-/-	-/-	-/-	-/-	-/-	-/-	-/-
	28.6%	33.3%	22.2%	50%	66.7%	45.5%	-	-	-	-	-	-	-	-	-
COOPER	5/16	5/19	7/22	5/20	3/17	1/9	-/-	-/-	-/-	-/-	-/-	-/-	-/-	-/-	-/-
	31.3%	26.3%	31.8%	25%	17.6%	11.1%	-	-	-	-	-	-	-	-	-

Final Punch Stat Report			
Total	Total Punches	Total Jabs	Power Punches
ALI	80/185	56/126	24/59
	43.2%	44.4%	40.7%
COOPER	60/211	34/108	26/103
	28.4%	31.5%	25.2%

74

12.

Just 77 days after beating Cooper for the second time, Ali returned to London to face the aptly named Brian London, a man Cooper had beaten three times, once by a first round knockout and twice on 15-round decisions for the British and Empire titles.

Born Brian Sydney Harper on June 19, 1934 in Hartlepool, the family moved to Blackpool when Brian was 16. (1) His father, John, who fought under the name "Jack London," amassed a record of 95-40-5 with two no-contests and 52 knockouts during his 18-year career, according to Boxrec. In his 123rd fight he captured the vacant British and Empire titles on points from future light heavyweight champion Freddie Mills. He lost those belts two fights later to Bruce Woodcock (KO by 6) and retired four-and-a-half years later.

Although Brian had his share of street fights, he didn't inherit his father's taste for "The Sweet Science." But when he joined the Royal Air Force as part of his two years of mandatory national service, he was stationed at the same camp his father had been.

"The guy that was running the camp said, 'so, you're Jack London's son. You'll be on the boxing team then, won't you?' " London told author Steve Brunt. Knowing that athletes are granted privileges such as better food and more time off, London accepted the invitation and began what would become a 87-2 amateur career. Unlike his father, who was known as a stylist, Brian was a straight-ahead brawler with a prominent jaw that was a tempting target for opponents. Upon turning pro in 1955, he adopted the "London" surname and set about contributing to the family business.

London's motivation for entering the pro game was purely financial.

"I had a taste for the money," London told Brunt. "What could I do then? I didn't have no degrees or nothing like that. What was I going to do? So I turned pro." (2)

London won his first 12 fights, all but one by KO. One of his initial victims was George "Jim" Cooper, the identical twin of Henry. Unfortunately for George, he also had Henry's bad history in terms of getting cut and that malady struck again against London, who stopped him in four rounds on cuts. Two fights later, however, Henry secured familial revenge by dusting London in a single round.

From there London won eight of his next 10 fights before stopping Joe Erskine in eight rounds to win the British and Empire titles. Three months later he avenged an earlier points loss to future light heavyweight champion Willie Pastrano by stopping him in five rounds, earning him a rematch with Henry Cooper. Despite losing to Cooper on points, his next fight was against world heavyweight champion Floyd Patterson, who was making the fourth defense of his title. London took the fight over the objections of the British Boxing Board of Control, who fined London 1,100 pounds for his defiance. (3) London shrugged his shoulders, paid the fine and flew to Indianapolis. Floored in rounds 10 and 11, the 10-to-1 underdog was stopped in the 11th.

Over the next seven years London faced other notable Americans, winning some (KO 7 Pete Rademacher, KO 6 Howard King, W 10 Von Clay, W 10 Tom McNeeley, W DQ 7 Amos Johnson) and losing some (KO by 7 Nino Valdes, KO by 5 Eddie Machen, L 10 Thad Spencer). London came within seconds of knocking out Ingemar Johansson when he floored the ex-champ in the waning seconds of their April 1963 12-rounder in Stockholm, but the bell saved the Swede, who was deemed the points winner by referee Andrew Smyth, the fight's lone scoring official. Johansson never fought again.

Three fights later London, nicknamed the "British Bulldog" for his rugged looks and fighting style as well as the "Blackpool Rock" for his adopted hometown and his previous job at a candy factory, lost to Cooper for the third time for the British, Empire and European titles. London won five of his next seven fights, the last of which was the seventh-round disqualification win over Amos Johnson, who was tossed out for excessive butting. At this point, London's record stood at 35-13 with 26 knockouts.

It was at this point that the 32-year-old London became the first post-war Briton to get a second crack at the heavyweight championship. Ali, facing troubles at home on multiple fronts that had potentially crippling financial and legal consequences, was in the midst of a whirlwind campaign through Europe that was starting to take a physical toll. During an interview with ABC's Howard Cosell, Ali said he had been feeling worn down due to his not taking enough iron in relation to his workout schedule. While he was taking iron tablets to remedy that issue he also cut down on his public sparring because Cooper and other London allies were filming his workouts. (4) Given these circumstances, it was not a shock that Ali scaled 209 1/2, eight more than for the Cooper rematch. For the record, London, who actually provided most of the pre-fight rhetoric, weighed 201 1/2 and was installed as a 17-to-5 underdog.

Those odds were also reflected by the light turnout at the Earl's Court Arena in London, for the 18,000-capacity building included approximately 7,000 empty seats. They were confirmed by the fight itself.

As soon as the opening bell sounded the vast differences in physique, technique and talent were made graphically apparent. The long and lithe Ali circled fluidly, punched sharply and executed his plan with a superstar's ease while the heavy-legged London looked slow, stiff and uncoordinated. Ali's blows sliced through London's guard with alarming regularity and landed forcefully enough to snap back the challenger's head. It was all London could do just to unleash a punch, much less land one. In the closing moments of round one, the area under London's left eye was already reddened.

After the first three minutes Ali had landed 22 of his 46 total punches, with his attack almost perfectly balanced between jabs (12 of 23, 52%) and power shots (10 of 23, 44%). London only punched 23 times, landing four for 17% accuracy and connecting on two of his nine power attempts (22%).

"That round Clay virtually used London as a punching bag, as a target, and yet he didn't really hurt him because he hasn't been punching hard," said color man Cosell, who mistakenly referred to Ali by his previous name. (5)

The first three minutes signaled to all, including London himself, that the writing was on the wall and that the worst was yet to come.

"I shouldn't ever tell, but I didn't really try," London admitted to Brunt. "I decided that he was too good for me. Not going in. I gave my best for two or three rounds. But then I realized that I was going to get one hell of a hiding. The way I fought, I was going to keep coming to him and throw punches and invariably I may catch him. But he was so fast. He was faster than I was, he was faster than most heavyweights in the world. Ever. I don't know of any faster heavyweight even now." (6)

The second round was more of the same: Ali slicing and dicing and London fruitlessly pursuing. The numbers in round two were nearly identical to the first -- Ali threw the same number of punches (46) and landed one fewer (21), threw two more jabs and landed one less and connected on the same number of power shots while attempting two fewer. London was even more futile as he landed one fewer punch with three while attempting the identical number of punches -- 23.

The end came swiftly in round three. Several seconds after he connected with a hook-right to the jaw, Ali used a series of beautifully executed hand and foot feints to maneuver London to his own corner pad. With London now trapped, Ali unleashed a blinding blaze of blows capped by a right to the temple that drove London to the floor. Lying on his right side, London didn't begin to stir until referee Harry Gibbs reached seven, and by then it was far too late. The 10-count was reached at the 40-second mark on round three, bringing the curtain down on an utterly dominant performance.

"He didn't throw any low punches, he did not grab and hold me, he did not try to butt me and did not break any rules," Ali said of London. "He's a gentleman." (7)

"He was big, he was fast and he could punch. I was smaller, fatter and couldn't punch," London cheekily said years later in the documentary "When Ali Came to Britain." "He stopped me in three rounds and that was it. I don't think I hit him."

The statistics say he actually landed seven punches, three jabs and four power shots. Unfortunately for him, Ali landed 50 -- 23 jabs and 27 power punches. The accuracy gaps favoring Ali were similarly wide: 47%-15% overall, 46%-12% jabs and 47%-19% power.

Though Ali produced outstanding numbers as well as aesthetics, he admitted the strenuous schedule was starting to get to him.

"I took on London too soon after the Cooper fight," Ali told RING founder and editor-in-chief Nat Fleischer months later. "Don't misunderstand me: London didn't touch me. But I downgrade nobody. I take nothing for granted. I had to rush my training for London, and noticed that I got tired. I was ordered to take vitamins. The Mildenberger fight gave me another rush job of training, and this meant reshaping my style to take care of Karl's southpaw stance." (8)

According to writer Thomas Georgiou, had London won he would have been the first winner of the Boxing News Gold Cup, which would have been awarded to the first British boxer to win the heavyweight title. The trophy, which was first purchased in the 1930s, had been kept inside a safe at an undisclosed location within London, and, unfortunately for the native son, it would have to remain in storage for the foreseeable future. (9)

This was the last fight Ali had under his managerial contract with the Louisville Sponsoring Group. Herbert Muhammad became his manager of record from this fight onward.

INSIDE THE NUMBERS: Ali featured a balanced attack against the overmatched London, landing 23 jabs (46%) and 27 power shots (47.4%). London landed 7 punches in 7:40 of ring time.

Date:	August 6, 1966				City: London, England			Venue: Earl's Court Arena								
Opponent:	Brian London																
Result:	Ali by KO at 1:40 of the 3rd round -- Retains World Heavyweight Title																

Referee:	Harry Gibbs															
Round	1	2	3	4	5	6	7	8	9	10	11	12	13	14	15	Total
Ali	X	X														2
London																0

Judge:	N/A															
Round	1	2	3	4	5	6	7	8	9	10	11	12	13	14	15	Total

Judge:	N/A															
Round	1	2	3	4	5	6	7	8	9	10	11	12	13	14	15	Total

MUHAMMAD ALI KO 3 BRIAN LONDON
08/06/66 - LONDON

Total Punches Landed / Thrown															
	1	2	3	4	5	6	7	8	9	10	11	12	13	14	15
ALI	22/46	21/46	7/15	-/-	-/-	-/-	-/-	-/-	-/-	-/-	-/-	-/-	-/-	-/-	-/-
	47.8%	45.7%	46.7%	-	-	-	-	-	-	-	-	-	-	-	-
LONDON	4/23	3/23	0/1	-/-	-/-	-/-	-/-	-/-	-/-	-/-	-/-	-/-	-/-	-/-	-/-
	17.4%	13%	0%	-	-	-	-	-	-	-	-	-	-	-	-

Jab Landed / Thrown															
	1	2	3	4	5	6	7	8	9	10	11	12	13	14	15
ALI	12/23	11/25	0/2	-/-	-/-	-/-	-/-	-/-	-/-	-/-	-/-	-/-	-/-	-/-	-/-
	52.2%	44%	0%	-	-	-	-	-	-	-	-	-	-	-	-
LONDON	2/14	1/11	0/1	-/-	-/-	-/-	-/-	-/-	-/-	-/-	-/-	-/-	-/-	-/-	-/-
	14.3%	9.1%	0%	-	-	-	-	-	-	-	-	-	-	-	-

Power Punches Landed / Thrown															
	1	2	3	4	5	6	7	8	9	10	11	12	13	14	15
ALI	10/23	10/21	7/13	-/-	-/-	-/-	-/-	-/-	-/-	-/-	-/-	-/-	-/-	-/-	-/-
	43.5%	47.6%	53.8%	-	-	-	-	-	-	-	-	-	-	-	-
LONDON	2/9	2/12	0/0	-/-	-/-	-/-	-/-	-/-	-/-	-/-	-/-	-/-	-/-	-/-	-/-
	22.2%	16.7%	0%	-	-	-	-	-	-	-	-	-	-	-	-

Final Punch Stat Report			
Total	Total Punches	Total Jabs	Power Punches
ALI	50/107	23/50	27/57
	46.7%	46%	47.4%
LONDON	7/47	3/26	4/21
	14.9%	11.5%	19%

13.

Even before Ali stepped into the ring with London, he already knew who his next opponent would be had he won: West Germany's Karl Mildenberger. And, as expected, Ali won.

The Mildenberger encounter was a fight of firsts on several levels. Not only was Mildenberger the first Ali opponent to fight out of a southpaw stance, he was the first left-hander ever to fight for the heavyweight championship. Also, their meeting was the first heavyweight title contest staged in Germany and the broadcast on ABC was the first time a sporting event delivered via satellite was shown in color. (1)

If one is to be truthful, however, Mildenberger wasn't a lefty by birth. Like two-time heavyweight titlist Michael Moorer nearly three decades later, the European heavyweight champion did everything right-handed but box. (2) In an era in which natural lefties were ordered to turn around in order to get fights, Mildenberger was a revolutionary. And, to this point, a successful revolutionary.

Mildenberger turned pro shortly after winning the national amateur heavyweight championship, capping a career that saw him win 52 of 64 fights. His success continued in the pros as he emerged victorious in 34 of his first 36 fights, 13 by knockout. Tellingly, both losses were by stoppage. The first came against Helmut Ball in a German light heavyweight title eliminator in his 12th fight in November 1959 while the second was a 155-second rout against Dick Richardson for the European title in February 1962 20 fights later.

Since then Mildenberger had gone 19-0-3, won the vacant European title against Santo Amonti (KO 1) and notched three successful defenses against Piero Tomasoni, Gerhard Zech and Ivan Prebeg, all by decision. Another tell: The three draws occurred against Americans Archie McBride, Zora Folley and Amos Johnson -- and all three fights were staged on home turf. The Folley result was particularly stunning; the European reporter for the Stars and Stripes saw Folley a 7-2-1 winner on the rounds system after the 78-fight veteran out-boxed, out-classed and battered the German into a bloody mess thanks to a gash over the right eye that was opened in the seventh. Since then, Mildenberger rolled off eight in a row -- including a 10-round decision over Eddie Machen two fights before meeting Ali (3) -- and the Prebeg fight in June served as a nice warm-up for the formidable task that awaited him. *

"I stand at the peak of my ability and condition," Mildenberger said when he learned he would challenge Ali. "We will see where I go from here. I know this: No fighter is invincible." (4)

For Ali, the Mildenberger fight was his fourth defense in a five-and-a-half month span, a pace that had not been seen since Joe Louis and his so-called "Bum of the Month Club." At 203 1/2, Ali was five-and-a-half pounds lighter than when he fought Brian London 35 days earlier while Mildenberger, at 195, was well within his usual envelope (he was 193 1/4 against Prebeg, 196 3/4 versus Machen and 194 against Zech).

The Ali-Mildenberger fight was an event of supreme importance in Germany and that was reflected by the attendance inside Frankfurt's open-air Waldstadion (between 50,000 and 60,000 according to Sports Illustrated's Martin Kane while RING founder Nat Fleischer estimated 45,000), the composition of two of the officials (Fleischer and referee Teddy Waltham, the secretary for the British Board of Control) and the introductions of Max Schmeling, Joe Louis and Ingemar Johansson moments before the opening bell.

Throughout his boxing life Ali had been thrown off by the southpaw stance and the first moments of the bout showed that remained the case because Ali, who normally circled clockwise, rotated mostly counter-clockwise here -- directly into the path of Mildenberger's power left. Ali said before the fight that the rightward movement was a strategy designed to confuse Mildenberger but, in reality, it hindered the champion's ability to jab effectively. In fact, Ali failed to land any of his 19 first-round jabs but his right hand accounted for most of his six power connects in 19 attempts. However, Mildenberger, the 10-to-1 underdog, made a good case for winning the round by throwing more (41 to 38), jabbing better (6 of 35 to Ali's 0 of 19) and landing three of his six power shots, one of which was a strong left cross following a triple jab in the closing minute that ignited an ear-splitting roar.

In round two, Ali, now moving more often to his left, was much more effective as he landed a fight-high 14 jabs and out-landed Mildenberger 19-11 overall, 14-7 jabs and 5-4 power. But most of Mildenberger's connects, whether jab or power punch, landed with surprising force and the cheers that accompanied each connect forwarded a narrative that the challenger was giving Ali more trouble than anyone had a right to expect. His best moments came when he briefly trapped Ali on the ropes or when Ali was moving in the strategically incorrect direction.

Mildenberger's high-water mark occurred in rounds three, four and most of the fifth as he went jab-for-jab with the taller, faster champion and landed several heavy lefts that earned Ali's attention -- and respect. In fact, Mildenberger out-landed Ali 31-26 overall and 16-11 power in the third and fourth while tying him with 15 jab connects. Moreover, Mildenberger's head movement kept Ali under 18% overall accuracy in three of the first five rounds, a laudatory accomplishment given the champion's immense hand speed.

The fight continued apace in the fifth, and even Cosell was puzzled as to why Ali insisted on moving to his right. A few moments later Mildenberger connected with two lefts to the chin, then another left and a one-two. Just as it appeared that Mildenberger was about to win another round, Ali, with only two seconds remaining, lashed out with a lead right that scored a flash knockdown, nullifying a round in which the challenger prevailed 15-9 overall and 9-4 power.

Ali's punches were inflicting more damage, for entering the sixth Mildenberger sported a gash over the right eye and a badly bruised left orb. As was the case with the two Cooper fights, Ali targeted the injured eye while also upping his work rate to a fight-high 67 punches. Still, Mildenberger proved an elusive target as Ali landed only 11 times overall (16%) and with six of his 25 power attempts (24%). Mildenberger, who was focused on survival, threw just 28 punches and landed six, both of which were his lows for the fight among completed rounds. Late in the round, Ali added a cut over the left eye.

Even as Ali was piling up rounds on the judge's scorecards, Mildenberger hung tough. He continued to pursue the champion and, from time to time, he landed the big left. In terms of stats, the action see-sawed: Ali took rounds six (11-6), eight (19-12) and 10 (14-13) while Mildenberger edged Ali in the seventh (16-15) and ninth (16-10). In addition to the fifth round knockdown, Ali floored Mildenberger in the waning moments of the eighth with a lightning right-left to the chin and near the end of the 10th with a crushing right to the point of the chin.

While the three knockdowns propelled Ali to a commanding lead on the scorecards -- referee Waltham had Ali up 7-2-2 while judges Fleischer and Felix Ohlert saw Ali up 8-3 and 6-3-2 respectively -- his statistical lead was much smaller. After 11 rounds, Ali clung to a 144-141 lead overall and a 66-52 gap in landed power shots. Surprisingly, Mildenberger out-jabbed Ali 89-78.

Shortly before the two-minute mark of the 12th, Ali finally solved the puzzle that was Mildenberger. A lead right landed heavily on the challenger's chin, after which he landed a double-jab that set up a swooping left uppercut to the jaw. A split-second after the uppercut landed chief second Angelo Dundee shouted "he's out!" Moments later, Ali proved his trainer correct as he connected with a flurry, maneuvered Mildenberger to the ropes and connected with a flush right to the jaw that sent the challenger tottering backward. The aftermath of that punch prompted referee Waltham to step between the combatants and declare the fight over.

"I knew from the start he was going to last a while," a subdued Ali said. "I did not take any chances. I never do. My best punch was my left. He tagged me a couple of times, mostly with his right. He was hard to get to and he had a pretty good punch. He was sharp. He was a real gentleman, though." (5)

Mildenberger, for the most part, was happy with his performance, a performance that lifted his fight with Ali to the third-place spot in THE RING's Fight of the Year race for 1966 behind Jose Torres-Eddie Cotton and Carlos Ortiz-Ultiminio "Sugar" Ramos. (6)

"I fought my best, but the cut under my left eye made it impossible," he said. "I really couldn't see from the ninth round on. I thought I was doing well except for the time he floored me, almost at the bell. I was happy with the way things were going. When he put me down at the end of the 10th, then that was when I knew I was in serious trouble." (7)

Mildenberger may have lost the fight, but his brave performance against Ali enhanced his reputation among German fans. Schmeling was, and always will be, the unquestioned legend of German boxing but for decades after his date with destiny Mildenberger occupied a high place in the national consciousness. In a very real way, Mildenberger may have lost the fight but he won an important personal war -- the war for self-respect as well as the respect of others.

The Mildenberger-Machen fight featured a rare referee switch. Jack Tree wrote in the May 1966 RING that referee Gerhard Seewald had to be replaced by Helmut Bertram in round seven after Machen's elbow accidentally nailed Seewald, who was trying to separate the boxers.

INSIDE THE NUMBERS: *Ali was out-landed in jabs (92-82) for only the second time among Ali fights counted by CompuBox to this point, landing just 19.9% overall. Mildenberger's 422 thrown jabs were the third most by an Ali opponent (444 by Holmes; 443 by Young) and his 92 landed were the fifth most by an Ali foe (Holmes' 205 was the most). Mildenberger landed 44.8% of his power shots, but landed an average of just 4.3 per round, throwing 9.7 per frame.*

Date: September 10, 1966   City: Frankfurt, Germany   Venue: Waldstadion/Radrennbahn
Opponent: Karl Mildenberger
Result: Ali by TKO at 1:30 of the 12th round -- Retained World Heavyweight Title

Referee: Teddy Waltham

Round	1	2	3	4	5	6	7	8	9	10	11	12	13	14	15	Total
Ali																7 (2E)
Mildenberger			X						X							2 (2E)

Judge: Felix Ohlert

Round	1	2	3	4	5	6	7	8	9	10	11	12	13	14	15	Total
Ali																6 (2E)
Mildenberger																3 (2E)

Judge: Nat Fleischer

Round	1	2	3	4	5	6	7	8	9	10	11	12	13	14	15	Total
Ali																8
Mildenberger																3

MUHAMMAD ALI TKO 12 KARL MILDENBERGER

09/10/66 - FRANKFURT

Total Punches Landed / Thrown												
	1	2	3	4	5	6	7	8	9	10	11	12
ALI	6/38	19/57	15/43	11/62	9/54	11/67	15/50	19/64	10/47	14/60	15/53	10/17
	15.8%	33.3%	34.9%	17.7%	16.7%	16.4%	30%	29.7%	21.3%	23.3%	28.3%	58.8%
MILDENBERGER	9/41	11/46	16/53	15/44	15/37	6/28	16/48	12/60	16/48	13/59	12/55	3/19
	22%	23.9%	30.2%	34.1%	40.5%	21.4%	33.3%	20%	33.3%	22%	21.8%	15.8%

Jab Landed / Thrown												
	1	2	3	4	5	6	7	8	9	10	11	12
ALI	0/19	14/39	7/29	8/51	5/47	5/42	11/43	7/40	6/31	5/28	10/37	4/6
	0%	35.9%	24.1%	15.7%	10.6%	11.9%	25.6%	17.5%	19.4%	17.9%	27%	66.7%
MILDENBERGER	6/35	7/37	6/35	9/31	6/25	5/26	15/46	8/46	12/41	7/42	8/41	3/17
	17.1%	18.9%	17.1%	29%	24%	19.2%	32.6%	17.4%	29.3%	16.7%	19.5%	17.6%

Power Punches Landed / Thrown												
	1	2	3	4	5	6	7	8	9	10	11	12
ALI	6/19	5/18	8/14	3/11	4/7	6/25	4/7	12/24	4/16	9/32	5/16	6/11
	31.6%	27.8%	57.1%	27.3%	57.1%	24%	57.1%	50%	25%	28.1%	31.3%	54.5%
MILDENBERGER	3/6	4/9	10/18	6/13	9/12	1/2	1/2	4/14	4/7	6/17	4/14	0/2
	50%	44.4%	55.6%	46.2%	75%	50%	50%	28.6%	57.1%	35.3%	28.6%	0%

Final Punch Stat Report			
	Total Punches	Total Jabs	Power Punches
ALI	154/612	82/412	72/200
	25.2%	19.9%	36%
MILDENBERGER	144/538	92/422	52/116
	26.8%	21.8%	44.8%

14.

Every so often, an athlete -- even one who long had been considered elite -- will produce a performance that shatters all pre-conceived limits of human accomplishment. At the 1968 Summer Olympics in Mexico City, Bob Beamon's first leap of the competition, a 29-foot 2 1/2-inch bomb, crushed the previous world record by an astonishing 21 3/4 inches. On March 2, 1962 in Hershey, Pa., Wilt Chamberlain smashed his own NBA single-game scoring record of 78 by pouring in 100 points, a mark that hasn't been seriously challenged since. And on September 28, 1951, L.A. Rams quarterback Norm Van Brocklin -- who that day was subbing for injured starter Bob Waterfield -- obliterated Johnny Lujack's single-game passing record of 468 yards by accumulating 554 yards on just 27 completions, a total that still stands despite the league's pass-happy approach in recent years. (1)

For Muhammad Ali, the peak was reached November 14, 1966 at the Houston Astrodome against Cleveland Williams. During seven minutes and eight seconds of ring action, the 24-year-old Ali's already balletic footwork soared to new heights thanks to his frequent use of the newly-created "Ali Shuffle" while his hands produced combinations that landed with stunning power and frequency. At the same time, he transitioned seamlessly between offense and defense to a degree never previously seen. When historians assess Ali's chances against other all-time greats, it's the Cleveland Williams fight they use, appropriately, to measure Ali at his best. Of that night, Howard Cosell later declared, "he was the most devastating fighter who ever lived." (2)

That said, even Ali conceded that the 33-year-old Williams wasn't the fighter he had been in the late-1950s and early 1960s. *That* fighter had been one of his era's most dangerous punchers -- and one of its most avoided.

Standing 6-foot-3 and owning an 80-inch wingspan, Williams could look Ali in the eye and also jab from equal distance. But it was his enormous two-fisted power that separated him from the pack as well as separated opponents from their senses. Entering the Ali bout, 53 knockouts adorned his 67-5-1 record, including 18 straight between March 1952 and January 1953. Yes, some of those victims had names like Graveyard Walters (KO 2), Baby Booze (KO 1) and Candy McDaniels (KO 2), but fights are fights, punches are punches and knockouts are knockouts.

While Williams made his bones knocking people out, his two most famous fights were the pair he lost to future champion Sonny Liston in April 1959 and March 1960. While Williams was stopped in rounds three and two respectively, he managed to stun "The Big Ugly Bear" in both bouts.

85

Since the Liston rematch in Williams' native Houston, "The Big Cat" had gone 20-1-1 with 14 knockouts. But Williams was a 15-year ring veteran who not only was growing long in the tooth, he also entered the Houston Astrodome ring with a policeman's .357 magnum bullet in his gut, the result of a confrontation with a Texas highway patrolman on November 29, 1964.

"Williams and three friends, two of them females, were arrested for drunken driving," wrote THE RING's Dan Daniel. "Cleve, who, according to (manager Hugh) Benbow, had had only a few beers, pleaded with the cop to let him go. He pleaded that his scheduled match with (WBA champion Ernie) Terrell (which had been announced just nine days earlier) would be in jeopardy if the news of his arrest got out. The patrolman refused and a scuffle ensued. Williams was shot.

"After an operation which lasted five-and-a-half hours, Cleve was sewed up and put to bed," Daniel continued. "Half an hour later he had to be operated on again, as he had been bleeding internally." (3)

According to the Associated Press, Williams was in critical condition for several weeks and underwent four operations over a seven-month period. Benbow later revealed that Williams had "died" three times during the initial operation and, during his recovery, his weight had plummeted to 158. (4)

In the end, Williams persevered.

"This man has an iron constitution, a body of steel," the chief surgeon said. "I believe he will be fighting again. But it will take some time." (5)

That time ended up being a little more than 14 months. Williams' first fight was a one-round blowout of Ben Black on February 8, 1966, which was quickly followed by victories over Mel Turnbow (an off-the-floor W 10) on March 22, Sonny Moore (W 10) on April 19 and Tod Herring (KO 3) on June 28, all of which were staged at the Sam Houston Coliseum in Houston. While the bout, on paper, appeared heavily tilted toward the defending champion, the matchup proved so attractive that it drew 35,460, which broke an indoor attendance record that had stood for a quarter-century. (6)

Despite the obvious differences in talent, career trajectory and ring wear, no one could have anticipated how severe a mismatch Ali-Williams would end up being.

Ali spent the first round on the move, firing a jab that easily sliced through Williams' guard and shooting power shots judiciously but accurately. Even this study-hall version of Ali left the far slower Williams at a loss, for he only got off 13 punches in the round, landing three. Meanwhile, Ali breezily landed 23 of his 50 total punches, 15 of his 33 jabs and 8 of his 17 power shots.

Of the 548 rounds Ali fought as a pro, round two of the Williams fight ranks as one of his very best. The statistics alone were awe-inspiring as he landed 38 of his 64 total punches (59%), 22 of his 38 jabs (58%) and 16 of his 26 power punches (62%). But the numbers only partially illustrated Ali's mind-boggling blend of speed and power.

Jabbing to the head, Ali bloodied the challenger's nose. Then, with 47 seconds remaining, Ali scored the first knockdown with a sudden one-two to the jaw. The determined Williams rose immediately but was soon staggered by a chopping right to the temple and dropped with a pinpoint right-left-right to the face. Again, Williams got up quickly and braced himself for the next wave.

With the end of the round fast approaching, Ali delivered the most picturesque combination of his career -- two flush hooks followed by a gorgeous right to the chin that left Williams flat on his back. In most jurisdictions the fight would have ended there, but since there was no three-knockdown rule, the challenger was given the opportunity to rise. Had the knockdown occurred earlier in the round, the semi-conscious Williams probably wouldn't have been able to do so, but because the bell sounded midway through referee Harry Kessler's count, Williams' manager and corner people were allowed to enter the ring and help their man back to his stool.

The 60-second rest only delayed the inevitable; for on this night Ali was unstoppable. As great as the second round was, the third was Muhammad Ali at his white-hot zenith.

It began with Ali jabbing Williams with spears, then, after yet another shuffle, bedazzling him a pair of four-punch combinations that landed hard and flush. An instant later, Ali scored the fourth knockdown with a missile of a right hand. Once again, Williams got up well before Kessler reached the halfway point of his count and once the fight resumed he tried his best to keep the Ali storm at bay.

He could not.

A right to the ear caused Williams to stumble, and after a final right crashed on Williams' jaw, the referee stopped the slaughter. In those 68 seconds, Ali threw 42 punches and landed 26 for 62% accuracy and connected on 22 of his 31 power punches, which translates to 71%.

Conversely, Williams threw just 12 punches in the round, striking Ali with only three. For the fight, Williams hit Ali 10 times, and eight of those were jabs. The Williams fight was Ali's fifth title defense of 1966 and his fourth straight knockout.

Ali's performance left observers awestruck. Many of the 35,460 that generated a $461,780 gate booed and hooted at Ali during his approach to the ring but once they witnessed the full array of Ali's talent they gave him an ovation upon leaving. (7)

RING founder Nat Fleischer, a longtime ally of Ali's, called his performance "splendid" and "the best of his career."

"I have seen, and been with, Clay on all of his foreign trips since the Rome Olympic Games, and at no time have I seen him unleash such power as against Williams," he wrote. "In contrast to other performances, Cassius was a fighting machine in Houston. Once he unlimbered his heavy artillery, he faced a confused, bewildered, floundering opponent who was baffled by what was taking place. The unexpected had happened and the fans saw a one-sided affair." (8)

Ali's display also caused some critics to change their tune.

"I kept saying he was a phony, a clay pigeon, but I take it all back," declared Benbow. "I apologize. He made a sucker out of me and my boy. He made a believer out of me. He's the real McCoy. I'm now convinced of his punching ability. He's a real champion. Let's not kid ourselves any longer." (9)

Ali's most surprising convert was none other than the legendary "Manassa Mauler," Jack Dempsey.

"He is fast, both with his hands and with his feet," he said. "His reflexes are amazing. You might expect them in a lightweight, but not in a man of his size. He showed he can take a man out. Williams was through when the bell saved him at the end of the second round. I guess we're lucky to have him around." (10)

He didn't win over everybody, however. In the same issue of THE RING in which Dempsey offered praise, Joe Louis opined an "as told to" article in which he detailed "How I Would Have Clobbered Clay." In fact, "The Brown Bomber's" article began on page six while Dempsey's started on page seven.

But while Benbow and Fleischer were amazed, Williams was puzzled.

"I didn't know what was going on after Clay smashed his right to my mouth in the second round," he said, "I don't remember the other knockdowns."

Asked whether he was ever hit harder, he said, "he was not the hardest hitter I've met." (11) It's only a guess, but that honor probably still belonged to Liston.

Years later, Williams gave voice to the most common criticism leveled against those who declared this Ali's best performance -- he fought a badly eroded version of the "Big Cat" that had so terrorized the heavyweight class years earlier.

"(Ali) wouldn't fight me before I got shot, him or Floyd Patterson," he said in 1979. "But when I did fight him, even a little kid could've beaten me." (12)

Despite Ali's tremendously accomplished 1966 campaign, THE RING's editors chose to bypass him -- and everyone else -- for the publication's Fighter of the Year award.

"Since 1963, Clay has disqualified himself for a repeat award with these demerits: 1. Cassius allied himself with the Black Muslims, who avowedly are not friendly toward the United States of America, and are not listed as a patriotic group; 2. Clay has entered a protest against his being drafted into the Army, and has laid claim to exemption from service, chiefly on the allegation that he is a student-preacher for the Mohammedan religion; 3. The champion boxer of the world has been guilty of utterances which have not redounded to the credit of boxing and which, arousing the vehement protests of the American Legion, Veterans of Foreign Wars and other patriotic organizations, forced cancellation of Clay's scheduled fight with Ernie Terrell in Chicago and had other bad repercussions." (13)

Dan Daniel, who wrote the editorial that appeared in the March 1967 issue, said that denying Primo Carnera of the 1933 award due to the shady nature of his management was adequate precedent for their stance against Ali, a stance which was said to have been received favorably by a 6-to-1 margin in the following month's edition. (14)

When asked for his reaction by RING founder and editor-in-chief Nat Fleischer, Ali was disappointed.

"I'm a fighting champion," he declared. "I'm sorry Nat Fleischer's magazine didn't award me the honor. My record for 1966 entitled me to be named. My religious belief should have not been considered. It has nothing to do with my fighting ability. Sportsmanship, ring achievement and clean living should decide. In those I know I stood out for the year 1966." (15)

Fifty years later, a new editor from a new generation opted to alter the record and retroactively bestow the honor on Ali.

"While many took issue with the Nation of Islam -- many still do -- we feel that athletes under consideration for such awards should be judged by their performance, not their political or religious affiliations," then-RING editor-in-chief Michael Rosenthal explained in the March 2017 issue. (16)

The Williams fight was the final one of Ali's 1966 campaign, and when his fighting career was suspended the following year, the Williams fight would stand out as an aching hint of what might have been had history unfolded differently.

INSIDE THE NUMBERS: Ali's numbers vs. Williams were spectacular. He landed personal bests among fights counted for total connect percentage (55.8% -- heavyweight average: 34%), jabs (50% -- more than doubling the division average of 25.5%) and power punches (62.2%, far above the divisional norm of 40.7%). Meanwhile the bedazzled Williams threw just 43 punches in 7:08 of ring time and landed just two power punches.

Date:	November 14, 1966				City: Houston, TX					Venue: Astrodome						
Opponent:	Cleveland Williams															
Result:	Ali by TKO at 1:08 of the 3rd round -- Retains World Heavyweight Title															

Referee:	Harry Kessler															
	Round	1	2	3	4	5	6	7	8	9	10	11	12	13	14	15	Total
	Ali	10	10														20
	Williams	9	7														16

Judge:	Jimmy Webb															
	Round	1	2	3	4	5	6	7	8	9	10	11	12	13	14	15	Total
	Ali	10	10														20
	Williams	9	7														16

Judge:	Ernie Taylor															
	Round	1	2	3	4	5	6	7	8	9	10	11	12	13	14	15	Total
	Ali	10	10														20
	Williams	9	7														16

MUHAMMAD ALI TKO 3 CLEVELAND WILLIAMS
11/14/66 - HOUSTON

Total Punches Landed / Thrown	1	2	3	4	5	6	7	8	9	10	11	12	13	14	15
ALI	23/50	38/64	26/42	-/-	-/-	-/-	-/-	-/-	-/-	-/-	-/-	-/-	-/-	-/-	-/-
	46%	59.4%	61.9%	-	-	-	-	-	-	-	-	-	-	-	-
WILLIAMS	3/13	4/18	3/12	-/-	-/-	-/-	-/-	-/-	-/-	-/-	-/-	-/-	-/-	-/-	-/-
	23.1%	22.2%	25%	-	-	-	-	-	-	-	-	-	-	-	-

Jab Landed / Thrown	1	2	3	4	5	6	7	8	9	10	11	12	13	14	15
ALI	15/33	22/38	4/11	-/-	-/-	-/-	-/-	-/-	-/-	-/-	-/-	-/-	-/-	-/-	-/-
	45.5%	57.9%	36.4%	-	-	-	-	-	-	-	-	-	-	-	-
WILLIAMS	3/10	2/8	3/11	-/-	-/-	-/-	-/-	-/-	-/-	-/-	-/-	-/-	-/-	-/-	-/-
	30%	25%	27.3%	-	-	-	-	-	-	-	-	-	-	-	-

Power Punches Landed / Thrown	1	2	3	4	5	6	7	8	9	10	11	12	13	14	15
ALI	8/17	16/26	22/31	-/-	-/-	-/-	-/-	-/-	-/-	-/-	-/-	-/-	-/-	-/-	-/-
	47.1%	61.5%	71%	-	-	-	-	-	-	-	-	-	-	-	-
WILLIAMS	0/3	2/10	0/1	-/-	-/-	-/-	-/-	-/-	-/-	-/-	-/-	-/-	-/-	-/-	-/-
	0%	20%	0%	-	-	-	-	-	-	-	-	-	-	-	-

Final Punch Stat Report	Total Punches	Total Jabs	Power Punches
ALI	87/156	41/82	46/74
	55.8%	50%	62.2%
WILLIAMS	10/43	8/29	2/14
	23.3%	27.6%	14.3%

15.

If the Williams fight was Ali at his phenomenal peak, his 15-rounder with Ernie Terrell laid bare the cruelty, vindictiveness and bitterness that swirled within him.

Terrell's crime: His refusal to address Ali by his Muslim name.

It wasn't as if Terrell wasn't warned about the consequences of his actions. After all, Floyd Patterson also called Ali "Cassius Clay" at every opportunity and, on fight night, was abused verbally and tortured physically by a vindictive champion determined to drive home a point.

Terrell didn't originally plan to pull the "name card." In fact, Terrell thought of Ali as a friend. Ali and Terrell were roommates for a week in Miami while the pair sparred together in 1962. Ali, then Clay, was preparing to fight Don Warner while Terrell was set to face Herb Siler on the undercard. The morning after both won their bouts, Clay drove Terrell from Miami to Louisville in his red Cadillac. (1)

Moreover, Terrell was one of Clay's sparring partners for the first Liston fight, and the photos published in the May 1966 issue of THE RING (thanks to an agreement the publication had with Jimmy Jacobs, the owner of the photos) suggested that Terrell more than held his own during the session at Miami's Fifth Street Gym, which was stopped after only one round. Three of the six photos showed Terrell firing punches over Clay's low guard while another depicted him landing a hard left to the chest.

On March 22, 1964, less than a month after Clay/Ali shook up the world, World Boxing Association president Ed Lassman stripped the new champion of its title, ostensibly for inking an immediate rematch with Liston, which went against the WBA's bylaws. Lassman added, however, that the title would be restored if Ali proved his eligibility through his conduct outside the ring, a not-so-veiled reference to his religious conversion and his recent political rhetoric. Two days later, Lassman reversed himself and restored the title to Clay, saying he would wait until August to give him and his colleagues sufficient time to consider the evidence presented in the March 19-31, 1964 Senate probe into boxing led by Sen. Phillip Hart of Michigan. (2) The WBA was true to its word because on August 29, moments after the site and date of the Ali-Liston rematch was announced and two days after the WBA unanimously voted to strip Ali of the title should a return match be made, the sanctioning body took back its belt. Interestingly, on that same day the WBA elected a new president, Merv L. McKenzie of Toronto. (3)

Although a four-man tournament involving Terrell, Cleveland Williams, Floyd Patterson and Doug Jones was initially called for, it never took place. Instead, Terrell won the vacant belt by out-pointing Eddie Machen in March 1965, then successfully defended against George Chuvalo (W 15) in November 1965 and Doug Jones (W 15) in June 1966. This despite the fact that McKenzie's successor as WBA president, Jim Deskin, the executive secretary of the Nevada State Athletic Commission, declared shortly after being elected in September 1965 that "the WBA's action earlier this year in removing its recognition of Clay as world heavyweight champion was premature and hurt the WBA and boxing in general. Clay is the champion to the people of the world." (4)

Ali and Terrell were originally set to unify the belts March 29, 1966 but a combination of factors led to the fight being canceled. The first was the New York State Athletic Commission's refusal to renew Terrell's license due to his association with Chicago-based manager Bernie Glickman, who was said to have ties with the mob and who had worked Terrell's corner for the Chuvalo defense when chief second Freddie Brown couldn't be located. (5) Those ties were all but confirmed when the FBI took Glickman into protective custody after he had been beaten by street toughs whose motives were not clear. (6) New York's move caused the proposed fight to be moved to Chicago.

The second, and most crucial, cause was Ali's draft reclassification from 1-Y to 1-A in February 1966 and the aftermath of his "Viet Cong" comment. Ali's refusal to apologize to the Illinois State Athletic Commission for his "unpatriotic remarks" caused the fight to be thrown out of the state. The fight gained approval in Montreal, but the Forum, the promoter's preferred site, was not available to host the bout. (7) The bout was then set for Toronto, but Terrell refused because he said the contract offered to him would have given exclusive rights to Main Bout Inc., which he said had strong Muslim affiliations. However, Mike Malitz, a shareholder in Main Bout, denied any such clause existed. "There was no lawyer with Terrell when he refused to sign for a Clay fight in Canada," he said. "I saw the contracts. There was no exclusive clause in them." (8)

Following failed bids by Maine and Kentucky, and after 180 of the 280 closed-circuit exhibitors withdrew following complaints by American Legion posts as well as other patriotic organizations, the fight was canceled. (9) Terrell went on to defend his WBA belt against Jones while Ali opted to fight Chuvalo.

For Terrell, the "Clay gambit" was just a way to get under an opponent's skin.

"I didn't consciously decide to call him 'Clay,'" Terrell told Hauser. "What happened was, when we signed to fight, the promoter told us, 'you'll both have to be in Houston two weeks ahead of time and complete your training there to help the promotion.' And he asked me, 'is that all right with you, Ernie?' And I said, 'it's all right with me if it's all right with Clay.' I wasn't trying to insult him. He'd been Cassius Clay to me all the time before when I knew him. Then he told me, 'my name is Muhammad Ali.' And I said fine, but by then he was going, 'why can't you call me

Muhammad Ali? You're just an Uncle Tom.' Well, like I said, I didn't mean no harm. But when I saw that calling him 'Clay' bugged him, I kept it going. To me it was just part of building up the promotion." (10)

Ali had long occupied the other side of the equation. To varying degrees, Ali insulted opponents in the name of goosing the gate, but here the roles were reversed -- and Ali didn't like it one bit.

The pre-fight tensions exploded during a joint interview conducted by ABC's Howard Cosell.

"I'd like to say something right here," the soft-spoken Terrell began. "Cassius Clay..."

"Why do you want to say 'Cassius Clay' when Howard Cosell and everybody is calling me 'Muhammad Ali?' " the champion asked. "Now why do you got to be the one of all people, who's colored, to keep saying 'Cassius Clay?' "

"Howard Cosell is not the one who's going to fight you. I am," Terrell answered.

"You're making it really hard on yourself now," an increasingly agitated Ali charged. "Why don't you keep the thing in the sport angle? Why don't you call me my name, man?"

"Well, what's your name?" Terrell asked. "You told me it was Cassius Clay a few years ago."

"I never told you my name was Cassius Clay," a glaring Ali shot back. "My name is Muhammad Ali and you will announce it right there in the center of that ring after the fight, if you don't do it now."

"For the benefit of this broadcast (I'll say) 'him,' all right?" a quiet but defiant Terrell said.

At this point Ali turned up the temperature considerably. As was the case with those who hurt him, Ali wanted to hurt his antagonist a thousand-fold. To do so here, Ali uttered the worst insult one African-American man could hurl at another.

"You are acting just like an old Uncle Tom," Ali spewed. "Another Floyd Patterson. I'm going to punish you!"

"Don't call me no Uncle Tom, man," Terrell warned.

"You are an Uncle Tom!" Ali repeated. "Uncle Tom!"

This incited a brief shoving match, and moments after a smiling Cosell declared the segment "perfect," Ali reached around and slapped Terrell's face.

While Terrell clearly touched a nerve in Ali, his physique and style presented potential style issues. At 6-foot-6 and owning an 82-inch reach, the 28-year-old Terrell was the first title-fight opponent to own both height and reach advantages over Ali. At his best, Terrell was an industrious sort who worked behind a very busy and effective jab. In stopping future light heavyweight king Bob Foster in 1964, Terrell averaged 82.2 punches per round, 50.2 jab attempts per round and 14.1 landed jabs, more than triple the heavyweight average. On the other hand, Terrell often fell into clinches and clamped on so strongly and frequently that he was dubbed "The Octopus." However unattractive the tactics, they resulted in 39 wins in 43 fights as well as 18 victories inside the distance. That said, Terrell's last KO victory came nearly two-and-a-half years earlier against Henry Wallitsch.

The atmosphere inside the Houston Astrodome was emotionally charged and Ali was at its epicenter. The booing for Ali began even before the ring announcer could finish his introduction, though the reaction to his name brought a mix of cheers and jeers. Ali talked to Terrell throughout the final instructions and at the sound of opening bell Ali asserted himself by firing a quick eight-punch flurry, most of which bounced off Terrell's high guard. Terrell, his straight-up stance accentuating the height difference, stiffly attempted to cut off the ring but also landed a few hard jabs to the face and thrice managed to corner the breathtakingly fluid champion. Thanks to several thumping body shots Terrell out-landed Ali 13-10 overall and won the round on the unofficial card of George Chuvalo, who was doing color commentary with Cosell.

Ali began the second taunting Terrell with a series of slapping rights more akin to shooing a pesky insect than repelling a world-class heavyweight. His intent was to belittle Terrell, who, to his credit, ignored the byplay and focused on blasting Ali's body in the clinches. Once again, Terrell edged Ali 10-9 in total connects as well as 8-3 in landed power shots. But make no mistake: While Terrell had forged in early statistical lead, the difference in talent favoring Ali was graphically apparent. Terrell was fighting at his best while Ali was content to bide his time and wait for the right moment to strike.

Terrell upped his aggression early in the third as he bore inside and fired repeated rights to the ribs as Ali held on. Ali responded by firing swift combinations highlighted by a normally ignored weapon, the right uppercut. Ali's jabs had created a tiny abrasion on the corner of Terrell's eye but with 30 seconds remaining Ali worsened it by rubbing Terrell's face on the uppermost rope, a maneuver that prompted a torrent of boos and caused Terrell to grimace and pull away.

"He rubbed my right eye against the ropes and thumbed my left eye so that from the third round on I couldn't see Clay to hit him," Terrell said after the fight. "I kept seeing two or three people." (11)

The third saw Ali increase his work rate from 32 to 50 punches while causing Terrell's to drop from 32 to 24. Ali also out-landed his titular counterpart 21-10 overall and 11-2 jabs.

An angry Terrell started the fourth by nailing Ali with a right to the chin and with thudding rights in the subsequent clinches. Ali, for his part, remained calm and methodically picked away at Terrell's injured eyes. Later in the round Ali deftly slipped three jabs and a right, then glided back to ring center, another example of his reflexes and fluidity. Moments later, a frustrated Terrell nearly hit Ali on the break with a right uppercut. Near the end of the round Terrell landed his best blow yet, a thudding hook to the jaw that made Ali's legs stutter for the briefest of moments. That blow capped off a round in which he out-landed Ali 11-8 overall and 9-5 power.

Aside from a 8-4 power connect lead in round five, it would be the last time Terrell would earn any kind of numerical advantage. The true degree of Ali's superiority emerged starting in the seventh, when he upped his output from 42 to 57 punches, out-landed Terrell 24-9 and 18-5 power and dramatically increased his marksmanship (from 33% to 42% overall and from 29% to 53% power). A right uppercut followed by a pair of hooks stiffened Terrell's legs and caused him to drape his upper body over the top rope, a maneuver that saved him from a knockdown. Ali leaped in and pounded Terrell with blinding combinations that opened cuts over both of Terrell's eyes and turned the left orb into a slit. Despite the searing pain, Terrell marched forward with both gloves covering his face, taking everything Ali was willing to dish out. In the final minute, the defiant Terrell lashed out at Ali and landed a strong right to the cheek. His courage, and Ali's temporarily ebbing gas tank, allowed Terrell to survive the round.

Ali's chief second Angelo Dundee told Cosell before the fight that the eighth round would be the last, but Ali was more intent on adding psychological wounds to Terrell's physical ones. Just before the two-minute mark, Ali suddenly and unexpectedly began to question Terrell.

"What's my name?"

Jab to the face and an overhand right to the side of the head.

"What's my name?"

Another four-punch flurry that prompted a clinch from Terrell.

"What's my name?"

Hook-right.

"What's my name?"

Jab to the face.

Again.

Jab to the face.

And again.

Right-left-right.

As the eighth round bell sounded, an infuriated Ali dropped his gloves, glared directly into Terrell's eyes and shouted, "What's my name, huh? What's my name, huh? *What's my name?!*"

Terrell said nothing.

Color analysts Chuvalo and Joe Louis chuckled at Ali's actions but for Ali the sequence was deadly serious. The final third of round eight had the look of a torture session in which Ali the inquisitor tried to beat a confession out of his subject. Failing to get the answer he wanted, Ali literally took matters into his own hands.

Ali continued to jab -- and jabber -- at Terrell in rounds nine and 10, venting his spleen but throttling down his physical attack in spots. Terrell tried to fight back, but Ali's head movement was simply too good. Louis and Chuvalo thought Ali was carrying Terrell to maximize the punishment as well as the humiliation. Terrell unleashed a rare spurt in the 10th when he trapped Ali on the ropes and pounded his body, but his punches lacked their earlier steam, if not their venom.

The final five rounds saw Ali let loose with his full arsenal in an attempt to insert the final exclamation point to a statement directed not just at Terrell but to the crowd that booed him inside the Astrodome, to the thousands that booed him around the various closed-circuit outlets and the legion of establishment forces that stripped him of the WBA title and threatened to imprison him for his anti-war stand.

In those five rounds Ali out-landed Terrell 144-39 overall and 104-26 power. In rounds 12-15 Ali averaged 68.8 punches per round, including 73 in the final three minutes. Through it all, Terrell stood, though he no longer had the energy to do much else. For him, survival was its own satisfaction.

Referee Harry Kessler (148-137) and judges Jimmy Webb (148-133) and Ernie Taylor (148-137) saw Ali a lopsided winner and the stats also reflected his control. Of his 293 total connects, 56% were accrued in the final six rounds.

"He was disappointing because he just kept holding and clinching all the time," Ali said. "But he had to have great courage to stay in the ring and take a whipping for 15 rounds." (12)

To the end, Terrell stood his ground.

"I don't hate the man as a fighter," he told Cosell shortly before the cards were announced. "I still dislike what he represents and what he said. I respect all fighters for ability, but not for nonsense."

As for whether he now would honor the champion's preferred name, Terrell said this:

"I say now his name is Cassius Clay."

So, at least in the immediate aftermath, Ali may have bent Terrell, but he didn't break him.

INSIDE THE NUMBERS: Uncharacteristically, Ali relied more on the power punch than the jab versus Terrell, as 447 of his 737 thrown punches (60.7%) were power shots and 184 of his 293 landed punches (62.8%) were power punches. In the 47 Ali fights tracked by CompuBox, 46.4% of his thrown punches were power shots and 52.9% of his landed punches were power punches.

Date:	February 6, 1967				City: Houston, TX				Venue: Astrodome							
Opponent:	Ernie Terrell															
Result:	Ali by unanimous decision -- Regains WBA Title															
Referee:	Harry Kessler															
	Round	1	2	3	4	5	6	7	8	9	10	11	12	13	14	15	Total
	Ali	10	9	10	10	9	10	10	10	10	10	10	10	10	10	10	148
	Terrell	10	10	9	9	10	9	8	9	9	9	9	9	9	9	9	137
Judge:	Jimmy Webb															
	Round	1	2	3	4	5	6	7	8	9	10	11	12	13	14	15	Total
	Ali	9	9	10	10	10	10	10	10	10	10	10	10	10	10	10	148
	Terrell	10	10	9	9	9	9	8	8	9	9	9	8	9	9	8	133
Judge:	Ernie Taylor															
	Round	1	2	3	4	5	6	7	8	9	10	11	12	13	14	15	Total
	Ali	10	10	10	9	9	10	10	10	10	10	10	10	10	10	10	148
	Terrell	9	9	9	10	10	9	9	9	9	9	9	9	9	9	9	137

MUHAMMAD ALI UD 15 ERNIE TERRELL
02/06/67 - HOUSTON

Total Punches Landed / Thrown															
	1	2	3	4	5	6	7	8	9	10	11	12	13	14	15
ALI	10/28	9/32	21/50	8/29	12/35	14/42	24/57	19/40	12/43	20/49	26/57	27/74	28/58	32/70	31/73
	35.7%	28.1%	42%	27.6%	34.3%	33.3%	42.1%	47.5%	27.9%	40.8%	45.6%	36.5%	48.3%	45.7%	42.5%
TERRELL	13/30	10/32	10/24	11/38	12/40	6/21	9/34	6/25	7/21	16/37	9/26	4/19	8/26	6/14	12/26
	43.3%	31.3%	41.7%	28.9%	30%	28.6%	26.5%	24%	33.3%	43.2%	34.6%	21.1%	30.8%	42.9%	46.2%

Jab Landed / Thrown															
	1	2	3	4	5	6	7	8	9	10	11	12	13	14	15
ALI	3/9	6/17	11/23	3/15	8/18	9/25	6/23	9/19	8/29	6/17	8/18	7/17	10/22	8/19	7/19
	33.3%	35.3%	47.8%	20%	44.4%	36%	26.1%	47.4%	27.6%	35.3%	44.4%	41.2%	45.5%	42.1%	36.8%
TERRELL	3/12	2/10	2/5	2/11	4/13	3/10	4/16	6/19	4/15	6/11	5/15	0/7	3/14	3/6	2/6
	25%	20%	40%	18.2%	30.8%	30%	25%	31.6%	26.7%	54.5%	33.3%	0%	21.4%	50%	33.3%

Power Punches Landed / Thrown															
	1	2	3	4	5	6	7	8	9	10	11	12	13	14	15
ALI	7/19	3/15	10/27	5/14	4/17	5/17	18/34	10/21	4/14	14/32	18/39	20/57	18/36	24/51	24/54
	36.8%	20%	37%	35.7%	23.5%	29.4%	52.9%	47.6%	28.6%	43.8%	46.2%	35.1%	50%	47.1%	44.4%
TERRELL	10/18	8/22	8/19	9/27	8/27	3/11	5/18	0/6	3/6	10/26	4/11	4/12	5/12	3/8	10/20
	55.6%	36.4%	42.1%	33.3%	29.6%	27.3%	27.8%	0%	50%	38.5%	36.4%	33.3%	41.7%	37.5%	50%

Final Punch Stat Report			
	Total Punches	Total Jabs	Power Punches
ALI	293/737	109/290	184/447
	39.8%	37.6%	41.2%
TERRELL	139/413	49/170	90/243
	33.7%	28.8%	37%

16.

With issues regarding his draft status nearing the day of reckoning, Ali continued his hyperactive ring schedule by meeting Zora Folley just 44 days after bludgeoning Terrell. It was to be Ali's eighth title fight since stopping Floyd Patterson exactly 16 months earlier, a pace only topped by Joe Louis' 10 between December 1940 and March 1942. Another improbable historic factoid: Ali-Folley would be the first heavyweight title fight staged at Madison Square Garden in more than 16 years, when Ezzard Charles stopped Lee Oma in 11 rounds. (1) For Ali, it would be his first appearance at MSG since out-pointing Doug Jones four years earlier.

Unlike Terrell, who drove Ali to what he believed was a righteous fury, Folley was such a gentle soul that even Ali had to dig deep to find any source of animosity. Folley, a father of eight and a decorated veteran of the Korean War, was one of the first fighters to call the champ "Muhammad Ali." Folley, ranked second by THE RING, (2) also profusely thanked Ali for giving him a title shot that had eluded him for nearly a decade.

The 35-year-old known for his clever boxing and sound defense was about to engage in the 86th fight of what had been a successful 13-plus year career. His record was a more-than-respectable 74-7-4 with 40 knockouts and his victims included Roger Rischer, Nino Valdes, Wayne Bethea (twice), Pete Rademacher, Henry Cooper (second fight), Alex Miteff, Eddie Machen, Mike DeJohn, Bob Cleroux (twice), George Chuvalo, Bob Foster and Oscar Bonavena. He drew with Karl Mildenberger and Machen and lost to the likes of Sonny Liston, Cooper, Doug Jones, Alejandro Lavorante, Ernie Terrell, Johnny Summerlin and, in December 1955, to someone named Young Jack Johnson.

The Ali that had generated massive interest with his ranting was subdued and respectful during the build-up.

"I expect him to be a good boxer," Ali said in an unusually flat and unenthusiastic voice. "I know he's punching good with both hands. He's not too fast on his feet, but he's clever and he's smart. I'll be moving fast and building up points, and if I see a knockout I'll try to get it.

"I'm not a puncher," the somber Ali added. "I don't hit too hard. I just keep my face smooth and dance and move fast and do all the hitting but I never get hit and then when I do hit I don't hit that fast. But if a knockout does come, it could come. I knocked out Cleveland Williams, I knocked out Archie Moore and I knocked out Brian London, some fall and some don't. In other words, different strokes for different folks."

A day-long snowstorm limited attendance to 13,780 but the gate was a record $244,471 thanks to $50 ringside seats, the highest price ever charged at the Garden. (3) The magnitude of the event was reflected by the men introduced in the ring beforehand: Sugar Ray Robinson, Joe Louis, Sandy Saddler, Willie Pep, Rocky Graziano, Emile Griffith, Ike Williams, Luis Rodriguez, Jose Torres, Pete Scalzo, Ernie Terrell, George Chuvalo, Jimmy Ellis and Roger Rouse. Folley's introduction was politely applauded while Ali's generated mostly boos.

For whatever reason -- Ali's hectic schedule, his lack of animus for Folley or the minimal danger the champion perceived -- the 25-year-old Ali fought deliberately, throwing just 19 punches in each of the first two rounds. Meanwhile, Folley, nine pounds lighter at 202 1/2, landed the right hand with surprising frequency and impact, a development that was enthusiastically cheered. The second round was even better for the challenger as he out-jabbed Ali 11-2 and connected with three of his seven power shots. Interestingly, Ali fought with his gloves in near-textbook position, a marked departure from the usual below-the-hips location. The mitts returned to their customary placement at the start of the third, in which Ali was content to play the hand-jive with Folley. As he did so, he circled the challenger like a hawk surveying its prey before beginning its final and fatal dive.

After three rounds, Ali trailed 28-11 overall, 19-7 jabs and 9-4 power. Folley's unexpectedly solid showing caused the crowd to remain patient despite the far-below-average output (38.7 per round for Folley, 20 per round for Ali).

The fight's sleepy trajectory shifted with startling suddenness shortly before the midway point in round four when a lashing lead right over Folley's double jab caused the challenger to turn around and fall on his stomach. Folley, at first motionless, stirred at four and alertly regained his feet at nine. With Folley bleeding from the nose Ali tried to press his advantage but Folley's caginess and respect-worthy power shots prevented him from finishing the job.

Ali chose not to chase the knockout in round five, for he didn't throw a single power punch during that three-minute span. Still, he landed 17 jabs, six more than Folley and three more than the challenger's total connects. The sixth was nearly as jab-heavy as it accounted for 11 of Ali's 13 connects and six of Folley's nine.

Told to "stop playing" by manager Herbert Muhammad, Ali obeyed orders by repeating -- and improving upon -- what he did in round four. Once again timing Folley's jab, Ali connected with two consecutive lead right hands and left Folley flat on his face. Folley remained motionless until the count of six but by the time he pirouetted himself into the corner pad time had run out.

The scene brought down the curtain to what had been curious combat.

"It was one of the strangest fistic exhibitions in my long experience " wrote RING founder Nat Fleischer. "Don't anybody question the bona fides of the KO. Folley tried as hard as he could.

But he was inadequate for the job. For a long time Folley -- kindly, gentlemanly, with a large family and no membership other than the healthy connection with a church -- was carried as the number two contender. But when Folley got into the ring he was about as futile as any heavyweight challenger had been going back to Johnny Paychek (who fought Joe Louis in March 1940).

"Folley could not hurt Cassius," he concluded. "Muhammad did not want to hurt Zora." (4)

Folley's early lead barely held up, for he out-landed Ali 66-61 overall and 22-16 power while the champion vaulted ahead 45-44 in landed jabs. Neither was particularly sharp as Ali led 32%-26% overall and 31%-22% jabs while Folley prevailed 36%-35% power.

"All I remember was a right-right to the chin," Folley said in his dressing room. "I don't remember anything else. I'll keep fighting. I still think I can beat any heavyweight but Clay. I'm not ashamed of my showing. I fought well. I gave it all I had." (5)

"Folley bothered me for a while," Ali admitted. "He was taking his time and stalking me, but he wasn't fast enough. He hit me low a couple of times, but he apologized for it."

Ali then offered the highest of praise for Folley.

"He's the best scientific boxer I ever met," he said. "If I'd met him 10 years ago, I know I'd have had a lot of trouble." (6)

We'll never know what would have happened if the 25-year-old Ali had met the 25-year-old version of Folley. We'll also never know what would have unfolded had Ali's next two scheduled fights had taken place -- Oscar Bonavena May 27 in Tokyo and Thad Spencer July 22 in San Francisco. (7)

What Ali suspected, but did not know fully, was that the double right hand that felled Folley would be the final two punches he would get to throw in a sanctioned boxing match for the rest of the decade.

Thirty-seven days after stopping Folley, Ali arrived at the United States Armed Forces Examining and Entrance Station. There, Ali, as expected, refused to step forward when the name "Cassius Marcellus Clay" was called. The New York State Athletic Commission immediately stripped Ali of his license in New York as well as its recognition of him as world heavyweight champion, prompting virtually all jurisdictions worldwide to do the same. Other entities, however, demonstrated thoughtful restraint. The British Boxing Board of Control recognized Ali until mid-1969 (8) while THE RING, despite hundreds of letters of protest, was determined to wait until all legal avenues were exhausted.

But even Fleischer and his other editors couldn't hold out for the entire duration of Ali's legal proceedings, which ended on June 28, 1971 when the Supreme Court voted unanimously to overturn his conviction. A combination of factors led THE RING to reverse itself on February 3, 1970. (9) First, the upcoming unification fight between NYSAC titlist Joe Frazier and WBA tournament winner Jimmy Ellis, which was to take place in 13 days. Second, Ali's announcement that he would present THE RING's championship belt to the winner of Frazier-Ellis at Madison Square Garden (an act that New York State Athletic Commission chairman Ed Dooley would not permit). Third, Ali shipping the RING belt to his alma mater, Central High School in Louisville, Ky., a deed Fleischer and his staff interpreted as a willful abandonment of the belt.

"It was the strong sentiment of the staff that Clay had given up the world championship of his free will and that THE RING had been released from its commitments on his behalf," Dan Daniel wrote on behalf of the editorial team. "THE RING decision was made without a dissenting voice. It also was voted that the winner of the Frazier-Ellis fight would be recognized by this magazine as the new heavyweight champion of the world. If, as many skeptics predict, Clay changes his mind about quitting the ring and the lush paydays which would become available to him if he were cleared by the Supreme Court, Cassius would have to appear as the challenger, and emphatically not as the champion." (10) Daniel compared Ali's situation to that of James J. Jeffries, who gave up the belt and appointed Marvin Hart and Jack Root to fight for his vacated belt. Hart won, lost the title to Tommy Burns, who, in turn, lost to Jack Johnson. When Jeffries returned to the ring six years later, he was installed as the challenger despite his status as the lineal champion going back to John L. Sullivan. By stopping Jeffries in round 15, Johnson assumed ownership of that line. Frazier, too, dearly wanted to own that line (which now extended back to the retired Rocky Marciano), for right after he stopped Ellis he said the following in his dressing room: "(Clay's) the man I want to fight...and no one else." (11)

Now shorn of all recognition of his championship, Ali had to play the hand as it was dealt.

Instead of jabs, hooks and crosses, Ali's life was consumed by briefs, hearings and trials. Now without the financial security that came with being the heavyweight champion of the world, Ali hustled to stay financially afloat. One short-lived venture was the Broadway musical "Buck White" in which he played the title role. Although Ali generally drew good reviews, the show closed December 6, 1969 after only seven performances. (12) He stopped by gyms and worked out from time to time, and in late 1968 he participated in a fantasy "computer match" with Rocky Marciano in which several different endings were filmed. In America, where Ali was seen as a pariah by many, audiences were shown a 13th round KO victory for Marciano while in Europe, where Ali was a more sympathetic figure, Ali stopped Marciano on cuts. (13)

As Ali's exile dragged on, so did the Vietnam War he opposed. With the casualties mounting daily, an increasing number of Americans realized that no end to the carnage was in sight, which caused them to turn against the war itself as well as those who had anything to do with it. Ali, on the other hand, was gaining respect from some of those same people for his willingness to stand firm despite financial hardship. With every passing day the public view of Ali was drifting from athletically gifted loudmouth to a political and social symbol whose influence transcended race, ideology, faith and geography.

The resulting momentum prompted numerous efforts to restore Ali's license, efforts that were snatched away at the finish line due to staunch resistance at the uppermost levels of political power.

Finally, there was a breakthrough -- and ironically, it occurred in Georgia, the heart of the Deep South. The opening resulted from the fact that while the state of Georgia had no athletic commission, individual municipalities within the state did, including Atlanta. Thanks to the efforts of Sen. Leroy Johnson, an African-American, and Sam Massell, Atlanta's first white Jewish mayor, Ali was given a license. (14) On September 15, 1970, four days after Ali signed to fight Quarry, Federal Judge Walter R. Mansfield ruled that Ali should be granted a boxing license in New York. (15)

Just like that, Ali was back in boxing.

On October 26, 1970, 55 days after Ali fought an eight-round exhibition against three opponents at Atlanta's Morehouse College (16), he was scheduled to meet Jerry Quarry -- THE RING's number-one contender and the WBA's third-rated heavyweight -- in a scheduled 15 round fight at the City Auditorium in Atlanta.

INSIDE THE NUMBERS: To say Ali went easy on Folley is a supreme understatement: He landed just 8.7 punches per round, 10.2 fewer per round than his nine other "Prime Ali" fights. His 27.6 punches thrown per round were 24 fewer than his nine other "Prime Ali" fights. Ali landed just 16 power shots in the 19:48 the fight lasted.

Date:	March 22, 1967					City: New York, NY			Venue: Madison Square Garden							
Opponent:	Zora Folley															
Result:	Ali by KO at 1:48 of the 7th round -- Retained WBA Heavyweight Title															

Referee:	Johnny LoBianco															
	Round	1	2	3	4	5	6	7	8	9	10	11	12	13	14	15	Total
	Ali			X	X	X	X										4
	Folley	X	X														2

Judge:	Frank Forbes															
	Round	1	2	3	4	5	6	7	8	9	10	11	12	13	14	15	Total
	Ali			X	X	X	X										4
	Folley	X	X														2

Judge:	Tony Castellano															
	Round	1	2	3	4	5	6	7	8	9	10	11	12	13	14	15	Total
	Ali				X	X	X										3
	Folley	X	X	X													3

MUHAMMAD ALI KO 7 ZORA FOLLEY

03/22/67 - NEW YORK

Total Punches Landed / Thrown															
	1	2	3	4	5	6	7	8	9	10	11	12	13	14	15
ALI	2/19	3/19	6/22	10/33	17/34	13/40	10/26	-/-	-/-	-/-	-/-	-/-	-/-	-/-	-/-
	10.5%	15.8%	27.3%	30.3%	50%	32.5%	38.5%	-	-	-	-	-	-	-	-
FOLLEY	8/29	14/47	6/40	9/48	14/43	9/27	6/23	-/-	-/-	-/-	-/-	-/-	-/-	-/-	-/-
	27.6%	29.8%	15%	18.8%	32.6%	33.3%	26.1%	-	-	-	-	-	-	-	-

Jab Landed / Thrown															
	1	2	3	4	5	6	7	8	9	10	11	12	13	14	15
ALI	1/13	2/15	4/17	5/19	17/34	11/33	5/16	-/-	-/-	-/-	-/-	-/-	-/-	-/-	-/-
	7.7%	13.3%	23.5%	26.3%	50%	33.3%	31.3%	-	-	-	-	-	-	-	-
FOLLEY	4/21	11/40	4/30	4/33	11/34	6/21	4/17	-/-	-/-	-/-	-/-	-/-	-/-	-/-	-/-
	19%	27.5%	13.3%	12.1%	32.4%	28.6%	23.5%	-	-	-	-	-	-	-	-

Power Punches Landed / Thrown															
	1	2	3	4	5	6	7	8	9	10	11	12	13	14	15
ALI	1/6	1/4	2/5	5/14	0/0	2/7	5/10	-/-	-/-	-/-	-/-	-/-	-/-	-/-	-/-
	16.7%	25%	40%	35.7%	0%	28.6%	50%	-	-	-	-	-	-	-	-
FOLLEY	4/8	3/7	2/10	5/15	3/9	3/6	2/6	-/-	-/-	-/-	-/-	-/-	-/-	-/-	-/-
	50%	42.9%	20%	33.3%	33.3%	50%	33.3%	-	-	-	-	-	-	-	-

Final Punch Stat Report			
	Total Punches	Total Jabs	Power Punches
ALI	61/193	45/147	16/46
	31.6%	30.6%	34.8%
FOLLEY	66/257	44/196	22/61
	25.7%	22.4%	36.1%

THE COMEBACK YEARS – QUARRY I THROUGH FRAZIER III

For a boxer, the combination of idle hands and the passage of time is corrosive. When Muhammad Ali finally stepped through the ropes in Atlanta to engage in his first sanctioned boxing match in more than three-and-a-half years, no one, even Ali, knew for sure what to expect. Would he be the same dancing master that bedeviled nine heavyweight title challengers between 1965 and 1967? Or would Ali, now in his late 20s, be a lesser force?

This phase of Ali's Career, the "Comeback Years," is made up of 21 fights, by far the largest sample of the four phases featured in "Muhammad Ali: By the Numbers." If Ali had his way, his road to regaining the title would've lasted just three fights but Joe Frazier, producing the greatest performance of his Hall of Fame career, decisively defeated Ali and forced the former champ to take the long way home.

Visually, Ali was markedly thicker of frame and slower of foot but in statistical terms, he hadn't lost a lot off his fastball. When one compares this version of Ali to the "Prime Ali," he was only 1% less accurate in total punches (35.6% versus 36.6%), almost the same in terms of power accuracy (43% versus 43.1%), somewhat less prolific with the jab (26.7 thrown/8.6 connects per round versus 31.8 thrown/10.5 connects per round) but nearly as accurate (32.2% versus 33%). In terms of activity and overall effectiveness, the numbers weren't all that different as the "Comeback Years" Ali averaged one punch less per round (50.6 versus 51.6) and connected on nearly one fewer punch each round (18 versus 18.9). Finally, Ali was a bit less precise with his power shots (39.2% versus 42.4%) but posted almost identical numbers as far as being hit with opponents' hooks, crosses and uppercuts (43% versus 43.1%).

Given the time he was away from the ring, the fact that Ali was this close to his prime years is remarkable. Yet his plus-minus rating was barely above even at plus-0.5 (35.6% for Ali, 35.1% for his opponents), a continued reflection of his ability to overcome defensive deficiencies as well as a lack of diversity in his offensive weaponry. As his leg speed slowed, the competitive drive and fighting spirit of Ali assumed a larger portion of his ring persona. He learned through his sparring sessions -- as well as the first Frazier fight -- that he owned one of the stoutest chins in boxing history, a nugget of knowledge that would prove disastrous over the long haul.

During this phase, Ali out-landed his opponents 4,235-3,366 overall and 2,021-779 in jabs but trailed 2,587-2,214 in power connects. Five men out-landed him in overall punches (Frazier in fight one, Norton twice, Ron Lyle and Foreman) but his opponents out-did him in power connects 12 times (Bonavena, Frazier in both fights, Buster Mathis Sr., Mac Foster, Chuvalo and Patterson in their respective rematches, Norton in both fights, Foreman, Wepner and Lyle). But jabbing was still Ali's game and in that department only four opponents managed to out-jab him (Bob Foster, Norton in fight one, Lyle and Bugner in the rematch). Of 235 possible rounds, Ali landed 10 or more jabs 84 times while opponents connected on 50% or more of their power punches 71 times.

Ali clearly benefitted from the whirlwind schedule leading up to the Foreman match because he remained match-ready while also proving he could handle a wide assortment of styles and attitudes. The story of the "long road back" for Ali is one that illustrates the value of persistence, patience and opportunism. The twists and turns of Ali's life, both inside and outside the ring, made for compelling watching and reading. To see why, read on.

17.

OCTOBER 26, 1970 - CITY AUDITORIUM, ATLANTA, GA
MUHAMMAD ALI KO 3 JERRY QUARRY I

In boxing terms, a 43-month break between fights is the equivalent of an Ice Age. The combination of age and inactivity has historically robbed fighters of their sharpness, their fluidity, their timing and their ability to perceive, process and act upon split-second openings. That was the challenge facing Muhammad Ali when he signed to fight Jerry Quarry in a 15-rounder, a nod to his status as the lineal champion. Yes, Joe Frazier held the belts thanks to his knockout victory over Jimmy Ellis, the winner of the WBA heavyweight title elimination tournament, but the undefeated Ali remained "the man who beat the man."

Up until this point in time, heavyweight history was replete with examples of champions failing to regain what they had lost following lengthy layoffs. John L. Sullivan lost his world heavyweight championship to James J. Corbett after not having fought for more than three years. Corbett, in turn, twice lost to James J. Jeffries following layoffs of 17 months and nearly three years while Jeffries emerged from almost six years of inactivity to lose to champion Jack Johnson. Joe Louis, who reigned as champion for nearly 12 years, was forced to return against his successor Ezaard Charles following a 27-month break. Although "The Brown Bomber" had his moments, he didn't have enough of them and ended up losing a lopsided 15-round decision.

The only man ever to regain the heavyweight title at this point was Floyd Patterson, who vaporized previous conqueror Ingemar Johansson with a ferocious left hook 370 days after their initial meeting. The overwhelming difference between Patterson and the others, beside the shorter break between fights, was his age: 25. Sullivan was one month short of 34 when he lost to Corbett while Corbett was 33 and 36 when he challenged Jeffries. Jeffries was 35 against Johnson while Louis was 36.

Entering the Quarry fight, Ali was three months shy of his 29th birthday, which meant that while he was still in his prime in terms of age he also was on the down slope of it. An additional challenge for Ali: In the 25-year-old Quarry, Ali was facing someone younger than himself for the first time in his professional career. In fact, Quarry was only the second Ali foe who had been born in the 1940s (Sonny Banks' birthday was June 29, 1940).

Moreover, "The Bellflower Belter" was a young veteran, for he came into the Ali fight with a 37-4-4 record that included 23 knockouts. His best punch was the left hook, the same punch Sonny Banks and Henry Cooper used to floor Ali. His victims included Brian London (W 10, KO 2), Alex Miteff (KO 3), Floyd Patterson (W 12 in their second fight), Thad Spencer (KO 12), Buster Mathis (W 12) and Mac Foster, the then-holder of the top spot in THE RING ratings who sported a 24-0 (24 KO) record before being stopped in six by Quarry, who took over the number-one slot with the win. (1) All of Quarry's four conquerors were of high quality: Eddie Machen, George Chuvalo, Ellis and Frazier, the latter two coming in heavyweight title fights. The upside: The Frazier loss was deemed THE RING's 1969 Fight of the Year. The downside: Two of Quarry's four losses were by stoppage, and cuts played a role in both defeats.

Best yet for Quarry: He was unafraid.

"None of the noise surrounding the fight bothered me," Quarry told author Thomas Hauser. "The more attention and publicity, the better. The crowd was 90 percent black and all for Ali, but that didn't motivate me or intimidate me either. When I got in the ring, it was just another fight, even though the opponent was Ali. I wasn't fighting against a symbol, I was fighting a fighter who had two arms and two legs just like me." (2)

Factually speaking, Quarry was correct. But in reality, Ali versus Quarry was much more than a boxing match; it was a social happening of the highest order. The names around ringside belonged on everyone's A-list: Actor Sidney Poitier, singers Diana Ross and Mary Wilson, Atlanta Braves slugger Hank Aaron, political figures Coretta Scott King, Julian Bond, Andrew Young and Jesse Jackson. Comedian Bill Cosby was blow-by-blow man Tom Harmon's color commentator for the closed-circuit broadcast that was beamed to 206 locations in the U.S. and Canada and was shown live to Asia, Australia, Europe and South America. The City Auditorium was filled to its 5,100 capacity (3) but no facility in the world could have held the number of people that *wanted* to be there.

While one side celebrated Ali's return to the ring, the other side seethed. Those who supported the Vietnam War believed Ali should not have been allowed to box again because, on June 20, 1967, he was convicted by a jury and then sentenced to pay a $10,000 fine and serve five years in a federal penitentiary. (4) Ali was allowed to await further legal developments outside of jail because he paid the bond, but despite the absence of prison walls, a legal and social cloud continued to hang over him. Because his case had not yet been fully resolved, the very thought of Ali inside a boxing ring, where he could generate millions of dollars for himself, made their blood boil.

"Onlookers treated the TV showing (of Ali-Quarry) as if they were watching an actual fight," THE RING's Nat Loubet opined in his fight report. "Clay was the king. Clay was the real world champion, and to hell with the Justice Department. Intertwined with the adulation of Clay was his having been made the leader of the anti-war fans. To millions he represents strident opposition to the fighting in Vietnam. That Clay is under Justice Department charge as a felon for refusal to accept draft into the Army is not a minus with millions. It is a howling 'hip hip hurrah' for the man who would not yield to the draft and all for which it stands, the United States of America included." (5)

To further illustrate the chasm between the two forces -- and to express its opinion of who best represented the ideals of America -- THE RING, in its January 1971 issue, ran a full-page black-and-white illustration by writer Ted Carroll of a "stars-and-stripes" shield accompanied by small drawings of Joe Louis and Jack Dempsey in fighting stances bookending a large bust drawing of a smiling Joe Frazier in the middle.

No matter how one felt about Ali's return to the ring, there was a palpable sense of curiosity and anticipation. The questions were plentiful: Would Ali be in shape? Would his legs have the same spring? Would his punches be delivered with sufficient timing and land with similar accuracy? Could Quarry connect with his formidable hook, and, if he does, would Ali be able to absorb it?

Ali weighed 238 pounds when he began training six weeks earlier (6) but when he stepped on the scale he was 216 1/2, five pounds heavier than he was against Folley and 18 1/2 pounds more than the 198-pound Quarry. Curiously, ring announcer Johnny Addie announced Quarry's weight as 197 1/2 and Ali's at 213 1/2.

"Who is the champion of the world?" a supercharged Ali yelled just before he weighed in.

"Jerry Quarry!" a sarcastic wag shouted from the back of the room.

"I got something for Quarry, and I got something for all of you!" Ali responded. "After tonight there will be no more Quarry. I'm sick and tired of it. All of this talk, taking my title, talking about new champs, all this phony stuff...This is the real game! This ain't no phony game! That's why I fight them all, regardless of risk. I'm a real fighter! All these chumps commercializing, you ain't nothin'! I'm the real one! And all will bow to me in a few days. You all will bow to me!" (7)

Ali was clearly in prime verbal form at the weigh-in, but would he be in prime form at the fight?

One marked change was how Ali was received. He was booed vociferously through much of his three-year reign but here the cheers were overwhelming. Yes, it was a partisan crowd but it also reflected the overall attitudinal shift in the country.

When the action started, it was evident that while Ali was markedly thicker and slightly slower than the whippet-like creature that bedeviled the likes of Liston and Cleveland Williams, his form was still more than good enough to handle the likes of Quarry. With each passing second, however, the rust that encased Ali's body began flaking off and by the start of the second minute he was raking Quarry's face with stabbing jabs and lightning one-twos. Every Ali connect brought forth a wave of adoring screams.

Ali's stilettos soon reddened Quarry's nose and by round's end Drew "Bundini" Brown, Ali's longtime court jester, was shouting "All night long!"

The end of the round ignited another wave of cheers that were part celebration and part relief. Indeed, Ali, even now, was not only good enough to hold his own against a leading title contender, he was good enough to dominate him. In round one Ali out-threw Quarry 61-18, out-jabbed him 16-2 and prevailed 41%-17% overall and 36%-9% power. For those who dearly wanted him to succeed, all was right in the world again.

During the break, Quarry's corner not only attended to the abrasion on his nose but also those underneath each eye, further evidence of Ali's effectiveness.

The first moments of round two were proof positive that Ali was in fine working order as two searing jabs popped back Quarry's head and his patented lean-back move allowed him to avoid a Quarry hook. The Californian determinedly pursued Ali behind his winging hooks, knowing that one flush connect would change not just the result of the fight but the arc of his life. But Ali was ready for everything Quarry tried and as a result most of his efforts produced a temporary breeze. By the final minute both fighters were bathed in perspiration, and though Ali controlled most of the round it was Quarry who landed the final punch, a long and heavy hook to the pit of the stomach.

While round two wasn't nearly as dazzling, it was almost as effective. Ali threw more (49-27 overall), landed more overall (20-8) and in jabs (15-2) but, thanks to a nice surge in the last 30 seconds, Quarry prevailed 6-5 in power connects.

The first part of round three saw both fighters settling in and preparing for a potentially long fight. That said, Quarry was doing a better job of closing the distance, slipping the jab, maneuvering Ali toward the ropes and landing an occasional power shot. Ali's output also was slowing a bit, which could have inspired post-mortem questions about his stamina. Yes, Ali's nervous energy had vaulted him to an early lead but could he be effective over the long haul?

That question, at least on this day, would go unanswered because one of Ali's knifing blows opened a gash over Quarry's left eye, a patch of red Ali attacked with relish. A chopping right to the face widened the wound (which needed 11 stitches to close) and another along the ropes deepened his duress. Quarry was never seriously hurt, but the fact he made it to the round-ending bell was certainly worthy of note.

The between-rounds period hadn't even reached its halfway point when an enraged Quarry bolted off his stool. After briefly working on the cut, Quarry's chief second Teddy Bentham told referee Tony Perez that the fight had gone far enough. Perez briefly looked at the cut, then waved off the fight. A furious Quarry pushed Bentham away and stomped around the ring, but by the time he neared Ali's corner he had calmed down to the point where he and Ali warmly embraced.

The statistics painted a bright picture for Ali. He led 57-17 in total connects, 38-4 in jabs and 19-13 in power connects while also being the more precise hitter (38%-25% overall, 38%-18% jabs and 40%-28% power). All in all, Ali couldn't have asked for a better first night back.

It didn't take long for Ali to address the one subject boxing fans wanted to hear about most -- a future showdown with Joe Frazier.

"I'm ready to settle the title," Ali said.

"We're ready to fight him as soon as we get rid of (Bob) Foster (Nov. 18) and as soon as Clay can get ready," Frazier's manager Yank Durham said at Frazier's training camp in East Stroudsburg, Pa. (8)

But before Ali and Frazier could get their hands on each other, the self-proclaimed "Greatest" had one more assignment to complete -- a December 7 date with Oscar Bonavena at Madison Square Garden.

INSIDE THE NUMBERS: The returning Ali resorted to his bread and butter against Quarry -- the jab. It comprised 68% of his thrown punches as well as 67% of his landed punches. Quarry managed to land just 4 jabs to 38 for Ali.

Date: October 26, 1970   City: Atlanta, GA   Venue: City Auditorium
Opponent: Jerry Quarry
Result: Ali by TKO after the 3rd round (corner retirement)

Referee: Tony Perez

Round	1	2	3	4	5	6	7	8	9	10	11	12	13	14	15	Total
Ali	X	X	X													3
Quarry																0

Judge: Lew Eskin

Round	1	2	3	4	5	6	7	8	9	10	11	12	13	14	15	Total
Ali	X	X	X													3
Quarry																0

Judge: Bill Graham

Round	1	2	3	4	5	6	7	8	9	10	11	12	13	14	15	Total
Ali	X	X	X													3
Quarry																0

MUHAMMAD ALI KO 3 JERRY QUARRY
10/26/70 - ATLANTA

Total Punches Landed / Thrown															
	1	2	3	4	5	6	7	8	9	10	11	12	13	14	15
ALI	25/61	20/49	12/39	-/-	-/-	-/-	-/-	-/-	-/-	-/-	-/-	-/-	-/-	-/-	-/-
	41%	40.8%	30.8%	-	-	-	-	-	-	-	-	-	-	-	-
QUARRY	3/18	8/27	6/23	-/-	-/-	-/-	-/-	-/-	-/-	-/-	-/-	-/-	-/-	-/-	-/-
	16.7%	29.6%	26.1%	-	-	-	-	-	-	-	-	-	-	-	-

Jab Landed / Thrown															
	1	2	3	4	5	6	7	8	9	10	11	12	13	14	15
ALI	16/36	15/39	7/26	-/-	-/-	-/-	-/-	-/-	-/-	-/-	-/-	-/-	-/-	-/-	-/-
	44.4%	38.5%	26.9%	-	-	-	-	-	-	-	-	-	-	-	-
QUARRY	2/7	2/8	0/7	-/-	-/-	-/-	-/-	-/-	-/-	-/-	-/-	-/-	-/-	-/-	-/-
	28.6%	25%	0%	-	-	-	-	-	-	-	-	-	-	-	-

Power Punches Landed / Thrown															
	1	2	3	4	5	6	7	8	9	10	11	12	13	14	15
ALI	9/25	5/10	5/13	-/-	-/-	-/-	-/-	-/-	-/-	-/-	-/-	-/-	-/-	-/-	-/-
	36%	50%	38.5%	-	-	-	-	-	-	-	-	-	-	-	-
QUARRY	1/11	6/19	6/16	-/-	-/-	-/-	-/-	-/-	-/-	-/-	-/-	-/-	-/-	-/-	-/-
	9.1%	31.6%	37.5%	-	-	-	-	-	-	-	-	-	-	-	-

Final Punch Stat Report			
	Total Punches	Total Jabs	Power Punches
ALI	57/149	38/101	19/48
	38.3%	37.6%	39.6%
QUARRY	17/68	4/22	13/46
	25%	18.2%	28.3%

113

18.

The week after a federal judge permitted New York state to issue Ali a boxing license in September 1970, it was announced that Ali would fight Oscar Bonavena at Madison Square Garden on December 7. Since Ali was originally set to face Bonavena in Tokyo two months after he stopped Folley, this fight would close a circle of sorts. But it also was designed to give Ali a chance to gauge himself against Frazier because the Argentine gave "Smokin' Joe" two of his toughest fights.

In the second round of their first encounter in September 1966, the then-South American champion twice drove Frazier to the floor and nearly had him out. But Frazier showed his mettle by sweeping the next four rounds on his way to capturing a demanding 10 round split decision, the first distance fight of the American prospect's 11-fight pro career. They met again in December 1968 and this time, Frazier, who was making the second defense of his New York State Athletic Commission title, was taken the 15-round distance for the first time. While Bonavena came out on the short end again, his physicality thoroughly tested Frazier's stamina.

Nicknamed "Ringo" for his floppy Beatles-like haircut, Bonavena loved to pound both hands against his opponents' ribs as much as Ringo Starr hammered his drum skins. His persistent aggression and unpredictable punching patterns often wrecked the timing of more skillful foes and helped him to match (and even exceed) the production of those who fought in similar fashion. His best wins came against George Chuvalo (a majority W 10), back-to-back victories against Tom McNeeley (KO 5) and Dick Wipperman (W 10) in his sixth and seventh pro bouts, Gregorio Peralta (W 12) for the South American title in their first of two fights, Karl Mildenberger (W 12) in Frankfurt as part of the WBA's heavyweight title tournament, Leotis Martin (W 10) and onetime title challenger Manuel Ramos (KO 1). The Ramos win was one of five straight KO wins Ringo rung up before meeting Ali, vaulting his record to 46-6-1 with 37 knockouts.

When Bonavena lost, it usually was to proven opponents, as four of his six defeats came against Jimmy Ellis (L 12) in the WBA heavyweight title elimination tournament, Frazier (L 10, L 15) and Zora Folley (L 10). It was telling that Bonavena's pro debut, a first-round knockout against Lou Hicks in January 1964, took place at Madison Square Garden, and entering the Ali fight his record there was 6-2 with four knockouts. As for Ali, his MSG mark was 3-0 with two knockouts.

Bonavena's wildness in the ring occasionally strayed beyond the Marquess of Queensberry rules. On one occasion, however, he ventured far beyond them. Like the time he bit an opponent during the finals of the 1963 Pan-American Games in Sao Paulo, Brazil.

"Sometimes, when athletes couldn't win, they bit back," Los Angeles Times writer Earl Gustkey opined in an August 1987 column. "A then little-known Argentine heavyweight boxer, Oscar Bonavena, was knocked down in the first round by American Lee Carr. Rising to his feet and spitting out his mouthpiece, the frustrated Bonavena promptly sank his teeth into Carr's forearm, and was disqualified." (1)

"Everybody asks about that," Bonavena told THE RING's Dan Daniel in February 1965. "I don't mind telling.

"Well, the American was tough," he began. "I hit him on the chin. As he fell he grabbed me. I tried to get free. He held on tighter, I was getting angrier by the second. Then I threw one and missed. I slipped. The referee ruled it a knockdown and started to count. I still could not get myself loose from Carr and then I did it. I bit him. Well, I bit myself out of the Pan-American championship. I since have been told by (trainer) Charley Goldman that in the professional ring a well-placed, hard bite doesn't count for a point. It was silly, and that's that." (2)

No matter how this "bite fight" unfolded, the Carr bout was one of only two losses in Bonavena's 48-fight amateur career, which included 36 knockout wins. (3) His wayward methods continued into his professional career, for two of his six defeats coming into the Ali fight were by disqualification (DQ 8 in his first fight against Jose Giorgetti, who Bonavena defeated by 10-round decision just 35 days later, and a seventh-round disqualification against Miguel Angel Paez for excessive low blows in January 1970, just six fights before meeting Ali).

Still, Bonavena entered the fight as the WBA's number-one contender, so, for Ali, the 6-to-1 favorite, (4) a victory not only would catapult him into the dream match with Frazier, it also would justify it.

The rugged Bonavena was expected to test Ali's conditioning, punching power and tolerance for rough fighting. Also, unlike Quarry, Bonavena was not a chronic cutter, so, if history held, Ali would not be given that potential shortcut ending.

As usual, Ali utilized his pre-fight shtick to generate interest and rattle his opponent, but Bonavena took everything in stride and eagerly returned the favor. His high-pitched voice, broken English and abundant charisma charmed both the press and Ali himself.

When the pair underwent their medical exam, Bonavena was comfortable, amiable and willing to go toe-to-toe with Ali rhetorically despite the language barrier. He pointed at his bulging bicep, saying, "Argentina is strong," and playfully stuck out his chin when Ali said Bonavena wouldn't hit him like he had Frazier. When Ali asked a Spanish interpreter to ask Bonavena which round he would score the knockout, Bonavena pointed to his head to indicate he had seen through Ali's ploy, smiled broadly and said, "no! Surprise!", a response that generated gales of laughter from the audience and earned a big grin from Ali. The final jousting saw Ali throw a series of jabs that fell inches short of Bonavena's face. When Ali slapped down Bonavena's left hand, the bemused Argentine's face darkened slightly. He then gave Ali a quick head-and-shoulder feint that made the ex-champ flinch, triggering another round of laughter and another smile from Ali. As Ali turned away he knew the South American had scored a rare win in the battle of wits. (5)

Ali's arrival was greeted with far more cheers than boos, a further indication of the shifting perceptual and cultural attitude toward the former champion, who, for the first time, sported red tassels on his shoes. Another indicator of his popularity was that an enormous crowd of 19,417 flowed into the Garden to see what would unfold. (6)

The profound contrast in style and ring temperament was made obvious within seconds as the athletically fluid Ali cut clockwise circles and the stiffly coiled Bonavena fired wild hooks with abandon. His crude but effective upper body movement allowed him to slip nearly as many blows as Ali as well as avert the former champion's vaunted jab throughout round one, a round that saw Ali go 11 of 38 to Bonavena's 10 of 37 as well as 5 of 18 in jabs to the South American's 3 of 16. A potential trouble spot for Bonavena: Low blows. One that connected in the first minute drew a caution from referee Mark Conn while another at the end of the round prompted a stronger warning.

Yank Durham, the manager of heavyweight champion Joe Frazier, was doing color commentary with ABC's Howard Cosell, and though he had an inherent bias his wizened eyes correctly foresaw that Ali was in for a rough evening.

One concession to Bonavena's physicality occurred early in round two when Ali opted to fight more flat-footedly instead of engaging in his trademark leftward circle, for even then he must have suspected that he would need to marshal his resources if he was forced to go longer than his predicted nine rounds. Even so, Ali's jab began to land more frequently (11 of 27) and accurately (41%) while Bonavena's performance level dropped slightly (7 of 37 overall, 19%, 6 of 18 power, 33%). At the bell, Bonavena dropped his arms and glared at Ali, who got a rise from the crowd when he responded with a dismissive wave of the glove.

The war of styles continued in the third, and while Ali got in a pair sharp one-twos and managed to keep the fight at long range and at ring center, Bonavena's quirky timing and roundhouse blows occasionally disrupted Ali's rhythm as well as the flow of the contest. Following the third round bell, moments after Bonavena whiffed on an awkwardly delivered hook, Ali pointed to the ground and yelled at Bonavena as if to say, "you're going down!"

But Bonavena didn't go down. In fact, he grew stronger.

The fourth was Bonavena's best to date as he charged Ali behind his whirlybird blows and forced him toward the ropes much more consistently. A growingly concerned Cosell perfectly summarized Bonavena when he called him "powerful, awkward, cumbersome, ponderous, but the aggressor." Ali initiated more of the clinches, prompting some to wonder whether Ali truly had enough gas in the tank to successfully navigate the 15-round distance. Cosell remarked that Ali had not looked this bad since the Karl Mildenberger fight in 1966, where the German's southpaw style had troubled Ali as few had before or since. In the fourth, Bonavena threw 56 punches and landed 17, both fight highs thus far, while Ali's output slipped to 26, landing 10.

The audience that had cheered Ali upon his arrival now buzzed with concern. They knew this wasn't the Ali that was universally acknowledged as the fastest heavyweight to ever live. Instead, this was a fighter that had to access other resources to get by. Had they met in 1967 as planned, that version of Ali probably would have easily out-speeded the South American en route to a wide points victory but here, more than three years later, the toll of Ali's forced inactivity and the erosion of his otherworldly skills were being laid bare. The harsh reality was that Ali no longer had all the poetry and the ballet at his disposal. If he was to win -- and the concept behind the word "if" was becoming more believable -- he would have to stand and *fight*.

Ali started round five with flashes of the float and sting but Bonavena was unmoved and unimpressed. He shrugged off Ali's arrows and continued to burrow inside with his cannonballs, one of which strayed below the belt and induced another warning from Conn. As the round closed, Ali resorted to a tactic he rarely employed: Jabbing to the body. Five landed in the final 30 seconds, which accounted for half of the jabs he landed in the round. Those 10 jab connects helped him forge a narrow 13-10 lead overall, but Bonavena's 8-3 bulge in landed power shots certified his effectiveness.

Durham was genuinely concerned that Frazier's showdown with Ali was in danger, saying "I'm a little afraid for Clay because Bonavena is going to get stronger. I see he's breathing hard over there. I don't think Clay could stand this pace."

Durham was right to be worried, and the disturbing pattern from his standpoint continued throughout the middle rounds as Bonavena gave as good as he got, and sometimes a bit better. A heavy hook early in the sixth drove Ali backward, inspiring one section of the crowd to begin chanting "Ringo! Ringo!" and for the usually optimistic Dundee to signal his puzzlement to Cosell. Drew "Bundini" Brown's cries of "the heavy bag" now had a pleading tone. A fight involving Ali was riveting in itself, but here two elements were introduced to the mix -- drama and suspense.

With every passing round those elements became more relevant. In fact, Bonavena exceeded Ali's total in overall connects in rounds eight through 13, a six-round stretch of success that once would have been unthinkable. That success also included the ninth, in which Ali had said Bonavena "would be mine."

To pull this fight out of the fire, Ali would have to rally.

Fortunately for him, his team and the millions who dearly wanted the Frazier fight to be made, he did. And, in typical Ali fashion, he did so with magnetism and flair.

With Brown repeatedly telling Ali to "close the show" throughout round 15, Ali connected with a pair of heavy hooks that suddenly sent Bonavena toppling to the floor and landing heavily on his left side. The crowd that had been sullen sprang to life, with one ringsider leaping up and down in rapturous joy. As usual, Ali never retreated to a neutral corner as Conn tolled the count, which reached five when Bonavena regained his feet. Ali's next punch, a right to the face, downed the dizzy Bonavena for the second time, prompting Ali to stand over his prey and raise his hands above his head. Conn tried to push Ali away but his efforts were futile. Ali was in full fighting fury and nothing, even the neutral corner rule that had been in effect since the 1920s, would deny him the finish he craved.

A big right hand to the face sent the near-helpless Bonavena to the canvas a third time, prompting Conn to wave off the fight, Ali to raise his arms in a victory pose and the Garden crowd to erupt in thunderous cheers. The concern that had enveloped them for so long was instantly replaced by a mixture of joy over the present and anticipation toward the future, a future that would now include Muhammad Ali versus Joe Frazier for the undisputed heavyweight championship.

Conn was the subject of post-fight criticism for the way he handled the 15th round knockdowns.

"In the 15th round, Conn failed to call the mandatory eight after Ringo had hit the deck for the first time, and also failed to order Clay to a neutral corner," wrote RING founder Nat Fleischer. "Came a second knockdown and the referee again forgot the mandatory eight and the order to go to a neutral corner. A third knockdown ended the fight under the rule which hangs up a KO against a fighter who has been decked twice in one round.

"When so prominent, able and reputable a referee as Conn becomes flustered in so important a fight, there is something radically wrong with the system. Especially as sloppy work is followed by no public reprimand from the chairman of the governing commission," Fleischer concluded. (7)

The final numbers were perilously close as Ali led 191-186 in total connects thanks to his 94-34 gap in landed jabs. Bonavena, for his part, landed far more power shots (152-97) and landed his hardest blows with more precision (38%-34%). The stats reflected the judgment of the Associated Press correspondent who had Ali ahead 7-6-1. (8) The official scorecards, however, indicated that Ali was never in any danger of defeat. Referee Conn had Ali up 12-2 while judges Joe Eppy (10-3-1) and Jack Bloom (8-5-1) scored similarly.

"The layoff bothered me," Ali told Cosell. "It showed up, I missed a lot of punches. But I'm glad it went 15, the word was I didn't have no stamina and I think I showed more than he did. Joe Frazier couldn't stop him. He was really out! Now we have a chance to see who the real champion of the world is."

Ali received one vote from the man who knew best: Oscar Bonavena.

"I'm sorry that I (called) you chicken," he said moments after Ali apologized to him about his own pre-fight rhetoric. "You (are) champion. You win with Frazier because you (are) better. You (are) boxing very well. You win with Frazier. Because you whipped me, you beat Frazier!" (9)

Frazier, of course, disagreed.

"Until the 15th I had given Oscar every round," Frazier said from his training camp in Monticello, N.Y. "I thought Clay fought dirty, pushing Oscar around and everything like that. I'll be ready for him." (10)

And the world would be ready for Ali versus Frazier.

> *INSIDE THE NUMBERS: Ali scored three knockdowns with just eight landed power punches in round 15. Ali tired down the stretch, averaging just 26.7 punches thrown per round over the last three rounds, landing 11 per round.*

Date: December 7, 1970   City: New York, NY   Venue: Madison Square Garden
Opponent: Oscar Bonavena
Result: Ali by TKO at 2:03 of the 15th round -- Won Vacant NABF Heavyweight Title

Referee: Mark Conn

Round	1	2	3	4	5	6	7	8	9	10	11	12	13	14	15	Total
Ali	X	X	X	X		X	X	X		X	X	X	X	X		12
Bonavena					X				X							2

Judge: Joe Eppy

Round	1	2	3	4	5	6	7	8	9	10	11	12	13	14	15	Total
Ali	X	X	X		X	X	X		X		X	X	E	X		10 (1E)
Bonavena				X				X		X			E			3 (1E)

Judge: Jack Bloom

Round	1	2	3	4	5	6	7	8	9	10	11	12	13	14	15	Total
Ali	X	X	X			X	X			X		X	X	E		8 (1E)
Bonavena				X	X			X	X		X			E		5 (1E)

MUHAMMAD ALI KO 15 OSCAR BONAVENA
12/07/70 - NEW YORK

Total Punches Landed / Thrown															
	1	2	3	4	5	6	7	8	9	10	11	12	13	14	15
ALI	11/38	17/44	9/37	10/26	13/41	12/37	21/51	12/44	18/47	10/30	13/42	12/43	11/26	11/28	11/26
	28.9%	38.6%	24.3%	38.5%	31.7%	32.4%	41.2%	27.3%	38.3%	33.3%	31%	27.9%	42.3%	39.3%	42.3%
BONAVENA	10/37	7/37	8/34	17/56	10/35	10/37	19/43	15/44	19/39	11/32	14/35	17/46	13/58	9/41	7/24
	27%	18.9%	23.5%	30.4%	28.6%	27%	44.2%	34.1%	48.7%	34.4%	40%	37%	22.4%	22%	29.2%

Jab Landed / Thrown															
	1	2	3	4	5	6	7	8	9	10	11	12	13	14	15
ALI	5/18	11/27	5/20	5/12	10/22	6/18	11/20	7/19	4/11	6/20	5/25	5/23	6/16	5/11	3/9
	27.8%	40.7%	25%	41.7%	45.5%	33.3%	55%	36.8%	36.4%	30%	20%	21.7%	37.5%	45.5%	33.3%
BONAVENA	3/16	1/19	1/12	0/13	2/13	4/14	3/13	0/8	2/5	3/13	1/4	6/19	6/33	0/7	2/7
	18.8%	5.3%	8.3%	0%	15.4%	28.6%	23.1%	0%	40%	23.1%	25%	31.6%	18.2%	0%	28.6%

Power Punches Landed / Thrown															
	1	2	3	4	5	6	7	8	9	10	11	12	13	14	15
ALI	6/20	6/17	4/17	5/14	3/19	6/19	10/31	5/25	14/36	4/10	8/17	7/20	5/10	6/17	8/17
	30%	35.3%	23.5%	35.7%	15.8%	31.6%	32.3%	20%	38.9%	40%	47.1%	35%	50%	35.3%	47.1%
BONAVENA	7/21	6/18	7/22	17/43	8/22	6/23	16/30	15/36	17/34	8/19	13/31	11/27	7/25	9/34	5/17
	33.3%	33.3%	31.8%	39.5%	36.4%	26.1%	53.3%	41.7%	50%	42.1%	41.9%	40.7%	28%	26.5%	29.4%

Final Punch Stat Report			
	Total Punches	Total Jabs	Power Punches
ALI	191/560	94/271	97/289
	34.1%	34.7%	33.6%
BONAVENA	186/598	34/196	152/402
	31.1%	17.3%	37.8%

19.

MARCH 8, 1971 - MADISON SQUARE GARDEN, NEW YORK, NY
JOE FRAZIER W 15 MUHAMMAD ALI I

Throughout the history of modern boxing, only a handful of fights could force the world to drop everything and focus only on what was happening inside a boxing ring. Some, like the first fight between Sugar Ray Leonard and Roberto Duran, the rematch between Evander Holyfield and Mike Tyson and the 2015 blockbuster between Floyd Mayweather and Manny Pacquiao, attracted attention because it pitted two outstandingly talented fighters with diametrically opposed styles and life stories. But others, like Jack Johnson-James J. Jeffries in 1910, Joe Louis-Max Schmeling II in 1938 and Larry Holmes-Gerry Cooney in 1982, boasted story lines whose tentacles reached far beyond the athletic arena. Johnson-Jeffries and Holmes-Cooney forced the public to confront racial tensions while Louis-Schmeling II was the sporting equivalent of the looming geopolitical conflict between Louis' America and Schmeling's Germany.

But if ever a fight epitomized the fusion of pugilism and politics, it was the first meeting between Joe Frazier and Muhammad Ali. Athletically speaking, it was the first time in history that two undefeated men with a legitimate claim to the undisputed heavyweight championship would meet head-to-head. Also, it featured two contrasting styles: Frazier, the blue-collar bob-and-weave aggressor who owned perhaps the greatest left hook the sport had ever known, and Ali, the balletic, stick-and-move speed merchant who did everything wrong but made it look right. Their personalities only added to the conflict; Frazier was a blunt, pugnacious, down-to-earth Christian who derived his greatest satisfaction from a job well done while Ali was a loquacious, charismatic, media-savvy Muslim who fearlessly spoke his mind and lost three-and-a-half of his best boxing years in the name of principle.

The backdrop described in the previous sentence vaulted Frazier-Ali I from an athletic spectacle to a confrontation of ideologies. While Ali sought and earned his place as an anti-establishment hero, Frazier, by default, was appointed the representative of the forces that opposed Ali and his counter-culture supporters. They were drawn to his pride, drive and soft-spoken nature but were won over by "Smokin' Joe's" ability to flatten opponents with his heat-seeking hook. While Ali specialized in ring science, Frazier's calling card was blunt force trauma.

As was the case before his first fight with Sonny Liston, Ali employed an extended psychological and verbal campaign against Frazier. For example, Ali was at ringside for Frazier's 15-round victory over Oscar Bonavena in December 1968, a pulsating action fight that Ali belittled due to its lack of science.

"It was a good slugging match, but not a championship fight," Ali said. He went so far as to boo Frazier even as he signed autographs for ringside admirers. (1)

121

Everywhere Joe went, there Ali was, haranguing him at every turn, much like Ali's hero Jack Johnson had done to then-champion Tommy Burns as he (with the financial help of a group of New York gamblers) pursued him around the world in the hopes of securing a title shot, a shot Johnson eventually got, and won. (2)

One such incident took place at a New York nightclub where Frazier was appearing. According to the manager of the club, Ali entered Frazier's dressing room and insisted on calling himself the champion. Somehow, during the commotion, the door came off its hinges. (3)

With every appearance he made with Frazier, Ali was spreading seeds of doubt in the public square: Yes, Frazier may hold the physical heavyweight championship belt but until he beats Ali he should never be considered the bona fide, undisputed world champion.

As the calendar turned from the 1960s to the 1970s, Ali dramatically turned up his boxing-oriented appearances as rumors swirled about his getting a license in this state or that state only for those rumors to be dashed just as quickly. Appetites were further whetted on January 20, 1970 when the film of a December 1968 "computer fight" between Ali and Rocky Marciano, the only other heavyweight champion to retire undefeated to that point in time, was shown inside movie theaters worldwide. One ending had Marciano winning by knockout while the other saw Ali prevailing on cuts, but the mere sight of Ali swapping punches, even faux ones, inside a boxing ring produced the intended effect: A growing desire to see the exile ended and for Ali to throw real punches at real opponents.

Every report ratcheted up the yearning and anticipation for a breakthrough, and when it finally happened in September 1970 the hopes of boxing fans shifted toward the ultimate showdown between Ali and Frazier. And now, finally, it was here, and the fervor that gripped the globe was palpable.

As the fight drew closer, battle lines were drawn between the fighters as well as the general public. Character assessments were made based on whether he or she supported Ali or Frazier, and the fighters did their best to stoke the strife.

"Frazier's no real champion," Ali declared. "Nobody wants to talk to him. Oh, maybe (U.S. President Richard) Nixon will call him if he wins. I don't think he'll call me. But ninety-eight percent of my people are for me. They identify with my struggle. Same one they're fighting every day in the streets. If I win, they win. I lose, they lose. Anybody black who thinks Frazier can whup me is an Uncle Tom. Everybody who's black wants me to keep winning." (4)

Frazier's words about Ali were cold, bitter and pointed.

"He's no good," Frazier declared shortly before the fight. "As far as I'm concerned, he's a phony. He don't really stand for all those things he talks about. He knows he's black, everybody else knows he's black. He's using his blackness to get his way. Preaching all that black talk! Clay called me an Uncle Tom! You going to tell me Clay don't have white friends? What color's his trainer, for example? Those black people who fall for him and believe him and follow what he says to do will be right where they are now 10 years from now.

"I couldn't be his friend. I wouldn't want to be his friend," he continued. "Clay has to be seen all the time, he says where he's going, what he's going to do, who's going to be there, what time he's going to leave. Me, I get in and out of places so quiet people don't even know I'm there. I don't have no trouble with police, with the businessmen, with people who want my autograph. I ain't trying to be good to make people love me. I don't *need* to be loved. When I get out there to do my roadwork, I'm alone. When I get in the ring, I'm alone. I go where I've got to go -- I'm always alone." (5)

Frazier scaled a fit 205 1/2 while Ali, who boasted considerable advantages in height (three-and-a-half inches) and reach (five inches), weighed 215. The unprecedented purses for the main event -- $2.5 million for each fighter -- prompted MSG executives to establish a never-before-used pricing scale: $150 for ringside tickets down to $20 for rafter seats. As a point of comparison, ringside tickets for Ali-Bonavena sold for $75 while the scale for Louis-Schmeling II ranged from $5.75 to $30. (6)

The scene inside Madison Square Garden the night of March 8, 1971 was nothing short of electrifying, so much so that one of the 20,455 spectators died of a heart attack. (7) The collection of celebrities, newsmakers and other sundry movers and shakers was extraordinary and the outfits adorning ringsiders strained the boundaries of convention. The roster of A-listers was nearly innumerable: Singer Diana Ross, astronauts Neil Armstrong, Michael Collins, Alan Shepard and Edwin E. "Buzz" Aldrin, talk show host David Frost, Playboy founder Hugh Hefner and his escort Barbi Benton, New York City mayor John Lindsay and so on. (8) The demand for tickets was so intense that the only way singer Frank Sinatra could gain entry was by being appointed the photographer for LIFE magazine. For the record, Frazier came out ahead 3-2 in a pre-fight poll of LIFE staffers. (9)

Fighters introduced to the crowd included Joe Louis, Archie Moore, Billy Conn, Gene Tunney, Jimmy Ellis, Dick Tiger, Buster Mathis, Joey Giardello, Jack Sharkey, Emile Griffith, Rocky Graziano and Oscar Bonavena. (10)

The air of anticipation, both inside MSG and inside the hundreds of closed-circuit outlets worldwide, was unlike anything that had been seen before because the styles, personalities and mutual animus virtually guaranteed a ring classic.

And a ring classic was exactly what they got.

Ali successfully exploited Frazier's tendency to start slowly by doubling the champion's output in round one (52 to 26), landing more than twice as many punches (21-10) and establishing

123

range with his jab (12 of 23 to Frazier's 1 of 5). The pattern continued in the second as Ali fired 63 punches to Frazier's 32, out-landed him 28-16 and shut him out 12-0 in jab connects. Not only was Ali whipping Frazier physically, he was also trying to do so verbally. The chatter was so pronounced that it could be heard through the microphone hanging above the ring, and, more than once, referee Arthur Mercante ordered them to "stop talking."

"They have time for that?" blow-by-blow commentator Don Dunphy asked in wonder.

By round three, the sufficiently warmed-up Frazier began to blast hooks to Ali's head and body, blows Ali repeatedly dismissed by pushing down on Frazier's neck, peering into the crowd and shaking his head. But while Ali postured, Frazier punched. In round three Frazier out-landed Ali 27-22 despite throwing fewer punches (40 to 55) and not even attempting a single jab. With Frazier now fully engaged, the war was truly on.

So far, the warfare reflected the extreme differences in their approaches. Through three rounds Frazier had thrown only 10 jabs and landed one while Ali had thrown 85 and connected on 32. Conversely, Frazier had landed 52 of his 88 power shots -- or 59% accuracy -- while Ali was 39 of 85 (46%). Ali worked far harder as he averaged 56.7 punches per round to Frazier's 32.7 but "Smokin' Joe's" precision kept him in the hunt.

By the latter stages of round four Frazier's hook had bloodied Ali's nose while in the fifth the confident champion began taunting the master trash-talker. At the end of round five Frazier swatted at the top of Ali's head, making evident that while Ali the talker had rattled Frazier's cage, Ali the fighter was someone with whom he could compete on nearly equal terms.

Shortly before entering the ring area Ali had predicted a sixth round knockout, but inside the ring the defiant champion enjoyed his best round to date as he landed 29 punches while Ali connected on 13, his lowest total of the bout thus far. Worse yet for Ali, Frazier led 28-7 in landed power shots and connected on 57% of his hooks and crosses to Ali's 30%.

The tremendous two-way action slowed in the middle rounds, mostly because Ali chose to use an embryonic version of the "Rope-a-Dope" that later ensnared George Foreman. It failed miserably against Frazier's powerful, pinpoint punching. In round eight Frazier enjoyed his most lopsided round as he out-landed Ali 31-14 overall and 31-3 in power connects. One particularly lengthy stay on the ropes brought loud boos from the crowd and at one point, a frustrated Frazier wrapped both gloves around Ali's wrists and forcibly pulled him out to ring center.

Some thought Ali's ploy was mere play-acting but Frazier knew better.

"Clowning?" he asked. "He couldn't move. Those body shots had slowed him down." (11)

Late in the ninth Ali suddenly zeroed in on Frazier's head, producing a salvo of flush punches that had the Ali supporters in a frenzy. Just three minutes after Frazier's best round to date, Ali recorded his as he landed 30 of his 87 punches while Frazier connected on 19 of 34. Convinced Frazier was finally slowing down, Ali yelled "he's out" to ringsiders during round 10, a notion proven wrong by the fact that Frazier edged Ali 26-23 overall, out-landed him 25-18 in power shots and connected on a sky-high 68% of his hooks, crosses and uppercuts.

Through 10 rounds the fight remained close, both in terms of the action inside the ring and the CompuBox statistics, which saw Ali with a slim 223-222 lead in total connects. With the final result still in doubt heading into the final third, it was up to one man to separate himself from his opponent.

That man would be Joe Frazier.

A short hook to the point of the chin buckled Ali's legs and nearly floored him in the final minute of round 11. * Frazier initially swarmed the stricken ex-champ but Ali's fertile mind conjured a series of moves that planted doubts about Ali's true state. In the final moments of a round that saw Frazier out-land Ali 36-16 and connect on 70% of his power shots, Ali's exaggerated wobble -- dubbed by some "the long walk" -- allowed Ali to make it to the bell, but just barely.

"He was on queer street in the 11th round," Ali's assistant trainer/cheerleader/witch doctor Drew "Bundini" Brown said after the bout. "I prayed for him." (12)

Frazier continued to punish Ali in round 12 and 13, the latter of which saw Frazier connect on 79% of his total punches and 82% of his power shots. In fact, the 45 power shots Frazier landed in the 13th was the most ever recorded by an Ali opponent in the 47 Ali fights tracked by CompuBox. Yet Ali, who now sported a badly swollen right cheek, somehow rallied to take the 14th with an inspired attack that earned him a 27-19 lead in total connects. But any doubts about the final result vanished early in the 15th round when Frazier countered Ali's right uppercut with a scorching hook to the swollen jaw. The punch drove Ali hard to the floor and as his tasseled shoes flapped about it appeared that the challenger -- at least for a moment -- was knocked out.

"I was hit, but I don't recall falling so it must have been hard," Ali said later. "I remember getting up. I was alert." (13)

To nearly everyone's shock, Ali not only scrambled to his feet by Mercante's count of four, he managed to stage a mini-rally in the bout's final minute. At the final bell, a bloody-mouthed Frazier yelled something at Ali, who turned away and walked to his corner.

"He called me a lot of names," Frazier said at the post-fight press conference. "I wanted him to come to me after the fight and apologize. But he just mumbled something and turned to his corner." (14)

The decision was unanimous as Frazier won 11-4, 9-6 and 8-6-1 under the rounds system. The margin of victory was largely earned in the fight's final five rounds, which saw Frazier out-land Ali 156-107 overall and 152-76 power. Frazier said his body attack was the key to victory, and the stats bore out his belief. Two-hundred fifteen of his 378 total connects struck Ali's flanks, the third highest total among the 47 Ali fights counted by CompuBox (Frazier's 237 in the Thrilla in Manila rated second while George Chuvalo's 267 in their first fight in 1966 was first).

For the first time since April 28, 1967 the world had an undisputed heavyweight champion, but in Frazier's mind there was never a doubt.

"I always knew who the champion was," he said. (15)

Ali didn't attend the news conference. He opted to remain in his dressing room for 30 minutes before leaving for Flower-Fifth Avenue Hospital for X-rays. According to the Times' Dave Anderson, Ali departed approximately 40 minutes later and left without bandages. (16)

"Don't worry, we'll be back," Ali said through a media statement delivered by Brown. "We ain't through yet." (17)

Ali was right. Although Frazier emerged victorious in this battle, both men knew their paths would cross again. The only blank left to fill was where and when their second act would take place.

* Note: LIFE sports editor Bill Bruns half-jokingly predicted that Frazier would stop Ali "at 2:21 of Round 11" Frazier's monstrous hook that nearly floored Ali connected just seven seconds before Bruns' projected end.

INSIDE THE NUMBERS: The punishment dished out in this fight was extraordinary. They combined to land 708 total punches, which translates to 47.2 connects per round, far above the 30.6 heavyweight norm. Another indicator of Frazier's fury inside the ring was that 96.6% of his landed punches were power shots (the CompuBox average is 72%) despite Ali landing an average of 9 of 29.3 jabs per round (the heavyweight averages are 5.3 of 20.4). They combined to land 34 or more power punches (including 75 in round 13) in twelve of the fifteen rounds (the heavyweight average is 20 combined). Frazier's 365 landed power shots are the most by an Ali opponent in the 47 Ali fights tracked by CompuBox. Frazier landed 45 of 55 power punches (81.8%) in round 13- (hvt. avg.: 9.9)- most by an Ali opponent. Frazier's 378 landed punches are the second highest total by an Ali opponent (Leon Spinks' 419 in fight one was number one). Frazier landed 59.9% of his total punches and 63.1% of his power punches, the highest percentage by an Ali opponent in both categories in the 47 Ali fights compiled by CompuBox.

Date:	March 8, 1971				City: New York, NY				Venue: Madison Square Garden							
Opponent:	Joe Frazier															
Result:	Frazier by unanimous decision -- For World Heavyweight Title															
Referee:	**Arthur Mercante Sr.**															
	Round	1	2	3	4	5	6	7	8	9	10	11	12	13	14	15	Total
	Ali	X	X				X	X		X	X		E				6 (1E)
	Frazier			X	X	X			X			X	E	X	X	X	8 (1E)
Judge:	**Artie Aidala**															
	Round	1	2	3	4	5	6	7	8	9	10	11	12	13	14	15	Total
	Ali	X	X							X	X			X	X		6
	Frazier			X	X	X	X	X	X			X	X			X	9
Judge:	**Bill Recht**															
	Round	1	2	3	4	5	6	7	8	9	10	11	12	13	14	15	Total
	Ali		X			X				X					X		4
	Frazier	X		X	X		X	X	X		X	X	X	X		X	11

JOE FRAZIER UD 15 MUHAMMAD ALI
03/08/71 - NEW YORK

Total Punches Landed / Thrown															
	1	2	3	4	5	6	7	8	9	10	11	12	13	14	15
FRAZIER	10/26	16/32	27/40	23/46	18/34	29/52	23/48	31/54	19/34	26/40	36/56	27/46	46/58	19/29	28/36
	38.5%	50%	67.5%	50%	52.9%	55.8%	47.9%	57.4%	55.9%	65%	64.3%	58.7%	79.3%	65.5%	77.8%
ALI	21/52	28/63	22/55	24/66	25/66	13/45	23/60	14/47	30/87	23/62	16/44	18/60	35/66	27/72	11/48
	40.4%	44.4%	40%	36.4%	37.9%	28.9%	38.3%	29.8%	34.5%	37.1%	36.4%	30%	53%	37.5%	22.9%

Jab Landed / Thrown															
	1	2	3	4	5	6	7	8	9	10	11	12	13	14	15
FRAZIER	1/5	0/5	0/0	1/4	2/5	1/3	0/5	0/2	3/7	1/3	1/6	1/2	1/3	1/3	0/0
	20%	0%	0%	25%	40%	33.3%	0%	0%	42.9%	33.3%	16.7%	50%	33.3%	33.3%	0%
ALI	12/23	12/35	8/27	12/38	16/42	6/22	10/26	11/30	12/47	5/24	4/21	8/34	5/17	10/31	4/23
	52.2%	34.3%	29.6%	31.6%	38.1%	27.3%	38.5%	36.7%	25.5%	20.8%	19%	23.5%	29.4%	32.3%	17.4%

Power Punches Landed / Thrown															
	1	2	3	4	5	6	7	8	9	10	11	12	13	14	15
FRAZIER	9/21	16/27	27/40	22/42	16/29	28/49	23/43	31/52	16/27	25/37	35/50	26/44	45/55	18/26	28/36
	42.9%	59.3%	67.5%	52.4%	55.2%	57.1%	53.5%	59.6%	59.3%	67.6%	70%	59.1%	81.8%	69.2%	77.8%
ALI	9/29	16/28	14/28	12/28	9/24	7/23	13/34	3/17	18/40	18/38	12/23	10/26	30/49	17/41	7/25
	31%	57.1%	50%	42.9%	37.5%	30.4%	38.2%	17.6%	45%	47.4%	52.2%	38.5%	61.2%	41.5%	28%

Final Punch Stat Report			
	Total Punches	Total Jabs	Power Punches
FRAZIER	378/631	13/53	365/578
	59.9%	24.5%	63.1%
ALI	330/893	135/440	195/453
	37%	30.7%	43%

20.

ALI'S ODYSSEY: THE LONG ROAD BACK - ELLIS THROUGH FRAZIER II

The loss to Frazier delivered a stinging reality check to the butterfly/bee: If he was to earn a second shot at the championship arbitrarily stripped from him in 1967, he would need to make his candidacy so decisive that Frazier -- or his potential successor -- would have no choice but to fight him. Tellingly, THE RING kept Ali as its number-one contender after the Frazier defeat, an acknowledgement of his courageous and highly competitive performance. (1)

The approach adopted by the iconoclastic Ali couldn't have been more old-fashioned: Fight anyone, anywhere, as often as possible, and win, win, win. Over the next 30 months Ali would fight 14 times, including one seven-month stretch in which he had six fights. Also, for someone who was fearful of flying, Ali racked up reams of frequent flier mileage. He fought twice in Houston, then jetted to Zurich, Tokyo, Vancouver, Las Vegas, Dublin, New York, Stateline (Nev.), Las Vegas again, San Diego, Inglewood (Calif.), Jakarta and New York a second time. He beat the stars and the unknowns, fought through a debilitating injury en route to his only loss during the stretch, defeated the man who inflicted that injury and loss six months later and ended the chase two fights after that by reversing the only other setback on his record in the same building in which it had taken place.

Ali also had another reason for the ambitious schedule.

"The whole thing is money," Ali said before his 1973 fight with Joe Bugner. "I don't need the title to get money, I keep them (the other contenders) from making money because I'm the one that the promoters want. I'm the one that can talk, write the poems, predict the rounds. I'm beautiful, they're ugly, they're slow, they can't talk. I'm the one! Having a trophy, having a gold medal, saying I'm the champion, that's kid stuff now, I'm above that. Muhammad Ali is bigger than the world title now. My title is 'Muhammad Ali.' So it doesn't mean anything to me to have a title." (2)

It could be argued that Ali achieved the biggest victory of his comeback even before he stepped into the ring for the first time in this stretch, which is often thought of as one unit and is why it is presented in this manner. On June 28, 1971, less than a month before Ali met childhood friend Jimmy Ellis in Houston, the U.S. Supreme Court voted 8-0 to reverse his conviction for draft evasion (Justice Thurgood Marshall removed himself from the vote because he was solicitor general when the government brought its case against Ali.) (3) According to Thomas Hauser's "Muhammad Ali: His Life and Times," the justices were initially 5-3 in favor of upholding the conviction but thanks to a compromise suggested by Justice Potter Stewart, the court was persuaded to reverse course.

In opposing Ali's request for conscientious objector status, Hauser wrote, the government had argued that Ali had not met any of the three requirements, which were: He was opposed to war in any form, that his opposition was based on religious training and belief and that his opposition was sincere. But during its arguments before the Supreme Court, the government conceded points two and three while basing its case solely on Ali's willingness to participate in jihad -- or holy war -- which indicated he wasn't opposed to *all* forms of war.

"Seizing on the discrepancy, Stewart pointed out that the draft appeal board had never indicated the specific basis on which Ali's request for conscientious objector status had been denied," Hauser wrote. "Thus, he argued, it was theoretically possible that the denial was based on a finding that Ali's position was not sincerely held or not based upon religious training or belief -- positions that the government itself now conceded were wrong.

"Stewart's argument appealed to the conservatives on the Court because it meant that Ali's conviction could be reversed without ruling that members of the Nation of Islam were entitled to conscientious objector status. Only Chief Justice Warren Burger refused to go along with the proposal; (but) in the end, he too succumbed to Stewart's logic." (4)

The reversal fully lifted the cloud that had shrouded Ali's life for nearly four years. World Boxing Association president Bill Brennan said he would recommend Ali be named its number-one contender after not being rated for the entirety of his legal wrangling while Edwin B. Dooley, chairman of the New York State Athletic Commission, also gave his blessing.

"The New York State Athletic Commission is grateful that the Muhammad Ali matter with reference to his selective service draft status has been finally qualified by the Supreme Court and he can pursue his career without further problems," Dooley said. (5)

*

With his legal issues behind him, Ali turned his attention to onetime WBA titlist Ellis, a close friend with whom he split two amateur meetings and, as Ali's stable mate, had served as his sparring partner. One unique side story was that this would be the first time since the Tunney Hunsaker fight more than 10 1/2 years ago in which Angelo Dundee would not be in Ali's corner. The reason: While he was the trainer for Ali he was the trainer *and* manager of Ellis, which meant that working Ellis' corner would earn Dundee a bigger share of the purse. (6) Recognizing Dundee's situation, Ali allowed his chief second and loyal friend to fatten his bank account, then hired Harry Wiley, who had worked with Henry Armstrong and Sugar Ray Robinson, to be his trainer on a one-fight-only basis. (7)

For the reasons stated in the previous paragraph, their July 26, 1971 fight at Houston's Astrodome had an intramural feel to it. Giving away 31 1/2 pounds to the 220 1/2-pound Ali, Ellis scored well in rounds one and three as he prevailed 15-4 and 17-7 overall but in the second minute of round four Ali put Ellis in his place with his most significant 60-second outburst of the fight (22 of 49 overall, 14 of 26 jabs, 8 of 23 power). Still, the statistics were fairly even through seven rounds (Ali led 87-83 overall) as Ali mostly concentrated on the jab, which accounted for 72 of his connects in that span. But Ali pulled away in rounds 8-11 (84-34 overall, 52-17 jabs, 32-17 power) before a final barrage rendered Ellis helpless and prompted referee Jay Edson to intervene just 50 seconds before the final bell.

Although the Associated Press said Ali produced "a brilliant exhibition of jabbing, footwork and precision punching," (8) the stats told a different story as he landed 32% of his total punches, 33% of his jabs (an excellent percentage) and 30% of his power shots while Ali tasted 27% overall, 22% jabs and 36% power. But because Ali was more active overall (50.7 per round to Ellis' 37.3) and had dominated the later rounds, he achieved leads of 189-118 overall, 131-63 jabs and 58-55 power.

Ali returned to Houston a little less than four months later to fight Buster Mathis Sr., who was coming off a decisive 12-round decision defeat to Jerry Quarry. Long criticized for his excess girth, Mathis, who scaled 300 in his pro debut, had been campaigning at impressively lighter weights. After stopping Mel Turnbow in seven rounds while scaling 247, Mathis worked off 20 1/2 pounds in less than three months and stopped James J. Beattie in the seventh. From there he weighed a career-low 220 1/2 (W 10 Amos Lincoln), 225 (W 10 Dick Wipperman) and 223 (KO 6 James J. Woody). The biggest win came a little more than four months after the Woody win when the 232-pound Mathis out-pointed George Chuvalo over 12 rounds, which set up the showdown with Quarry just 52 days later. Again, Mathis was in shape (234 1/2), but his unique blend of speed and nimbleness was no match for Quarry's crunching power, which registered a knockdown in round two and helped him pound out a lopsided victory.

A disheartened Mathis didn't fight again for nearly 32 months, and he couldn't have asked for a more difficult comeback opponent than Ali, even an Ali that weighed 227, the heaviest of his career to that point. Meanwhile, Mathis scaled 256 1/2, still relatively svelte compared to past fights but considerably heavier than during his run in the late 1960s. Active and battle-tested, Ali moved better than his weight, was far more industrious (64.2 punches per round to Mathis' anemic 30.3) and won the battle of the jabs by miles (39.5 thrown/9.2 connects per round to Mathis' 9.7 thrown/1.8 connects). As was the case with Ellis, Ali did most of his scoring with the jab but his power punching was unusually inaccurate as he landed just 21% of his hooks, crosses and uppercuts. That said, Ali produced a strong finish by flooring Mathis two times in the 11th and twice more in the 12th, a feat that required just 23 power connects to achieve. Thanks to Ali's compassion, Mathis managed to last until the final bell but he was a thoroughly beaten fighter physically, statistically and professionally. Mathis fought just two more times before hanging up the gloves for good (KO 3 Claude McBride on Sept. 5, 1972, and KO by 2 Ron Lyle 24 days later). Meanwhile, Ali's campaign continued.

Just 39 days after disposing of Mathis, Ali traveled to Zurich to fight German Juergen Blin, a one-time national heavyweight titlist who had twice lost on points in bids for the European belt, the first against the 30-0 Jose Manuel Urtain and, seven fights later, against Joe Bugner. The 28-year-old Blin (27-9-6) was coming off a two-round stoppage of journeyman George "Scrap Iron" Johnson, only his sixth win inside the distance.

In Steven Brunt's book "Facing Ali," Blin saw himself as an overachiever.

"If I had had a punch to go with my dedication, I would have been pretty good," Blin told Brunt. "I just didn't have the talent." (9) He did have enough talent to make it to the final of the German Olympic trials in 1964, where he lost on points to Hans Huber. Huber, in turn, advanced to the Olympic final against an American who only made the team because the original representative, Mathis, was injured -- Joe Frazier. (10)

The fight, appropriately, was staged on Boxing Day 1971 at the Hallenstadion. Stung by the criticism for allowing the stricken Mathis to last until the final bell, Ali predicted a first-round knockout by, according to ringside commentator Reg Gutteridge, holding up one finger as he approached the ring. By now, however, Ali's prognostications were more show business than sporting guarantee. The graphic gulf in talent was evident from the first moment as Ali skillfully worked behind a jab that registered double-digit connects in four of the first five rounds while Blin tried to nail Ali with purposeful but wildly inaccurate swings. One of those swings nearly knocked out Ali's mouthpiece in round two but that would prove to be his only moment of semi-glory. In round three, Blin picked up a most unusual injury: The follow-through on one of his reckless left hooks along the ropes opened a cut on his right elbow.

Blin, who worked as a butcher in a sausage factory when he wasn't boxing, (11) fought to the best of his ability but that ability didn't even begin to measure up against an Ali who was largely operating on autopilot. After out-landing Blin 11-1 in round four, Ali locked down full control of the contest by upping his work rate from 34 punches in the fourth to 60 in the fifth, landing a fight high 20 jabs and stinging him with occasional but accurate power shots (9 of 20, 45%). Ali throttled down in the sixth, allowing Blin to out-land him for the only time in the fight (10-9) and even allowing the German to tie him with six landed jabs. In the seventh, Ali said enough was enough and went for the kill shot.

A one-two to the jaw sent Blin tottering to the ropes, after which he slumped to the canvas and took referee Sepp Suter's 10-count. That event closed out a fight in which Ali nearly tripled Blin's total connects (116-41), almost quadrupled his opponent's landed jabs (78-20) and was much more precise in all categories (36%-15% overall, 34%-19% jabs and 39%-13% power).

"I could have gone on," Blin told Brunt. "Maybe I should have. But then I would have been knocked out in the ninth or 10th in a bad way. So I live to fight another day." (12)

Indeed he did. In fact, two fights after losing to Ali, Blin avenged his defeat to Urtain and won the European title by unanimous decision before Urtain's home fans in Madrid. But he was unable to reverse his loss to Bugner when they met four months later in London, for the young Hungarian-turned-Brit stopped Blin in the eighth. Like Mathis, Blin's career ended with a second-round KO defeat to Ron Lyle in Denver.

On April Fool's Day 1972 the top-rated Ali trekked to Tokyo to fight a scheduled 15-rounder against the ninth-ranked Mac Foster, (13) which marked the first time two top-10 heavyweights faced each other on the Asian continent. Foster, a Vietnam veteran and Marine who served 18 months and participated in 13 missions, began his career by scoring 24 consecutive knockouts, a string which helped him earn THE RING's "Progress Award" for 1969. (14) That streak was stopped cold by fellow power puncher Jerry Quarry, who halted Foster in the sixth in June 1970. To Foster's credit, he came into the Ali fight off four straight knockout wins over the aged Zora Folley (KO 1), the 13-0 Mike Boswell (KO 4), journeyman Billy Joiner (KO 5) and Giuseppe Ros (KO 8) on the Ali-Blin undercard.

Ali had predicted a fifth-round knockout and he further emphasized it by entering the ring with the fifth-round placard in tow. (15)

Unlike the Blin fight, Ali tried his hardest to make his soothsaying stick. In rounds one through five Ali averaged 77.2 punches per round, firing 86, 98 and 94 punches in the third, fourth and fifth. But Foster not only hung tough, he got in his fair share of punches, especially to the body. In round two Foster landed 22 body shots (half of which were jabs) and he racked up a fight-high 46 total connects as well as 32 power shots while the resting Ali was just 11 of 32 overall and 5 of 15 power. From round six forward, Ali dominated as he pleased and recovered when he felt like it. In round six he prevailed 20-2 while in the seventh Foster produced his last big burst to landing 37 of 58 power shots (64%), connecting 27 times to the body and out-landing Ali 38-11. For the fight Foster landed 154 times to the body, the third most body shots to date behind Chuvalo's 267 in their first fight and Frazier's 215 in 1971's "The Fight of the Century." Despite that punishing number, Ali, whose exceptional good looks obscured the fact that he was one of the toughest men ever to step inside a boxing ring, never allowed the body shots to affect his ability to dance.

When Ali decided to fight hard, his talent was far too much for Foster to handle. Ali's repeated blows in the ninth (35-13 overall, including a fight-high 24 of 82 jabs) opened a cut on Foster's forehead.

After Foster apparently won the 10th by out-landing Ali 29-15 overall and 28-7 power, Ali pulled away in the final five rounds (142-48 overall, 98-12 jabs, 44-36 power) to extend his final margins to 380-285 overall and 239-58 jabs. Foster did out-perform Ali in power shots (227-141) and he was the more accurate hitter (41%-34% overall, 44%-34% power). The judges agreed with the level of superiority the numbers projected, for under the five-point must system Ali prevailed 75-67, 74-66 and 73-65.

Exactly one month later, Ali fought George Chuvalo in Vancouver a little more than six years after their bruising (and hastily arranged) heavyweight championship fight in Toronto. Back then Chuvalo gave as good as he got verbally and nearly did the same physically as he relentlessly hammered Ali's body and never came close to hitting the canvas despite Ali landing what would be a career high 474 punches overall and 274 jabs.

Chuvalo remained active since losing to Ali as he fought 37 times, winning 32 to raise his record to 66-17-2 with 57 knockouts. All five losses were to quality fighters -- Oscar Bonavena, Joe Frazier, Buster Mathis Sr., George Foreman and Jimmy Ellis -- and though Frazier and Foreman stopped Chuvalo neither was able to drive him to the floor. Ali's, whose shot-for-shot power paled in comparison to that of "Smokin' Joe" and "Big George," was determined to become the first.

"I'm not gonna let it be said there was ever a heavyweight that didn't fall," he said. "They have pictures showing my heels. Jack Johnson fell. Jack Dempsey fell. Sugar Ray Robinson fell. Joe Frazier fell, and George Chuvalo is gonna fall." (16)

"I'm a better fighter than I was in 1966 and he's not as good a fighter as he was then," Chuvalo shot back. (17)

According to Chuvalo's autobiography "A Fighter's Life," Chuvalo separated a couple of ribs and may have torn cartilage when a partition separating the fighters unexpectedly collapsed when Chuvalo playfully lunged at Ali when the ex-champ invaded Chuvalo's gym. (18)

Ali, surely remembering the hard fight Chuvalo had given him six years earlier, was all business at the weigh-in, both in attitude and poundage. At 217 1/2, Ali was nearly 10 pounds lighter than he was against Foster the previous month and was at his lowest poundage since the first Frazier fight. Chuvalo, at 221, had logged just two fights and eight rounds of ring time since out-pointing a 38-year-old Cleveland Williams on the Ali-Mathis undercard. But, like most Ali opponents, just seeing "The Greatest" across the ring was enough motivation to produce one's best effort.

As was the case in their first fight, Chuvalo attacked the body hard (110 of his 152 power connects hit the flanks) but this time Ali was focused, serious and energetic throughout. The Chuvalo rematch was one of the few fights during "The Long Road Back" in which Ali was compelled to fight at his highest level every second of every round. Ali was on his toes almost constantly and his jab worked like a dream. He registered double-digit connects in every round (extending his streak to 17 straight rounds) and his performance in rounds six through nine (21 of 48, 20 of 36, 23 of 40 and 33 of 59) rates as perhaps the best four-round stretch of jabbing of his fistic life. In a sport in which 30% jab accuracy is considered exceptional, Ali topped that standard in every round, exceeded 40% 10 times and 50% an incredible six times. In the final two rounds Ali prevailed 32-0 in landed jabs. But just as he would do in all of his 93 fights before retiring in 1978, Chuvalo proudly remained on his feet.

While there was much to like about Ali's performance in the Chuvalo rematch, his defense still left much to be desired as Chuvalo landed 39% of his total punches and 51% of his power shots, mostly because of his great success to the body. Digging deeper into his power numbers, Chuvalo exceeded 50% accuracy seven times, including 78% in round one and 60% in round 12. Because Ali took the punishment unflinchingly and made sure to reply with dispatch, Chuvalo's excellent work was largely ignored by the judges, who saw Ali a lopsided winner (60-46, 59-51, 58-51 under the five-point must).

Ali continued his breakneck schedule by engaging in another rematch, this time against Quarry, just 57 days after beating Chuvalo. Although Ali won their first fight inside three rounds, some believed Ali was losing considerable energy when the fight was stopped due to Quarry's cut over the left eye. The critics had a point, for while Ali fired 61 and 49 punches in the first two rounds he logged only 39 in the third as well as a fight-low 12 overall connects.

This card held at the Convention Center in Las Vegas was dubbed "The Soul Brothers versus The Quarry Brothers" because the co-feature to Ali-Quarry II was Bob Foster's light heavyweight title defense against younger sibling Mike, who, at 21, was among the youngest fighters ever to challenge for the 175-pound championship. Foster held up his end of the bargain by spearing the feisty challenger with laser-sharp punches before ending the fight in round four with a horrific hook that produced instant unconsciousness. As for Ali, he was less destructive than his fellow "soul brother," but, then again, Foster set an incredibly high bar.

When Ali fought Quarry the first time, he felt a need to make a big opening statement because it was his first round following a three-and-a-half-year exile and he wanted to show he was still the "real" heavyweight champion. This time, Ali, more comfortable with his place in boxing as the number-one contender to Frazier's crown, mostly played with the second-ranked Quarry during the first nine minutes, even allowing the Californian to take round two with a 18-9 outburst that included 17 of 28 power shots, or 61% accuracy. Starting in round four, however, Ali began to show the fullness of his abilities and demonstrated how wide the talent gap between them had grown in the past couple of years. Ali's sizzling jabs cut through Quarry's guard with impressive frequency (11 of 42, 26% in the fourth, 16 of 50, 32% in the fifth) while the two-time title challenger barely got in a punch edgewise. Ali, who averaged 63.5 punches per round in rounds four and five to Quarry's 24, out-landed his antagonist 41-14 overall, 27-3 jabs and 14-11 power during that stretch.

Ali shifted into overdrive in the sixth as he unloaded a nearly ceaseless fusillade. In all he threw 101 punches and landed 38 while the beleaguered Quarry got off only 35 punches, landing a respectable 14. As round seven began, the ever-perceptive Ali sensed something was awry with Quarry. After landing a clean combination he beckoned referee Mike Kaplan to stop the fight. When he didn't, Ali landed another salvo that persuaded Kaplan to step in. In that round, Ali landed seven of his eight power shots, or 88%.

"I definitely could have gone on," Quarry said, sounding an awful lot like Blin. "But it wouldn't do any good. My brother's fight took it all out of me." (19)

Too bad Quarry couldn't have seen what happened after his fight with Ali. That's because, according to the Natchez News Leader, brother Mike had recovered sufficiently enough from the Foster KO to engage in one of the post-fight scuffles. (20)

With Ali generating incredible career momentum -- as well as excellent income -- he continued his roll by fighting Alvin "Blue" Lewis in Dublin just 22 days after dispatching Quarry. Ali entered the fight with a head cold -- a malady broadcaster Reg Gutteridge dubbed "The Ali Snuffle" -- but he also appeared to carry a level of animus that hadn't been seen in years. A possible reason was cited by Gutteridge: Two years earlier, Ali fired Lewis after "Blue's" robust body shots injured Ali's ribs. With that past in mind, Ali expanded his hitting zone as never before.

One oft-cited objection to Ali's style is his lack of body punching, a justifiable criticism for most of his fights. Here, however, Ali specifically targeted the pit of Lewis' stomach, particularly with the jab. Of his 170 jab connects, 60 were to the body. If one added his 14 power connects to the torso, his 74 landed body shots is, by far, the most he ever accumulated in his 47 CompuBox-tracked fights.

"For the only time I ever saw him fight, Ali punched to the body," referee Lew Eskin wrote in Boxing Illustrated. "In fact, I warned him once to keep them up." (21)

Ali scored the fight's only knockdown in round five and though Ali's corner people complained bitterly about what they saw as a "long count," Eskin said his actions were well within the rules.

"I made a special point of informing Ali that there would be a timekeeper, but that he had been instructed not to begin his count until I did, and that if he was to score a knockdown I was not going to begin that count until he went to and stayed in a corner," he wrote. "I told him that there was no way that I would tolerate him running around the ring during a count!'

"He looked at me and sort of half-smiled, but had a stern look on his face and said 'are you telling *me*?' I said, "yes I am!'"

Then, when Ali did score the knockdown, Ali did what he usually did. Then Eskin made good on his pre-fight promise.

"Ali stood there as he went down and looked at him," Eskin recalled. "I looked at Ali and said 'go to the corner.' He just stood there for a second, saw that I was not counting, turned and went to a corner as I started to count. He stayed there too, and as Ali got up, just as I said, I wiped off his gloves and then the bell rang." (22)

From round five onward, Ali administered a sustained beating. He averaged 82.8 punches per round in rounds 5-10, a stretch that saw him out-land Lewis 252-98 overall, 99-46 jabs and 153-52 power and achieve 50% or better power accuracy in every round. Lewis bravely plugged away but even the toughest man -- at least the toughest man not named George Chuvalo -- has a breaking point. For Lewis, that came in the 11th as Ali went 15 of 25 overall (including 14 of 24 jabs) while Lewis missed each of his five punches. Eskin, seeing no need for the slaughter to continue, stepped in at the 1:15 mark.

Two months and a day later, Ali fought former two-time champ Floyd Patterson for the second time, his third rematch in his last four fights. Ali's relationship with Patterson had always been a multi-layered one; at times he treated Patterson with immense respect and deference, even allowing him to call him "Clay" without much complaint. But when they met in November 1965 for Ali's heavyweight championship, the mutual tension was at its zenith. In one corner was Patterson, who declared that "Cassius Clay must be beaten and the Black Muslims' scourge removed from boxing" while in the other corner was Ali, who was bound and determined to make Patterson pay for his insolence. Instead of wiping out Patterson in short order, Ali chose to either ridicule him or dazzle him with his otherworldly hand and foot speed, hitting him just enough to win rounds and to hurt him, but not enough to put him away. Adding to the spectacle was Patterson's injured back, which was stretched several times between rounds. The unseemly contest mercifully ended late in the 12th when referee Harry Kessler finally stepped in.

The hard feelings subsided with time and by the time they met again in September 1972 the two future Hall of Famers were at opposite points in their careers. While the 30-year-old Ali was in the midst of a spectacularly productive year, Patterson was now 37 and nearing the end of a highly successful in-ring life. He was, however, on a good run, for since losing a hotly disputed decision to then-WBA titlist Jimmy Ellis, Patterson had won nine in a row, including wins over Terry Daniels (W 10), Oscar Bonavena (W 10) and, most recently, Pedro Agosto (KO 6) a little more than two months earlier. At 188 1/2, Patterson was at his lightest weight since he scaled 186 against Charley "Devil" Green, his first opponent since losing to Ellis two years and one day earlier. While Patterson looked fit and ready, Ali appeared to be raring to go as well as he scaled 218, only a half-pound heavier than the Lewis fight.

With his back fully healed and armed with plenty of reasons to be motivated, including a throng of 17,378 that rooted strongly for him, Patterson dominated the first two rounds, partly because he was able to fight better against Ali than had been the case in 1965 and partly because the playful Ali gave away the opening six minutes, attempting just one power shot (which missed) in that span. Ali perked up a little in rounds three, four and five but the plucky Patterson still got the best of the action as he connected with hard blows that ignited the heavily pro-Patterson crowd. In fact, Patterson out-landed Ali in each of the first six rounds and in rounds four and five the gap was 39-14 overall and 38-6 power.

Any visions of a Patterson upset evaporated in the sixth as Ali finally woke up, then opened up. The sixth saw Ali throw 68 punches (nearly matching the combined 72 he logged in rounds four and five combined) and inflict heavy damage to Patterson's left eye, which became cut, then swollen. While Patterson still out-landed Ali 13-10 in the sixth, the momentum had shifted.

The seventh was even better for Ali and even worse for Patterson as Ali out-threw the ex-champ 56-24, out-landed him for the only time in the fight (17-11 overall and 9-7 power) and had Patterson in duress. Ever determined, Patterson refused to hit the canvas and made it back to his corner. Unfortunately for him, the ringside physician refused to let him out of the corner for round eight because the left eye was now nearly closed.

The statistics reflect both Patterson's success and Ali's confidence, for Ali allowed Patterson to build huge statistical leads (90-39 overall, 83-22 power in the first six rounds) before stirring himself and reeling in the defiant veteran.

"Patterson is a great, great fighter," a gracious Ali said. "I thought he'd be nothing, but he surprised me. I didn't knock him out. I didn't get him on a TKO. All I did was close his eye." (23)

Although Patterson never announced his retirement, the Ali rematch would be his last official fight. Both he and Ali would be among the inaugural class for the International Boxing Hall of Fame, but while Patterson's in-ring story was at an end, Ali's was only gaining more steam.

Ali's incredible 1972 ended with a showdown against reigning light heavyweight champion Bob Foster November 21 at Stateline, Nev. Foster had been extraordinarily dominant against fellow 175-pounders but every time he stepped up to fight the big boys his spindly 6-foot-3 frame couldn't put on the necessary weight to effectively compete. Such was the case here when he scaled 180, only five above the light heavyweight championship limit. The blows that rendered his light heavyweight compatriots senseless -- just ask Dick Tiger, Mike Quarry and Vicente Rondon -- merely ticked the chins of Ernie Terrell (KO by 7), Zora Folley (L 10) and Joe Frazier (KO by 2), whose titanic hook left Foster a supine, semi-conscious mess.

Although both were the same height, Ali's 41 1/4-pound weight advantage made Foster look frail in comparison. Heeding his past history with heavyweights, Foster did his best to keep Ali at bay with a busy and very productive jab. In fact, Foster was one of the few fighters to out-jab Ali (he led 69-48 for the fight) and the blow produced another first for Ali -- a cut. The swelling around his left eye broke open in the fifth and Ali, who had been playful to this point turned serious. Deadly serious.

Ali scored four knockdowns in round five thanks to the three-knockdown rule being waved and also to a right cross and a trifecta of left hooks. Incredibly, Ali landed more power punches in round five -- 22 -- than was the case in the previous four rounds, 18. Ali jabbed his way through the sixth, a round that saw Foster go 4 of 16 -- all jabs -- before throttling up again in the seventh by scoring two knockdowns. The latter of the two knockdowns perfectly illustrated Foster's conundrum: After Foster hit Ali with three of his hardest right hands -- right hands that had destroyed his light heavyweight peers -- Ali broke into a fake wobble, then dropped Foster with a cuffing hook, one of only six power shots he would land in the round.

By the eighth Foster was too far gone. Ali's only connect of the round -- a tap of a right to the chin -- put the future Hall of Famer down for the 10 count. The final margins for Ali with the judges were reflective of his control (35-27, 35-28 twice) but because of Ali's long stretches of inaction the CompuBox stats were much closer (94-87 overall). Foster was also the more accurate hitter in all three phases (37%-29% overall, 37%-25% jabs, 38%-33% power), but in boxing, like in life, size truly does matter. Foster certainly thought so.

"I don't know if I could have beaten Muhammad if I had had more weight," Foster said. "But I do know that my handicap of more than 40 pounds beat me. He was too big for me, too heavy, too strong, with a defense that challenged my attack and came off better than mine. However, I am what I am, with 180 pounds the best I can produce, and that's how it is and how it will continue to be.

"Muhammad is quick," he observed. "For a man weighing around 220, he was quick beyond words." (24)

All this time Ali's ultimate goal had been a rematch with Frazier for the undisputed championship. But 23 days before Ali's first fight of 1973, a scheduled 12-rounder against young veteran Joe Bugner, Frazier shockingly lost the title to 3 1/2-to-1 underdog George Foreman, who scored six knockdowns en route to a smashing second-round TKO victory in Kingston, Jamaica. The victory lifted Foreman's record to 38-0 with 35 knockouts, and, just like that, the heavyweight world was turned on its ear much like Foreman had turned Frazier on his ear.

With his new target in mind, Ali entered the Convention Center ring in Las Vegas with a spectacularly sequined robe with the words "People's Choice" on the back. It was a gift from Elvis Presley, who, at one time, was as much of a monarch in his business as Ali had been in his. (25) While Ali and Presley remained huge stars, they were still seeking to regain what had been lost over time.

Bugner vaulted onto the world-class scene in March 1971 by capturing a narrow but unanimous decision over Henry Cooper to become the new British, Commonwealth and European champion, a verdict that still inspires heated debate. Four months after successfully defending against Blin (W 15), Bugner shockingly lost all three belts on points against veteran southpaw Jack Bodell. Coming into the Ali fight Bugner had won nine straight, including a TKO win over Blin to regain the European title, and a successful defense against Rudi Lubbers (W 15) three fights later. Though still a month shy of his 23rd birthday, Bugner (43-4-1) was about to engage in his 49th professional fight.

Bugner said in his autobiography that he had the benefit of sparring with Ali as a 19-year-old and during that time he not only studied Ali's strengths and weaknesses, he also observed how the champion conducted his business around the camp. Unlike most foes, Ali didn't try to antagonize Bugner, who had always been respectful. (26) Still, Ali predicted that he would stop Bugner in seven.

In the ring, however, the absence of overly harsh words didn't help Bugner much against Ali, though he was fiercely competitive from first bell to 12th. Bugner refused to be Ali's foil and thus forced the ex-champ to compete instead of clown. Still, the only time Ali really opened up was in the 10th, where he shut out Bugner 33-0 overall and fired a fight-high 70 punches.

ABC blow-by-blow man Howard Cosell, a notoriously hard-to-please observer, was impressed by Bugner's courage and drive, telling Dundee "this kid is no chump." Statistically speaking, Bugner held his own in the first five rounds as Ali led 66-52 overall, 39-31 jabs and 27-21 power but from the sixth round forward Ali's greatness enabled him to pull away (140-41 overall, 64-18 jabs, 76-23 power). Ali was precise (47% overall, 46% jabs, 48% power), balanced (224 jabs, 216 power attempts and 103 connects in both departments) and unusually hard to hit (25% overall, 21% jabs, 29% power). The scorecards were close (57-54, 56-53, 57-52 under the five-point must), which earned Bugner credibility in defeat.

Forty-eight days after beating Bugner, Ali met someone else he initially met in the gym: A well-muscled Marine named Ken Norton.

According to Eddie Futch, Ali and Norton first met in the Hoover Street Gym in Los Angeles during Ali's exile. It was customary for Ali to travel with gym equipment in tow and on this day he sparred a few rounds with George "Scrap Iron" Johnson, Howard Smith and a third fighter whose name escaped Futch's memory. After doing so, someone pointed out Norton and Ali decided to work with him.

Norton followed Futch's instructions to work with Ali rather than fight him. But as the round approached its conclusion, Ali decided to up the ante.

"Near the end of the round, Ali stepped back and announced to Norton and the crowd, 'OK, boy, I'm through playing with you, I'm going to put something on you.' Ali really starts punching but Norton goes right with him. What a round that was, a wild round.

"The thing was, Ali didn't think Norton could counter because Norton had been working along with him earlier," Futch told Dave Anderson in his book "In the Corner." "But when Ali started punching harder, Norton countered. Norton embarrassed him, and Ali didn't expect that. Ali didn't like that at all. The next day Ali walked into the gym screaming, 'I want that Norton, where's that Norton?' But I had told Norton to stay in his street clothes. Ali looked over and saw Norton standing around in his street clothes, then he looked at me and said, 'Ain't he going to work today?' I said, 'No.' He said, 'Why not?' I said, 'Yesterday you came in here looking for a workout. Today you came in here looking for a fight. When this kid fights you, he's going to get paid. And paid well.' " (27)

Indeed he would be, but virtually no one could have known that their March 31, 1973 fight staged before 11,884 at the San Diego Sports Arena would send shock waves throughout the sporting world and would spawn a celebrated trilogy. Futch and Norton, however, strongly believed they had the formula to beat Ali. Futch had long been an avid Ali-watcher; he had worked with Charlie Powell when he fought the then-Cassius Clay in 1963 and had helped Yancey Durham prepare Joe Frazier for their 1971 showdown. In essence, Futch's blueprint centered around jabbing with Ali while keeping his right hand high, something Ali didn't do.

"His jab will pop into the middle of your glove and then your jab will come right down the pipe into the middle of his face," Futch told Norton in Anderson's book. "Every time he starts to punch, don't pull back, go forward toward him. That's what Norton did. That's what destroyed Ali's rhythm."

The second part of Futch's master plan was what to do when Ali was on the ropes.

"I told him, 'if you start from the center of the ring, it'll take you only three moves to get Ali on the ropes. Every time you jab, step in and make him jab again. Then do the same thing.' With both of them being big heavyweights, I knew if Norton was in the center of the ring when he countered Ali's jab, those three moves would back Ali into the ropes. When he got Ali on the ropes, I told him, 'don't do like all the other guys do. Don't throw your hook to the head. He'll pull back against the ropes and when you're off balance, he'll pepper you with counterpunches. When he's on the ropes, instead of going to the head with the left hook, start banging his body with both hands. I don't care whether you land or not. Make him, in order to protect his body, bring his elbows down and his head down. That gives you a shot to the head.' Simple. So simple." (28)

The sixth-rated Norton's anonymity was such that the fight was aired live on ABC, the first time in six years that an Ali fight had not been shown on closed-circuit. (29) What had been considered a tune-up for Ali, the 5-to-1 favorite, quickly turned into a struggle for survival, not just strategically but physically. That's because sometime during the fight Ali suffered a broken jaw, likely from a Norton right cross. Dundee believed the injury happened in round one while Futch thought it might have happened in round 11. More neutral observers split the difference, saying it occurred sometime during the middle rounds.

Ali showed the most distress during the 12th round, where Norton prevailed 29-9 overall and 24-4 power. It was the only time in the fight when one doubted whether Ali could make it to the final bell, but make it he did.

According to Dr. Gary Manchester, who performed the 90-minute operation to wire Ali's jaw together, described the break thusly: "The bone which was broken had three or four jagged edges and they kept poking into his cheek and mouth. It was a very bad break." (30)

Dr. Ferdie Pacheco, Ali's personal physician, graphically described Ali's physical challenges.

"Every time you turn your head, there's pain. Every time you get hit, there's pain. Hell, if you take a punch on your shoulder it hurts. This guy showed remarkable courage just to hang in there. I don't want to take anything away from Kenny Norton. He has a lot of guts and a tremendous future. But he could never come close to beating a healthy Ali." (31)

No matter when it happened, Norton emerged with a split decision that, given the lopsidedness of the stats (233-171 overall, 109-93 jabs, 124-78 power and percentage gaps of 43%-26% overall, 41%-22% jabs and 45%-33% power) should have been unanimous.

Dundee, the eternal optimist, was philosophical and congratulatory.

"We've had our share of the good days and you have to be able to take the bad with the good," he said. "This day belonged to Ken Norton and to the people of San Diego...it was a great win for both!" (32)

Norton, for his part, began to believe the upset was possible as the fight hit the halfway point, telling Futch after round six, 'I'm going to beat this guy." (33) From that point forward, Norton let Ali know just how good he was feeling about his chances.

"Sitting ringside you could hear Norton taunt him with 'come on sucker, give me a fight!' and 'watch it, here comes one.' Another time on a break, Norton playfully gave Ali a backhand and laughed, 'wheeee!' " wrote RING reporter John Greensmith. (34)

Ali's supporters scrambled for explanations. The broken jaw was the most obvious but others believe Ali came into the ring in a compromised state because he allegedly turned an ankle while doing roadwork at a golf course six days earlier. The injury reportedly forced Ali to abandon his running and gym work the following day, but during the bout Ali appeared to move normally, albeit a bit more slowly. (35)

Other members of Team Ali admitted their man simply wasn't in proper condition.

"Ali just didn't get in shape for Norton and I told you long before the fight that he had better be in better condition than he was for Joe Bugner," said promoter/writer Harold Conrad. "He wasn't though, and this was the big thing. I think he's gone stale and maybe this will be a lesson for him." (36)

While Norton zoomed up to second in THE RING rankings following his landmark victory, (37) Ali and Frazier, within the span of two months, lost a huge payday. As part of the deal to help put together the first Ali-Frazier fight, Cooke had the right to stage the rematch at Cooke's Forum in Inglewood, Calif., with both fighters set to make $3.2 million. (38) But with Frazier's stunning second-round defeat to Foreman in January and Ali's even more stunning loss to Norton, those plans were shattered, figuratively and, in Ali's case, quite literally.

Ali accepted the defeat graciously, accepting Norton's offer to shake hands in the ring after the fight as well as allowing a visit to his hospital room following surgery, a visit Norton believed cemented their friendship. Norton's fans, however, weren't so magnanimous. In Norton's autobiography "Going The Distance," Ali was handed a brown paper bag with the following message: *The butterfly has lost its wings. The bee has lost its sting. You are through, you loud-mouthed braggart. Your mouth has been shut up for all time. It's a great day for America. You are finished!"* (39)

Instead of throwing the bag away, Ali taped the bag on the wall of his gym so he could see it during every workout. (40) It, in part, helped Ali work himself into incredible condition for the rematch, which was staged a little more than five months later at the Forum in Inglewood, Calif. Both appeared primed for the challenge.

"I'm not the kind of a guy who brags and I'm not cocky. But I feel I'll knock out Ali this time," Norton wrote in THE RING. "There's a line between confidence and over-confidence. I think positive and have confidence in my ability to back it up. Ali has respect for me as a fighter and it might even work to his disadvantage. I showed him that I could not only hit with either hand but that I could move and box pretty good myself. He's basically a very defensive fighter who does little on offense while he's concentrating on defense. He has to be thinking about the broken jaw, even if it's in his subconscious.

"Eddie and I know just what to expect from Ali and will try to be well prepared as we were the first time. We will train purposefully with a plan and all I have to do is execute," he concluded. "I'm a flexible fighter and can change if necessary. I don't think we'll have to." (41)

"I have nobody to blame but myself for my loss to Ken Norton," Ali wrote in the same issue. "I didn't train properly because I really didn't think Ken was that great a fighter. I was wrong. This time things will be different. You'll see the real Muhammad Ali. I can beat Norton by moving. Keeping on my toes, dancing and sticking -- that's the way I'm going to beat Norton. I danced for a couple of rounds at San Diego. Rounds three and 11 I won easily but I just wasn't ready to keep it up. I should weigh about 215 or 216 for Norton this time. I was a little sluggish at 221 at San Diego. I have fought some good fights coming in around 220 but I am fast and comfortable at about 216." (42)

Ali stunned observers -- and perhaps himself given his pre-fight words -- by scaling a greyhound-quick 212 pounds, nine pounds lighter than for their first meeting and his lowest poundage since the Oscar Bonavena fight nearly three years earlier, when he also weighed 212. Norton, who weighed 210 in March, was a svelte 205 for the rematch.

This was a fight told in two halves. The first six rounds saw Ali move with a speed and consistency not seen since the late 1960s, when he was the fastest heavyweight ever to walk the earth. Statistically speaking, however, Ali's lead was perilously narrow (70-67 overall and 42-31 jabs to offset Norton's 36-28 edge in landed power shots). By the seventh, the fight began to turn as Norton's steady pressure and accurate power hitting eroded Ali's movement and forced him into risky exchanges. Norton out-landed Ali in rounds seven through 11 and his margins of victory were far larger than those built by Ali. During that span Norton prevailed 116-77 overall and 95-44 power to offset Ali's 33-21 lead in landed jabs. Going into the 12th, it appeared to be anyone's fight.

Digging into his reservoir of experience, talent and immense pride, Ali overcame his obvious fatigue and won the final round going away. He out-threw Norton 69-39, out-landed him 28-14 overall and 19-13 power as well as out-jabbed him 9-1. Still, Norton ended the fight with leads of 197-175 overall and 144-91 power as well as percentage gaps of 40%-28% overall, 28%-24% jabs and 48%-34% power.

Once again the decision was split. This time, Ali came out the winner.

Referee Dick Young saw Ali a 7-5 winner while judge George Latka viewed Norton ahead 6-5. The deciding vote was cast by judge John Thomas, whose card read 6-5 for Ali.

Six months ago, the 31-year-old Ali's career was in peril, but now, thanks to his gut-check 12th round performance, which won him the round on all three cards, he was back on track.

An exhausted Ali had nothing but praise for his rival.

"Ken Norton is the best man I have ever fought," Ali declared. "No man could hit me as much as Norton did in the shape that I am. Frazier couldn't do it...Foreman wouldn't do it. I imagine if you watched films of my old fights, I'm not too much slower, but I can't be 22 again. I'm satisfied with my comeback. I've trained hard for 15 weeks and I am very tired." (43)

Tired as he was, there was still more work to do. With one defeat avenged, Ali still needed to square the other.

Forty days after beating Norton, Ali defeated Rudi Lubbers of the Netherlands over 12 rounds in Jakarta, Indonesia, a fight Ali later called the easiest fight of his career.

"Man didn't do nothin' " Ali told writer Dave Anderson. (44)

Of all the fights Ali waged between the Doug Jones bout in March 1963 and his final fight against Trevor Berbick in December 1981, the Lubbers fight is the only one in which complete footage is not available. Thus, it was excluded from this statistical study.

Although the site of the bout, Bung Karno Stadium, boasted a capacity of 120,000 only 23,000 seats were filled. The fight held special meaning for Ali because the crowd was reportedly 98 percent Muslim, and though he did his best to fulfill his prediction of a fifth-round knockout he ended up going the full 12. Ali belted Lubbers at will, bloodying his nose and nearly shutting his opponent's right eye, all despite limiting his use of the right hand.

"I had to save the right for Joe Frazier," Ali said. (45)

Since beating Ali, Frazier had fought just four times to Ali's 13 -- a pair of fourth round knockouts over massive underdogs Terry Daniels and Ron Stander, the disastrous KO loss to Foreman and a 12-round decision over Bugner in London on July 2, 1973. With neither man holding a world championship, their $850,000 base purses paled to the $2.5 million they each earned for their first fight and the $3.2 million each they stood to make had Frazier and Ali cleared all hurdles, but the venomous feelings that defined their 1971 showdown only intensified with the passage of time.

Frazier, for his part, went after the one thing guaranteed to infuriate Ali: The name game.

"Clay and I, we want each other bad," Frazier said. "I still call him Clay; his mother named him Clay. If you've been around this guy long enough, you can have a lot of hate in your heart when the bell rings, but otherwise you kind of look at him and you laugh. There's something wrong with this guy. I'm aware now that the guy's got a couple of loose screws someplace." (46)

Ali also went for the jugular by questioning Frazier's intelligence, with "ignorant" being the insult of choice.

Because of previous commitments at Madison Square Garden, the fight was moved up from February 4 to January 28, 1974. (47) Given the heat between the two, it was for the best.

Five days before the fight Ali and Frazier visited ABC's studios in New York City to review their first fight with Howard Cosell for "Wide World of Sports." Futch objected to the idea based on past sit-downs but in Dave Anderson's book "In the Corner" Cosell told Futch he would sit between the fighters. Futch was unconvinced but allowed the event to proceed to show an associate that his concern about a brawl breaking out would come true. (48)

Sure enough, it happened. Cosell, breaking his word to Futch, was seated to the left while the fighters were positioned side-by-side. As the video of round 10 was being shown Ali complained about being hit low 95 times, to which Frazier, turning toward Cosell, said "that's when he went to the hospital," knowing that was a sore point with Ali.

"Don't talk about no hospital," Ali said. "You were wrong for bringing up the hospital. I ain't gonna say nothing about no hospital."

"You don't wanna mention it," a smirking Frazier told Ali.

"I went to the hospital for 10 minutes, you went for a month," a clearly irritated Ali shot back. "Now be quiet."

The temperature in the studio was clearly rising and wasn't far from the boiling point.

Frazier: "I was resting."

Ali: "Oh, yeah, you went to the hospital to rest..."

Frazier: "...in and out."

Ali: "That's embarrassing. Don't nobody go to the hospital to rest. I wasn't going to bring up the hospital. That just shows how dumb you are. He brought up the hospital!"

Cosell tried to steer the conversation back to the fight and Frazier, having gotten his dig in, wanted to do the same. But Ali, his pride wounded, dearly wanted to retaliate. And retaliate he did.

"He's gonna bring up the hospital, see how ignorant the man is."

As soon as Ali uttered the word "ignorant" the fuse was lit.

An incensed Frazier ripped off his earpiece, stood up, glowered down on the seated Ali and asked, "why do you think I'm ignorant?" Frazier's intimidating move caused Ali's mood to instantly shift toward peacemaking mode.

"Sit down," Ali said with a calmer tone. "Sit down, Joe. Sit down, Joe."

But Joe was having none of it as he brushed away Futch's hand and turned his attention to Ali's younger brother Rahaman Ali, who walked onto the set and stood near Frazier.

"You wanna get in on this too?" Frazier asked Rahaman.

Ali then suddenly bolted up from his seat and wrapped his left arm around Frazier's neck in what appeared to be a half-serious, half-playful wrestling move. All that did was push Frazier over the cliff emotionally. His upper body strength and lower center of gravity allowed him to push Ali down and onto his back. Had mixed martial arts been in vogue then, he might have tried to put Ali into a guillotine or an arm bar but instead members of the crew did their best to pull them apart. An infuriated Frazier left the studio while Ali remained on set and reviewed the remainder of the fight with Cosell. Both men were fined $5,000 by the New York State Athletic Commission for "deplorable conduct demeaning to boxing."

But the forfeiture of money could not even begin to quiet the storms that swirled within Frazier.

"I'm just sick of listening to him," Frazier wrote in THE RING. "He's just a phony anyway, with punch and tongue, and I don't care what he says or thinks. I'll do my talking in the ring. I'm just anxious to get it on. I'm not one for predicting -- that's his game -- but I think I'll knock him out." (49)

In his own first-person article, Ali said he didn't hate Frazier -- "I don't really bear a grudge against Joe Frazier. He's a nice man and a good fighter" -- but he dearly wanted to even the score with Frazier just as much as we wanted to do so against Norton.

"Joe Frazier represents a goal for me," he wrote. "I don't even look beyond him. I have to teach him a lesson and the only way to do it is to give him a solid whupping. I'm sure he feels the same way about me. I will win because I'm the better fighter and always was. In his heart, Joe Frazier knows this. But Joe has courage and stamina and it will be a tough, hard fight and there can be only one winner." (50)

Ali created a stir at his Deer Lake training camp eight days before the fight when reporters noticed Dundee applying a substance to Ali's right hand, which apparently was injured during the Norton rematch. Reporters noticed an oversized jar of Theraffin inside the gym and when they addressed the subject Ali lowered his voice to a whisper and declared, "Joe Frazier is gonna feel the hand." (51)

"It's an astringent," said Dr. Edwin Campbell, a representative of the state athletic commission, who said he would X-ray the hand mid-week. "It's supposed to be used to stop inflammation. I know that Ali's had problems before with the cartilage around his right knuckle, but I hadn't heard of anything lately." The doctor expressed surprise when told Ali had been using the waxy substance on a daily basis.

He was not the only person surprised by the development.

"I never seen a guy train that way," said former featherweight champion Willie Pep, a frequent visitor to the camp during this training cycle. "He's not throwing no punches." (52)

Ali, ranked first by THE RING to Frazier's number two (53), was a 7-to-5 favorite on fight night (54) and just like the first fight, the Garden was sold out. In fact, Teddy Brenner, the director of boxing at MSG, believed that the fight would have sold out a 60,000-seat arena. (55) But while the hatred remained real and raw, the rematch was fought much differently than their classic first encounter. Ali remained on the move almost constantly, stayed away from the ropes, pulled down on Frazier's neck -- 133 times by Futch's count (56) -- and repeated the pattern once referee Tony Perez separated them. Ali shocked observers by wobbling Frazier badly in the final moments of round two but Ali's momentum was halted by Perez, who thought he had heard the bell.

Ali's tactics slowed Frazier's pace to a mere 34 per round while Ali fired a comfortable 60. But while Ali was the unquestioned ring general, the statistics portrayed a much closer fight as Ali landed only nine more punches (181-172) and was the much less accurate fighter (Frazier led 42%-25% overall, 18%-14% jabs and 44%-31% power). The round-by-round breakdown revealed that Ali and Frazier were tied 5-5-2 overall, with Frazier leading 8-4 in power connects and Ali holding a 11-0-1 bulge in landed jabs. Worse yet for Ali, he landed just 37 jabs in 12 rounds. Had they fought this way three years earlier, boxing would have been greatly harmed and the world probably would have never seen a second fight, much less a third.

In the end, the decision was unanimous for Ali, and rightfully so. Ali did what he needed to do to win and nothing more while Frazier, perhaps compromised by the Foreman beating, didn't spew the same "smoke" that left Ali choking on his dust nearly three years earlier.

At long last, Muhammad Ali stood at the doorstep of his ultimate goal. All possible obstacles to a second chance at the heavyweight championship had been cleared. Now, the only roadblock standing between Ali and his dream was a foreboding figure carrying the name of George Edward Foreman.

INSIDE THE NUMBERS: Ali famously avoided the body in most of his fights, but that wasn't the case against Al "Blue" Lewis. In that fight he landed 74 body punches -- of which 60 were jabs. Both are, by far, the highest totals Ali compiled in the 47 fights tracked by CompuBox. Other single-round bests Ali achieved during this 14-fight stretch include the following: 113 total punches thrown in round 11 against Mac Foster, 82 attempted jabs in round nine against Mac Foster, 57 total punches landed in round seven against Al "Blue" Lewis, 37 landed jabs in round seven against Al "Blue" Lewis. Finally, Ali threw the most punches of this 47-fight study -- 1,132 -- against Mac Foster.

Date: July 26, 1971   City: Houston, TX   Venue: Astrodome
Opponent: Jimmy Ellis
Result: Ali by TKO at 2:10 of the 12th round -- Won Vacant NABF Heavyweight Title

Referee: Jay Edson

Round	1	2	3	4	5	6	7	8	9	10	11	12	13	14	15	Total
Ali	10	10	10	10	10	10	10	10	10	10	10					110
Ellis																102

Judge: Earl Keel

Round	1	2	3	4	5	6	7	8	9	10	11	12	13	14	15	Total
Ali																108
Ellis																102

Judge: Ernie Taylor

Round	1	2	3	4	5	6	7	8	9	10	11	12	13	14	15	Total
Ali																107
Ellis																104

Date: November 17, 1971   City: Houston, TX   Venue: Astrodome
Opponent: Buster Mathis
Result: Ali by unanimous decision -- Retains NABF Heavyweight Title

Referee: Chris Jordan

Round	1	2	3	4	5	6	7	8	9	10	11	12	13	14	15	Total
Ali	10	10	10	10	9	10	10	9	10	10	10	10				118
Mathis	10				10		10									105

Judge: Ernie Taylor

Round	1	2	3	4	5	6	7	8	9	10	11	12	13	14	15	Total
Ali	10	10	10	10	9	10	10	9	10	10	10	10				118
Mathis	10				10		10									104

Judge: Earl Keel

Round	1	2	3	4	5	6	7	8	9	10	11	12	13	14	15	Total
Ali	10	10	10	10	10	10	9	10	10	10	10	10				119
Mathis	10				10	10		10								108

Date: April 1, 1972   City: Tokyo, Japan   Venue: Nippon Budokan
Opponent: Mac Foster
Result: Ali by unanimous decision

Referee: John E. Crowder

Round	1	2	3	4	5	6	7	8	9	10	11	12	13	14	15	Total
Ali	5	5	4	5	5	5	5	5	5	4	5	5	5	5	5	73
M. Foster			5							5						65

Judge: Takeo Ugo

Round	1	2	3	4	5	6	7	8	9	10	11	12	13	14	15	Total
Ali	5	5	5	5	5	5	5	5	5	5	5	5	5	5	5	75
M. Foster																67

Judge: Hiroyuki Tezaki

Round	1	2	3	4	5	6	7	8	9	10	11	12	13	14	15	Total
Ali	10	10	10	10	10	10										74
M. Foster																65

Date: May 1, 1972   City: Vancouver, Canada   Venue: Pacific Coliseum
Opponent: George Chuvalo
Result: Ali by unanimous decision -- Retained NABF Heavyweight Title

Referee: Dave Brown

Round	1	2	3	4	5	6	7	8	9	10	11	12	13	14	15	Total
Ali																59
Chuvalo																51

Judge: Tommy Paonessa

Round	1	2	3	4	5	6	7	8	9	10	11	12	13	14	15	Total
Ali	5	5	5	5	5	5	5	5	5	5	5	5				60
Chuvalo																46

Judge: Tommy Keyes

Round	1	2	3	4	5	6	7	8	9	10	11	12	13	14	15	Total
Ali																58
Chuvalo																51

Date: June 27, 1972   City: Las Vegas, NV   Venue: Las Vegas Convention Center
Opponent: Jerry Quarry
Result: Ali by TKO at 0:19 of the 7th round -- Retained NABF Heavyweight Title

Judge: Art Lurie

Round	1	2	3	4	5	6	7	8	9	10	11	12	13	14	15	Total
Ali	5	5	5	5	5	5										30
Quarry	4	5	4	4	4	4										25

Judge: Ralph Mosa

Round	1	2	3	4	5	6	7	8	9	10	11	12	13	14	15	Total
Ali	5	5	5	5	5	5										30
Quarry	4	5	4	4	4	4										25

Judge: Barry Pearlman

Round	1	2	3	4	5	6	7	8	9	10	11	12	13	14	15	Total
Ali	5	5	5	5	5	5										30
Quarry	4	4	4	4	4	4										24

Date: September 20, 1972   City: New York, NY   Venue: Madison Square Garden
Opponent: Floyd Patterson
Result: Ali by TKO after the 7th round (corner retirement) -- Retained NABF Heavyweight Title

Referee: Arthur Mercante Sr.

Round	1	2	3	4	5	6	7	8	9	10	11	12	13	14	15	Total
Ali	X		X	X	X	X	X									6
Patterson		X														1

Judge: Jack Gordon

Round	1	2	3	4	5	6	7	8	9	10	11	12	13	14	15	Total
Ali		X	X	E		X	X									4 (1E)
Patterson	X			E	X											2 (1E)

Judge: Tony Castellano

Round	1	2	3	4	5	6	7	8	9	10	11	12	13	14	15	Total
Ali			X		E	X	X									3 (1E)
Patterson	X	X		X	E											3 (1E)

Date: November 21, 1972   City: Stateline, NV   Venue: Sahara Tahoe Hotel

Opponent: Bob Foster

Result: Ali by KO at 0:40 of the 8th round -- Retained NABF Heavyweight Title

Judge: Wally Rusk

Round	1	2	3	4	5	6	7	8	9	10	11	12	13	14	15	Total
Ali	5	5	5	5	5	5	5									35
B. Foster	4	4	5	4	3	5	3									49

Judge: Anthony Smercina

Round	1	2	3	4	5	6	7	8	9	10	11	12	13	14	15	Total
Ali	5	5	5	5	5	5	5									35
B. Foster	4	4	4	5	3	4	3									27

Judge: Bill Stremmell

Round	1	2	3	4	5	6	7	8	9	10	11	12	13	14	15	Total
Ali	5	5	5	5	5	5	5									35
B. Foster	4	4	4	5	3	4	3									27

Date: February 14, 1973   City: Las Vegas, NV   Venue: Las Vegas Convention Center

Opponent: Joe Bugner

Result: Ali by unanimous decision

Judge: Roland Dakin

Round	1	2	3	4	5	6	7	8	9	10	11	12	13	14	15	Total
Ali										5	5	5				57
Bugner										4	4	4				54

Judge: Lou Tabat

Round	1	2	3	4	5	6	7	8	9	10	11	12	13	14	15	Total
Ali										5	5	5				56
Bugner										4	4	4				53

Judge: Ralph Mosa

Round	1	2	3	4	5	6	7	8	9	10	11	12	13	14	15	Total
Ali										5	5	5				57
Bugner										4	4	4				52

Date: March 31, 1973   City: San Diego, CA   Venue: San Diego Sports Arena

Opponent: Ken Norton

Result: Norton by split decision -- Lost NABF Heavyweight Title

Referee: Frank Rustich

Round	1	2	3	4	5	6	7	8	9	10	11	12	13	14	15	Total
Ali	1	0	1	0	0	0	1	1	0	0	1	0				5
Norton	0	2	0	1	1	0	0	0	1	1	0	1				7

Judge: Hal Rickards

Round	1	2	3	4	5	6	7	8	9	10	11	12	13	14	15	Total
Ali	0	0	1	0	1	0	0	1	0	0	1	0				4
Norton	0	1	0	1	0	0	0	0	1	1	0	1				5

Judge: Fred Hayes

Round	1	2	3	4	5	6	7	8	9	10	11	12	13	14	15	Total
Ali	1	0	1	0	0	1	1	1	0	1	0	0				6
Norton	0	1	0	1	0	0	0	0	1	0	1	1				5

Date:	September 10, 1973					City: Inglewood, CA				Venue: Inglewood Forum						
Opponent:	Ken Norton															
Result:	Ali by split decision -- Regained NABF Heavyweight Title															

Referee: Dick Young

Round	1	2	3	4	5	6	7	8	9	10	11	12	13	14	15	Total
Ali	1	1	1	1	0	1	0	0	1	0	0	1				7
Norton	0	0	0	0	1	0	1	1	0	1	1	0				5

Judge: John Thomas

Round	1	2	3	4	5	6	7	8	9	10	11	12	13	14	15	Total
Ali	1	1	1	0	0	1	0	0	1	0	0	1				6
Norton	0	0	0	0	1	0	1	1	0	1	1	0				5

Judge: George Latka

Round	1	2	3	4	5	6	7	8	9	10	11	12	13	14	15	Total
Ali	1	1	1	0	1	0	0	0	0	0	0	1				5
Norton	0	0	0	0	0	1	1	1	1	1	1	0				6

Date:	October 20, 1973					City: Jakarta, Indonesia				Venue: Bung Karno Stadium						
Opponent:	Rudi Lubbers															
Result:	Ali by unanimous decision															

Judge: Lim Kee Chan

Round	1	2	3	4	5	6	7	8	9	10	11	12	13	14	15	Total
Ali	5	5	5	5	5	5	5	5	5	5	5	5				60
Lubbers																45

Judge: Leon Johannes

Round	1	2	3	4	5	6	7	8	9	10	11	12	13	14	15	Total
Ali																59
Lubbers																52

Judge: Chris Scinneder

Round	1	2	3	4	5	6	7	8	9	10	11	12	13	14	15	Total
Ali	5	5	5	5	5	5	5	5	5	5	5	5				60
Lubbers																40

Date:	January 28, 1974					City: New York, NY				Venue: Madison Square Garden						
Opponent:	Joe Frazier															
Result:	Ali by unanimous decision -- Retained NABF Heavyweight Title															

Referee: Tony Perez

Round	1	2	3	4	5	6	7	8	9	10	11	12	13	14	15	Total
Ali	X	X		E	X	X			X		X					6 (1E)
Frazier			X	E			X	X		X		X				5 (1E)

Judge: Tony Castellano

Round	1	2	3	4	5	6	7	8	9	10	11	12	13	14	15	Total
Ali	X	X	X	E		X			X		X	X				7 (1E)
Frazier				E	X		X	X		X						4 (1E)

Judge: Jack Gordon

Round	1	2	3	4	5	6	7	8	9	10	11	12	13	14	15	Total
Ali	X	X		X	X	X			X	X	X					8
Frazier			X				X	X				X				4

153

MUHAMMAD ALI UD 12 JIMMY ELLIS
07/26/71 - HOUSTON

Total Punches Landed / Thrown												
	1	2	3	4	5	6	7	8	9	10	11	12
ALI	4/23	10/44	7/18	26/66	10/47	18/42	12/57	21/59	19/56	25/71	19/60	18/54
	17.4%	22.7%	38.9%	39.4%	21.3%	42.9%	21.1%	35.6%	33.9%	35.2%	31.7%	33.3%
ELLIS	15/38	7/23	17/56	11/45	11/34	9/39	13/37	11/40	12/50	5/27	6/41	1/9
	39.5%	30.4%	30.4%	24.4%	32.4%	23.1%	35.1%	27.5%	24%	18.5%	14.6%	11.1%

Jab Landed / Thrown												
	1	2	3	4	5	6	7	8	9	10	11	12
ALI	4/20	7/33	7/12	16/36	10/43	18/39	10/39	14/36	12/36	12/42	14/40	7/25
	20%	21.2%	58.3%	44.4%	23.3%	46.2%	25.6%	38.9%	33.3%	28.6%	35%	28%
ELLIS	8/20	4/15	8/39	4/25	8/22	5/29	8/24	4/23	9/40	1/16	3/25	1/6
	40%	26.7%	20.5%	16%	36.4%	17.2%	33.3%	17.4%	22.5%	6.3%	12%	16.7%

Power Punches Landed / Thrown												
	1	2	3	4	5	6	7	8	9	10	11	12
ALI	0/3	3/11	0/6	10/30	0/4	0/3	2/18	7/23	7/20	13/29	5/20	11/29
	0%	27.3%	0%	33.3%	0%	0%	11.1%	30.4%	35%	44.8%	25%	37.9%
ELLIS	7/18	3/8	9/17	7/20	3/12	4/10	5/13	7/17	3/10	4/11	3/16	0/3
	38.9%	37.5%	52.9%	35%	25%	40%	38.5%	41.2%	30%	36.4%	18.8%	0%

Final Punch Stat Report			
	Total Punches (Body Landed)	Total Jabs (Body Landed)	Power Punches (Body Landed)
ALI	189 (7)/597	131 (3)/401	58 (4)/196
	31.7%	32.7%	29.6%
ELLIS	118 (59)/439	63 (18)/284	55 (41)/155
	26.9%	22.2%	35.5%

MUHAMMAD ALI UD 12 BUSTER MATHIS SR.
11/17/71 - HOUSTON

Total Punches Landed / Thrown												
	1	2	3	4	5	6	7	8	9	10	11	12
ALI	9/39	11/63	11/58	10/46	13/57	19/76	17/59	9/57	14/68	15/81	23/88	21/78
	23.1%	17.5%	19%	21.7%	22.8%	25%	28.8%	15.8%	20.6%	18.5%	26.1%	26.9%
MATHIS SR.	7/24	8/33	12/43	5/22	10/32	9/21	8/26	19/45	10/33	10/36	5/27	5/21
	29.2%	24.2%	27.9%	22.7%	31.3%	42.9%	30.8%	42.2%	30.3%	27.8%	18.5%	23.8%

Jab Landed / Thrown												
	1	2	3	4	5	6	7	8	9	10	11	12
ALI	8/37	11/53	3/27	8/37	7/30	17/53	16/49	6/30	5/34	8/43	14/46	7/35
	21.6%	20.8%	11.1%	21.6%	23.3%	32.1%	32.7%	20%	14.7%	18.6%	30.4%	20%
MATHIS SR.	4/16	5/23	3/13	3/14	1/7	3/8	0/11	0/3	1/4	1/10	0/3	1/4
	25%	21.7%	23.1%	21.4%	14.3%	37.5%	0%	0%	25%	10%	0%	25%

Power Punches Landed / Thrown												
	1	2	3	4	5	6	7	8	9	10	11	12
ALI	1/2	0/10	8/31	2/9	6/27	2/23	1/10	3/27	9/34	7/38	9/42	14/43
	50%	0%	25.8%	22.2%	22.2%	8.7%	10%	11.1%	26.5%	18.4%	21.4%	32.6%
MATHIS SR.	3/8	3/10	9/30	2/8	9/25	6/13	8/15	19/42	9/29	9/26	5/24	4/17
	37.5%	30%	30%	25%	36%	46.2%	53.3%	45.2%	31%	34.6%	20.8%	23.5%

Final Punch Stat Report		
	Total Punches (Body Landed)	Total Jabs (Body Landed)	Power Punches (Body Landed)
ALI	172 (7)/770	110 (0)/474	62 (7)/296
	22.3%	23.2%	20.9%
MATHIS SR.	108 (53)/363	22 (7)/116	86 (46)/247
	29.8%	19%	34.8%

MUHAMMAD ALI KO 7 JUERGEN BLIN
12/26/71 - ZURICH

Total Punches Landed / Thrown												
	1	2	3	4	5	6	7	8	9	10	11	12
ALI	14/58	14/42	17/50	11/34	29/60	9/33	22/49	-/-	-/-	-/-	-/-	-/-
	24.1%	33.3%	34%	32.4%	48.3%	27.3%	44.9%	-	-	-	-	-
BLIN	9/35	9/44	6/57	1/20	5/40	10/58	1/18	-/-	-/-	-/-	-/-	-/-
	25.7%	20.5%	10.5%	5%	12.5%	17.2%	5.6%	-	-	-	-	-

Jab Landed / Thrown												
	1	2	3	4	5	6	7	8	9	10	11	12
ALI	12/41	12/38	9/30	11/33	20/40	6/25	8/21	-/-	-/-	-/-	-/-	-/-
	29.3%	31.6%	30%	33.3%	50%	24%	38.1%	-	-	-	-	-
BLIN	5/17	4/17	2/21	0/7	3/13	6/27	0/6	-/-	-/-	-/-	-/-	-/-
	29.4%	23.5%	9.5%	0%	23.1%	22.2%	0%	-	-	-	-	-

Power Punches Landed / Thrown												
	1	2	3	4	5	6	7	8	9	10	11	12
ALI	2/17	2/4	8/20	0/1	9/20	3/8	14/28	-/-	-/-	-/-	-/-	-/-
	11.8%	50%	40%	0%	45%	37.5%	50%	-	-	-	-	-
BLIN	4/18	5/27	4/36	1/13	2/27	4/31	1/12	-/-	-/-	-/-	-/-	-/-
	22.2%	18.5%	11.1%	7.7%	7.4%	12.9%	8.3%	-	-	-	-	-

Final Punch Stat Report		
	Total Punches (Body Landed)	Total Jabs (Body Landed)	Power Punches (Body Landed)
ALI	116 (2)/326	78 (1)/228	38 (1)/98
	35.6%	34.2%	38.8%
BLIN	41 (11)/272	20 (8)/108	21 (3)/164
	15.1%	18.5%	12.8%

MUHAMMAD ALI UD 15 MAC FOSTER
04/01/72 - Tokyo

Total Punches Landed / Thrown															
	1	2	3	4	5	6	7	8	9	10	11	12	13	14	15
ALI	19/76	11/32	32/86	36/98	34/94	20/50	11/59	25/75	35/108	15/41	40/113	25/79	28/74	29/89	20/58
	25%	34.4%	37.2%	36.7%	36.2%	40%	18.6%	33.3%	32.4%	36.6%	35.4%	31.6%	37.8%	32.6%	34.5%
FOSTER	13/38	46/78	25/69	23/50	24/53	2/19	38/65	24/54	13/34	29/78	8/27	17/50	6/26	12/41	5/22
	34.2%	59%	36.2%	46%	45.3%	10.5%	58.5%	44.4%	38.2%	37.2%	29.6%	34%	23.1%	29.3%	22.7%

Jab Landed / Thrown															
	1	2	3	4	5	6	7	8	9	10	11	12	13	14	15
ALI	8/40	6/17	20/60	19/55	8/32	18/46	8/39	22/56	24/82	8/23	17/54	20/49	24/63	21/56	16/44
	20%	35.3%	33.3%	34.5%	25%	39.1%	20.5%	39.3%	29.3%	34.8%	31.5%	40.8%	38.1%	37.5%	36.4%
FOSTER	3/12	14/32	9/25	7/14	5/11	1/13	1/7	1/6	4/7	1/5	1/5	3/12	2/13	5/17	1/5
	25%	43.8%	36%	50%	45.5%	7.7%	14.3%	16.7%	57.1%	20%	20%	25%	15.4%	29.4%	20%

Power Punches Landed / Thrown															
	1	2	3	4	5	6	7	8	9	10	11	12	13	14	15
ALI	11/36	5/15	12/26	17/43	26/62	2/4	3/20	3/19	11/26	7/18	23/59	5/30	4/11	8/33	4/14
	30.6%	33.3%	46.2%	39.5%	41.9%	50%	15%	15.8%	42.3%	38.9%	39%	16.7%	36.4%	24.2%	28.6%
FOSTER	10/26	32/46	16/44	16/36	19/42	1/6	37/58	23/48	9/27	28/73	7/22	14/38	4/13	7/24	4/17
	38.5%	69.6%	36.4%	44.4%	45.2%	16.7%	63.8%	47.9%	33.3%	38.4%	31.8%	36.8%	30.8%	29.2%	23.5%

Final Punch Stat Report			
Total	Total Punches	Total Jabs	Power Punches
ALI	380/1132	239/716	141/416
	33.6%	33.4%	33.9%
FOSTER	285/704	58/184	227/520
	40.5%	31.5%	43.7%

MUHAMMAD ALI UD 12 GEORGE CHUVALO
05/01/72 - VANCOUVER, B.C.

Total Punches Landed / Thrown												
	1	2	3	4	5	6	7	8	9	10	11	12
ALI	18/44	20/46	21/39	16/37	23/45	40/96	27/50	28/53	54/105	21/53	28/77	45/105
	40.9%	43.5%	53.8%	43.2%	51.1%	41.7%	54%	52.8%	51.4%	39.6%	36.4%	42.9%
CHUVALO	14/32	9/27	12/33	10/35	9/36	6/29	18/45	16/40	27/55	20/50	15/34	21/41
	43.8%	33.3%	36.4%	28.6%	25%	20.7%	40%	40%	49.1%	40%	44.1%	51.2%

Jab Landed / Thrown												
	1	2	3	4	5	6	7	8	9	10	11	12
ALI	13/32	15/33	15/26	14/27	16/31	21/48	20/36	23/40	33/59	10/27	15/44	17/42
	40.6%	45.5%	57.7%	51.9%	51.6%	43.8%	55.6%	57.5%	55.9%	37%	34.1%	40.5%
CHUVALO	7/23	2/15	1/12	0/13	2/18	1/14	5/14	3/15	3/13	1/7	0/7	0/6
	30.4%	13.3%	8.3%	0%	11.1%	7.1%	35.7%	20%	23.1%	14.3%	0%	0%

Power Punches Landed / Thrown												
	1	2	3	4	5	6	7	8	9	10	11	12
ALI	5/12	5/13	6/13	2/10	7/14	19/48	7/14	5/13	21/46	11/26	13/33	28/63
	41.7%	38.5%	46.2%	20%	50%	39.6%	50%	38.5%	45.7%	42.3%	39.4%	44.4%
CHUVALO	7/9	7/12	11/21	10/22	7/18	5/15	13/31	13/25	24/42	19/43	15/27	21/35
	77.8%	58.3%	52.4%	45.5%	38.9%	33.3%	41.9%	52%	57.1%	44.2%	55.6%	60%

Final Punch Stat Report			
	Total Punches (Body Landed)	Total Jabs (Body Landed)	Power Punches (Body Landed)
ALI	341 (15)/750	212 (3)/445	129 (12)/305
	45.5%	47.6%	42.3%
CHUVALO	177 (110)/457	25 (1)/157	152 (109)/300
	38.7%	15.9%	50.7%

MUHAMMAD ALI TKO 7 JERRY QUARRY
06/27/72 - LAS VEGAS

Total Punches Landed / Thrown												
	1	2	3	4	5	6	7	8	9	10	11	12
ALI	7/34	9/30	13/45	19/62	22/65	38/101	7/9	-/-	-/-	-/-	-/-	-/-
	20.6%	30%	28.9%	30.6%	33.8%	37.6%	77.8%	-	-	-	-	-
QUARRY	6/24	18/37	8/27	6/27	8/21	14/35	0/1	-/-	-/-	-/-	-/-	-/-
	25%	48.6%	29.6%	22.2%	38.1%	40%	0%	-	-	-	-	-

Jab Landed / Thrown												
	1	2	3	4	5	6	7	8	9	10	11	12
ALI	6/28	7/23	9/31	11/42	16/50	13/36	0/1	-/-	-/-	-/-	-/-	-/-
	21.4%	30.4%	29%	26.2%	32%	36.1%	0%	-	-	-	-	-
QUARRY	2/5	1/9	1/4	1/8	2/4	0/8	0/0	-/-	-/-	-/-	-/-	-/-
	40%	11.1%	25%	12.5%	50%	0%	0%	-	-	-	-	-

Power Punches Landed / Thrown												
	1	2	3	4	5	6	7	8	9	10	11	12
ALI	1/6	2/7	4/14	8/20	6/15	25/65	7/8	-/-	-/-	-/-	-/-	-/-
	16.7%	28.6%	28.6%	40%	40%	38.5%	87.5%	-	-	-	-	-
QUARRY	4/19	17/28	7/23	5/19	6/17	14/27	0/1	-/-	-/-	-/-	-/-	-/-
	21.1%	60.7%	30.4%	26.3%	35.3%	51.9%	0%	-	-	-	-	-

Final Punch Stat Report			
	Total Punches (Body Landed)	Total Jabs (Body Landed)	Power Punches (Body Landed)
ALI	115 (1)/346	62 (0)/211	53 (1)/135
	33.2%	29.4%	39.3%
QUARRY	60 (43)/172	7 (4)/38	53 (39)/134
	34.9%	18.4%	39.6%

159

MUHAMMAD ALI TKO 11 AL LEWIS
07/19/72 - DUBLIN, IRELAND

Total Punches Landed / Thrown												
	1	2	3	4	5	6	7	8	9	10	11	12
ALI	13/44	36/61	19/49	18/55	38/69	46/93	57/90	29/69	38/69	44/107	15/25	-/-
	29.5%	59%	38.8%	32.7%	55.1%	49.5%	63.3%	42%	55.1%	41.1%	60%	-
LEWIS	12/38	9/46	12/55	7/36	12/46	17/43	14/45	18/44	25/67	12/38	0/5	-/-
	31.6%	19.6%	21.8%	19.4%	26.1%	39.5%	31.1%	40.9%	37.3%	31.6%	0%	-

Jab Landed / Thrown												
	1	2	3	4	5	6	7	8	9	10	11	12
ALI	8/21	31/47	6/26	12/38	22/39	11/29	37/56	3/20	11/21	15/49	14/24	-/-
	38.1%	66%	23.1%	31.6%	56.4%	37.9%	66.1%	15%	52.4%	30.6%	58.3%	-
LEWIS	8/24	4/37	6/39	4/20	6/34	6/26	9/32	8/29	11/36	6/27	0/5	-/-
	33.3%	10.8%	15.4%	20%	17.6%	23.1%	28.1%	27.6%	30.6%	22.2%	0%	-

Power Punches Landed / Thrown												
	1	2	3	4	5	6	7	8	9	10	11	12
ALI	5/23	5/14	13/23	6/17	16/30	35/64	20/34	26/49	27/48	29/58	1/1	-/-
	21.7%	35.7%	56.5%	35.3%	53.3%	54.7%	58.8%	53.1%	56.3%	50%	100%	-
LEWIS	4/14	5/9	6/16	3/16	6/12	11/17	5/13	10/15	14/31	6/11	0/0	-/-
	28.6%	55.6%	37.5%	18.8%	50%	64.7%	38.5%	66.7%	45.2%	54.5%	0%	-

Final Punch Stat Report		
	Total Punches (Body Landed)	Total Jabs (Body Landed)	Power Punches (Body Landed)
ALI	353 (74)/731	170 (60)/370	183 (14)/361
	48.3%	45.9%	50.7%
LEWIS	138 (32)/463	68 (11)/309	70 (21)/154
	29.8%	22%	45.5%

MUHAMMAD ALI TKO 7 FLOYD PATTERSON
09/20/72 - NEW YORK

Total Punches Landed / Thrown												
	1	2	3	4	5	6	7	8	9	10	11	12
ALI	1/24	4/25	10/41	8/33	6/39	10/68	17/56	-/-	-/-	-/-	-/-	-/-
	4.2%	16%	24.4%	24.2%	15.4%	14.7%	30.4%	-	-	-	-	-
PATTERSON	9/23	14/36	15/40	18/62	21/41	13/29	11/24	-/-	-/-	-/-	-/-	-/-
	39.1%	38.9%	37.5%	29%	51.2%	44.8%	45.8%	-	-	-	-	-

Jab Landed / Thrown												
	1	2	3	4	5	6	7	8	9	10	11	12
ALI	1/23	4/25	3/24	8/30	0/19	1/17	8/24	-/-	-/-	-/-	-/-	-/-
	4.3%	16%	12.5%	26.7%	0%	5.9%	33.3%	-	-	-	-	-
PATTERSON	3/7	1/8	1/9	1/21	0/2	1/3	4/7	-/-	-/-	-/-	-/-	-/-
	42.9%	12.5%	11.1%	4.8%	0%	33.3%	57.1%	-	-	-	-	-

Power Punches Landed / Thrown												
	1	2	3	4	5	6	7	8	9	10	11	12
ALI	0/1	0/0	7/17	0/3	6/20	9/51	9/32	-/-	-/-	-/-	-/-	-/-
	0%	0%	41.2%	0%	30%	17.6%	28.1%	-	-	-	-	-
PATTERSON	6/16	13/28	14/31	17/41	21/39	12/26	7/17	-/-	-/-	-/-	-/-	-/-
	37.5%	46.4%	45.2%	41.5%	53.8%	46.2%	41.2%	-	-	-	-	-

Final Punch Stat Report		
Total Punches (Body Landed)	Total Jabs (Body Landed)	Power Punches (Body Landed)
ALI		
56 (1)/286	25 (0)/162	31 (1)/124
19.6%	15.4%	25%
PATTERSON		
101 (55)/255	11 (0)/57	90 (55)/198
39.6%	19.3%	45.5%

MUHAMMAD ALI KO 8 BOB FOSTER
11/21/72 - STATELINE, NV

Total Punches Landed / Thrown												
	1	2	3	4	5	6	7	8	9	10	11	12
ALI	13/51	16/56	6/26	17/52	22/63	8/38	11/38	1/6	-/-	-/-	-/-	-/-
	25.5%	28.6%	23.1%	32.7%	34.9%	21.1%	28.9%	16.7%	-	-	-	-
FOSTER	6/21	16/41	15/45	21/43	7/35	4/16	17/32	1/1	-/-	-/-	-/-	-/-
	28.6%	39%	33.3%	48.8%	20%	25%	53.1%	100%	-	-	-	-

Jab Landed / Thrown												
	1	2	3	4	5	6	7	8	9	10	11	12
ALI	10/43	10/40	1/11	14/37	0/0	8/35	5/21	0/3	-/-	-/-	-/-	-/-
	23.3%	25%	9.1%	37.8%	0%	22.9%	23.8%	0%	-	-	-	-
FOSTER	5/20	16/39	9/31	17/36	3/16	4/16	14/27	1/1	-/-	-/-	-/-	-/-
	25%	41%	29%	47.2%	18.8%	25%	51.9%	100%	-	-	-	-

Power Punches Landed / Thrown												
	1	2	3	4	5	6	7	8	9	10	11	12
ALI	3/8	6/16	5/15	3/15	22/63	0/3	6/17	1/3	-/-	-/-	-/-	-/-
	37.5%	37.5%	33.3%	20%	34.9%	0%	35.3%	33.3%	-	-	-	-
FOSTER	1/1	0/2	6/14	4/7	4/19	0/0	3/5	0/0	-/-	-/-	-/-	-/-
	100%	0%	42.9%	57.1%	21.1%	0%	60%	0%	-	-	-	-

Final Punch Stat Report			
	Total Punches (Body Landed)	Total Jabs (Body Landed)	Power Punches (Body Landed)
ALI	94 (1)/330	48 (0)/190	46 (1)/140
	28.5%	25.3%	32.9%
FOSTER	87 (27)/234	69 (18)/186	18 (9)/48
	37.2%	37.1%	37.5%

162

MUHAMMAD ALI UD 12 JOE BUGNER
02/14/73 - LAS VEGAS

Total Punches Landed / Thrown												
	1	2	3	4	5	6	7	8	9	10	11	12
ALI	18/29	13/33	12/23	13/25	10/21	20/57	23/49	13/20	10/24	33/70	15/37	26/52
	62.1%	39.4%	52.2%	52%	47.6%	35.1%	46.9%	65%	41.7%	47.1%	40.5%	50%
BUGNER	7/31	10/43	9/34	16/45	10/42	2/23	8/44	10/28	6/20	0/10	4/23	11/37
	22.6%	23.3%	26.5%	35.6%	23.8%	8.7%	18.2%	35.7%	30%	0%	17.4%	29.7%

Jab Landed / Thrown												
	1	2	3	4	5	6	7	8	9	10	11	12
ALI	9/16	6/17	12/20	7/14	5/12	12/24	5/16	13/19	8/17	12/27	7/25	7/17
	56.3%	35.3%	60%	50%	41.7%	50%	31.3%	68.4%	47.1%	44.4%	28%	41.2%
BUGNER	3/19	6/27	4/20	11/31	7/29	1/15	6/29	4/14	3/12	0/5	2/13	2/15
	15.8%	22.2%	20%	35.5%	24.1%	6.7%	20.7%	28.6%	25%	0%	15.4%	13.3%

Power Punches Landed / Thrown												
	1	2	3	4	5	6	7	8	9	10	11	12
ALI	9/13	7/16	0/3	6/11	5/9	8/33	18/33	0/1	2/7	21/43	8/12	19/35
	69.2%	43.8%	0%	54.5%	55.6%	24.2%	54.5%	0%	28.6%	48.8%	66.7%	54.3%
BUGNER	4/12	4/16	5/14	5/14	3/13	1/8	2/15	6/14	3/8	0/5	2/10	9/22
	33.3%	25%	35.7%	35.7%	23.1%	12.5%	13.3%	42.9%	37.5%	0%	20%	40.9%

Final Punch Stat Report		
	Total Punches (Body Landed)	Total Jabs (Body Landed)	Power Punches (Body Landed)
ALI	206 (12)/440	103 (5)/224	103 (7)/216
	46.8%	46%	47.7%
BUGNER	93 (41)/380	49 (16)/229	44 (25)/151
	24.5%	21.4%	29.1%

KEN NORTON SD 12 MUHAMMAD ALI
03/31/73 - SAN DIEGO

Total Punches Landed / Thrown												
	1	2	3	4	5	6	7	8	9	10	11	12
ALI	15/63	12/46	11/53	9/29	15/64	13/56	12/51	13/57	9/49	17/50	36/92	9/45
	23.8%	26.1%	20.8%	31%	23.4%	23.2%	23.5%	22.8%	18.4%	34%	39.1%	20%
NORTON	14/31	34/54	10/22	23/69	22/57	15/36	13/34	10/27	30/55	23/53	10/36	29/68
	45.2%	63%	45.5%	33.3%	38.6%	41.7%	38.2%	37%	54.5%	43.4%	27.8%	42.6%

Jab Landed / Thrown												
	1	2	3	4	5	6	7	8	9	10	11	12
ALI	9/36	7/33	8/39	0/11	9/46	2/30	8/37	12/42	7/34	9/31	17/54	5/23
	25%	21.2%	20.5%	0%	19.6%	6.7%	21.6%	28.6%	20.6%	29%	31.5%	21.7%
NORTON	11/23	17/31	4/11	8/28	14/33	11/26	10/20	4/14	15/29	7/22	3/14	5/15
	47.8%	54.8%	36.4%	28.6%	42.4%	42.3%	50%	28.6%	51.7%	31.8%	21.4%	33.3%

Power Punches Landed / Thrown												
	1	2	3	4	5	6	7	8	9	10	11	12
ALI	6/27	5/13	3/14	9/18	6/18	11/26	4/14	1/15	2/15	8/19	19/38	4/22
	22.2%	38.5%	21.4%	50%	33.3%	42.3%	28.6%	6.7%	13.3%	42.1%	50%	18.2%
NORTON	3/8	17/23	6/11	15/41	8/24	4/10	3/14	6/13	15/26	16/31	7/22	24/53
	37.5%	73.9%	54.5%	36.6%	33.3%	40%	21.4%	46.2%	57.7%	51.6%	31.8%	45.3%

Final Punch Stat Report		
Total Punches (Body Landed)	Total Jabs (Body Landed)	Power Punches (Body Landed)
ALI		
171 (0)/655	93 (0)/416	78 (0)/239
26.1%	22.4%	32.6%
NORTON		
233 (0)/542	109 (0)/266	124 (0)/276
43%	41%	44.9%

MUHAMMAD ALI SD 12 KEN NORTON
09/10/73 - INGLEWOOD,CA

Total Punches Landed / Thrown												
	1	2	3	4	5	6	7	8	9	10	11	12
ALI	11/40	7/42	10/37	10/40	14/42	18/57	11/43	16/66	20/70	12/52	18/60	28/69
	27.5%	16.7%	27%	25%	33.3%	31.6%	25.6%	24.2%	28.6%	23.1%	30%	40.6%
NORTON	3/11	7/15	9/24	15/34	16/42	17/48	26/66	26/54	23/60	14/36	27/61	14/39
	27.3%	46.7%	37.5%	44.1%	38.1%	35.4%	39.4%	48.1%	38.3%	38.9%	44.3%	35.9%

Jab Landed / Thrown												
	1	2	3	4	5	6	7	8	9	10	11	12
ALI	5/23	7/33	6/22	7/29	8/22	9/38	8/29	6/36	7/44	7/32	5/19	9/25
	21.7%	21.2%	27.3%	24.1%	36.4%	23.7%	27.6%	16.7%	15.9%	21.9%	26.3%	36%
NORTON	0/5	3/7	5/15	8/24	5/22	10/26	6/20	2/12	8/31	4/15	1/4	1/8
	0%	42.9%	33.3%	33.3%	22.7%	38.5%	30%	16.7%	25.8%	26.7%	25%	12.5%

Power Punches Landed / Thrown												
	1	2	3	4	5	6	7	8	9	10	11	12
ALI	6/17	0/9	4/15	3/11	6/20	9/19	3/14	10/30	13/26	5/20	13/41	19/44
	35.3%	0%	26.7%	27.3%	30%	47.4%	21.4%	33.3%	50%	25%	31.7%	43.2%
NORTON	3/6	4/8	4/9	7/10	11/20	7/22	20/46	24/42	15/29	10/21	26/57	13/31
	50%	50%	44.4%	70%	55%	31.8%	43.5%	57.1%	51.7%	47.6%	45.6%	41.9%

Final Punch Stat Report			
	Total Punches (Body Landed)	Total Jabs (Body Landed)	Power Punches (Body Landed)
ALI	175 (5)/618	84 (0)/352	91 (5)/266
	28.3%	23.9%	34.2%
NORTON	197 (62)/490	53 (5)/189	144 (57)/301
	40.2%	28%	47.8%

MUHAMMAD ALI UD 12 JOE FRAZIER
01/28/74 - NEW YORK

Total Punches Landed / Thrown												
	1	2	3	4	5	6	7	8	9	10	11	12
ALI	10/49	15/58	12/49	14/47	13/47	17/69	13/50	8/50	30/96	9/67	21/73	19/65
	20.4%	25.9%	24.5%	29.8%	27.7%	24.6%	26%	16%	31.3%	13.4%	28.8%	29.2%
FRAZIER	7/19	12/26	13/40	14/28	15/37	10/27	17/34	14/31	12/32	20/35	19/39	19/58
	36.8%	46.2%	32.5%	50%	40.5%	37%	50%	45.2%	37.5%	57.1%	48.7%	32.8%

Jab Landed / Thrown												
	1	2	3	4	5	6	7	8	9	10	11	12
ALI	1/10	1/16	2/11	3/18	2/17	6/34	4/18	0/19	8/35	3/34	4/26	3/20
	10%	6.3%	18.2%	16.7%	11.8%	17.6%	22.2%	0%	22.9%	8.8%	15.4%	15%
FRAZIER	0/1	0/3	1/6	0/2	1/4	0/1	0/3	0/1	0/1	2/2	1/2	0/2
	0%	0%	16.7%	0%	25%	0%	0%	0%	0%	100%	50%	0%

Power Punches Landed / Thrown												
	1	2	3	4	5	6	7	8	9	10	11	12
ALI	9/39	14/42	10/38	11/29	11/30	11/35	9/32	8/31	22/61	6/33	17/47	16/45
	23.1%	33.3%	26.3%	37.9%	36.7%	31.4%	28.1%	25.8%	36.1%	18.2%	36.2%	35.6%
FRAZIER	7/18	12/23	12/34	14/26	14/33	10/26	17/31	14/30	12/31	18/33	18/37	19/56
	38.9%	52.2%	35.3%	53.8%	42.4%	38.5%	54.8%	46.7%	38.7%	54.5%	48.6%	33.9%

Final Punch Stat Report			
	Total Punches (Body Landed)	Total Jabs (Body Landed)	Power Punches (Body Landed)
ALI	181 (0)/720	37 (0)/258	144 (0)/462
	25.1%	14.3%	31.2%
FRAZIER	172 (0)/406	5 (0)/28	167 (0)/378
	42.4%	17.9%	44.2%

21.

OCTOBER 30, 1974 - STADE DU 20 MAI, KINSHASA, ZAIRE
MUHAMMAD ALI KO 8 GEORGE FOREMAN

When Ali emerged from an exile that lasted a little more than 43 months, more than a few believed the 28-year-old would quickly reclaim the throne that had been his during the prime years of his athletic life. That all changed March 8, 1971 when Joe Frazier, the man who seized the crown in Ali's absence, used his powerful hooks and gargantuan will to win their one-of-a-kind showdown at Madison Square Garden.

That defeat forced Ali to continue what would become a seven-year odyssey to regain the undisputed heavyweight title. But even for a man accustomed to producing sporting magic, Ali couldn't have fathomed a more theatrical end to his championship chase: Fighting in the heart of central Africa against one of history's most dangerous punchers in champion George Foreman, Ali reacquired the title -- by knockout -- with the most extraordinary example of strategic improvisation ever produced inside a boxing ring, a tactic Ali later dubbed the "Rope-a Dope." The sight of referee Zach Clayton waving off the fight with just two seconds remaining in round eight unleashed a tidal wave of joy that instantly enveloped the globe. The deafening cheers and arm-waving celebrations of the 62,000 souls that jammed into Stade du 20 Mai in Kinshasa, Zaire reflected similar unseen displays at dozens of closed-circuit outlets worldwide. In that moment, because of the weight of his feat and the magnitude of the prize he had just regained, Muhammad Ali the athlete was transformed into Muhammad Ali the icon.

Thanks in part to the machinations of a frizzy-haired ex-con named Don King, Foreman versus Ali was instantly changed from dream fight to reality. Even before financing was secured for the fight, King convinced Foreman and Ali to sign on the dotted line, after which the funds were guaranteed through four entities: Video Techniques, Panama's Risnella Investment, the British-based Hemdale Film Corporation and Zaire's dictator Mobutu Sese Seko, who wanted to use the fight to vault his nation into the financial mainstream. (1) Both fighters were promised a record $5 million purse, twice the amount Ali and Frazier each made four years earlier, but, according to biographer Thomas Hauser, Ali received $5.45 million. (2)

For Ali, the Foreman match must have been a case of deja vu, for while his antagonists were different individuals, they presented a similar set of obstacles. At the same time, however, Ali was forced to address several changes in his own ability level.

In the waning days of his life as Cassius Marcellus Clay, Ali won his first heavyweight championship from Charles "Sonny" Liston, who, coming in, was regarded by many as the most fearsome force the division had ever seen. Against Foreman, however, Ali faced an even more daunting physical and chronological challenge.

167

The 22-year-old Clay was 11 years younger than Liston and was light years ahead of the champion in terms of hand and foot speed, but against Foreman the 32-year-old Ali was seven years older and was noticeably slower than the version that dethroned "The Big Ugly Bear." At 6-foot-3 1/2-inches, Foreman stood three inches taller than Liston and sported a more powerful physique. While Liston operated behind an underrated jab, Foreman was a search-and-destroy volume puncher that crushed most opponents in short order. Going into the Ali fight, Foreman's record was 40-0 and of his 37 knockouts, of which 21 occurred within the first two rounds -- including his last seven fights. Among those seven victims were Frazier and Norton, the only two men to defeat Ali. Not only did Foreman beat them, he pulverized them; he floored Frazier six times and Norton three times before finishing them off in a combined 10 minutes 26 seconds of ring time. Worse yet for Ali, most of their falls were of the spectacular, highlight reel variety. Many Ali fans feared the same fate for their hero.

Foreman was installed as a relatively narrow 3-to-1 favorite but the general sentiment at the time placed even greater odds against Ali. The following quote by the *New York Times'* Dave Anderson reflected that conventional wisdom:

"George Foreman might be the heaviest puncher in the history of the heavyweight division. For a few rounds, Ali might be able to escape Foreman's sledgehammer strength, but not for 15 rounds. Sooner or later, the champion will land one of his sledgehammer punches, and for the first time in his career, Muhammad Ali will be counted out. That could happen in the first round." (3)

In honor of his mentor Liston, with whom Foreman sparred occasionally, the intrinsically amiable Texan amplified his frightful in-ring performances by projecting a brooding, intimidating persona. He often wore a sneer while giving brief, violence-laden answers to reporters' questions.

"My opponents don't worry about losing," Foreman said. "They worry about getting hurt." (4)

In his autobiography "By George," Foreman revealed he contemplated killing an opponent to answer all questions about his worth as a fighter.

"Having demolished Joe Frazier, I didn't expect to hear doubts about my skill. But there they were. 'George fought a tomato can' some people said after the Joe Roman fight. What's he so scared of?' I realized such comments were motivated by my growing reputation as the champ you loved to hate. But I couldn't ignore them. In too many ways I was still the kid from Fifth Ward, fighting to be king of the jungle. I intended to convince every last doubter. 'I'm going to kill one of these fools,' I decided. 'Then everyone'll shut up.' The 'fool' I chose was Ken Norton." (5)

The neck-wrenching uppercuts that flattened Norton were a scary sight and after the fight he looked down at Ali, who was doing color commentary for ABC, and said, "I'm going to kill you." (6) Foreman saw fear in Ali's eyes that night but the former champ sure didn't act like it as he proceeded to launch a full-frontal verbal and psychological assault that harkened back to his first fights against Liston and Frazier.

His multi-pronged attack began by ingratiating himself with the local populace through frequent public workouts, humor-filled press conferences and removing all walls between himself and his admirers. Ali repeatedly said that the Zairian people were "my people" and held up their country as a positive example of black leadership. After learning the Lingala word for "kill him" -- "bomaye" -- he made the "Ali, bomaye" chant a staple of his public appearances.

Another part of the master plan was to dub Foreman "The Mummy" for his heavy-legged stalking and his slow, easily countered punches.

"George telegraphs his punches," Ali said. "Look out, here comes the left. Whomp! Here comes the right. Whomp! Get ready, here comes another left. Whomp! I'm not scared of George. George ain't all that tough." (7)

Foreman wasn't without his supporters but they were dwarfed by those who threw their full-throated support to Ali. Foreman virtually ceded Ali the "home crowd" advantage by staying in isolation most of the time, and during the rare times he ventured out he was accompanied by guard dogs. Although Foreman long had an affinity for the German Shepherd breed, to the locals it reminded them of the unpleasant days of Belgian colonial rule. (8)

While Foreman dealt with being made into public enemy number one, other parts of the promotion struggled to establish a solid foothold. A fight poster declaring the fight to be "from the slave ship to the championship" had to be replaced following a public outcry and the first set of tickets had to be shipped back and reprinted because Mobutu's name was misspelled. (9) But those snafus paled in comparison to what happened down the homestretch.

The fight originally was to begin at 3 a.m. September 25 to ensure live prime-time coverage in the U.S. but eight days out the fight was postponed after a stray elbow from sparring partner Bill McMurray sliced open the area above Foreman's right eye. The fight was rescheduled for 4 a.m. October 30 and both Ali and Foreman remained in Zaire for the duration. (10) While Foreman sulked, Ali took full advantage of the situation by ramping up his already robust PR campaign while also drawing spiritual strength from his African surroundings.

The surroundings inside the soccer stadium hosting the bout spawned a new crisis just hours before the fight was to begin. Ali's chief second Angelo Dundee and public relations guru Bobby Goodman stopped by the stadium to check out the ring. What they saw horrified them: One side of the ring had sunk into the muddy pitch, the foam rubber padding had become mushy because of the severe heat and humidity and the ropes -- which were made for a 24-foot square ring instead of the 20-footer they had -- sagged toward the floor.

Seeing this, the two future Hall of Famers became part of an impromptu ring maintenance crew. They placed concrete slabs under the corner posts to balance the ring and placed resin on the canvas to deal with the new surface's slipperiness.

"(To fix the ropes) we took off the clamps, pulled the ropes through the turnbuckles, lined everything up, and cut off the slack," Goodman told Hauser. "We took about a foot out of each rope and retightened the turnbuckles by hand so they could be tightened more just before the fight. Angelo even told the ring chief that, right before the first bout, he should tighten the ropes by turning the turnbuckle. And then, before the main event, they were supposed to tighten them again. That never happened. They just didn't do it, so by the time Ali got in the ring the ropes were slack, but there was nothing underhanded in what Angelo did. In fact, Dick Sadler and Archie Moore, who were Foreman's corner men, saw us that afternoon in the ring. Angelo and I were sweating our butts off, cutting the ropes with a double-edged razor blade because nobody could find a knife. We were pulling them through, taping up the ends. And we said, 'come on! You know, you guys can help.' But it was hot and they wouldn't give us a hand." (11)

With massive rain clouds hovering over the stadium and dozens of traditional African dancers and percussionists adding to the exotic atmosphere, Ali, as the challenger, was the first to emerge from his dressing room. Even though he flashed a small smile from time to time as he navigated the lengthy soccer pitch he looked focused and ready to fight. Team Foreman chose to make Ali wait inside the ring for an uncomfortably long time, but once the champion came out he and his team *jogged* toward the ring. Both appeared in perfect condition as Ali scaled 216.7 pounds to Foreman's 220, 30 pounds lighter than what the defending champion scaled in August. (12)

Following the introductions, each man tried to secure one final psychological advantage: Ali by chattering, Foreman by fixing a stony stare. That battle went down as a draw but the one that followed had a decisive winner.

Ali's original plan was to move constantly, use his quicker hands to beat Foreman to the punch and extend the fight to exploit Foreman's questionable stamina. Although his stick-and-move tactics won Ali the opening round, his surroundings and his opponent's tactics demanded a dramatic shift in strategy.

First, Ali realized the heavily padded canvas would deaden his legs long before the end of the scheduled 15-rounder. Second, if the canvas didn't empty his gas tank the oppressive heat and humidity -- both of which were in the 80s even at 4 a.m. -- would. Finally, Foreman proved himself quite adept at cutting off the ring, which meant Ali would expend more energy getting to his escape routes than Foreman would by blocking them. Even worse for Ali: The available space inside the ropes was 19 feet square instead of the usual 20. (13)

Foreman's first-round effectiveness was reflected in the statistics, which saw Foreman land 17 of 43 punches, including 14 of 35 power shots. Ali, for his part, attempted only 30 punches, landing nine, and his jab was limited to just 3 of 13.

To Ali, every equation added up to disaster. Thus, Ali's fertile mind produced an antidote that, on the surface, was suicidal but in practice was a stroke of genius.

One minute into round two, Ali retreated to the ropes and appeared to give Foreman exactly what he wanted -- a stationary target ready to absorb massive punishment. Eager to shut Ali's mouth as well as prove his manhood to all the world, Foreman tore into Ali with ferocious body shots and huge swings aimed at Ali's head. For Ali's corner it was their worst nightmare come true and writer George Plimpton, who was seated at ringside, thought he was witnessing a fix. (14)

The stats, however, told a different story. Yes, Foreman still out-landed Ali 18-14 in the second and 24-20 in the third, but Ali was striking the champion with stunning regularity. His sprightly counters enabled Ali to land 41% of his total punches in the second (including 46% of his jabs, 10 of 22) and 57% across the board in the third (20 of 35 overall, 12 of 21 jabs and 8 of 14 power punches). Meanwhile, Foreman, thrilled at the prospect of a stationary Ali, shrugged off the challenger's blows and kept on firing. Given that Foreman had landed 38% of his power punches in the second and 52% of them in the third, he had good reason to feel that way.

For all of Foreman's early numerical success, Ali had created a tempting mirage and Foreman, thirsting for another career-defining knockout victory, willingly fell under its spell. No longer the dancing master of the late-1960s, Ali compensated for the ravages of age by learning how to fight off the ropes during numerous sparring sessions. There, he learned how to pick off blows with his arms, pivot his torso ever so slightly to minimize the impact of body blows and formulate the proper counters for the punches coming at him. Those sparring sessions enabled Ali to create an entirely new map from which to operate and he had the confidence -- and the bravery -- to apply that map during one of the most critical moments of his fighting life.

In retrospect the components of the "Rope-a-Dope" addressed every problem Ali encountered in round one. By staying stationary Ali preserved enough strength in his legs to move only when necessary while simultaneously prompting an overanxious Foreman to drain his gas tank. Second, the looser-than-normal ropes enabled Ali to lean back far enough to remove his head from the plane of Foreman's bombs. Third, Ali's energy-saving maneuvers neutralized the effects of the weather for him while exacerbating them for Foreman. Finally, the tactic allowed Ali to exploit Foreman's predatory mindset, which knew nothing about pacing oneself for a 15-round fight, while Ali, a veteran of long fights, could take his time and assess his options.

"Starting in the second round, I gave George what he thought he wanted," Ali recalled. "And he hit hard. A couple of times he shook me bad, especially with the right hand. But I blocked and dodged most of what he threw, and each round his punches got slower and hurt less when they landed. I was on the ropes, but he was trapped because attacking was all he knew how to do. By round six, I knew he was tired. His punches weren't as hard as before." (15)

Foreman agreed with the principles behind Ali's inspired strategy.

"When you're young like that and you've had so many knockouts, you don't want to win by points, you want to knock them out," Foreman told NBC's Marv Albert in 1990. "If I had to do it all over again, I'd just win the fight on points and not worry about it. If he didn't want to come out in the middle of the ring, forget him. If he don't want the championship of the world... that kind of thing. He fought just like your initial bum, just lay on the ropes and take a whipping. That's normally what a bum would do. But this time he did it with character. He said, *'I'm going to weather this storm and I'm going to whip George Foreman.'* (The "Rope-a-Dope" didn't surprise me at all) because normally when I fight a guy that's all he can do anyway; just get on the ropes and just hope that he doesn't get hurt. And if you happen to lay on the ropes, and George Foreman becomes a dope, you win the fight." (16)

Lying on the ropes alone didn't win the fight for Ali; it just created the environment by which he *could* win. As Foreman whaled away with impunity -- and growing inaccuracy -- a wide-eyed Ali scanned for openings and seized on almost every one of them. Foreman's ever-wider punches created a causeway down the middle for Ali's spearing jabs and lightning-quick right leads that snapped the champion's head and puffed his face.

The fourth round saw Ali out-land Foreman for the first time in the bout (15-12 overall) and his wickedly accurate counter shots connected at a 75% rate (12 of 16). Foreman, however, went all out in the fifth as he landed 26 of his 93 total punches and 23 of his 65 power shots, all fight highs. Statistically speaking, Ali answered Foreman's surge with stiletto-sharp punching. In round five Ali was 19 of 37 overall (51%) and 10 of 17 with his power punches (59%). But as much as Ali's punching affected Foreman, his mouth dished out even more punishment. Every time the fighters fell into a clinch Ali leaned in and dug verbal daggers that pierced Foreman's psyche.

"Hit harder! Show me something, George," Ali demanded. "That don't hurt. I thought you were supposed to be bad." Then, twisting the knife even further, he asked Foreman, "is that all you got?"

"Yep, that's about it." Foreman recalled thinking at that moment. (17)

For Foreman, one particular moment in round three inflicted untold psychological damage. During a round that was one of Foreman's best, the champion landed a series of crunching body shots that he felt would be enough to finish the job.

"I went out and hit Muhammad with the hardest shot to the body I ever delivered to any opponent," Foreman told Hauser. "Muhammad cringed; I could see it hurt. And then he looked at me, he had that look in his eyes, like he was saying *'I'm not gonna let you hurt me'*. And to be honest, that's the main thing I remember about the fight. Everything else happened too quick. I got burned out." (18)

As that round closed, Ali rattled in a right-left-right to the face that allowed him to escape the ropes and a stinging one-two at ring center that landed painfully flush. When the bell sounded, Ali whirled around and fixed a defiant stare that said, *"I will not be denied."*

The remainder of the fight was a fast-paced series of skirmishes marked by Ali's counters, clinches and chatter and Foreman's increasingly slower and more ponderous punches. Despite his growing exhaustion, Foreman never stopped throwing and at times he looked awkward as he tried to push his gloves past the thicket of Ali's arms. By the sixth Ali was hitting Foreman virtually at will and by the eighth the older and lighter Ali was able to maneuver the monstrous champion into any position he chose.

Following his peak performance in the fifth, Foreman sagged to 12 of 50 overall in the fifth and 16 of 49 in the sixth. Ali, on the other hand, continued to puncture Foreman with well-aimed spears as he landed 45% of his jabs in the fifth (9 of 20) and sixth (13 of 29) while his power punching was downright surgical (10 of 17, 59%, in round five and 6 of 8, 75%, in the sixth).

The pattern of the fight was stunning and the wisdom of Ali's strategy was finally dawning on the shocked audience. Despite the crippling exhaustion that enveloped him, Foreman continued to charge in because he knew no other way to fight. In the seventh he out-landed Ali 16-13 only because he nearly doubled Ali's output (49-26). Meanwhile, Ali continued to strike with impressive precision (13 of 26, 50% overall, 6 of 9, 67% power).

While many believed the fight would not go the full 15 rounds, nearly everyone believed the champion would be the one who would apply the finisher. Now, with Foreman hurtling toward exhaustion, the possibility of Ali emerging victorious in a shortened fight was a growing likelihood.

To the world's utter astonishment, that likelihood soon became reality.

With 20 seconds remaining in round eight, Ali began his final assault by landing a lancing right that nailed the onrushing Foreman. That was followed by a right to the temple that turned Foreman's body and left it draped over the top rope. As Ali pivoted toward ring center he landed a third right to the forehead, then a devastating hook-cross to the face that sent Foreman stumbling and falling heavily to the canvas on his right side. As the crowd exploded in celebration, Ali calmly stood in the neutral corner as referee Clayton stood over the champion and tolled his count. Foreman finally began to stir at six and by eight he managed to climb to a knee. But Clayton, for reasons only known to him, crisscrossed his arms after tolling eight and stopped the fight.

Technical questions aside, the awe-inspiring force of the moment was overwhelming. Members of the "Ali Circus" rushed the ring and Ali's brother Rahaman tried to lift the new champion in the air, but a clearly agitated Ali slapped his sibling's arm away with his left glove, then sat on the canvas to get away from the swirl of joy that orbited him. Dozens of spectators flooded the ring and several of them broke into dance. The scene soon spiraled out of control as a ring stool was tossed toward Ali and dozens of white-helmeted riot police struggled to quell the pandemonium. As a sad, dejected and depleted Foreman exited the ring, the triumphant Ali led another round of "Ali, bomaye" chants.

At the time of the stoppage Ali led on all three scorecards -- 70-67 according to Tunisian judge Nourridine Adalla, 69-66 on American James Taylor's card and 68-66 by Clayton's account. Foreman's ferocious, but ultimately futile, attack still allowed him to out-land Ali 138-125 overall and 109-63 in power shots but Ali's dominant jab (62-29), searing accuracy (48% overall, 40% jabs, 58% power) and ability to block most of Foreman's bombs (30% overall, 19% jabs, 35% power) created a fusion of circumstance that led to a wondrous and historic victory.

At long last, Ali's odyssey had reached its end. Ali became only the second man to date to regain the heavyweight championship and unlike many of those who would follow him his claim was undisputed.

As he did after he stopped Liston more than a decade earlier, Ali took time to chide his doubters.

"Everybody stop talking now. Attention!" he said in the dressing room. "I told you, all of my critics, I told you all that I was the greatest of all times when I beat Sonny Liston. I told you today I'm still the greatest of all times. Never again defeat me, never again say that I'm going to be defeated, never again make me the underdog until I'm about 50 years old." (19)

Ironically, it would be Foreman who would still be in boxing until nearly age 50. Long after Ali retired, came back and retired for good after back-to-back losses to Larry Holmes and Trevor Berbick, Foreman emerged from a 10-year layoff, lost a stirring challenge of Evander Holyfield at age 42 then, wearing the same trunks he wore two decades earlier in Kinshasa, fired the right hand heard around the world and regained the heavyweight championship from Michael Moorer at the age of 45 years, 310 days. The 20-year gap between championship reigns is -- and probably will forever be -- the longest in boxing history. But more importantly for Foreman, the victory allowed him to exorcise the ghosts that had haunted him since his nightmarish experience in the African jungle.

Now it was Foreman's turn to feel the rush Ali must have when he scored his massive upset two decades earlier. The crowd inside the MGM Grand produced noise so cacophonous that it could be heard far beyond its confines. The commotion was at least the equal of the post-fight scene in Zaire and that, in effect, helped close the circle for Foreman.

Armed with his religious faith, the incisive perspective of a middle-aged man who had seen it all and done it all and the peace that came with his historic triumph over Moorer, Foreman -- who once had blamed the Ali loss on poisoning -- had a different outlook on what transpired against Ali.

"When I look back on it, devastated at that time as I was from losing the fight, I'm just happy that I didn't win it," Foreman told "Facing Ali" author Steven Brunt. "I'm just happy that I didn't land that big shot and knock him out. Boy, am I happy about that. Because you could have changed everything then. The second chances. Even now, with Muhammad Ali being proclaimed The Greatest. Everything could have been messed up.

"It's harmony to me when I hear people say Muhammad Ali is The Greatest," he continued. "When they call him The Greatest and he walks around and people give him standing ovations, I'm thinking he deserves it. He *deserves* it. Life is a rough journey with a lot of problems. A lot of things happen to you. If a person can leave with some applause, amen to them. I think of the Sonny Liston fight, maybe the Joe Frazier Thrilla in Manila, and the George Foreman fight -- you take any pieces of that puzzle away and you don't crown him that. Then I get a second chance to come back because of the devastation with that fight. It forced me to just turn over every stone. *'What's wrong? I'm not supposed to lose. Something is wrong here.'* I couldn't figure that out. And eventually having a fight with Jimmy Young, trying to become the number-one contender, pushing myself to my limits just to go 12 rounds made me fall into the hands of God. And if any one of those little things....it was that fragile, that one little thing (beating Ali) could have messed the whole thing up. And my world could have been totally different. Muhammad Ali's world, Joe Frazier's. All of us. The world could have been different for us. Because of the trials Muhammad is going through, he should have that (being called "The Greatest"). I wouldn't want anyone else to be that, especially myself." (20)

In that vein, it can fairly be said that, by beating Foreman, Ali had erected the final pillar of his fistic legacy, not just by regaining the championship, but doing so as an older fighter against a younger, stronger and more ferocious version of Sonny Liston. The long march to regain the crown taken from him by outside forces was now complete. The argument of his merit as a fighter was now settled. What he said from the very beginning of his career -- even before he had logged one notable accomplishment -- still applies now: When one combines in-ring feats with worldwide fame that transcends boxing's confines, Muhammad Ali cemented himself as the greatest star boxing had ever known -- and may ever know.

INSIDE THE NUMBERS: Ali landed 66% or higher with his power punches in four of the last five rounds -- 75% in the 4th (12 of 16); 75% in the 6th (6 of 8); 66.7% in the 7th (6 of 9) and 68.8% in the 8th (11 of 16) -- far higher than the heavyweight average of 40.8%. Ali landed 57.8% of his power punches in the fight, his second highest percentage of the 47 fights tracked by CompuBox (his 62.2% accuracy in the Cleveland Williams fight was the highest). The weary Foreman landed just 28 power punches in the last three rounds after landing 54 in the previous three rounds.

Date:	October 30, 1974					City: Kinshasa, Zaire				Venue: Stade du 20 Mai							
Opponent:	George Foreman																
Result:	Ali by KO at 2:58 of the 8th round -- Regained World Heavyweight Title																
Referee:	**Zach Clayton**																
	Round	1	2	3	4	5	6	7	8	9	10	11	12	13	14	15	Total
	Ali																68
	Foreman																66
Judge:	**Nourridine Adalla**																
	Round	1	2	3	4	5	6	7	8	9	10	11	12	13	14	15	Total
	Ali	10	10	10	10	10	10	10									70
	Foreman																67
Judge:	**James Taylor**																
	Round	1	2	3	4	5	6	7	8	9	10	11	12	13	14	15	Total
	Ali																69
	Foreman																66

MUHAMMAD ALI KO 8 GEORGE FOREMAN
10/30/74 - ZAIRE

Total Punches Landed / Thrown

	1	2	3	4	5	6	7	8	9	10	11	12	13	14	15
ALI	9/30	14/34	20/35	15/32	19/37	19/37	13/26	16/32	-/-	-/-	-/-	-/-	-/-	-/-	-/-
	30%	41.2%	57.1%	46.9%	51.4%	51.4%	50%	50%	-	-	-	-	-	-	-
FOREMAN	17/43	18/58	24/57	12/50	26/93	12/50	16/49	13/61	-/-	-/-	-/-	-/-	-/-	-/-	-/-
	39.5%	31%	42.1%	24%	28%	24%	32.7%	21.3%	-	-	-	-	-	-	-

Jab Landed / Thrown

	1	2	3	4	5	6	7	8	9	10	11	12	13	14	15
ALI	3/13	10/22	12/21	3/16	9/20	13/29	7/17	5/16	-/-	-/-	-/-	-/-	-/-	-/-	-/-
	23.1%	45.5%	57.1%	18.8%	45%	44.8%	41.2%	31.3%	-	-	-	-	-	-	-
FOREMAN	3/8	5/24	2/15	3/17	3/28	2/14	5/15	6/30	-/-	-/-	-/-	-/-	-/-	-/-	-/-
	37.5%	20.8%	13.3%	17.6%	10.7%	14.3%	33.3%	20%	-	-	-	-	-	-	-

Power Punches Landed / Thrown

	1	2	3	4	5	6	7	8	9	10	11	12	13	14	15
ALI	6/17	4/12	8/14	12/16	10/17	6/8	6/9	11/16	-/-	-/-	-/-	-/-	-/-	-/-	-/-
	35.3%	33.3%	57.1%	75%	58.8%	75%	66.7%	68.8%	-	-	-	-	-	-	-
FOREMAN	14/35	13/34	22/42	9/33	23/65	10/36	11/34	7/31	-/-	-/-	-/-	-/-	-/-	-/-	-/-
	40%	38.2%	52.4%	27.3%	35.4%	27.8%	32.4%	22.6%	-	-	-	-	-	-	-

Final Punch Stat Report

Total	Total Punches	Total Jabs	Power Punches
ALI	125/263	62/154	63/109
	47.5%	40.3%	57.8%
FOREMAN	138/461	29/151	109/310
	29.9%	19.2%	35.2%

22.

MARCH 24, 1975 - RICHFIELD COLISEUM, RICHFIELD, OH

MUHAMMAD ALI KO 15 CHUCK WEPNER

For Ali, the Foreman fight was the apex of his fistic career. While winning the title from Sonny Liston was an earth-shaking upset, beating "Big George" was an even more massive accomplishment because he defeated a younger, larger and even more fearsome version of "The Big Ugly Bear" with a strategy that defied all conventional wisdom. It was, in a word, magical.

However, all mountaintop moments are followed by the tedium of valleys, and, for world boxing champions, that means getting on with the rest of one's athletic life. All long-reigning champions must repel challengers that are perceived to be no-hopers, journeymen, or, for those who wish to be particularly insulting, bums. More often than not, it is this type of fighter who is served up as the first sacrificial lamb for a popular champion who wants to get his new title reign off on the right foot.

On the surface, Charles William "Chuck" Wepner, was delivered directly from Central Casting. At age 35, Wepner, born in New York City but raised in New Jersey, was nearly three years older than Ali, and while his weight ranged between 215 and 228 and was spread over a 6-foot-5 frame, his somewhat soft-looking physique disguised the truth that he was a professional athlete. His receding hairline, Fu Manchu moustache, thick legs and hairy torso was the polar opposite of Ali's movie-star looks and his hard New Jersey accent aptly expressed the toughness within him.

His crude and awkward style was amplified by his frequent forays into the darker arts of boxing such as low blows, elbows, head butts and especially rabbit punching, which, for the uninitiated, is the term used for a sharp blow to the back of the head. While Ali sported a glittering record of 45-2 with 32 knockouts, Wepner's ledger of 30-9-2 with 12 knockouts reflected the hardscrabble road he had faced inside the squared circle. Like Ali, Wepner had fought a young Foreman and an old Liston but while Ali defeated both Wepner lost to both thanks to his most glaring weakness -- cuts.

Wepner's propensity to cut was even more severe than that of Henry Cooper, so much so that he was dubbed "The Bayonne Bleeder." Thanks to the approximately 300 stitches he had incurred over the years, (1) the area above his eyes were caked with scar tissue, tissue so tender that the lightest of touches could break it open and turn potential victory into bitter defeat. Besides his bouts with Liston and Foreman, cuts played a role in his setbacks to Buster Mathis Sr., Joe Bugner and Jerry Judge. That said, Wepner hadn't bled in a fight in approximately two-and-a-half years following an operation on his brows, and it was no coincidence that he had won every fight in that span.

178

"That's all in the past," declared Wepner's manager Al Braverman. "Not even Ali will make him bleed this time. And don't think my man won't give Ali a hard fight. Chuck is gonna be all over him. If Ali thinks it's gonna be easy, he's in for a surprise." (2)

While Wepner had plenty of shortcomings in terms of innate talent, he earned his share of successes. The onetime Marine was unbeaten in 65 amateur fights (3) and his honors included the 1964 New York Golden Gloves novice heavyweight championship. His best pro victories included a six-round split decision over Ray Patterson (the younger brother of two-time heavyweight champion and Hall of Famer Floyd Patterson), points wins over Pedro Agosto, Manuel Ramos and Ernie Terrell as well as a 2-1 series lead against the cerebral yet rugged Randy Neumann. He also was a two-time New Jersey heavyweight champion and was in the midst of an eight-fight winning streak, the longest of his career. That streak included his two victories over Neumann (W 12, KO 6) and he came into the Ali fight off a wild TKO win over the 37-3-2 Terry Hinke in Salt Lake City. Billed as a fight for the "American Heavyweight Title," Wepner was deducted four points for various fouls but made up for it by scoring three knockdowns, including the finisher in round 11.

As if his look and his ring work wasn't enough to certify his blue-collar status, Wepner continued to work as a liquor salesman throughout his boxing career.

Boxing is a sport that is built on contrasts, and if any fight in history illustrated that truism, it was Muhammad Ali versus Chuck Wepner. Incredibly, this was the first heavyweight championship fight on U.S. soil since Joe Frazier stopped Ron Stander in Omaha in May 1972.

Pittsburgh Post Gazette writer Al Abrams reported that neither Ali or Wepner had done little training for the fight.

"The champion talked all about the ice cream and pastries he wolfed down, while the challenger spent a lot of time at Thistledown, a horse track," he wrote. "Strange behavior for title bout contenders." (4)

Wepner's $100,000 purse was 10 times more than his previous high-water mark. Thus, it was fitting that Ali was installed as a 10-to-1 favorite. Still, Wepner was so confident of victory that he made a promise to his wife shortly before he left for the venue, the Richfield Coliseum in Richfield, Ohio.

"That night, before the title bout, I bought my wife a powder blue negligee and I gave it to her," he said in June 2016. "I said, 'wear this to bed tonight, because tonight you're going to be sleeping with the heavyweight champion of the world.' Anyway, after the fight, I come back to the room, I walked in, and she's sitting on the edge of the bed in the negligee. She says, 'am I going to Ali's room, or is he coming to mine?' " (5)

Yes, Wepner lost the fight. But his persistence, defiance and bravery in the face of overwhelming odds touched the hearts of many, including an aspiring writer/actor named Sylvester Stallone that used the fight as the basis for his film "Rocky," which won three Oscars, including Best Picture, the following year.

At the weigh-in, which was carried live on ABC, a noticeably thicker but highly playful Ali scaled 223 1/2. In the five months since the Foreman fight Ali's weight had ballooned to 245 and though he wanted to scale 220, he ended up being slightly heavier. Reports indicated that Ali had trained hard only during the week before the bout.

"I don't have to train hard for Wepner," yelled Ali. "I'll whup him without even hitting him in the face!" (6)

Meanwhile, Wepner was 225, the same poundage he carried in the Hinke fight but six pounds heavier than his recent fights with Charley Polite, Neumann and Terrell. A smiling Wepner rolled with the jokes better than he had rolled away from most punches and, at Ali's prompting, promised to whip Ali, throw the champion into the second row and "mess up that pretty face."

Ali didn't throw his first punch -- a right over the head while in a clinch -- until nearly two minutes had elapsed. Meanwhile, the deadly serious Wepner chased after Ali and curled in nearly a dozen rabbit punches, prompting a furious Ali to respond with four blatant ones of his own while also berating referee Tony Perez. Because Wepner also dug in some body shots in the clinches, he out-landed Ali 15-2 and won the first round virtually by default.

It was clear Ali could hit and hurt Wepner whenever he chose but for reasons only known to him he chose to play with the challenger for long stretches over the first eight rounds. His jab was the primary weapon, for he recorded eight, 13, 13, 16, 14 and 12 connects in rounds two, three, four, five, seven and eight. Conversely, Wepner plodded after Ali to the best of his ability, whacked him with right hands to the body (as well as more rabbit shots) and threw punches at every opportunity. Best yet for Wepner, his eyes held up for six rounds. But in round seven, the proverbial razors in Ali's gloves finally broke the skin above Wepner's left eye.

Because Wepner was so much busier over the first eight rounds (70.5 punches per round -- including 93 in the sixth -- to Ali's 30.8, including just nine in the sixth), the challenger had built connect leads of 140-110 overall and 124-33 power. Of course, those leads were forged only because Ali permitted it. Surely, this trend wouldn't last. Surely, Ali wouldn't lose this fight...would he?

Then came round nine and the single event that would vault this event from exhibition to memorable point in time.

As the ninth neared the two-minute mark, Wepner landed a long right under the heart, which caused Ali to suddenly fall back-first onto the bottom strand of rope. To everyone's surprise, Perez began to count over Ali, which officially added Wepner to the roll call of fighters who had scored knockdowns over Ali -- Sonny Banks, Henry Cooper and Joe Frazier.

"He fell backward and went under the bottom rope," Wepner recalled. "I went back to the corner and I said 'Al, start the car. We're going to the bank, we're millionaires.' But he said to me, 'Chuck, you better turn around. He's getting up and he looks pissed off.' I turned around and he had a shocked look on his face, and Drew 'Bundini' Brown was going nuts." (7)

A photograph printed in the Cleveland Plain Dealer proved Wepner's punch wasn't the sole reason Ali went to the canvas. At the same time he landed the punch, Wepner's foot was on top of Ali's, preventing the champ from fully regaining his balance.

"Everybody says, 'oh, you stepped on his foot,' but let me tell you something: If you're in a world title fight or any battle and the guy drops you and steps on your foot, the first thing you do after you get up is tell the ref, 'hey ref, he stepped on my foot.' " Wepner said. "But he never said that. He took the eight-count and then he kept fighting, because he knew it was the punch under the heart that knocked him down." (8)

While one can debate whether Wepner's fist or his foot created the historic moment, one other part of the story was undeniably true: Ali was angry and he wanted to make Wepner pay for embarrassing him.

In rounds nine through 14, Ali upped his work rate from 30.8 to 52, out-landed Wepner 144-77 overall and connected on 54% of his power shots (87 of 161). But while Ali was doing his best to knock Wepner out, the challenger defiantly kept his feet. Meanwhile, Wepner, who had never fought beyond round 12, was losing steam.

"By the 13th round my legs were starting to give out on me a little bit," Wepner recalled years later. "I was getting tired in my legs, and I remember after the 14th round, I come back to the corner just before the 15th round and I said to (chief second) Al (Braverman), 'take my mouthpiece out.' I was going to fight the 15th round without a mouthpiece to help me breathe more. And Al says, 'I'm not doing that, leave your mouthpiece in, and just go out and do the best you can.' " (9)

His best was good enough to get him *to* the 15th round, but his best wasn't enough to get him *through* the 15th round. With less than 40 seconds remaining in the fight, Ali hurt Wepner with a combination, then dropped him with a flush right hand to the jaw that left him tangled in the ropes. Wepner courageously struggled to regain his feet, and he probably would have, albeit shakily, had Perez not waved off the fight at his count of six.

Wepner, who dearly wanted to go the distance with Ali, fell just 19 seconds short. But while he failed to achieve his stated goals, Wepner should take pride in the following statistical milestones: Of all the fighters involved in this statistical study, no Ali opponent threw more total punches (1,021) or more power punches (688) than he did.

Ali's rally resulted in connect leads of 276-225 overall and 142-25 jabs while Wepner prevailed 200-134 in power connects. The champion was supremely accurate (45% overall, 41% jabs, 51% power) while Wepner struggled to draw a bead (22% overall, 8% jabs, 29% power).

"I knocked him down," a battered and bruised Wepner told the press. "I've had tougher fights. Sonny Liston was much tougher. But he's a great champion and he's a great fighter. I feel no shame in losing to a man of Muhammad Ali's caliber." (10)

"My main thing is to find an opening, tag him and really convincingly win this round (the 15th)," Ali told Cosell on ABC's Wide World of Sports. "My objective was to stay on him, annihilate him, cool him off, keep him numb, keep him shook up, realizing another fight with Foreman or Frazier laid on this. (As the final right landed) I knew I had won the fight with no doubt. I figured the referee might let it go but I was glad when he counted him out because the man really wasn't in no condition to keep going."

Ali complained bitterly about Wepner's rabbit punching as well as Perez's officiating and his objections were so vociferous that Perez filed a $20 million lawsuit that went to trial. Ali won, but years later he and Perez resolved their differences. (11)

Though beaten, Wepner's effort earned praise from some of the pundits that had panned the match beforehand.

"Wepner lost, as expected. But in losing he gained a victory," wrote one scribe. "He gained a victory over all those who mocked him, who ridiculed him, who derided him. And he gained it by having a carload of courage and an abundance of dignity. Chuck Wepner will never be a classic fighter. He never claimed to be. At times he looked amateurish against Ali. But he never -- not for a moment -- retreated or allowed himself to be psyched by Ali, as so many of Muhammad's other opponents have. Chuck Wepner may not have the physical skills to defeat a Muhammad Ali, but he made up for that lack with *heart*.

"To Chuck Wepner, this fight wasn't a joke and he didn't treat it as such," the writer continued. "He viewed it as an opportunity and made the best of that opportunity. Sure, he took his lumps, his stitches. But he never asked for more than a shot. He made no excuses. He didn't need any. There are many people in sports who, by their actions, invite ridicule. Chuck Wepner is not one of those. Chuck Wepner is a man, no more no less, who has paid his dues in blood for the chance to grasp at a rainbow. We think Chuck Wepner has a lot to be proud of and we think people now understand what Al Braverman meant when he said Chuck was a fighter with 'two hearts.' "(12)

As for Wepner, his fame remained strong decades after his retirement in 1978. His link to the "Rocky" franchise and the memories of his determined performance as a massive underdog has resulted in multiple projects depicting his life, the latest of which was a biopic starring Liev Schrieber first titled "The Bleeder," then re-titled "Chuck." Incredibly, Wepner, as of May 2017, still worked as a liquor salesman for the same company that employed him all those years ago.

"If I was to drop dead now, I still had a great life," Wepner told Newsday. "I've lived it to the fullest." (13)

For someone who experienced more than his share of ups and downs -- in the ring and out -- Wepner was able to land perfectly on his feet.

INSIDE THE NUMBERS: Wepner threw a Rocky-like 1,021 total punches (68.1 per round, markedly above the 44.8 division average) and 688 power shots (61 more than Joe Frazier threw in Manila). Those totals are the most by an Ali opponent in both categories in the 47 Ali fights tracked by CompuBox. The Bayonne Bleeder also missed nearly 800 punches. Ali, looking for the KO following the ninth round "knockdown," landed 61% of his power punches in round eleven and 63% in round twelve. Ali landed 51.3% of his power punches, his fifth highest percentage from the 47 fights tracked by CompuBox.

Date:	March 24, 1975				City: Richfield, OH				Venue: Richfield Coliseum							
Opponent:	Chuck Wepner															
Result:	Ali by TKO at 2:41 of the 15th round -- Retained World Heavyweight Title															

Referee:	Tony Perez															
	Round	1	2	3	4	5	6	7	8	9	10	11	12	13	14	15	Total
	Ali	9	10	10	10	10	9	10	9	8	10	10	10	10	10		135
	Wepner	10	9	9	9	9	10	9	10	10	9	9	9	9	9		130

Judge:	Jackie Keough															
	Round	1	2	3	4	5	6	7	8	9	10	11	12	13	14	15	Total
	Ali	9	10	10	10	10	9	10	10	8	10	10	10	10	10		136
	Wepner	10	9	9	9	9	10	9	9	10	9	9	9	9	9		129

Judge:	Sam Taormina															
	Round	1	2	3	4	5	6	7	8	9	10	11	12	13	14	15	Total
	Ali	10	10	10	10	10	9	10	10	9	10	10	10	10	10		138
	Wepner	9	9	10	9	9	10	9	9	10	9	9	9	9	9		129

MUHAMMAD ALI TKO 15 CHUCK WEPNER
03/24/75 - RICHFIELD, OH

Total Punches Landed / Thrown															
	1	2	3	4	5	6	7	8	9	10	11	12	13	14	15
ALI	2/5	16/35	19/44	20/37	21/41	2/9	18/50	12/25	19/50	26/55	23/42	24/46	22/52	30/67	22/52
	40%	45.7%	43.2%	54.1%	51.2%	22.2%	36%	48%	38%	47.3%	54.8%	52.2%	42.3%	44.8%	42.3%
WEPNER	15/55	29/88	21/81	22/88	13/48	19/93	11/68	10/43	11/62	10/62	10/76	15/60	14/69	17/80	8/48
	27.3%	33%	25.9%	25%	27.1%	20.4%	16.2%	23.3%	17.7%	16.1%	13.2%	25%	20.3%	21.3%	16.7%

Jab Landed / Thrown															
	1	2	3	4	5	6	7	8	9	10	11	12	13	14	15
ALI	0/0	8/17	13/34	13/23	16/34	1/6	14/41	12/23	9/30	12/29	9/19	12/27	6/20	9/26	8/20
	0%	47.1%	38.2%	56.5%	47.1%	16.7%	34.1%	52.2%	30%	41.4%	47.4%	44.4%	30%	34.6%	40%
WEPNER	3/20	3/34	3/27	1/29	1/18	1/27	3/28	1/14	0/22	2/19	2/20	1/20	1/24	2/20	1/11
	15%	8.8%	11.1%	3.4%	5.6%	3.7%	10.7%	7.1%	0%	10.5%	10%	5%	4.2%	10%	9.1%

Power Punches Landed / Thrown															
	1	2	3	4	5	6	7	8	9	10	11	12	13	14	15
ALI	2/5	8/18	6/10	7/14	5/7	1/3	4/9	0/2	10/20	14/26	14/23	12/19	16/32	21/41	14/32
	40%	44.4%	60%	50%	71.4%	33.3%	44.4%	0%	50%	53.8%	60.9%	63.2%	50%	51.2%	43.8%
WEPNER	12/35	26/54	18/54	21/59	12/30	18/66	8/40	9/29	11/40	8/43	8/56	14/40	13/45	15/60	7/37
	34.3%	48.1%	33.3%	35.6%	40%	27.3%	20%	31%	27.5%	18.6%	14.3%	35%	28.9%	25%	18.9%

Final Punch Stat Report			
Total	Total Punches	Total Jabs	Power Punches
ALI	276/610	142/349	134/261
	45.2%	40.7%	51.3%
WEPNER	225/1021	25/333	200/688
	22%	7.5%	29.1%

23.

For any other fighter in history, the sight of a boxer lying on the ropes and hiding behind a defensive shell should have been a cause for celebration. But ever since Muhammad Ali used what would be become known as the "Rope-a-Dope" to improbably regain the heavyweight championship from George Foreman, rival fighters and trainers viewed the tactic much as a vampire would a clove of garlic --something to be feared and to be avoided at all costs.

Fifty-three days after his off-the-floor victory over Chuck Wepner, Ali faced Ron Lyle at the Convention Center in Las Vegas. Decades earlier, Lyle's trainer Chickie Ferrara mentored a young Philadelphian named Angelo Dundee, a gesture that cemented Dundee's everlasting loyalty and appreciation. After Dundee earned worldwide acclaim for his work with Carmen Basilio, Luis Rodriguez, Jose Napoles and Ali, he made sure to include Ferrara in his corner whenever possible, not just as a "thank you" for past kindnesses but also because Ferrara remained one of the smartest and most versatile corner men the sport has ever known. One example of his worth: He was one of the seconds working feverishly over the-then Cassius Clay when a substance got into the challenger's eyes during the first fight with Liston.

This time, however, Ferrara and Dundee would occupy opposite corners, and as Ferrara prepared Lyle for Ali his biggest concern was how to neutralize the "Rope-a-Dope."

Ferrara's answer was novel: Do nothing.

"I told Ron not to wear himself out throwing useless punches," Ferrara said. "I told him 'make him come off the ropes. Stand there and motion for him to get off the ropes and fight.' The referee will take care of the rest." (1)

If Lyle didn't engage with Ali, Ali would have no choice but to engage with Lyle, who possessed fight-ending power in both hands.

"I'm not going to try to kill him; I'm not going to fight him like everybody else has fought him," Lyle told ABC's Howard Cosell the morning of the fight. "Liston tried to kill him. Frazier was more successful because he put more pressure on him. Foreman tried to kill him. Bugner tried to kill him. Norton tried to kill him. And when you're trying to kill him, you can't get the good leverage shots that you really need to hurt him effectively. I'm going to have to make him come to me. I'm going to go after him but eventually I'm going to make him come to me too."

When asked about the "Rope-a-Dope," Lyle continued his narrative of non-engagement.

185

"It's not my job to worry about the ropes, that's the referee's job," Lyle said. "My job is to fight and be in control of myself at all times, just as it's the referee's job to be in control of the fight at all times. I'm not going to try to kill him; I'm going to beat him. And that's how you win. There's no certain amount of margin (that) you win a horse race; if you win by *that much* the horse wins. If you win by one point in a basketball game, you win. There's no certain way to win, the only thing to do is to win."

The 34-year-old man who spoke so serenely, so reasonably and so intelligently to Cosell about not killing his opponent and remaining calm in the heat of competition was a man who learned his lessons from hard experience. In 1961 Lyle got involved in a gang fight because a member of his group was being assaulted by 21-year-old rival member Douglas Byrd. After Byrd was killed from gunfire, Lyle, who said he was being attacked with a lead pipe and wasn't the one who pulled the trigger, was tried for first-degree murder but was convicted for second-degree murder. He was sentenced to 15 to 25 years at the Colorado State Penitentiary and it was there that he began boxing.

"When I first went into the penitentiary, they were holding fights on the Fourth of July," Lyle told Cosell. "The guys were fighting and I looked at it and said to myself 'it doesn't look hard; I think I can try that.' And I did." Lyle approached Lt. Cliff Mattax, the prison's athletic director, and joined the prison boxing team, launching an amateur career that would see him compile a 25-4 record that included 17 knockouts. While in prison, Lyle dreamed of eventually becoming heavyweight champion, but that dream -- and his life -- was almost snuffed out after he was stabbed in the abdomen. He spent more than seven hours on the operating table and his condition was so dire that one doctor had already signed his death certificate. Fortunately for Lyle, another surgeon kept working on him and was able to save his life.

Thirty-five pints of blood were used to keep Lyle alive during the procedure and when he awakened only Mattax was at his bedside. That event proved transformative for Lyle.

"He asked me how I was," Lyle recalled. "Man, here was a white man worrying about me. I cried. He was depending on me for the baseball team and I had let him down before and it hurt me. Right then and there I changed my whole outlook on life and people." (2)

Lyle wasn't only gifted as a boxer. His 20-points-per-game average led the basketball team and he regularly batted over .400 for the baseball squad. He played quarterback and defensive end for the football team and one time he kicked a 60-yard field goal. (3)

Following his recovery Lyle resumed his amateur boxing career, which saw him win several titles: The National AAU, the North American Amateur and the International Boxing League. Lyle won them all in 1970, not long after he was paroled from prison after serving seven-and-a-half years on November 22, 1969.

Lyle joined the pro ranks at the extraordinarily late age of 30 but he proved to be a quick study and an enormously effective hitter. He rolled off 19 straight wins, 17 by knockout, before losing a 12-round decision to the veteran Jerry Quarry in February 1973. Lyle recovered by going 11-0-1 in his next 12 fights, and his victims included Gregorio Peralta (W 10), Jose Luis Garcia (KO 3), Juergen Blin (KO 2), Larry Middleton (W 10), Oscar Bonavena (W 12), Jimmy Ellis (W 12) and Boone Kirkman (KO 8). The lone draw came against the tricky 115-fight veteran Peralta in a rematch, a foreshadowing for what happened in his next fight against the quicker and slicker Jimmy Young, who scored a dominant 10-round decision. Despite the lopsided loss, Lyle was named Ali's next opponent, which forced Lyle to answer questions about his worthiness.

"I don't think it really matters what you do while you're coming, it's what you do when you get there," Lyle told Cosell during a joint interview with Ali. "The opportunity is here. It is my turn. (Ali's) had his turn. He's been an inspiration to a lot of people..."

"Have been?" Ali asked.

"He still is," Lyle replied, correcting himself as Ali nodded his approval. He said he wasn't afraid of Ali just as Cosell shouldn't be afraid of other sportscasters and their abilities. When asked if he was afraid of his peers, the ever-modest Cosell replied, "that'll be the day."

The 33-year-old Ali was convinced he would stop Lyle, whose two losses in 33 fights were on points.

"(Between rounds) one and eight, it'll be all over," Ali told Cosell with a trace of slurring in his voice. "The man's never been knocked out. George Foreman's never been knocked out, Chuck Wepner's never been knocked out, and this man's never been out, so it gives me something to fight for."

Ali then revealed to Cosell that he planned to fight Lyle the same way he fought Foreman, which, for the first time, he dubbed the "Rope-a-Dope," saying the "dope" is in honor of the guy who chases him to the ropes.

"But what if Lyle doesn't pursue you into the ropes?" Cosell asked. "What if he backs off?"

Ali replied that he would cover up at ring center, move in and force Lyle to punch, a tactic he called "The Mirage."

"The Mirage is used when they won't come to me on the ropes," Ali explained later. "I walk to the middle of the ring and cover up. The guy punches away, but never lands any real hard shots. But he thinks he's hurting me. He's just seeing things, like a man on a desert who thinks he sees water. That's my Mirage." (4)

As Ali approached the ring, a contingent of Lyle fans started chanting the challenger's name, a sound that surely lifted the spirits of Lyle and his team. The battle of minds between Dundee and Ferrara promised to be more intriguing than that between their respective charges, for the odds-makers installed Ali as the solid 10-to-1 favorite. Just before the fight Ali added a new dimension to his pre-fight prediction; not only did he declare that he would stop Lyle in the eighth, but that he'd do so between 2:35 and 2:43 of the round.

The bout began with both men fulfilling their pre-fight promises: Ali immediately backing toward the ropes and covering up, Lyle falling into a clinch and refusing to engage. Next, with Ali at ring center, he tried the "Mirage" and again, Lyle jabbed lightly, landed a feathery right to the body and circled away. When Ali tried the "Rope-a-Dope" again, Lyle landed a light hook to the ribs, dropped his arms and waited for Ali's next move, which was to push him off.

The crowd of 6,875, which immediately recognized that it was watching a game of chicken rather than a boxing match, voiced its displeasure. For the remainder of the round, Lyle did what little fighting was done and won the round by default.

As time has gone on, more of Ali's fights were waged in this manner. Instead of applying the skills that had made him a global phenomenon, he chose to treat his fights as glorified sparring sessions in which he clowned, rested and did everything but fight consistently. The first round against Lyle was an extreme example of his laziness, for he threw just three punches, none of which landed, while Lyle was an industrious 13 of 69 overall and 11 of 27 power, the latter figure being enough to draw blood from Ali's right nostril.

Ali was slightly more spirited in the second, but only because the bar he set in round one was so low. Lyle, for his part, expended more energy when Ali planted himself on a corner pad but even then Lyle fired punches on his own terms, leaned in heavily enough to collect the needed rest and landed enough (12-5 overall, 9-3 power) to secure the round.

In the third, Ali tried to goad Lyle into falling into his trap by talking to him but, as Dr. Ferdie Pacheco said, Lyle and Ferrara were too smart and too disciplined to be drawn into Ali's counterintuitive "fight" plan.

This was a fight that a pacifist might have tolerated, for one refused to punch much at all while the other purposefully withheld his massive punching power so as to not empty his gas tank.

Statistically speaking, rounds four through six featured more of the same for Ali as he landed none of his seven punches in the fourth, 3 of his 30 in the fifth and 5 of his 18 in the sixth. Lyle, for his part, was much more productive as he landed 37 of his 151 punches and led Ali 28-2 in landed power shots during that span.

Late in the fifth, Ali woke up the crowd by abandoning his shell defense, dancing in the old Ali style and popping Lyle's head back with a jab, his heaviest punch of the night thus far. Even then, however, Lyle was wary of Ali's intent. He backed away and waited for Ali to settle down and return to within arm's reach, which he did in the final seconds when he put his back against the ropes and allowed Lyle to land a few power shots.

Ali threw in the shuffle at the start of the sixth, and while Ali didn't use his hands much his fluid movement was much more interesting to watch. Still, it was Lyle who was the smarter, more disciplined fighter as well as the more productive man.

Because of this, Lyle, who had no fear of Ali coming in, had even more reason to feel emboldened. With Ali falling behind on the scorecards, one had to wonder when -- or if -- he would finally spring to life.

By the seventh, Ali gave up the ghost on the "Rope-a-Dope" and the "Mirage" and tried to fight Lyle for real. The dance-master Ali threw 40 punches and landed 10, both highs for the fight by far. Lyle, for his part, also shifted into a higher gear and for the seventh consecutive round he out-landed Ali as he went 15 of 74 overall, out-jabbed Ali 5-1 and led 10-9 power. After seven rounds Lyle had opened substantial statistical leads of 84-28 overall, 21-11 jabs and 63-17 power. At the end of the seventh, however, Ali maneuvered Lyle to the ropes and landed a stinging right to the face. It was the first time Ali had shown any interest in retaining his championship and his fans hoped that blow would ignite a fight-changing surge similar to the one he produced after being floored by Wepner.

It would, but in round eight his primary motivation was to fulfill his unusually precise pre-fight prediction, which prompted ABC to show a running clock during most of the round. At long last, this was the Ali the fans had wanted to see and for the first time he let loose with his entire arsenal. But while he unleashed a fight-high 69 punches, of which he landed 22, they weren't enough to dislodge Lyle, who not only stood up to the punishment but fired back with gusto. Better yet for Lyle, he rebounded strongly in the ninth (18-5 overall, 13-1 power) while Ali recovered from the exertion of the previous round.

Ali's mathematical hole appeared to deepen dangerously following the 10th round, which saw Lyle out-throw Ali 77-8 overall and out-land the champion 21-2 overall and 16-1 power. After 10 rounds Lyle was up 49-43 on judge Bill Kipp's card, but his colleagues Art Lurie (46-45 Lyle) and John Mangriciana (46-46) obviously were more spellbound by Ali's magnetism and box-office appeal than what was happening inside the squared circle.

As Cosell was interviewing comedian Alan King -- whose tennis tournament at Caesars Palace was to be televised by ABC the next day -- Ali produced boxing's equivalent of a 150 mile-per-hour ace as Ali served up a rocket of a right hand that found Lyle's sweet spot, the tip of his chin. The blow caused Lyle's body to instantly stiffen and reel back toward the ropes, prompting Ali to move in for the kill.

Now it was Lyle's turn to employ the "Rope-a-Dope" as he crouched down and hid behind his upraised gloves. Ali, thinking Lyle was turning the tables on him, took a step back to assess the situation, then started raking Lyle with long, strafing punches. A barrage drove Lyle to the neutral corner pad and the glassiness of the challenger's eyes prompted Ali to look toward referee Ferd Hernandez, a former fighter who had out-pointed an aged Sugar Ray Robinson nearly a decade earlier. When Hernandez didn't move in, Ali connected with another volley capped by a left that snapped Lyle's head straight back. This time, Hernandez had seen enough. He stepped between the fighters and declared the bout over at the 1:08 mark of round 11. A bewildered Lyle glared at Hernandez and the crowd who had sensed a titanic upset was on the horizon registered its displeasure.

Ali's assault was clinical and precise, for he landed 22 of his 49 punches (45%) and exactly half of his 42 power shots while Lyle, who was 1 of 3 in the round, managed just one weak jab during the final sequence. The ending wiped out Lyle's considerable statistical leads of 137-79 overall, 35-25 jabs and 102-54 power.

Lyle, as expected, disagreed with the stoppage.

"Sure it was stopped too soon," Lyle said. "It shouldn't have been stopped at all. I don't mean this with any racial overtones, but stopping the fight was like saying, 'hey, n******, you can't have that (the title).' He called it the way he saw it, but that doesn't make it right." (5)

Ferrara, whose master plan had helped Lyle get to the doorstep of the championship, was aghast, saying "you do that in four-round fights, not championship ones.

"Ron only made one mistake," he continued. "Some people can make thousands and get away with them, but Ron dropped his left too low while he was still within striking distance and the old pro, Ali, put across that big right hand." (6)

Ali sensed Lyle was near the end once he landed the decisive right hand.

"I didn't want to hurt the man. That's why I asked the referee to stop the fight," he said. "I never want to hurt any man. I couldn't live with myself if I seriously injured an opponent. The referee did a good job in stopping the fight." (7)

The Ali fight would be Lyle's only chance at the heavyweight championship. Meanwhile, Ali already knew the date, place and identity of his next title defense: June 30, Malaysia and Joe Bugner.

INSIDE THE NUMBERS: Another dismal offensive performance by Ali, who landed 21 power punches in round eleven after landing just 33 in the previous ten rounds. Ali landed just 79 total punches (7.2 per round) versus Lyle, who did not co-operate with Ali's "Rope-a-Dope" antics. Ali averaged just 27.6 punches thrown against Lyle, markedly less than the 54.2 per round a 39-year-old Ali averaged in his final fight against Trevor Berbick.

Date:	May 16, 1975				City: Las Vegas, NV				Venue: Las Vegas Convention Center							
Opponent:	Ron Lyle															
Result:	Ali by TKO at 1:08 of the 11th round -- Retained World Heavyweight Title															

Judge: Bill Kipp

Round	1	2	3	4	5	6	7	8	9	10	11	12	13	14	15	Total
Ali	4	4	4	4	5	4	5	5	4	4						43
Lyle	5	5	5	5	5	5	5	4	5	5						49

Judge: Art Lurie

Round	1	2	3	4	5	6	7	8	9	10	11	12	13	14	15	Total
Ali	4	5	4	4	5	5	4	5	5	4						45
Lyle	5	4	5	5	4	5	5	4	4	5						46

Judge: John Mangriciana

Round	1	2	3	4	5	6	7	8	9	10	11	12	13	14	15	Total
Ali	4	5	5	4	5	5	4	5	5	4						46
Lyle	5		5	5			5	4		5						46

MUHAMMAD ALI KO 11 RON LYLE
05/16/75 - LAS VEGAS

Total Punches Landed / Thrown															
	1	2	3	4	5	6	7	8	9	10	11	12	13	14	15
ALI	0/3	5/22	5/14	0/7	3/30	5/18	10/40	22/69	5/26	2/8	22/49	-/-	-/-	-/-	-/-
	0%	22.7%	35.7%	0%	10%	27.8%	25%	31.9%	19.2%	25%	44.9%	-	-	-	-
LYLE	13/69	12/42	7/60	8/73	15/35	14/43	15/74	13/52	18/59	21/77	1/3	-/-	-/-	-/-	-/-
	18.8%	28.6%	11.7%	11%	42.9%	32.6%	20.3%	25%	30.5%	27.3%	33.3%	-	-	-	-

Jab Landed / Thrown															
	1	2	3	4	5	6	7	8	9	10	11	12	13	14	15
ALI	0/1	2/16	2/10	0/7	2/25	4/16	1/19	8/26	4/18	1/5	1/7	-/-	-/-	-/-	-/-
	0%	12.5%	20%	0%	8%	25%	5.3%	30.8%	22.2%	20%	14.3%	-	-	-	-
LYLE	2/42	3/22	2/51	4/57	4/17	1/16	5/48	4/26	5/26	5/49	0/1	-/-	-/-	-/-	-/-
	4.8%	13.6%	3.9%	7%	23.5%	6.3%	10.4%	15.4%	19.2%	10.2%	0%	-	-	-	-

Power Punches Landed / Thrown															
	1	2	3	4	5	6	7	8	9	10	11	12	13	14	15
ALI	0/2	3/6	3/4	0/0	1/5	1/2	9/21	14/43	1/8	1/3	21/42	-/-	-/-	-/-	-/-
	0%	50%	75%	0%	20%	50%	42.9%	32.6%	12.5%	33.3%	50%	-	-	-	-
LYLE	11/27	9/20	5/9	4/16	11/18	13/27	10/26	9/26	13/33	16/28	1/2	-/-	-/-	-/-	-/-
	40.7%	45%	55.6%	25%	61.1%	48.1%	38.5%	34.6%	39.4%	57.1%	50%	-	-	-	-

Final Punch Stat Report			
	Total Punches (Body Landed)	Total Jabs (Body Landed)	Power Punches (Body Landed)
ALI	79 (3)/286	25 (1)/150	54 (2)/136
	27.6%	16.7%	39.7%
LYLE	137 (80)/587	35 (9)/355	102 (71)/232
	23.3%	9.9%	44%

24.

As was the case with many contests involving Muhammad Ali, the fight at hand served as an infomercial for the next episode of "The Ali Circus," the swirling storm of activity that orbited Ali in the ring as well as beyond the ropes. This was particularly true during Ali's whirlwind schedule in 1966 and 1967 and also during his "long road back" campaign in the early 1970s. In some ways, Ali's life was a precursor to the reality-show culture that overwhelms today's American entertainment scene. Not only was Ali a global sporting figure, he was a celebrity whose every move was recorded for posterity. Ali, for his part, more than held up his end of the bargain because he was arguably the most accessible superstar athlete in history.

Thus, even before Ali stepped inside the ring to fight Joe Bugner a second time in Kuala Lumpur, Malaysia, all knew that the champ's next assignment would be a rubber match against his greatest rival, Joe Frazier. In fact, Frazier was at ringside not only to witness Ali-Bugner II but also to be present during the post-fight press conference when a presumably victorious Ali would announce Ali-Frazier III.

By accepting the fight, Bugner, by definition, saw himself as the roadblock to those well-laid plans. On paper, he had reason to believe he could produce an even better showing than when he first faced Ali in February 1973. At 25, Bugner was still approaching his chronological prime while the 33-year-old Ali was years past his. His 6-foot-5 frame had also matured and thickened. At 230, he was 11 pounds heavier than he was against Ali the first time while the 224 1/2-pound Ali, seven pounds more than he was in fight one, might be slowed by the extra weight. Also, while Ali had endured physically demanding fights with Norton (twice), Frazier (twice) and Foreman, Bugner came into the rematch on an eight-fight winning streak that included defenses of his European title against Giuseppe Ros (W 15), Mario Baruzzi (KO 10) and Dante Cane (KO 5) as well as wins over Mac Foster (W 10), Jose Luis Garcia (KO 2) and Jimmy Ellis (W 10) that lifted his record to 51-6-1 with 31 knockouts.

However, although Bugner was confident in his boxing ability, his mental state wasn't at its absolute peak. In "Joe Bugner: My Story," Bugner said his relationship with the British press had been rocky ever since his razor-thin victory over national treasure Henry Cooper in 1971 and, like Larry Holmes years later after succeeding Ali, Bugner felt he couldn't generate any praise no matter what he did because he was the man who had beaten a beloved legend. That sustained negativity ate at his psyche, as did the sauna-like conditions at the open-air Merdeka Stadium -- a 105-degree temperature and soul-sapping humidity.

Thanks to "The Rumble in the Jungle," Ali was better prepared to handle the muggy working conditions. Somewhat surprisingly, Ali took the fight to Bugner in the opening round as he backed the larger Brit to the ropes, landed several hard blows and initiated virtually every attack. This was a far different Ali than the one who sleepwalked against Ron Lyle, and while he fought before an estimated 22,000 spectators, (1) Ali really was performing for an audience of one -- Joe Frazier.

Frazier, who was doing color commentary with blow-by-blow man Don Dunphy and was acting as the telecast's "unofficial official," appeared to be a man bedeviled by mixed feelings. His hatred for Ali as a man was quite real -- and, to many, quite justified -- yet because he was to be his next opponent, and the source of his next big paycheck, he had to root for Ali's success. Following a round in which Ali out-landed Bugner 16-7 overall and nearly doubled the challenger's output (45-24), Frazier said he gave the stanza to Ali, who he repeatedly called "my man."

Ali shifted into dancer mode in the second, though he occasionally leaped in behind a flurry. Meanwhile, the straight-up Bugner remained in reactive mode as he either followed Ali around the ring or fended off his attacks. Bugner found marginal success with a series of impressively quick jabs but just when it appeared he had generated some momentum he retreated to the ropes and balled up into a semi "Rope-a-Dope."

Between rounds two and three, a small but very vocal British contingent chanted Bugner's name, which caused Ali to rise from his stool and glare at that section. Ali responded by putting more power into his punches and keeping the ultra-defensive Bugner on the back foot. A nifty right-left-right to the jaw near the end of the third generated a deafening roar from the already energetic crowd.

Between rounds three and four, it was the Ali partisans' turn to chant for their man and the support continued to pour in round after round. Ali responded by being much more aggressive. After Bugner refused to bite on a brief "Rope-a-Dope" late in the fourth, Ali jumped in, threw a combination and backed Bugner to the ropes. Ali then retreated to the ropes and covered up, prompting Bugner to stand 15 feet away and beckon him in. Ali had no choice but to comply but he made Bugner pay by throwing a couple of more combinations before the bell.

Aside from the sixth (in which Bugner narrowly out-landed Ali for the first time in the fight), and especially the 12th when Bugner produced his only significant surge (21-5 overall, 17-2 power), Ali was in full command of the proceedings and did pretty much as he pleased before being declared the unanimous decision winner (73-67, 73-65 and 72-65 under the five-point must). Ali also was the far stronger finisher in the final three rounds because, first, he accelerated his work rate from 14 in the 12th to 41, 41 and 49 while Bugner throttled down from 46 to 18, 22 and 18; second, Ali out-landed Bugner 53-18 overall and 41-11 power in the 13th through 15; and, third, Ali recorded a fight-high 25 total connects and 16 landed power shots in the final round while Bugner was mired in single digits (six total connects, four landed power shots).

More remarkably, Ali was extraordinarily aggressive in terms of his punch selection as he threw far more power punches than jabs (372 versus 146), a dramatic reversal from the norm. Against Lyle, Ali had thrown 14 more jabs than power shots (150 versus 136) while the gaps were larger against Wepner (349 jabs versus 261 power shots), Foreman (154 versus 109) and Norton (416 versus 239 in the first fight, 352 versus 266 in the rematch). Entering the Bugner rematch, Ali had averaged 52.7 punches per round, of which 29.6 were jabs and 23 were power punches, so his willingness to throw hard and often in this bout was noteworthy.

While Ali's jab was immensely accurate (38% for the fight), he never reached double-digit connects. His high-water mark occurred in the 15th when he landed nine of his 14 jabs but before that he landed no more than six and in rounds 8-14 he failed to get to five. In fact, Bugner actually out-jabbed Ali 63-55, a prop bet that surely would have garnered a nice payout had it been available. For the fight, Ali averaged just 9.7 jab attempts per round, a stunningly low number for a stick-and-mover who was known as much for the stick as for the move.

For all of Ali's kinetic activity, the raw numbers indicated a slow-paced fight as Ali averaged 34.5 punches per round to Bugner's 23.1, well below the 44.6 heavyweight average.

THE RING's Nat Loubet was deeply unimpressed by the proceedings. He pointedly summed up the bout by listing four immutable facts:

"One: Nobody got hurt. Two: Nobody got cut. Three: Nobody got knocked down. Four: Nobody wants to go back here for another fight." (2)

Bugner was roasted by the British press with more intensity than the Malaysian sun could ever produce.

"Any fighter given the rare opportunity to bear the most prized crown in sport should be prepared to die in the attempt," wrote Colin Hart, who, appropriately, opined for The Sun newspaper. "He (Bugner) should never have enough surplus energy left to cavort in bathing trunks like a package holiday tourist. A comprehensive points defeat is no cause for a celebration party. Never once did he give the impression he was about to abandon caution -- break the rules and go down kicking. Going out with a flourish is better than finishing a flop."

The scorn deeply hurt Bugner's then-wife Melody so much that she wanted to move to America. While Bugner offered no comment on that score, he said the following about his performance against Ali:

"I still think I could have beaten him anywhere else in the world. I had Ali whipped but the conditions beat me. I believe what I did against Ali was correct. But the pressurization got to me. It was no use giving all my guts by, say, the fifth round and leaving them in the ring." (3)

From Ali's perspective, the Bugner rematch couldn't have gone much better: He got in 15 rounds of work without having to expend himself too severely, he won decisively on all three scorecards and he showed Frazier that he was ready, willing and able to go to war with him.

The war of words between the two old antagonists began even before the Bugner fight was over because between rounds 14 and 15 Ali walked across the ring, peered down and Frazier and started to taunt him. As has been the case over all the years, Frazier gave it right back to his rival, pointing his finger and saying repeatedly "you are going to get it."

With his second "W" over Bugner now safely in Ali's column, the world was about to get it too.

INSIDE THE NUMBERS: Bugner, obviously bothered by the 105-degree heat and humidity, threw just 346 punches, an average of 23.1 per round. That's the lowest total by an Ali opponent in 11 of his title fights that went the 15 round distance. In a rare occurrence, Ali had a sizeable advantage in power connects (130-58) over Bugner.

Date:	June 30, 1975				City: Kuala Lumpur, MY					Venue: Merdeka Stadium						
Opponent:	Joe Bugner															
Result:	Ali by unanimous decision -- Retained World Heavyweight Title															
Referee:	Takeo Ugo															
	Round	1	2	3	4	5	6	7	8	9	10	11	12	13	14	15	Total
	Ali																73
	Bugner																67
Judge:	Ken Brady															
	Round	1	2	3	4	5	6	7	8	9	10	11	12	13	14	15	Total
	Ali																72
	Bugner																65
Judge:	Lt. Col. Suthee Promjara															
	Round	1	2	3	4	5	6	7	8	9	10	11	12	13	14	15	Total
	Ali																73
	Bugner																65

MUHAMMAD ALI UD 15 JOE BUGNER
06/30/75 - KUALA LUMPUR

Total Punches Landed / Thrown	1	2	3	4	5	6	7	8	9	10	11	12	13	14	15
ALI	16/45	7/21	12/29	8/25	11/34	8/27	15/41	12/34	13/46	13/37	12/34	5/14	13/41	15/41	25/49
	35.6%	33.3%	41.4%	32%	32.4%	29.6%	36.6%	35.3%	28.3%	35.1%	35.3%	35.7%	31.7%	36.6%	51%
BUGNER	7/24	3/13	7/13	8/15	7/19	11/44	5/15	8/26	8/22	10/25	8/26	21/46	4/18	8/22	6/18
	29.2%	23.1%	53.8%	53.3%	36.8%	25%	33.3%	30.8%	36.4%	40%	30.8%	45.7%	22.2%	36.4%	33.3%

Jab Landed / Thrown	1	2	3	4	5	6	7	8	9	10	11	12	13	14	15
ALI	5/9	5/7	6/11	4/12	2/6	1/8	5/11	4/11	3/14	3/6	2/11	3/6	0/7	3/13	9/14
	55.6%	71.4%	54.5%	33.3%	33.3%	12.5%	45.5%	36.4%	21.4%	50%	18.2%	50%	0%	23.1%	64.3%
BUGNER	7/23	3/13	5/9	2/6	7/18	4/34	4/14	4/17	6/18	3/10	7/23	4/18	1/10	4/13	2/9
	30.4%	23.1%	55.6%	33.3%	38.9%	11.8%	28.6%	23.5%	33.3%	30%	30.4%	22.2%	10%	30.8%	22.2%

Power Punches Landed / Thrown	1	2	3	4	5	6	7	8	9	10	11	12	13	14	15
ALI	11/36	2/14	6/18	4/13	9/28	7/19	10/30	8/23	10/32	10/31	10/23	2/8	13/34	12/28	16/35
	30.6%	14.3%	33.3%	30.8%	32.1%	36.8%	33.3%	34.8%	31.3%	32.3%	43.5%	25%	38.2%	42.9%	45.7%
BUGNER	0/1	0/0	2/4	6/9	0/1	7/10	1/1	4/9	2/4	7/15	1/3	17/28	3/8	4/9	4/9
	0%	0%	50%	66.7%	0%	70%	100%	44.4%	50%	46.7%	33.3%	60.7%	37.5%	44.4%	44.4%

Final Punch Stat Report	Total Punches	Total Jabs	Power Punches
ALI	185/518	55/146	130/372
	35.7%	37.7%	34.9%
BUGNER	121/346	63/235	58/111
	35%	26.8%	52.3%

25.

October 1, 1975 - Araneta Coliseum, Manila, Philippines
Muhammad Ali KO 14 Joe Frazier III

When Ali committed to meet Frazier for the third time, promoter Don King billed the fight as "The Saga of Our Lifetime," but Ali, ever the brilliant marketer, had a better idea. He came up with perhaps the best nickname ever given to a boxing match: "The Thrilla In Manila."

"It'll be a killa, a chilla, and a thrilla when I get 'the Gorilla' in Manila," boasted Ali. After making fun of Frazier's diction at a press conference, Ali reached into his pocket and pulled out a black rubber gorilla.

"This here is Joe Frazier's conscience. I keep it everywhere I go," he told reporters. Then, as he pounded the toy's face with his right fist he said, "This is the way he looks when you hit him. All night long, this is what you'll see. Come on 'Gorilla,' we in Manila. Come on 'Gorilla,' this is a thrilla." (1)

As King and the assembled media chuckled at Ali's childish taunts, Frazier had long surpassed the boiling point. In his mind, Ali had crossed several lines. While it's fairly common for a boxer to make light of his opponent's fighting ability, few ever dared to mock his foe's speech pattern or use imagery with such overtly racial overtones. By now Frazier was used to Ali's barbs but here the acidity had reached a new level.

"It's real hatred," Frazier said shortly before the fight. "I want to hurt him. I don't want to knock him out. I want to take his heart out. If I knock him down, I'll stand back, give him a chance to breathe, to get up." (2)

While the emotions on both sides were genuine, many observers wondered if either still had the talent to match the hype. To be sure, both fighters were past their prime, and that mutual erosion led to the fight being seen as a pick-'em affair. The odds-makers installed Ali as a narrow 6-to-5 favorite and an article that rated the fighters on a five-point scale in 20 categories saw Frazier with a narrow half-point lead (85.0-84.5) . That system, by the way, foresaw Ali's victory over Foreman as Ali prevailed 83.5-80. (3)

The numbers further illustrated the state of their respective careers going into the match.

Ali had fought four times since the second fight with Frazier: The stunning eighth-round KO over George Foreman in "The Rumble in the Jungle;" his Sylvester Stallone-inspiring 15th round KO over Chuck Wepner; a bore-snore 11th round TKO of Ron Lyle; and a 15-round decision over previous victim Joe Bugner in the searing heat and humidity of Malaysia. In those fights,

198

Ali averaged only 34.2 punches per round, probably because he spent extended time propped against the ropes or clowning around. Ali's punch-per-round pace in these fights was markedly slower than the 55 he averaged in the 12 fights between the first and second fights with Frazier, and his jab wasn't nearly the weapon (16.3 thrown/5.8 connects per round) that it had been (33 thrown/10.7 connects per round).

But when Ali chose to fight, he still did so with breathtaking accuracy. He landed a combined 40% of his total punches, 36% of his jabs and 44% of his power punches while taking 26% overall, 14% jabs and 35% power. His offensive numbers were far higher than the figures he recorded in the 12 CompuBox-tracked fights between Frazier I and Frazier II (34% overall, 32% jabs, 36% power), while the superior quality of his post-Frazier I opponents resulted in Ali absorbing more punishment (34% overall, 26% jabs, 41% power).

Ali knew from past experience that he couldn't get past Frazier throwing only 34 punches per round; "Smokin' Joe's" style demanded full effort from his opponents. The big question for Ali was how much effort he could still produce. After all, he was a 15-year pro who was a little more than three months away from his 34th birthday and was about to engage in his 51st professional fight.

Meanwhile, Frazier had fought only twice since losing to Ali, and both were knockout victories over previous opponents Jerry Quarry (KO 5) and Jimmy Ellis (KO 9). Frazier-Quarry I was an epic slugfest that won THE RING's 1969 Fight of the Year, but in the rematch only Frazier had any semblance of his previous form. Quarry did his best to fight intelligently in the early going but once Frazier drew him into a trench war, his fate was sealed. In rounds four and five Frazier out-landed Quarry 51-10 overall, 15-1 jabs and 36-9 power, a beating so graphic that Frazier implored referee Joe Louis to stop the contest. When the "Brown Bomber" refused, Angelo Dundee, an analyst for the broadcast, dropped his headset and screamed at Louis to step in. Instead, a badly cut Quarry and his corner were forced to give in.

Frazier feasted on Quarry's porous defense as he landed 53% of his total punches, 42% of his jabs and 55% of his power shots while Quarry connected on 25%, 5% and 31% respectively. Thanks to his surge in the final one-and-a-half rounds, Frazier prevailed 138-70 overall, 20-3 jabs and 118-67 power. Against the badly faded Ellis, who had gone 1-4-1 in his last six fights and would fight only once more before retiring, Frazier took his sluggishness in training into the ring; he averaged just 24.3 punches in the first three rounds, which saw Ellis average 45.3 and out-land Frazier 42-27 overall and 22-7 jabs. Starting in the fourth, however, Frazier accelerated to 54 punches to Ellis' 30 and landed with more regularity. In rounds four through nine, Frazier out-landed Ellis 122-46 overall and 107-23 power before a barrage of unanswered blows prompted Dundee -- Ellis' manager and Ali's trainer -- to ask the referee, recently-retired light heavyweight champion Bob Foster, to stop the contest. While Frazier was his usually accurate self (41% overall, 34% jabs, 42% power), he was much easier to hit as Ellis landed 41% of his power shots. That would be bad news against a sharpshooter like Ali.

A common misconception is that Frazier was a bad defensive fighter in general and was even worse during this stage of his ring life. The numbers indicate the opposite, for in the four fights after meeting Ali for the first time (KO 4 Terry Daniels, KO 4 Ron Stander, KO by 2 George Foreman and W 12 Joe Bugner), Frazier absorbed just 25% overall, 14% jabs and 33% power while landing 51%, 30% and 55% respectively. Take away the Foreman bout, where he took 50% overall, 45% jabs and 54% power, and the defensive numbers are even better: 23% overall, 11% jabs and 31% power, all of which were well below the heavyweight averages of 34%, 26% and 41% and were markedly better than his six CompuBox-tracked fights before meeting Ali for the first time (30% overall, 17% jabs, 38% power). Indeed, the bob-and-weave defense worked well against most opponents and Frazier's bad rap on defense comes mostly from his performances against Foreman and Ali.

If the heavyweight championship of the world wasn't a big enough prize, two other rewards loomed for the winner. First, the privilege of being perceived by historians as the better fighter pound-for-pound. And second: Bragging rights for the rest of their lives.

"When it came down to Manila, (it) wasn't (just for) the heavyweight championship of the world," Hall of Fame writer Jerry Izenberg declared. "Ali and Frazier were fighting for something more important than that. They were fighting for the championship of each other." (4)

To accommodate American TV, the fight began at 10:45 a.m. local time. Despite the early hour, conditions inside the Araneta Coliseum in Quezon City (which was located within the Metro Manila area) were oppressive. The aluminum roof, the lack of air conditioning, and the body heat generated by thousands of spectators turned the arena into a sauna. Sitting in it was bad enough; imagine having to fight either Joe Frazier or Muhammad Ali in that environment.

Aware of Frazier's reputation as a slow starter -- and knowing he had stunned "Smokin' Joe" late in the second round of their rematch -- Ali began the fight flat-footed and eager to exchange while Frazier, wearing a smiling sneer, ducked Ali's punches and sought to bang the body. With 20 seconds remaining, Ali landed a compact hook that wobbled Frazier. Ali gunned for the early finish but Frazier avoided most of the incoming and, at round's end, even playfully tugged at the bottom of Ali's trunks before walking to his corner.

Unlike his recent fights with Wepner and Lyle, Ali was all business in round one as he fired 80 punches, landed 34 of them and connected on 26 of 58 power shots. Conversely, Frazier threw 35 and landed 15 total punches as well as nine power shots.

Encouraged by his early success, Ali continued to attack. But when Frazier started to land more often, Ali resorted to his oft-used tactic of placing his glove on the back of his opponent's neck and pushing down. Before the fight, Eddie Futch, Frazier's chief second, complained bitterly about Ali's move and made sure that referee Carlos Padilla was made aware of it. Futch's lobbying worked: Padilla made a point of stopping the action and issuing a stern warning the first time Ali tried the maneuver.

Without the stalling tactic at his disposal, the fighters exchanged more freely -- and Frazier actually got the better of the action in round two as he out-landed Ali 22-17 overall and landed 69% of his power shots (20 of 29) to Ali's 50% (14 of 28).

The fighters continued to pound each other in rounds three through five, and although Frazier got in his fair share of blows, Ali out-landed the challenger 77-72 overall and 73-72 in power shots in those sessions. Despite the torrid heat, the pace was faster than anyone had a right to expect as Ali averaged 61.6 punches per round to Frazier's 45.4 through the opening five. Frazier more than made up for his lower output by landing 51% of his power shots while Ali connected on 44% of his.

While the first third of the fight belonged to Ali, the second five-round segment was clearly Frazier's. Just seconds into the sixth, Frazier landed a massive hook to the jaw that forced Ali to cover up, then connected with a half-dozen more throughout the rest of the round to drive home the point. Statistically speaking, round six was a landslide for Frazier as he out-landed Ali 32-15 overall and connected on 56% of his power punches to Ali's 36%.

Knowing Frazier had seized the momentum, Ali tried to turn it back his way in the seventh by suddenly shifting into butterfly mode. Ali attempted a fight-high 44 jabs and landed 25 of them, also his highest total for the fight, and those jabs enabled him to land 21 of his 37 power shots, which resulted in a brilliant 46 of 81 round overall. But Ali's movement barely deterred Frazier, who went 25 of 50 overall and connected on 23 of his 47 power shots.

Ali returned to his flat-footed self in the eighth and traded with Frazier, whose face was noticeably swollen. But because the champion couldn't maintain the pace, Frazier won the round's second half by digging in and blasting Ali with meaty power shots whose effects reverberated through his body. While the totality of round eight was nearly even -- Ali led 41-39 in total connects and 39-38 in power shots -- the flow of the action had clearly shifted toward Frazier.

For Ali, rounds nine and 10 were hell on earth. As Ali rested on the ropes Frazier hammered him with punches that had the look and feel of payback.

"You call me an Uncle Tom?" Whack! *"I'm a gorilla?"* Boom! *"I'm so ugly that I should donate my face to the U.S. Bureau of Wildlife?"* Wham! One could almost hear the James Brown tune "The Payback" in the background as Frazier settled into his brutal groove.

Only Ali's massive pride kept him upright under the assault. But his even more gigantic fighting heart prompted him to fire back. While Frazier out-landed Ali 30-8 in round nine (including 30-5 in power shots), Frazier's leads in the 10th were only 36-32 overall and 33-32 power. That said, the power behind each of Frazier's blows dramatically drained Ali's gas tank, so much so that Ali was forced to confront his own mortality.

"Man, this the closest I've ever been to dying," Ali told Dundee between rounds.

He had every reason to feel that way. In rounds 6-10 Frazier upped his work rate from 45.4 to 53.8 and out-landed the champion 162-142 overall and 155-111 power, landing 70.4% of his non-jabs in round eight and 66.7% in round nine.

And yet, sometime during that rest period, Ali tapped into a reservoir accessible to only the greatest of fighters. That reservoir not only injected renewed energy into Ali's arms and legs, it also revitalized his spirit.

Given the pounding he absorbed in rounds nine and 10, Ali improbably began the 11th by dancing, firing snappy jabs and raking Frazier with lashing combinations that raised welts on the challenger's forehead to accompany his swelling eyes. Round 11 saw Ali land 47 punches overall -- his highest total of the contest to date -- and his 39-29 lead in power connects marked only the fourth time that Ali prevailed in that category. His 65% power accuracy also was his best of the match to date.

It was a rally whose strength and effectiveness was breathtaking, especially considering how far gone Ali had looked just minutes earlier. Still, Frazier continued to fire back. In fact, he landed 29 of 57 overall (51%) and 29 of 55 power shots (53%) in the 11th, figures that any fighter would have been proud to produce. It was apparent, however, that the tide had turned in a most consequential way. If Frazier wanted to become the third man ever to regain the heavyweight championship, he had to find a way to stem Ali's surge.

Ali's ferocious finishing kick continued in the 13th as a sharp right to the face sent Frazier's bloody mouthpiece flying out of the ring. In the round's final minute, another right caused Frazier to stumble backward. By round's end the damage Ali inflicted was devastating: He led 40-19 in overall connects while doubling Frazier in landed power shots (36-18) and connecting on 62% of his power shots to Frazier's 46%.

As bad as the 13th had been for Frazier, the 14th was even worse. Frazier's eyes had been pounded into slits, the left side of his head was misshapen and blood poured from his mouth. He could no longer hold his arms high enough to defend himself and his trademark bob-and-weave was a distant memory. Meanwhile, Ali tore into his nearly helpless foe like a typhoon and the punishment was ceaseless.

Ali's 14th round dominance was extraordinary. He threw 74 punches to Frazier's 32. He landed 50 total punches to Frazier's eight and he connected with 68% of his overall punches as well as

68% of his power shots to Frazier's 25% and 24% respectively. At the bell, Padilla had to guide Frazier toward his corner, where the man leading it was waiting for him.

That man, Eddie Futch, had seen enough.

"I'm going to stop it," Futch told Frazier. The proud former champion tried to convince Futch to let him finish the fight but offered no resistance when his chief second pressed down on his shoulder. Futch then turned to Padilla and waved off the fight.

"I thought the fight should be stopped because he (Frazier) was being belted with too many clean shots," Futch said. "He was blind in his right eye and couldn't see Ali's left hand coming at him. I felt that Joe was going to pieces, was worn down after two bad rounds." (5)

The pain Ali inflicted in rounds 11-14 was prodigious. During that stretch Ali averaged 72.3 punches per round to Frazier's 44.5 and out-landed the challenger 173-83 overall and 141-81 power. In rounds 13 and 14 alone the connect gaps were 90-27 overall and 68-25 power.

But while Frazier didn't want to quit, Ali nearly did. Years later, it was revealed in HBO's documentary "Thrilla in Manila" that Willie "The Worm" Monroe, a member of Frazier's camp who was seated near Ali's corner, had overheard Ali telling Dundee to cut the gloves off, a story later confirmed by Ali corner man Wali Muhammad, personal physician Dr. Ferdie Pacheco and Ali himself to author Tom Hauser. (6) Monroe frantically gestured toward the Frazier corner but his actions went unseen. Had they been, would Futch have waited out the rest period to see if Ali would pull the parachute? We'll never know.

After being pushed to his physical and emotional limits, Ali had nothing but praise for his rival.

"He is tough," Ali declared. "He is a great fighter. I'm so tired I don't want to do nothing. I want to rest for one week. My arms are sore, my legs are sore, my sides are sore. He is the best fighter there is -- except (for) me." (7)

THE RING deemed Ali-Frazier III its Fight of the Year (8) and in 1996, the magazine rated it the number-one fight of all time. (9) Ali earned his third Fighter of the Year honor in the last four years (10) and his status as one of history's most resilient heavyweights was cemented for all time.

Frazier, too, would be fondly remembered for his considerable contributions to the trilogy. He joined Ali as a charter member of the International Boxing Hall of Fame's inaugural class in 1990 and in September 2015, nearly four years after his death, his adopted hometown of Philadelphia unveiled a 12-foot bronze statue in his likeness. (11) Though born in South Carolina, Frazier will forever personify the special drive and determination of "The Philadelphia Fighter."

One of the greatest signs of respect a series of fights can be given is to have each of the fighter's surnames separated by a hyphen. Robinson-LaMotta, Zale-Graziano, Gatti-Ward, Barrera-Morales, Vazquez-Marquez and Bowe-Holyfield are only six such examples but as wondrous as those multi-fight series were, all must cede the top spot to Ali-Frazier, which was, as Ali would say, "the greatest of all time."

INSIDE THE NUMBERS: Frazier's relentless pressure and vicious body attack forced Ali to fight Smokin' Joe's fight, as 712 of Ali's 917 thrown punches (77.7%) were power punches. Compare that ratio to Ali's career breakdown: 53.6% jabs thrown and 46.4% power shots thrown. Ali and Frazier combined to land 797 total punches (56.9 combined landed per round, nearly double the combined heavyweight average of 30.6) and 702 power punches (50.1 combined landed per round, MORE than double the combined heavyweight average of 20). Even more brutality: 88.1% of their combined landed punches were power shots. Ali's 365 power connects (165 more than his previous high of 200 vs. Chuvalo I) and 712 power attempts (250 more than his previous high of 462 vs. Frazier II and 17.8 more per round by Ali than in any other fight tracked by CompuBox.) were the high totals for the 47 of his fights tracked by CompuBox. Ali's 917 thrown punches is the third highest total behind the 1,132 he threw against Mac Foster and the 1,038 he attempted in the first George Chuvalo fight. His 443 landed punches ranks as the second most in the study, topped only by his 474 landed in the first Chuvalo fight. Ali landed 46 or more punches in three different rounds vs. Frazier and he landed 36 or more power punches in three different rounds. Ali's 48.3% connect percentage was surpassed only by his masterful performance versus Cleveland Williams nine years earlier, when he landed 55.8% of his total punches. Frazier's 354 landed punches was the third highest by an Ali opponent behind Leon Spinks' 419 in their first fight and Frazier's 378 in their initial meeting. Frazier's 53.7% power accuracy was the second highest percentage landed by an Ali opponent -- and Frazier holds the number-one slot with 59.9% in fight one. Frazier's 337 landed power punches was surpassed only by his 365 landed in their first fight for the most landed by an Ali opponent. Frazier gave Ali's body a hellacious beating, as a whopping 62% of his landed punches were to Ali's flanks -- more than double the CompuBox average. In fact, in the three meetings between these two all-time greats, 63.2% of Frazier landed punches were body shots. In their three fights, Ali and Frazier combined to land 1,858 of 4,241 punches (43.8%), a combined average of 45.3 landed and 103.4 thrown per round. For the record, the divisional averages are a combined 30.6 connects and 89.6 punches thrown. Needless to say, "The Thrilla in Manila" was savagery personified and the numbers prove that beyond doubt.

Date:	October 1, 1975					City: Manila, Philippines			Venue: Araneta Coliseum							
Opponent:	Joe Frazier															
Result:	Ali by TKO after the 14th round (corner retirement) -- Retained World Heavyweight Title															

Referee: Carlos Padilla

Round	1	2	3	4	5	6	7	8	9	10	11	12	13	14	15	Total
Ali																66
Frazier																60

Judge: Larry Nadayag

Round	1	2	3	4	5	6	7	8	9	10	11	12	13	14	15	Total
Ali																66
Frazier																62

Judge: Alfredo Quiazon

Round	1	2	3	4	5	6	7	8	9	10	11	12	13	14	15	Total
Ali																67
Frazier																62

MUHAMMAD ALI KO 14 JOE FRAZIER
10/01/75 - MANILA, PHILLIPINES

Total Punches Landed / Thrown

	1	2	3	4	5	6	7	8	9	10	11	12	13	14	15
ALI	34/80	17/41	24/61	31/65	22/61	15/47	46/81	41/85	8/42	32/65	47/76	36/64	40/75	50/74	-/-
	42.5%	41.5%	39.3%	47.7%	36.1%	31.9%	56.8%	48.2%	19%	49.2%	61.8%	56.3%	53.3%	67.6%	-
FRAZIER	15/35	22/37	26/60	22/47	24/48	32/57	25/50	39/56	30/45	36/61	29/57	27/47	19/42	8/32	-/-
	42.9%	59.5%	43.3%	46.8%	50%	56.1%	50%	69.6%	66.7%	59%	50.9%	57.4%	45.2%	25%	-

Jab Landed / Thrown

	1	2	3	4	5	6	7	8	9	10	11	12	13	14	15
ALI	8/22	3/13	1/4	1/8	2/5	1/8	25/44	2/6	3/23	0/5	8/16	2/7	4/17	18/27	-/-
	36.4%	23.1%	25%	12.5%	40%	12.5%	56.8%	33.3%	13%	0%	50%	28.6%	23.5%	66.7%	-
FRAZIER	6/13	2/8	0/5	0/2	0/1	1/2	2/3	1/2	0/0	3/3	0/2	0/0	1/3	1/3	-/-
	46.2%	25%	0%	0%	0%	50%	66.7%	50%	0%	100%	0%	0%	33.3%	33.3%	-

Power Punches Landed / Thrown

	1	2	3	4	5	6	7	8	9	10	11	12	13	14	15
ALI	26/58	14/28	23/57	30/57	20/56	14/39	21/37	39/79	5/19	32/60	39/60	34/57	36/58	32/47	-/-
	44.8%	50%	40.4%	52.6%	35.7%	35.9%	56.8%	49.4%	26.3%	53.3%	65%	59.6%	62.1%	68.1%	-
FRAZIER	9/22	20/29	26/55	22/45	24/47	31/55	23/47	38/54	30/45	33/58	29/55	27/47	18/39	7/29	-/-
	40.9%	69%	47.3%	48.9%	51.1%	56.4%	48.9%	70.4%	66.7%	56.9%	52.7%	57.4%	46.2%	24.1%	-

Final Punch Stat Report

Total	Total Punches	Total Jabs	Power Punches
ALI	443/917	78/205	365/712
	48.3%	38%	51.3%
FRAZIER	354/674	17/47	337/627
	52.5%	36.2%	53.7%

PAST PRIME ALI: COOPMAN THROUGH BERBICK

With the "Thrilla in Manila" behind Ali, those closest to him, particularly Dr. Ferdie Pacheco, felt the time had come for the great fighter to bow out gracefully and enjoy the fruits of his spectacular labor. But he and everyone else connected with the Ali Circus knew that Ali was the one and only ringmaster and that only he had the power to close down the show. His decision to keep going not only was dictated by finances, it also was fueled by his continuous love of the limelight.

Ali knew the risks. He felt the heaviness of age in his arms and legs. He perceived the dullness of thought in his mind and the thickness of speech from his tongue. Worse yet, he also knew the zest for training that had defined his younger years was long gone. For him, the sit-ups, the medicine ball drills, the rope-jumping and the sparring had become necessary evils instead of ways of burning off the excess energy of youth. But the drudgery was still worth it. He loved the hype. He loved the cheers. And he loved the heavyweight title and all that came with it.

In all, the Ali Circus played 10 more dates. Most would leave a sour taste. More than any grouping of fights, these Past Prime fights likely exacerbated the health issues that would leave Ali tragically damaged and rendered him virtually silent for the final few decades of his life. One statistic that could graphically explain his post-career neurological difficulties can be found in the following statistic: In the 20 fights before the Thrilla in Manila Ali absorbed 71.9 punches to the head per fight but in the 10 fights following the Thrilla, the average number of head shots he took nearly doubled to 142.3

Ali's relatively leisurely approach to training was enough to get him through the first fight of the Final Ten, his fifth round TKO over the hopelessly overmatched "Lion of Flanders," Jean-Pierre Coopman. The next nine, however, would see Ali absorb horrific damage.

Of those nine bouts, Ali was out-landed in seven of them and the margins Ali's foes racked up are staggering. In those seven fights (which did not include his decision victories over Alfredo Evangelista or his rematch win over Leon Spinks, the fights in which Ali prevailed in overall connects), Ali's foes averaged nearly 14 more punches thrown per round (57.1 to Ali's 43.4), almost 11 more total connects each round (22.5 versus Ali's 12) and more than doubled Ali's per-round power connects (15.3 versus 7), figures most people believed unthinkable during his better years.

Worse yet, Ali's usually woeful defense was even more so while his accuracy wasn't anywhere near that of his zenith. While Ali connected on 28% of his total punches and 34% of his hooks, crosses and uppercuts in his seven worst fights, his opponents in those bouts landed 39% overall and a sky-high 48% of their power punches. The unkindest cut of all was that those seven antagonists -- Jimmy Young, Richard Dunn, Ken Norton (fight three), Earnie Shavers, Leon Spinks (first fight), Larry Holmes and Trevor Berbick -- collectively out-jabbed the man considered by many the best jabber in heavyweight annals. Ali threw 22.5 jabs per round, landing 4.9 for 22%. But his opponents fired 25.5 per round and landed 7.2 for 28% accuracy.

The plus-minus rating, marginal even during the best of times, was an abysmal minus-8.2 in these 10 fights as Ali landed 28.3% of his total punches to their 36.5%. Most telling was the even larger gap in power percentage -- Ali's 33.8% to his opponents' 44.2%.

The raw numbers further illustrate the damage that had been wrought. In the final 10 fights Ali was out-landed 2,230-1,471 in total punches and 1,565-833 in power shots. In 45 of the 120 total rounds in this phase, or 37.5%, Ali's foes landed at least 50% of their power punches while Ali's jab, such a prolific weapon in his prime, was a shadow, for only 16 times in his last 10 fights did he register 10 or more connects in a round. In his prime fights, which also numbered 10 bouts, he reached that threshold 39 times. Moreover, his jab landed only 5.3 times per round compared to 8.6 for the "Comeback Years" Ali, 10.5 for the Prime Ali and 6.4 for the Young Clay. While 5.3 is a good number for most fighters, it was a clear step down for one of the best jabbers in history.

The wear-and-tear of age could be also seen in his far slower trigger. While the Young Clay averaged 64.8 punches per round and the Prime and "Comeback Years" Ali threw 51.6 and 50.6 per round respectively, the Past Prime Ali produced just 43.4. Also, his total connects per round were dramatically down. Up until now Ali had been remarkably consistent, for in the other phases he had logged 18.9, 18.9 and 18 connects per round. Here, however, his average plunged to 12.3. Meanwhile, his opponents' success surged as they averaged 18.6 connects per round against the Past Prime Ali compared to 12.3 against the Young Clay, 11.7 versus the Prime Ali and 14.3 against the "Comeback Years" Ali.

As bad as these figures are -- and they are -- they are only part of the story. What can't be measured is the punishment Ali absorbed during hundreds of sparring sessions during training camp as well as countless exhibitions in which the intensity varied widely. Some, like a very young Michael Dokes and NFL player Lyle Alzado, fought to the best of their ability and forced Ali to push himself harder than he should have because of the unspoken ground rules that dictate such situations. Others heeded those dictates and placed fun over competition.

James "Smitty" Smith, veteran broadcaster and the star of the long-running series "In This Corner," had a up-close and personal view of Ali's sparring sessions at the Fifth Street Gym in Miami. He first met Ali at age 11 and their shared boldness created an instant bond that ended up lasting decades.

"I gained access because of my access to Ali," Smith said in a July 2017 phone interview. "Ali would tell his people to let 'my main man, the little white boy' underneath the little rope that cordoned off the fans from the fighters. After a while -- because Ali let me -- I knew it wouldn't be hard for me to get underneath the rope and get access to do pretty much what I wanted.

"Beginning with the first Frazier fight I watched him spar several times a week, on the days that I was out of school as well as the days when my sixth-grade teacher, Mr. Wilson, let me skip school in order to watch him train," he continued. "He let me do it as kind of a school project and also because he loved Ali and wanted to know how he was preparing for that mega-fight with Frazier. Ali sparred *a lot* for that fight."

Smith maintained this ritual for the next several fights until Ali moved his operations to Deer Lake, Pa. In many of those Miami workouts he saw Ali practice what would become the "Rope-a-Dope."

"(I saw him do that) all the time," he said. "I marveled at how he would let his sparring partners hit underneath his elbows. Sometimes he totally exposed his body and lifted up his arms. When Angelo would see any of that, he would kind of say, 'cut that crap out, stop that,' and Bundini Brown would be yelling the same thing. I witnessed Ali taking *way* too many shots to the body, unguarded shots by Levi Forte, middleweight Nat King, and at other times with other heavyweights. He would tell them to hit him to the body, and then later on, depending on the day or even the session or the round, he would (tell them to) do the same thing to the head. Now, he would put his guard up, but in no way firing back, not counter-punching, kind of doing the 'Rope-a-Dope' thing even before he popularized it and made it famous and legendary against George Foreman. Anybody that has boxed, or even sparred, knows that you hold those hands up. If you get in there with guys that can punch, it rattles your brain."

While most observers associate the "Rope-a-Dope" with the second half of his career, its origins date back to the mid-1960s. Ali allowed George Chuvalo to whale away at his body for the first five rounds of their 1966 fight before switching gears and dominating the rest of the fight, and one apparently knowledgeable letter-writer to Boxing Illustrated claimed the tactic dated back to before the first Liston fight.

"Those who remember Ali's training regimen for his title-winning fight with Sonny Liston will also recall that Ali, after going several warm-up rounds with Jimmy Ellis, would retreat to the ropes and permit a heavy-hitting spar-mate named Shotgun Sheldon to whale away at his head and body while he practiced covering up," wrote Donn-Wayne Bridges of La Puente, Calif. in the October 1977 issue. "Ali felt that if Liston were to survive his middle-rounds assault, he would, in turn, have to defend against Liston's counter-attack by laying on the ropes, blocking Liston's shots and conserving his energy for a big, closing-rounds rally. As it turned out, such tactics never had to be employed." (1)

Joe Bugner and Eddie Mustafa Muhammad were just two of the dozens who helped Ali prepare for his fights, and each bore witness to the unusual protocol Ali demanded.

"He used to instruct me to hit him solidly around the body, to build up his resistance to heavy body hits from Frazier and Foreman," Bugner wrote in his autobiography. "For five rounds in Zaire in 1974, George Foreman gave him the beating of his life. It was only because Ali was young and healthy that he was able to put up with so much punishment." (2)

Mustafa Muhammad met Ali through friends from Newark, N.J. who worked security for the champ. Ali then invited him to train for his March 1980 title shot against then-WBA light heavyweight champion Marvin Johnson at Deer Lake -- free of charge -- while also helping Ali to prepare for his fights with Holmes and Berbick (where Mustafa Muhammad stopped Michael Hardin in eight rounds on that undercard). Ali's deteriorated state was the justification used to establish ground rules.

"I was always told (by Bundini Brown and Wali "Youngblood" Muhammad) not to hit him in the head," Mustafa Muhammad said in a July 2017 phone interview. "That was cool because I was a great body puncher and that's the way I went to work. The only time that I would actually hit him in the head was with a jab and even then I'd only hit him on top of the headgear. He wore Everlast headgear and I would hit him right on the 'Everlast' (logo on his forehead). I would never hit him in the face because they told me just to go easy on his head. Ali knew nothing about the order I was given."

It was an instruction that Mustafa Muhammad eagerly accepted and applied because Ali was a personal hero as well as a Muslim brother (Mustafa Muhammad, the former Eddie Gregory, didn't announce his name change until after he knocked out Johnson in the 11th to win the WBA championship). Also, Mustafa Muhammad believed his restraint was the morally right thing to do.

"It was my way of showing respect," he said. "I respected everything that he had done for me in my life and in my lifetime."

That prohibition, however, didn't apply to other sparring partners that included future heavyweight titlists Tony Tubbs and Tim Witherspoon.

"Everybody else could try to hit him (in the head) because they were heavyweights and they were much slower," he said. "They realized that I was a quick, fast light heavyweight and that I could punch with both hands. I knocked out a lot of guys at Deer Lake -- light heavyweights and cruiserweights -- and Ali witnessed that. So, when he boxed me, he wore 16-ounce gloves and they gave me 20-ounce gloves, which says a lot right there. They respected my punching ability. But I didn't care; I just wanted the opportunity to swap punches with the greatest heavyweight of all time."

Like Mustafa Muhammad, Smith's admiration and gratitude was such that he didn't initially object to the champ's sparring tactics.

"Not at first. I was so in awe of Ali, I idolized him, and he could do no wrong at first with me," he recalled. "I absolutely deluded myself into thinking he beat Frazier the first time. I was a kid, and a kid who had all-access to the greatest, most famous athlete on the planet. At the same time I'm a ball-boy for the (Miami) Dolphins and I'm with Paul Warfield all the time -- maybe the greatest wide receiver at the time. I was in awe of all this and if anything even remotely popped into my mind of 'that's not good,' (I rationalized it by saying) it was Ali doing it. So if it wasn't good, it's good if Ali was doing it. It's got to be OK, right?"

Time and maturity taught Smith that these sparring sessions may have laid the foundation for the health troubles that defined the second half of Ali's life.

"I wasn't there for Bonavena or Quarry but I say (the preparation for the first Frazier fight) was the beginning of the downfall," Smith said. "Ali never was the same after that fight. People talk a lot of the 'Thrilla in Manila' but that fight, *that fight*, was the start. By the way, Frazier would never be the same either. They gave parts of their careers and their lives in that fight."

Smith, whose broadcasting experience has enabled him to notice subtle changes in fighters' speech patterns, spotted erosion in Ali's diction.

"(As Ali aged) everything was measured," he said. "It was apparent when he was getting ready to fight Larry Holmes. There was a period a year or two before that fight, if you watch the preparation before the fight, it was just *unbelievable*. It was a precipitous decline from that point on. I would talk to Angelo Dundee on my radio show later on and at that time everybody wanted to deny that boxing had anything to do with it. But the truth of the matter was that boxing had *everything* to do with it. It was not just his speech, but his movement. It was the difference between a guy whipping around saying (quickly and crispy), 'hey, it's my main man' to 'heeey, it's my maaaain maaaan.' "

It's been said that water droplets, if given enough time, could eventually break the strongest stone. While Ali's chin remained sturdy, his brain cells and internal organs eventually gave way.

"He did everything wrong and we would say Ali got away with it, but he really didn't get away with it," Smith opined. "For every punch Ali avoided, the second or third shots that got through, even the ones that didn't get through cleanly, were still being landed by guys who were heavyweights. In taking the punches, whether it be in the gyms or against Frazier, or Shavers, or Norton, or Foreman, it had the most deleterious effect that it could have on a prizefighter or a human being. Before the exile, Ali was getting hit but not as much because he had the legs to move away then. Those three years (away from boxing) took a lot out of him. His legs weren't the same, he wasn't as fast, he wasn't as swift. When you're at that level and fighting the way he did, just split-seconds can be the difference. Think of a guy hitting the speed bag and how many punches can be thrown. It was those split-seconds (lost by age) that allowed him to be hit with those shots (and) would do the terrible damage. The fights themselves would have taken one hell of a toll, but I think what pushed it over the edge was the gym and getting hit during sparring. That was simply too much water in the pan and it spilled over.

"I never thought Ali would die, which is silly, but I thought he would always be in my life," he concluded. "He was like the Santa Claus figure to me. As you get older and wiser, you realize that there is no 'Santa Claus.' Having said that, he was that type of figure and will always be. Ali told me in the last interview I did with him that if he could have changed anything (in his life) he wouldn't have. He had his blueprint and he was very happy with it. But if I could go back, I'd yell up to him in the ring and say 'stop taking all those punches, champ. You don't need to.'"

For decades afterward, Pacheco portrayed Ali as the ultimate cautionary tale for fighters who opt to fight on too long. The numbers listed in the first several paragraphs of this section and expanded upon in the fights to follow show just how right he was. Because of Ali's choice to fight long beyond "The Thrilla in Manila," the world was robbed of a happy, healthy and eloquent elder statesman. What a shame. And worse yet, it was an avoidable shame.

26.

FEBRUARY 20, 1976 - ROBERTO CLEMENTE COLISEUM, SAN JUAN, PR
MUHAMMAD ALI KO 5 JEAN-PIERRE COOPMAN

Given Ali's "near-death" experience against Frazier in the "Thrilla in Manila," he could be excused for wanting to fight a less demanding opponent. However, few heavyweight title challengers have ever been more lightly regarded than Jean-Pierre Coopman, a sculptor and stone cutter who had fought outside his native Belgium only once, a six-round decision loss to the 1-0 Harald Skog in Oslo in his fifth pro outing. It was one of three defeats Coopman had suffered to this point (the others came against Ireno Werleman, who stopped Coopman in two four fights after Skog, and Rudi Lubbers, who scored a 10-round decision win in fight 16).

Since then, however, Coopman had won his last 11 to push his record to 24-3 with 14 knockouts. During the streak he defeated Charley "Devil" Green (KO 8) and onetime title challenger Terry Daniels (W DQ 7). But while those names were somewhat familiar to the hard-core U.S. fans, the best of the rest were total strangers -- the 16-0-1 Bernd August (W 10), the 12-3 Karsten Honhold (KO 6) and the 28-8-2 Jan Lubbers (W 10) -- much less other fighters he beat in his career like Ferenc Kristofcsak (W DQ 3), Lino Finotti (KO 4), Domingo Silveira (W 10) or Lisimo Obutobe (KO 7), Coopman's last opponent before meeting Ali.

The task of marketing Coopman as a viable title challenger fell to veteran matchmaker George Kanter, a native of Belgium who was at ringside when Coopman stopped Green. Kanter got the gig when, after meeting Coopman's manager following the Green fight, he convinced Ali that Coopman would be the perfect first post-Thrilla opponent.

"European heavyweights weren't much at the time and the heavyweights in Belgium were even less," Kanter told author Thomas Hauser. "And Coopman was perfect."

Just before the opening press conference in New York, Kanter still hadn't figured out a way to sell Coopman to the American media.

"It occurred to me: Belgium is cut up into three parts," he said. "There's Flanders, there's Brussels and there's the Walloon country. Coopman was from Flanders, and on their flag -- it's a yellow flag with a lion on it -- I said to myself, 'well, this is the obvious thing; we'll call him 'The Lion of Flanders.' " (1)

The nickname was a winner with the press but everything else about Coopman as a heavyweight challenger was out of phase. Kanter told Hauser that one public sparring session against a woefully out-of-shape and ring-rusty foe had to be stopped because Coopman was being beaten so badly (the official excuse: Jet lag) and that Coopman was so star-struck by Ali that he wanted to kiss him more than hit him. (2)

"He is one of the nicest men I've met in the ring," Ali said later. "He has a nice trainer, and a lovely and friendly wife." (3)

Later, Kanter told Hauser that he hired a famous witch based in Puerto Rico, ostensibly to conjure the spirits of a dead general and his army to serve as back-up during the Ali fight, which, since Coopman believed in witches, wholeheartedly embraced. (4) At the very least, it made for good pre-fight copy.

Coopman looked no better in subsequent sessions but by weigh-in time he had worked himself into passable condition. At 226, Ali was just one pound under his career high to date while Coopman, at 206, was a full 20 pounds lighter than the champion. That was only one of several deficits the challenger faced, both physical (three-and-a-half inches in height, five inches in reach) and in terms of athletic talent, the gap of which could have been measured in parsecs rather than inches. The odds-makers, whose sole interest was to attract two-way action, deemed Coopman a 20-to-1 underdog, only the fourth time in nearly 35 years that a heavyweight championship challenger was that distant a choice (Tony Musto and Ron Stander were 20-to-1 dogs against Joe Louis and Joe Frazier respectively while no official odds were posted for Pete Rademacher, who challenged Floyd Patterson in his professional debut). (5)

According to Mark Kram of Sports Illustrated, ringside tickets were selling for $200. Because it was Ali and because boxing was (and still is) a major sport in Puerto Rico, sales were brisk. (6)

The stare-down between Ali and Coopman was uneventful, a rarity in an Ali fight. Then came the first round bell, which quickly delivered a hard reality check to all involved -- most of all Coopman.

"Until the bell had sounded, I thought I could win," Coopman told author Stephen Brunt. "But two seconds after the bell, he knew that I was nothing more than a fly. I wanted to spend four or five rounds just putting on the pressure and blocking the shots. But against Ali it didn't work. It came from all sides, from all angles." (7)

Even with Ali entering the ring with a mild cold, it took him less than a minute for his jabs to redden Coopman's face and it required only a little more time for Ali to figure out he could afford to fight with his hands below his waist and to throw in an "Ali Shuffle" whenever he felt like it -- just like the good old days. If that wasn't enough, Ali rubbed Coopman's backside with his right glove during a clinch. Coopman, perhaps the happiest man ever to endure a leather shower, took it all in stride.

The first round numbers adequately described the degree of Ali's command: 26 of 59 (44%) for Ali, 5 of 43 (12%) for Coopman.

There was one department in which Coopman had Ali beaten: While Ali drank water, Coopman rinsed with champagne.

"I had heard a story that Joe Frazier used to wash his mouth between rounds with champagne to get rid of the slime and so on," Coopman told Brunt. "Frazier, he was my idol, he was my man. Frazier, he spit the champagne out. I had always tried to get pointers and tips from everywhere. So I tried it out. I found that cleaning your mouth with champagne actually worked very well. During the first four or five rounds (in past fights) I just spit it out. And from round five or six on, I swallowed a bit of champagne, which made me feel a little bit euphoric, and made me go faster and faster." (8)

With today's post-fight testing, such a tactic would draw a fine at least and title revocation at worst. But for Coopman, it probably helped dull the pain.

Midway through the second, a stinging right lead from Ali opened a cut over Coopman's left eye, but unlike past fights Ali didn't invest full attention on the injury. That's because he was having too much fun hitting Coopman everywhere else.

When guest broadcaster Don Dunphy joined CBS' Pat Summerall and Tom Brookshier between rounds two and three, he was asked to assess Coopman's performance.

"Ali has had more trouble with some of his sparring partners than he's had with Jean-Pierre Coopman," the future Hall of Famer opined. "The Lion of Flanders may leave here as the Pussycat of Ponce Playa Beach."

Ouch.

By the first minute of round three, the Coliseo Roberto Clemente was awash in boos and derisive whistles, for by now it was evident Ali-Coopman was a profound mismatch. Ali landed right leads with impunity and at one point he connected on a quadruple jab-right hand to the forehead. Coopman managed to hit Ali from time to time but every landed punch carried the force of a foam pillow. It wasn't as if Coopman was executing horribly by his standard because, for him, this *was* the standard.

The margins for rounds two and three were similar to that of round one (22-7 and 24-8 overall) but in round four Ali bore down and throttled up by firing 80 punches and landing 35. Coopman also achieved his best numbers in the fourth, but those were 51 punches and nine connects.

"Coopman said before the fight 'I really don't know how good I am,' " Summerall said during the fourth. "He's finding out."

"What a way to learn," Brookshier replied. "On-the-job training with the heavyweight champion."

As Ali stood in his corner between rounds four and five, he looked as relaxed as a defending champion could ever be. That's because he was secure in the knowledge that, for the first time in years, he was about to make a knockout prediction come true. Coopman tried his best to cut down the ring on the floating Ali but he lacked the speed to get to the spot before Ali could.

The end came after Ali fired a four-punch combination capped by a right uppercut to the eye that felled Coopman in his own corner. Tellingly, referee Ismael Quinones Falu lightly pushed down on Coopman's shoulder with his left hand while counting over him with his right. He, like everyone else, just wanted it to be over.

And so it was, at the 2:46 mark of round five. As soon as Falu finished his count Ali immediately walked over to Coopman, draped his right arm over the challenger's shoulder, patted it with his glove and did his best to console the challenger, who spoke no English. No one, most of all Ali, had reason to dislike him personally. This time, the beating he inflicted and the knockout he scored was not the product of malice; it was just business.

In terms of statistics, it was good business for Ali indeed. He out-landed Coopman 122-33 overall, 52-4 jabs and 70-29 power and enjoyed percentage gaps of 42%-17% overall, 34%-5% jabs and 50%-27% power. Of Coopman's 33 connects, only five struck Ali's head. At age 34 and with the years of punishment beginning to take its toll, Ali couldn't have asked for a better outcome in terms of physical punishment.

A kind-hearted Ali told Brookshier this was "a tough fight."

"I may not look like it but the man hit hard," he added. "He was awkward and he could take a lot of punches. I enjoyed the fight and everything was nice."

Coopman had no problems with how the fight ended.

"It was just in time," he told Brunt. "Just in time to get out safe. Surviving the fight was more important than the result. In the dressing room afterward, a lot of Americans were poking around, asking questions. The general feeling was relief. It was never a question of winning or losing. Just surviving. Yes, I lost the fight. But most of them do against Ali. But surviving the fight, that was OK." (9)

What was more OK was that nearly 13 months after losing to Ali, Coopman achieved his dream of becoming European champion when he knocked out Jose Manuel Urtain in the fourth in front of his home nation crowd in Antwerp. His reign lasted all of 56 days, for Frenchman Lucien Rodriguez out-pointed him over 15 rounds, again in Antwerp.

Incredibly, after initially retiring in 1981, Coopman, whose subsequent sculptures and paintings earned positive feedback, came back for one final fight after nearly 18 years on the shelf. According to Boxrec.com, the 52-year-old Coopman faced 50-year-old Freddy De Kerpel before 4,000 fans in Vlaanderen, Belgium. The result: A six-round majority draw. Even better: He weighed one pound *lighter* than he did when he faced Ali 23 years earlier. In boxing terms, the De Kerpel fight qualifies as a pretty happy ending.

One well-worn boxing truism is that anyone who has the courage to walk up the ring steps and box another person deserves utmost respect. But anyone who does so knowing that a far superior opponent awaits him -- one that is ready to deliver a prodigious beating -- possesses an even higher level of fortitude and merits even more regard. For this reason, it can be said that Jean-Pierre Coopman, at least on the night of February 20, 1976, was the bravest man on earth.

INSIDE THE NUMBERS: The overmatched Coopman landed in single digits in all five rounds and landed just 33 total punches. Conversely, Ali landed 52 jabs. Coopman landed just 16.8% of his total punches; only Juergen Blin (15.1%) and Brian London (14.9%) landed at a lower percentage versus the normally defense-challenged Ali.

Date:	February 20, 1976				City: San Juan, PR			Venue: Coliseo Roberto Clemente								
Opponent:	Jean-Pierre Coopman															
Result:	Ali by KO at 2:46 of the 5th round -- Retained World Heavyweight Title															

Referee:	Ismael Quinones Falu															
	Round	1	2	3	4	5	6	7	8	9	10	11	12	13	14	15	Total
	Ali	10	10	10	10												40
	Coopman																

Judge:	Ismael Wiso Fernandez															
	Round	1	2	3	4	5	6	7	8	9	10	11	12	13	14	15	Total
	Ali	10	10	10	10												40
	Coopman																

Judge:	Roberto Ramirez Sr.															
	Round	1	2	3	4	5	6	7	8	9	10	11	12	13	14	15	Total
	Ali	10	10	10	10												40
	Coopman																

MUHAMMAD ALI KO 5 JEAN-PIERRE COOPMAN
02/20/76 - SAN JUAN

Total Punches Landed / Thrown	1	2	3	4	5	6	7	8	9	10	11	12	13	14	15
ALI	26/59	22/50	24/56	35/80	15/46	-/-	-/-	-/-	-/-	-/-	-/-	-/-	-/-	-/-	-/-
	44.1%	44%	42.9%	43.8%	32.6%	-	-	-	-	-	-	-	-	-	-
COOPMAN	5/43	7/39	8/45	9/51	4/19	-/-	-/-	-/-	-/-	-/-	-/-	-/-	-/-	-/-	-/-
	11.6%	17.9%	17.8%	17.6%	21.1%	-	-	-	-	-	-	-	-	-	-

Jab Landed / Thrown	1	2	3	4	5	6	7	8	9	10	11	12	13	14	15
ALI	11/34	7/20	14/37	9/27	11/34	-/-	-/-	-/-	-/-	-/-	-/-	-/-	-/-	-/-	-/-
	32.4%	35%	37.8%	33.3%	32.4%	-	-	-	-	-	-	-	-	-	-
COOPMAN	1/22	0/16	0/18	1/21	2/11	-/-	-/-	-/-	-/-	-/-	-/-	-/-	-/-	-/-	-/-
	4.5%	0%	0%	4.8%	18.2%	-	-	-	-	-	-	-	-	-	-

Power Punches Landed / Thrown	1	2	3	4	5	6	7	8	9	10	11	12	13	14	15
ALI	15/25	15/30	10/19	26/53	4/12	-/-	-/-	-/-	-/-	-/-	-/-	-/-	-/-	-/-	-/-
	60%	50%	52.6%	49.1%	33.3%	-	-	-	-	-	-	-	-	-	-
COOPMAN	4/21	7/23	8/27	8/30	2/8	-/-	-/-	-/-	-/-	-/-	-/-	-/-	-/-	-/-	-/-
	19%	30.4%	29.6%	26.7%	25%	-	-	-	-	-	-	-	-	-	-

Final Punch Stat Report	Total Punches (Body Landed)	Total Jabs (Body Landed)	Power Punches (Body Landed)
ALI	122 (1)/291	52 (0)/152	70 (1)/139
	41.9%	34.2%	50.4%
COOPMAN	33 (28)/197	4 (3)/88	29 (25)/109
	16.8%	4.5%	26.6%

27.

For Muhammad Ali, 1976 promised to be an extraordinarily busy year. Even before facing Coopman in February, Ali knew what lay ahead: Jimmy Young in April, Richard Dunn in May, a boxer-wrestler exhibition against Antonio Inoki in June and the rubber match with the top-rated Ken Norton in September. Because each assignment also required considerable preparation inside the gym, Ali had precious little time to recharge his batteries, and, at 34, that process required much more time – and, in retrospect, more energy – than he had at his disposal.

Ali's potential reward for successfully navigating this ambitious schedule was massive: A gross take that would exceed $10 million, of which $6 million would come from the Inoki match alone (though he ended up being paid $2.2 million). (1) Business was booming, and the business of being Muhammad Ali was, at least on the surface, even better.

History states that Ali avoided defeat in 1976 as he turned back Young, Dunn and Norton while also emerging with a draw against Inoki. Had Ali fought the same fights in the present day, however, Ali may have come out with a 1-3 record. To most eyes, Young and Norton had done more than enough to win the title from Ali while Inoki's kicks inflicted so much damage that Ali was fortunate not only to walk out of the ring under his own power but to fly home without the resulting blood clots killing him. (2) As it was, he had to be hospitalized for several weeks.

Until the late-1980s, the conventional wisdom in boxing was that a challenger had to almost annihilate the defending champion in order to win the title by decision. The common phrase used to describe this concept was that a challenger had to "take it from the champion." Entering 1976, only four times in heavyweight championship history had a challenger won the title on points from a defending champion. The first occurred in February 1906 when Tommy Burns out-pointed Marvin Hart over 20 rounds. The second happened in September 1926 when Gene Tunney overwhelmingly out-boxed the beloved Jack Dempsey over 10 rounds while the third saw Jack Sharkey beat defending champion Max Schmeling by split decision in their June 1932 rematch. The most recent example was when Max Baer virtually handed the title to "Cinderella Man" James J. Braddock with his excessive clowning before losing over 15 rounds. Even then, one judge, George Kelly, still saw fit to score the fight 7-7-1 under the rounds system before deeming Braddock the winner on the supplemental points system. Thankfully, Kelly was overruled by referee Johnny McAvoy (9-5-1) and judge Charley Lynch (11-4), both of whom scored the fight in the ring instead of the mythical belt around Baer's waist.

An added barrier for Ali opponents was that Ali was boxing's biggest star as well as its greatest source of cash flow. He attracted massive media coverage before and after each fight, generated enormous ancillary income for the cities that hosted his matches, produced incredibly high Nielson ratings that, in turn, resulted in huge advertising revenue for the TV networks lucky enough to air his fights. Finally, Ali's fights kept boxing near the top of the pecking order in terms of visibility and relevance. The depth and breadth of his celebrity extended into books and movies as well as other avenues inaccessible to other fighters, such as fast food chains and, in the future, comic books, commercials and a Saturday morning cartoon series. For these reasons, conventional wisdom stated that once Ali's championship reign died, so would boxing as a whole.

For those charged with the responsibility of scoring Ali's fights, this one-two punch of historical precedent and present-day circumstance presented an integrity-based quandary. If Ali's less charismatic opponent out-fought him in a given round, would that judge acknowledge it or would Ali's "champion's advantage" be applied? Since most distance fights have a number of "swing rounds" that are open to interpretation, that advantage could rob the challenger of a close but deserved victory. All of these factors appeared to be in play on April 30, 1976 at the Capitol Center in Landover, Md. when Young challenged Ali.

The 27-year-old Young was the only child of William (an expert welder) and Ruth, and while Young always felt he was a good athlete he didn't join any teams in high school. Young turned to boxing because he felt it was the best way to deal with his expanding waistline.

"I was overweight and I just went down to the Police Athletic League Center gym on 22nd and Columbia in Philly to work out with some guys I knew and lose weight," he said.

Young showed enough talent to take his pursuit to the next level -- an amateur career. There, he compiled a modest 15-6 record which included two New Jersey Golden Gloves titles. (3) Young then turned pro with a first-round TKO over Jimmy Jones October 28, 1969 at Philadelphia's legendary Blue Horizon.

Despite the sensational result in his maiden voyage, Young was a Philadelphia fighter who didn't fight in the city's classically combative style. He was the quintessential "cutie" who put defense above offense, fed off opponent's mistakes with piercing jabs and sharp counterpunches and specialized in making his opponents look bad. That resulted in paydays so sporadic and minimal that between fights he served as a sparring partner for Joe Frazier and Oscar Bonavena as well as future opponents Earnie Shavers and Ken Norton.

"I worked as a sparring partner for Norton before his second fight with Ali and gave him problems," Young recalled. "He never hit me hard, not that he tried to, but I could see then that if Norton was qualified to fight for the championship, eventually my time was coming too." (4)

Young's best victories came against Ron Lyle (W 10), Richard Dunn (KO 8) and Jose Luis Garcia (W 10) but he also experienced setbacks. Shavers crushed Young in three rounds and held him to a draw in the rematch while Clay Hodges, Randy Neumann and Roy Williams accounted for the other defeats.

Young's 17-4-2 record boasted only five knockouts and his personality, while pleasant, couldn't hold a candle to Ali's in terms of attracting and sustaining media attention. For those who appreciated the nuances of self-defense, Young was a delight. For the masses, however, he was a dud. So, if the atmospherics and attitudes of the boxing world in general weren't enough of an impediment to Young's potential ascension, his comparatively bland demeanor and unattractive ring style presented two more possible roadblocks to upending the great Ali.

Ali, of course, won the pre-fight press conference going away.

"I'm so fast, I'll hit you before God gets the news," Ali told Young, a line that got big laughs from the assembled press. "Boy, I'll hit you so hard it'll jar your kinfolks in Africa."

"Aren't you tired of repeating all that?" Young asked, chiding Ali for repeating old lines. "That's been played out."

"No, I'm not tired. As long as I got new heads to beat on, they're gonna listen," Ali shot back. "And your head is new."

Young's best attempt at humor was when he addressed Ali as a "tramp" instead of a champ. The line barely registered with the reporters. (5) He also didn't impress the odds-makers, who saw Young as a 15-to-1 underdog. (6)

What Ali did not win was the weigh-in. Not only did Young show a much more playful side, the gelatinous champion scaled an unsightly 230, three pounds more than his previous career high of 227 against Buster Mathis Sr. more than five years earlier. Meanwhile, Young was a fit 209, six pounds lighter than for his most recent fight, a 10 round decision over onetime title challenger Jose "King" Roman.

After the top-rated Norton stopped Ron Stander in the fifth and Larry Holmes, a frequent Ali sparring partner, advanced his record to 21-0 by out-pointing Roy Williams, Ali and Young took center stage and put on a most unexpected show.

Speaking of sparring partners, the title fight wasn't the only time Young ever stepped inside the ring with Ali. On January 27, 1972 at the Hampton Roads Coliseum in Norfolk, Va., Young was one of four fighters who shared the ring with Ali during an eight-round exhibition. Young, along with Jeff Merritt and James Tracy Summerville of Miami as well as Buffalo's Johnny Gauss, sparred two rounds each with Ali before approximately 3,700 fans. Jersey Joe Walcott, who infamously officiated Ali's rematch with Sonny Liston, was the referee here, and chief second Angelo Dundee flew up from Miami to be in Ali's corner.

When Ali was introduced to ringside physician Dr. Albert Thompson, Ali said, "I don't need a doctor. Joe Frazier needs a doctor." (7)

Ali made $15,000 for the exhibition while Young made considerably less. Here, however, the purses were far better: $1.6 million for Ali (plus $200,000 in training expenses), $85,000 for Young. (8)

The contrast in energy level and sharpness was graphic in round one, but unlike Ali-Coopman it was Young that displayed the skills and Ali who was his willing foil. Ali's most threatening punch of the round was a sloppy hook that badly missed the target and threw Ali off-balance. Then again, there wasn't much from which to choose because he threw just five of them -- and none of them landed. Meanwhile, Young was spry, engaged and active. The evidence: Young fired 74 punches and landed 18, including 16 power shots that connected at a 62% rate. Although Ali failed to land a single blow and barely tried to attempt one, referee Tom Kelly and judge Larry Barrett called the first round even while judge Terry Moore correctly judged the round for Young.

Rounds two and three were more of the same -- Young fighting and Ali playing. While Young's punches carried little steam, they did land, and, unlike Ali, he was fully engaged and trying to win. Ali was content to raise his arms over his head and point a glove at his stomach and invited Young to hit it -- which he did. Not only that, Young eagerly seized upon every opening Ali made available to him. Conversely, Ali continued his antics, such as leaning heavily and comically against the ropes while drowning Young in endless verbiage. Despite Young's command of the action (17-6 overall, 9-1 jabs, 8-5 power and a 57%-36% lead in power accuracy), Kelly and Moore saw Ali the winner while Barrett judged it for Young.

The perceptual malady that apparently afflicted the scorers also infected several members of the media. ABC's Howard Cosell reported that while reporters gave Young the first two rounds, the consensus was that the third was even, a round in which Young tripled Ali in total attempts (78-26) and total connects (21-7). As for the "official" officials, Barrett scored the round even while Kelly and Moore saw Ali the 5-4 winner. Why? Although the first "Star Wars" movie wouldn't be released until a year later, Ali had apparently mastered the Jedi Mind Trick.

Entering the sixth, Ali had yet to out-land Young in any round and his statistical deficits were daunting -- 76-35 overall and 58-19 power. Young averaged 68.3 punches per round in the first nine minutes to Ali's 17 before Ali perked up to 43.5 and Young decelerated to 34 in rounds four and five. One would have thought that Ali, having given away the first third of the fight, would have felt a sense of urgency. He did not. That's because past experience taught Ali that he could flip the switch anytime he wished and pull himself away from the fire. After all, Ali whiled away most of the first 10 rounds against Lyle before polishing him off in the 11th and he ceded most of the first eight rounds to Wepner until a flash knockdown in the ninth stirred him from

222

his slumber. If he could do that against Lyle and Wepner, why shouldn't he have felt the same about Young? To Ali, Young was just another fighter who was fated to fail.

Ali finally showed signs of life in the sixth and seventh rounds as the reality of his situation began to sink in. Here, Ali fought with more purpose while Young descended into a defensive shell. Still, Ali's punches lacked the snap and accuracy of past fights, plus Young's fluid upper body movement made the champion's punches look even more ponderous. In comparison to the first five rounds, however, Ali was fighting much better while Young was not. The seventh saw Ali throw 81 punches, which would be his highest total for the contest. It was Ali's best round yet, but even so he led by only 14-13 in total connects and landed 14 of 62 power shots (23%) to Young's 10 of 17 (59%).

It was also in the seventh that Young committed what was construed as his greatest sin. With 43 seconds remaining in the session and Ali belaboring him with blows for the first time in the fight, Young leaned sideward and intentionally stuck his head between the top and middle ropes. It was an act he would repeat several more times, and ultimately it played to his detriment, not just during the fight but in its aftermath.

Nevertheless, Young was still fighting well enough to win rounds. With each passing minute the unthinkable prospect of a new champion became more real. Ali's corner watched in stony silence, as did most of the crowd. That changed when Ali began to dance midway through round nine, and though he missed most of his punches, this resurgence and the cheers that accompanied it signaled that maybe all was still right in the world, that Ali would find a way to remain champion. It didn't matter that Young landed the hardest punch of the sequence, a flush counter right over Ali's overextended jab, or that Young out-landed Ali 10-6 overall and 5-1 power. All that mattered was that Ali was fighting better. The evidence: All three judges gave Ali the round. No matter what Ali did (or didn't do) it dominated the viewer's eye to the point that the opponent was rendered irrelevant, if not invisible.

Ali's dancing continued in the 10th, movement that helped conceal Young's 9-2 lead in overall connects in the eyes of the jurists, two of whom voted for Ali while the third saw it even. Ali then moved forward in the 11th, but while he threw 16 punches and landed four (including an excellent right to the jaw, his best blow of the fight thus far) Young, though backpedaling, landed 15 of 67. Young finally broke through here as he won the round on all three cards -- the first time he had done so in the entire fight.

Norton, the man who stood to lose the most with a Young victory, joined Cosell on commentary in the 12th. He was as astonished as anyone at Ali's lack of timing, conditioning and sharpness but he was heartened when, in the final minute, Ali pushed Young to the neutral corner pad and tried to drown him in leather. Ali's rally broke open what had been a close round and allowed him to take a narrow 17-16 lead in total connects. The exclamation point at the end of the sentence happened in the round's final moments when Young ducked his entire upper body through the ropes to get away from Ali's assault, a move that prompted referee Kelly to call a standing knockdown.

"They counted laying outside the ropes as a knockdown," Ali said afterward. "That hurt him. I don't think he would have done it if he realized that. That was his mistake." (9)

"(I did it) to keep the pressure off me," the counterpunching Young countered. "That was part of my strategy. I even used some of the 'Rope-a-Dope.' " (10) Curiously, despite the penalty, all three judges scored the 12th 5-4 for Ali, not 5-3.

That didn't stop Young from doing it again when Ali trapped him on the ropes at the start of the 13th, then again seconds later. While Kelly didn't issue a count either time, the crowd booed loudly and, worse yet, the cowardice Young's maneuver projected couldn't have helped his cause. Young connected with a booming right and a follow-up one-two in the final seconds that forged his own 17-16 lead in total connects. While Barrett and Kelly saw the round 5-4 for Young, Moore scored it 5-4 for Ali.

Suspecting he needed the final two rounds to pull off the massive upset, Young dug down and produced the far superior numbers in the 14th: 23 of 77 versus 5 of 36. A pair of flush rights to the chin late in the round stunned Ali and forced him to back toward the ropes, which he followed with another right lead that snapped back his head. It was enough to impress all three judges, who rightly gave Young the round.

By the start of round 15, the crowd rose as one, sensing that it might be sitting in on history. So did Norton, who exhorted Ali throughout the entire rest period.

Young got off to a horrible start by ducking his body through the ropes for the fourth time. But he more than made up for it by attacking Ali with a previously unseen consistency. It was quite an impressive effort for a man who, until tonight, had never fought past the 10th round.

Despite Young's good work, the overarching question of whether Young did enough to "take" the title still hung over the proceedings.

"The only thing that can cost Jimmy Young is the frequency of defensive tactics," Cosell told Norton. "I think you made an effective point (about) taking the title away from the man."

The 15th round numbers suggested he did enough -- more than enough: 23 of 56 overall for Young, 7 of 37 for Ali. The final figures also foreshadowed a Young victory; he threw more punches (752-594), landed more in every category (222-113 overall, 65-27 jabs, 157-86 power) and did so far more precisely (30%-19% overall, 15%-12% jabs, 51%-24% power). He finished stronger than Ali (46-12 overall, 32-7 power in the final·two rounds) and the round-by-round breakdowns saw Young out-land Ali in 12 of the 15 rounds overall and compile cavernous edges in the other two categories (11-2-2 in jabs and 11-4 in power shots). Although Cosell reported that scores around ringside were mixed, the reporter covering the fight for the Associated Press saw the fight 69-66 for Young. (11)

By every measurable indicator, Young should have been declared the winner and new heavyweight champion.

Except he wasn't. Even more outrageously, the margins in Ali's favor were almost criminal -- under the five-point must system referee Kelly saw Ali a 72-65 winner (10-3-2 in rounds) while judge Moore turned in a 71-64 score (11-4 in rounds). The only man in the building who gave Young any sort of credit -- though not nearly enough -- was judge Barrett, who saw Ali leading 70-68 (7-5-3).

The crowd loudly booed the verdict and one famous picture of Young that was snapped the moment Ali was declared the winner said it all: Eyes wide, mouth agape and his glove covering his cheek. It was the essence of shock and disappointment.

"I thought I won the fight," Young said. "I really thought you had a new heavyweight champion. I've been hurt more in the gym (by sparring partner Mike Koranicki). I didn't daze him but I thought I shocked him with a couple of punches. I deserve a rematch." (12)

Referee Arthur Mercante Sr. strenuously objected to the scoring of referee Kelly, who somehow scored the first 10 rounds 50-41 for Ali.

"The referee was way off in his scoring up to that point," he told World Boxing's editor-in-chief Peter King. "The whole fight was a farce anyway. Actually, it was an exhibition."

Harold Lederman, a respected New York state official and future "unofficial official" for HBO, also believed the wrong man's hand was raised.

"I think Jimmy Young won the fight," the future Hall of Famer told King. "It really shouldn't matter that it's a heavyweight championship fight. The winner should be the man who does the most. I think Young did more. Ali just didn't do enough to warrant his winning the fight."

Veteran scribe Lester Bromberg of the New York Post, who felt Young won 10 rounds, called the verdict "a travesty on judging. Jimmy took command early and only intermittently surrendered it. The bout was a throwback to the classic class of bad decisions."

New York Daily News sports editor Dick Young agreed, scoring the bout 11 rounds to 4 for the challenger. (13)

However, THE RING's editor-in-chief Nat Loubet not only confirmed the "champion's advantage" that saved Ali's title, but justified it.

"Many at ringside believed that Young had won," he wrote. "If there was a point of difference it would seem that a challenger should take a champion's title away from him and not win it running away, and there was no doubt but that Young ran to live another day. We must not take away from Young the point that he lasted fifteen rounds with an inept champion, but he looked like a little boy against the heavy boned champion. Young looked more like a light heavyweight at his 211 pounds (sic) and never gave the impression of being overly dangerous." (14)

In other words, in Loubet's eyes, Young wasn't deemed a suitable successor to the mighty Ali because his style wasn't the "right" style and his look wasn't the "right" look. Thus, Young was denied his dream and Ali was granted the privilege of continuing his reign.

Ali admitted that he had fought "the worst fight of my career."

"He hit me with a hook and burst my right eardrum," he said. "I don't remember which round. I hurt it in the Philippines once before and he reopened it. I was hurt twice. He hit me with two right hands. I saw stars and my knees started to buckle." (15)

To his credit, Ali mostly blamed himself for his poor showing.

"I weigh 230 pounds, just what I weigh when I'm in terrible shape," he said. "I'm 34 and I'm telling you what I did was a miracle, going 15 rounds and beating that young man. I've been eating too much pie, too much ice cream. You wouldn't believe the things I do in training." (16)

Training that, thanks to his packed schedule, was becoming much more chore than privilege.

"I made a mistake by contracting myself to fight too much this year," Ali confessed. "The training is getting so boring. Do you realize that I have to go back in training two days from now? I really don't want to train." (17)

But the win over Young gave him no choice; he had to train, no matter what. Moreover, he was now obligated to fly 4,200 miles from Landover to Munich, West Germany to defend his championship against England's Richard Dunn -- and that fight was just 24 days away.

> INSIDE THE NUMBERS: *Ali landed just 19% of his total punches -- his lowest percentage in the 47 Ali fights tracked by CompuBox. Ali landed just 27 jabs in 15 rounds, less than two per round. Conversely, he averaged 7.9 landed jabs per round in this statistical study. Ali never landed more than five jabs in any round against Young and was mired in single digits in terms*

of total connects in eleven of fifteen rounds. Ali landed just 113 punches, his lowest total in a 15 round fight.

Date:	April 30, 1976				City: Landover, MD				Venue: Capitol Center							
Opponent:	Jimmy Young															
Result:	Ali by unanimous decision -- Retained World Heavyweight Title															

Referee:	Tom Kelly															
	Round	1	2	3	4	5	6	7	8	9	10	11	12	13	14	15	Total
	Ali	5	5	5	5	5	5	5	5	5	5	4	5	4	4	5	72
	Young	5	4	4	4	4	4	4	4	4	4	5	4	5	5	5	65

Judge:	Larry Barrett															
	Round	1	2	3	4	5	6	7	8	9	10	11	12	13	14	15	Total
	Ali	5	4	5	5	5	5	5	5	5	5	4	5	4	4	4	70
	Young	5	5	5	4	4	4	4	4	4	5	5	4	5	5	5	68

Judge:	Terry Moore															
	Round	1	2	3	4	5	6	7	8	9	10	11	12	13	14	15	Total
	Ali	4	5	5	5	5	5	5	5	5	5	4	5	5	4	4	71
	Young	5	4	4	4	4	4	4	4	4	4	5	4	4	5	5	64

MUHAMMAD ALI UD 15 JIMMY YOUNG
04/30/76 - LANDOVER, MD

Total Punches Landed / Thrown

	1	2	3	4	5	6	7	8	9	10	11	12	13	14	15
ALI	0/5	6/20	7/26	6/45	6/42	10/51	14/81	7/43	6/40	2/32	4/16	17/52	16/68	5/36	7/37
	0%	30%	26.9%	13.3%	14.3%	19.6%	17.3%	16.3%	15%	6.3%	25%	32.7%	23.5%	13.9%	18.9%
YOUNG	18/74	17/53	21/78	11/43	9/25	6/28	13/40	14/41	10/33	9/35	15/67	16/48	17/54	23/77	23/56
	24.3%	32.1%	26.9%	25.6%	36%	21.4%	32.5%	34.1%	30.3%	25.7%	22.4%	33.3%	31.5%	29.9%	41.1%

Jab Landed / Thrown

	1	2	3	4	5	6	7	8	9	10	11	12	13	14	15
ALI	0/2	1/6	2/7	2/18	1/21	2/17	0/19	3/22	5/36	1/27	1/8	2/7	2/8	3/19	2/17
	0%	16.7%	28.6%	11.1%	4.8%	11.8%	0%	13.6%	13.9%	3.7%	12.5%	28.6%	25%	15.8%	11.8%
YOUNG	2/48	9/39	3/48	1/25	3/13	1/13	3/23	3/23	5/23	4/22	4/45	7/27	6/31	9/40	5/23
	4.2%	23.1%	6.3%	4%	23.1%	7.7%	13%	13%	21.7%	18.2%	8.9%	25.9%	19.4%	22.5%	21.7%

Power Punches Landed / Thrown

	1	2	3	4	5	6	7	8	9	10	11	12	13	14	15
ALI	0/3	5/14	5/19	4/27	5/21	8/34	14/62	4/21	1/4	1/5	3/8	15/45	14/60	2/17	5/20
	0%	35.7%	26.3%	14.8%	23.8%	23.5%	22.6%	19%	25%	20%	37.5%	33.3%	23.3%	11.8%	25%
YOUNG	16/26	8/14	18/30	10/18	6/12	5/15	10/17	11/18	5/10	5/13	11/22	9/21	11/23	14/37	18/33
	61.5%	57.1%	60%	55.6%	50%	33.3%	58.8%	61.1%	50%	38.5%	50%	42.9%	47.8%	37.8%	54.5%

Final Punch Stat Report

	Total Punches	Total Jabs	Power Punches
ALI	113/594	27/234	86/360
	19%	11.5%	23.9%
YOUNG	222/752	65/443	157/309
	29.5%	14.7%	50.8%

28.

MAY 24, 1976 - OLYMPIAHALLE, MUNICH, WEST GERMANY
MUHAMMAD ALI KO 5 RICHARD DUNN

Boxing is a sport that requires its participants to endure physical pain as well as emotional stress. Few mastered that better than Muhammad Ali, who fought with a broken jaw against Ken Norton and summoned an improbable late-round rally in the "Thrilla in Manila" despite feeling as if death was at his doorstep. As he began his preparations to fight Richard Dunn, the source of his stress was more mental than physical. Even though he had not yet reached the midpoint of his turbulent 1976 schedule, Ali, in the immediate aftermath of the controversial Young fight, admitted he was bored with training and dreaded the prospect of having to return to the gym just two days after surviving Young. Not exactly the ideal attitude to have when one has to defend his title in just 24 days' time.

But Ali, as always, rose to the moment. He somehow melted off 10 pounds and, at 220, he was at his lightest weight since a 216 1/2-pound Ali regained the championship from George Foreman nearly 19 months earlier. He also had enough energy to hype the Dunn fight, which included a satellite appearance on ITV's "This is Your Life."

One major selling point to potential ticket-buyers was that Dunn was to be only the second southpaw Ali had faced as a pro and, as such, could trouble the champion the way Karl Mildenberger did nearly a decade earlier.

"I read in the London Times the other day. My friend (promoter) Jarvis Astaire sent me an article talking about your wife -- I see she's a fight expert now," Ali said in a half-mocking tone as Dunn and his wife Janet listened in amusement before a live audience. "She has said that I had trouble with Karl Mildenberger and he was a southpaw and I'm going to have trouble with you because you're a southpaw. I don't care if it's a northpaw, a southpaw, an eastpaw or a westpaw, it ain't gonna matter what paw I get on you because whatever paw lands on you is gonna do you real good."

Referencing Dunn's time as a Territorial Army paratrooper, Ali finished by saying, "so you've taken 67 parachute drops. Well, I want you to mark this down: You have one more big drop to come...I mean a big, hard drop. It's gonna be the longest short drop you've ever had."

Dunn also did his share of pre-fight hype. Before he entered the ring inside the Olympiahalle in Munich, West Germany, Dunn presented a sealed envelope containing his pre-fight prediction to NBC's Joe Garagiola, who opened the letter during the opening segment.

229

"It is the eighth round," Garagiola began after scanning down what colleague Dick Enberg characterized as a master's thesis. "And as Ali tries his 'Rope-a-Dope' trick, I get mad and try to force him out of the ring. I hammer him onto the ropes and we're a tangle of legs and arms. Suddenly the referee stops the fight. I hold my hands up, and the next thing I know I wake up in a sweat, convinced that I am the new champion."

Ali had his own prediction, revealed only after the fight when he donated his gloves to former light heavyweight title challenger Chris Finnegan, who had recently lost an eye. "Ali wins" it read inside one glove while the other read "Round five."

Which was exactly what happened. But it wasn't easy.

The fight almost didn't happen. The German promoters ran into money problems and thanks to Top Rank's Bob Arum (and Ali) the fight was saved. Arum helped put the show back together for NBC while Ali not only paid Dunn's hotel bill but also purchased 2,000 tickets to pump money into the struggling promotion. (1)

The sleeker Ali began the fight on his toes while Dunn pursued him in straight lines and sought to land his best weapon, the left cross. Because he knew Dunn's lefty stance would limit the effectiveness of his jab -- the right glove was in perfect position to block the punch -- Ali concentrated on throwing lead rights. But it soon became evident that Ali hadn't learned from the Mildenberger fight because he insisted on circling to his right and directly into the path of Dunn's left, the same cardinal sin that made the Mildenberger fight harder than it needed to be. Because Ali chose to repeat this tactical error, the same thing happened against Dunn.

Although Ali landed several strong rights to Dunn's prominent jaw, Dunn also popped Ali's head back with a snappy right jab, connected with several heavy lefts to the breadbasket and showed the champion he was unafraid as he waded in and fired freely. In round one Dunn more than doubled Ali's output (57 punches to Ali's 24), out-jabbed the champ 5-1 and prevailed 14-12 in total connects. However, Ali landed 11 of his 20 power shots (55%), a bad sign given that eight of Dunn's nine losses to date had been by knockout.

The second round was Dunn's best as he rifled in left crosses with surprising ease while a more stationary Ali covered up and allowed the challenger's storm to swirl about him. Late in the round, Ali connected with a pair of robust rights that stunned Dunn but instead of falling down as expected the challenger stood his ground and fired back with everything he had. The toe-to-toe action had the Munich crowd roaring at full volume, and had there been a noise ordinance they surely would have been cited given that the bout began shortly before 3:30 a.m.

Dunn felt so good about his second-round performance that between rounds he looked down and winked at the NBC broadcasting crew. He had reason to feel that way because he landed 21 of his 90 punches while keeping Ali to 11 of 36. He also out-jabbed the champ (7 of 60, 12% to 2 of 13, 15%), earned a 14-9 edge in power punches and connected in 47% of his hooks, crosses and uppercuts to Ali's 39%. Dunn had successfully drawn Ali into the brawl he wanted, but in order to make his dream come true he'd need to hang one on Ali before Ali could hang one on him.

Dunn certainly tried his hardest in round three. As Ali circled more to his left than to his right -- finally -- and connected with a big right to the jaw, Dunn instantly retaliated with a lashing left that knocked Ali off-balance and drove him to the corner pad. Ali beckoned the challenger in with a quick wave of the glove but Dunn, with visions of George Foreman and the "Rope-a-Dope" flashing through his brain, thought better of it and retreated to ring center.

A moment after Dunn landed yet another left, Ali's counter right opened a cut over Dunn's brow. Again, Dunn pushed the crisis to the side and kept fighting back, and by round's end he had out-landed Ali for the third consecutive round (19-11 overall and 11-3 jabs while tying 8-8 in power connects) and pushed his connect leads to 54-34 overall, 23-6 jabs and 31-28 power.

"Beautiful!" Dunn's trainer George Vittles told Dunn between rounds. "You keep doing that and you're going to win. Keep it up!" Enberg reported that the veteran writers at ringside wore expressions of surprise; they were convinced that Dunn couldn't possibly trade with Ali and survive.

In round four, however, the dream that propelled Dunn's self-belief during training and fueled his unexpectedly strong start was replaced by the boxing ring's unsentimental reality. The combination of Dunn's adrenaline rush and Ali's tactical carelessness was enough to get Dunn past the first nine minutes, but Ali proved that the brave Brit would have needed a far deeper reservoir to keep it up for 36 more, much less the five it actually went.

Just 15 seconds into the fourth, Ali connected with a lead right to the chin that reverberated through Dunn's body as if he had been struck by lightning. Dunn tried mightily to stay upright, but his quivering legs let him down as he fell to his knees. Because Ali refused to go to the correct neutral corner, referee Herbert Tomser suspended his count at three, pushed the champion toward the correct location, completed the mandatory eight and allowed the fight to continue 15 seconds after Dunn had hit the floor.

Though shaky, the defiant Dunn continued to exchange with the champion. Another Ali right to the chin froze Dunn in his tracks but not only did his teetering legs regain their strength, the challenger charged in and drove Ali backward with a series of dangerous-looking punches, which, fortunately for Ali, mostly missed.

With 28 seconds remaining in a wild round, Ali connected with another massive lead right to the jaw that dumped Dunn with a thud. While still on his knees, Dunn turned toward his corner and held out both gloves in an "I'm-still-all-right" gesture, then shifted his attention to Tomser's count, which reached five when Dunn unsteadily arose. Again, Dunn ran toward Ali, who met him with yet another right lead to the jaw that forced Dunn to take a slow-motion knee. Mercifully for Dunn, the subsequent count, the third of the stanza, allowed the clock to run out on what had been a nightmarish round.

In round four, Ali connected on 22 of his 39 power shots (56%) to Dunn's 14 of 34 (41%) and forged a 25-21 lead in total connects. While the raw numbers were close, Ali had violently turned the momentum in his favor.

Vittles and his team feverishly worked to revive Dunn while a relaxed and confident Ali rejected the stool and surveyed the scene before him with arms stretched over both sets of strands. Shortly before the fifth-round bell, Ali pointed his right glove at Dunn and warned him that an even worse fate was about to befall him. Dunn, now standing, took the news with both hands on his hips and a grim expression on his face. Then, he used both gloves to command Ali to come forward.

Despite the fourth-round disaster, it was Dunn who pushed Ali backward and hammered him with power shots and the champion who was clinching to stop his momentum. It was, in reality, Dunn's last stand; if he was to go down, he was going to go down giving everything he had. He even had time to say something to Ali after maneuvering him to a corner pad near NBC's microphones.

Yes, Dunn controlled the first two minutes of the round. But Ali was simply biding his time. The fourth round showed him that he owned the poison pellet that would do in Dunn -- the right lead. The first one turned Dunn's knees to jelly, after which the second one dropped the challenger for the fourth time in the fight. Dunn bravely rose at seven and as he charged yet again at the champion, Ali rotated his right arm in bolo-style, then threw a punch with the meanest of intentions. That right landed on Dunn's left glove but the next one hit the bull's-eye and caused the challenger to fall forward and onto his knees. Again, Dunn got up, this time at three, while Ali stood in the corner and began whirling his right arm. Although Dunn seemed ready to continue, Tomser saw something in the challenger's eyes that prompted him to wave off the fight at eight. With victory secured, Ali's triumphant arm-whirling reached a feverish pitch, a comical end to what had been an unexpectedly exciting fight.

Dunn's early lead helped him retain a 100-73 lead in total connects and his southpaw advantage was such that Ali was limited to 12 landed jabs while Dunn more than tripled Ali with 37. But Ali's power surge in rounds four and five got him to within 63-61 in terms of power connects. Ali's accuracy was searing as he landed 44% of his total punches and 51% of his power punches but Dunn performed admirably as he landed 29% overall and 43% of his hooks, crosses and uppercuts.

"I'm so happy that I trained and I got in shape," Ali told Enberg as Dunn listened at the champion's left shoulder. "This man is a world top contender. He's a young man yet. I predict he's going to be a top-notch contender. He gave me more trouble than I expected. If I was in the same shape this month like I was last month, I would have lost the fight with no doubt because he's a great fighter. He's better than I thought he was, and I predict you'll hear a lot about Richard Dunn."

Ali's kind-hearted prediction didn't play out, for Dunn fought just twice more before retiring in September 1977: A first-round knockout defeat to Joe Bugner for the British, Commonwealth and European titles and a fifth round stoppage loss to Kallie Knoetze in Johannesburg. But Dunn's brave effort earned accolades while also creating a marvelous lifetime memory.

"Muhammad was so quick," Dunn told the Daily Mail's Patrick Collins in 2009. "He went backwards, forwards, sideways, on his toes all the time. He was up for it, all right. Yet, I really enjoyed it. I wished it had gone on longer. But the punch that finished it -- cracking right hand, wasn't it? Nearly took my bleeding head off. For a split-second I thought I was all right, then my brain said, 'go down, you daft bastard.' I tried my best, and my best wasn't good enough. But I gave it what I had. And that's all I had." (2)

As scheduled, Ali flew to Tokyo the next month and met Japanese wrestling legend Antonio Inoki in what turned out to be a farcical contest that ended in a 15-round draw. Ali threw just six punches and landed two while the crouching Inoki's powerful kicks inflicted horrific damage to Ali's legs, legs that he would need to fend off his next challenger, the formidable Ken Norton.

> *INSIDE THE NUMBERS: Dunn fought a spirited fight, averaging 70.2 punches thrown per round -- 25 more than the heavyweight average and 30 more per round than Ali's 46 other opponents tracked by CompuBox. The southpaw Brit out-landed Ali in jabs 37-12 and 100-73 in total punches. Ali landed 33 of 59 power punches (55.9%) over the last two rounds.*

MUHAMMAD ALI TKO 5 RICHARD DUNN
05/24/76 - MUNICH

Total Punches Landed / Thrown												
	1	2	3	4	5	6	7	8	9	10	11	12
ALI	12/24	11/36	11/29	25/47	14/30	-/-	-/-	-/-	-/-	-/-	-/-	-/-
	50%	30.6%	37.9%	53.2%	46.7%	-	-	-	-	-	-	-
DUNN	14/57	21/90	19/70	21/69	25/65	-/-	-/-	-/-	-/-	-/-	-/-	-/-
	24.6%	23.3%	27.1%	30.4%	38.5%	-	-	-	-	-	-	-

Jab Landed / Thrown												
	1	2	3	4	5	6	7	8	9	10	11	12
ALI	1/4	2/13	3/11	3/8	3/10	-/-	-/-	-/-	-/-	-/-	-/-	-/-
	25%	15.4%	27.3%	37.5%	30%	-	-	-	-	-	-	-
DUNN	5/38	7/60	11/43	7/35	7/30	-/-	-/-	-/-	-/-	-/-	-/-	-/-
	13.2%	11.7%	25.6%	20%	23.3%	-	-	-	-	-	-	-

Power Punches Landed / Thrown												
	1	2	3	4	5	6	7	8	9	10	11	12
ALI	11/20	9/23	8/18	22/39	11/20	-/-	-/-	-/-	-/-	-/-	-/-	-/-
	55%	39.1%	44.4%	56.4%	55%	-	-	-	-	-	-	-
DUNN	9/19	14/30	8/27	14/34	18/35	-/-	-/-	-/-	-/-	-/-	-/-	-/-
	47.4%	46.7%	29.6%	41.2%	51.4%	-	-	-	-	-	-	-

Final Punch Stat Report			
Total	Total Punches	Total Jabs	Power Punches
ALI	73/166	12/46	61/120
	44%	26.1%	50.8%
DUNN	100/351	37/206	63/145
	28.5%	18%	43.4%

29.

More than a few great fighters have that one opponent that disrupts his rhythm, short-circuits his wires and earns better results than anyone could have expected given the perceived gap in talent. For Jack Dempsey, that opponent was "Fat" Willie Meehan, who improbably went 2-1-2 in their quintet of four-round fights between March 1917 and September 1918. For Joe Louis it was Arturo Godoy, who pushed "The Brown Bomber" to a split decision in their first meeting for the heavyweight title in February 1940 and required seven more rounds of figuring before Louis finally put him away in round eight of their rematch four months later.

For Muhammad Ali, that fighter was Ken Norton. Yes, Norton eventually joined Ali in the International Boxing Hall of Fame and was a presence near the top of the division for seven years, but his reputation was largely forged by the angst he caused Ali. It is true that Norton had far more physical tools and athletic ability than Meehan and Godoy. He earned 10 letters while at Jacksonville (Ill.) High School as a pitcher and centerfielder in baseball, a wingback in football, at forward in basketball and, in track, as a discus thrower and hurdler. Those talents earned him a full scholarship to Northeast Missouri State Teachers College. (1)

With teaching not a viable financial option, Norton ended his college career in 1963 and enlisted in the Marines. It was at Camp Lejeune in North Carolina that Norton discovered boxing.

"I think I was intrigued by both the individuality and brutality of the sport," Norton recalled. (2)

Norton's athletic talent was such that he won 24 of his 25 amateur fights as well as an impressive collection of championships -- the All-Marine title in 1965, 1966 and 1967, the North Carolina Golden Gloves championship and the AAU title. He even took part in several international competitions. (3)

Norton earned worldwide prominence with his shocking, jaw-breaking split decision over Ali in March 1973 and despite losing the rematch by split verdict nearly six months later he proved his initial success was no fluke. His Adonis-like physique, crushing two-fisted power and off-kilter timing was a pungent blend not just for Ali, but for most of the world's heavyweights. Coming into the Ali fight, the 32-year-old Norton's record stood at 37-3 with 30 knockouts.

The third Norton fight was the eighth defense of Ali's second reign, and at 34, he was showing signs of wear following his "near-death" experience at the "Thrilla in Manila." Knockout wins over Jean-Pierre Coopman and Richard Dunn were overshadowed by his flat and uninspired effort against Jimmy Young, a fight many observers thought he should have lost.

Conversely, Norton was riding a wave of success following his crushing two-round loss to George Foreman, which took place six months after the second Ali fight. The heavily muscled Marine rebuilt his career with seven straight knockout wins, the best of which were back-to-back fifth-round stoppages against Jerry Quarry and previous conqueror Jose Luis Garcia. Three more knockouts against Pedro Lovell (KO 5), Ron Stander (KO 5) and Larry Middleton (KO 10) set the stage for Norton's rubber match against Ali set for September 28, 1976 at Yankee Stadium. It was the first heavyweight title fight staged at baseball's shrine in more than 17 years, when, in June 1959, Ingemar Johansson savagely snatched the crown from Floyd Patterson's head thanks to a torrent of "toonderous" right hands.

Despite Ali's obvious decline, Norton's surge and the challenger's troublesome style, the defending champion was installed a solid 2-to-1 favorite. (4)

Most fight nights have an air of anticipation but this one had the stench of probable chaos. That's because striking New York Police Department officers used the fight as a platform for their pay demands as well as to show how an absence of their crowd control skills would impact a marquee event.

"Preceding the fight, the police came out with pickets in hand, shouted at the top of their lungs, blew whistles, banged on drums and purposefully blocked traffic in front of Yankee Stadium," Earnie Shavers wrote in his book "Welcome to the Big Time." According to Shavers, who stopped Henry Clark in two rounds on the undercard, Ali's limousine was blocked from entering the property while a mob jumped on his front fender and rear hood. Because the driver was forced to inch the car forward Ali didn't reach his dressing room until just 45 minutes before fight time. (5)

"We all came uptown on buses provided by the promoters and they hustled us into the stadium," Hall of Fame writer Ed Schuyler recalled in 2010. "It was nasty. They were picketing outside and they were letting all these bums in. They weren't being professional police officers in any sense of the word. A lot of non-New Yorkers wouldn't have dared try to get to the fight through the subway." (6)

More than 10,000 stormed into the unprotected stadium and once they gained entry they committed all sorts of vile acts on people and property. This, combined with the police's inaction, had a profound impact on impulse ticket sales. The official attendance was listed at 30,289, but according to Bob Arum, only eight walk-up tickets were sold at the 108 booths the night of the fight. (7)

"The real story of the fight was what was going on behind me because anything that happened during the fight was going on in the stands," Schuyler said. "I didn't realize all the muggings that were going on and Joe Frazier's car was damaged. Press row during the fight was OK, but there was no real security that I can remember. After the fight the crowd flooded press row and a few typewriters were stolen. I'm not sure about this, but I recall that somebody pulled a knife on (legendary columnist) Red Smith. My sports editor held a chair over my head while I dictated my story." (8)

Once Ali and Norton were in the ring, the champion did his best to pour on the psychology. When he wasn't glaring at Norton, he was leading chants of "Norton must fall" while wind-milling his arm like an out-of-control helicopter blade.

Ali surprised many by opening the bout flat-footed and landing several sharp rights to the face while Norton was content to survey from a distance. Ali also found time to jabber at Norton, asking him "is that all you got?" After the first round ended, a round in which Ali out-landed Norton 15-9 overall and 12-5 power, Ali led another round of "Norton must fall" chants instead of listening to chief second Angelo Dundee while Norton stood in his corner with a blue robe draped over his shoulders, a practice he maintained for the entire fight. The prideful Ali chose to do the same, even in the late rounds when the effects of Norton's punishment left him exhausted. Ali's ego was such that he couldn't allow Norton to enjoy any kind of edge.

Norton revved up his offense in the second as he jabbed to the body and slung overhand rights to the side of Ali's head. One of them caused Ali to break into a shimmy, after which he covered up behind his elbows, forearms and gloves. Norton attacked Ali's body with both hands and he spat out some verbal venom after sinking in a pair of hooks to the liver. Not only was Norton punishing, he was precise: In round two the challenger landed 52% of his total punches (26 of 50), 40% of his jabs (10 of 25) and 64% of his hooks, crosses and uppercuts (16 of 25). Ali was accurate as well, but he couldn't match Norton's output (13 of 32 overall, 41%; 7 of 17 jabs, 41% and 6 of 15, 40% power).

The third saw Ali continue to rake Norton's face with long right leads while the challenger whipped in overhand rights and body shots. Norton's unrelenting pressure forced Ali to work every second and after absorbing a strong first-minute Ali rally in the fourth Norton stormed back by cornering the champion and whaling away with full-shouldered shots. In the third Norton landed 7 of 12 power shots (58%) while in the fourth he was 11 of 15 (73%).

Norton's attack shifted into a higher gear in the fifth and sixth rounds while Ali was content to cover up, recline on the ropes and wiggle his hips. Ali's playfulness almost cost him dearly in the waning moments of the sixth when Norton's knifing hook to the liver doubled over Ali. The numbers favoring Norton during that six-minute period were stunning: 54-11 overall, 10-4 jabs and 44-7 power.

After throwing a combined 30 punches in the fifth and sixth to Norton's 143, Ali bore down more in the seventh and eighth by throwing 111 to Norton's 90 but still trailed 50-32 overall and 38-23 power thanks to the challenger's ferocious body attack and stunningly flush head shots.

Sensing he might be behind on the scorecards, Ali turned back the clock -- at least for a round-and-a-half -- by showing a slightly slower version of his float and sting. The tactic worked well as he slowed Norton's momentum while sparking his own. In rounds nine and 10 Ali out-threw Norton 98-41 but only out-landed him 20-19 overall.

In the 11th, a confident Norton tried to turn the tables on Ali by retreating to the ropes and teasing Ali while executing an exaggerated bob-and-weave. Norton thought he might have one-upped Ali in the psychology department but in reality he diminished himself and his chances by entering Ali's world instead of sticking to business.

Though Norton continued to apply pressure throughout the championship rounds, Ali significantly upped his work rate in rounds 11-14 (from 54 in round 10 to 64.8 per round in the next four) and the momentum seemed to switch by the round, and, on occasion, by the moment. Norton edged the 11th 24-22, dominated the 12th 23-14 and out-landed Ali 20-13 in the 14th while Ali got by Norton 24-22 in the 13th. Although the punch stats heavily favored Norton, Ali's aura allowed him to win enough close rounds to put him virtually even entering the 15th.

As was the case in their second meeting three years earlier, Ali essentially won the fight in the final round. Norton inexplicably throttled down his offense by throwing just 10 punches in the first two minutes while Ali got on his toes and let his hands go. Norton rocked Ali in the final 15 seconds but it wasn't enough to off-set what Ali had done in the first two-and-a-half minutes. That didn't matter to Norton, who, after the final bell, woofed at Ali before launching a wild celebration with his corner. Meanwhile, the champion and his retinue appeared concerned and somber.

Their reactions were justifiable, for the writers for the New York Times and the Philadelphia Daily News saw it 10-5 and 8-6-1 Norton while the scribe for the London Daily Mirror had it 6-6-3. Of 21 sportswriters polled after the fight, 17 believed Norton should have been awarded the decision. (9) The numbers, which were compiled off video years later, were heavily in favor of Norton (286-199 overall and 192-128 power as well as percentage gaps of 45%-28% overall, 33%-21% jabs and 56%-35% power). That said, Ali did most of his punching in the final minute; of his 709 total punches 287 were fired in the final 60 seconds compared to Norton's 235 of 635. Ironically, the power-punching Norton landed more jabs (94-71) while the boxing-oriented Ali threw more power shots (364) than jabs (345). One not so ironic stat was that Norton landed 84 body shots to Ali's five.

Norton's jubilation and Ali's reserve proved ill-placed. That's because judges Harold Lederman and Barney Smith had Ali up 8-7 under the rounds system while referee Arthur Mercante Sr. saw it 8-6-1 for the winner -- and still -- champion.

A heartbroken Norton openly wept in his corner. Norton's manager Bob Biron declared his fighter "the uncrowned champion." Trainer Bill Slayton called for an investigation of the New

York officials. (10) The public outrage was such that CBS aired a tape of the fight a week later and had a panel of celebrity judges score the bout. (11) Their verdict: A draw. (12)

But had Norton fought full-bore those last three minutes, the two 8-7 scores that belonged to Ali might have flipped to Norton, something that aggrieved Norton for the rest of his days.

"As far as my third fight with Ali is concerned, I look back and wish I could fight that last round over again," he told author Thomas Hauser. "I wasn't tired; I was in good shape. I could have fought the whole three minutes all-out and won it easily, but my corner said I had the fight won and don't take any chances. That's why I was so cautious. And if you saw the look on Ali's face at the end, he knew I beat him. He didn't hit me hard the whole fight. Then they announced the judges' decision and I was bitter, very bitter. Not toward Ali...he'd done his job, he was just there to fight. But I was hurt, I was mad, I was angry, I was upset...and it still upsets me." (13)

Schuyler, who scored the fight 9-6 for Ali, believed Ali's "champion's advantage" played a pivotal role in the outcome, especially during those rounds that were extremely close.

"Ali's reputation was a weapon," he said. "A close round with Muhammad Ali was most often going to Muhammad Ali and that's because judges and fans saw the Ali who beat Liston, the Ali of the 1960s who was the dancing master and the man who could float like a butterfly and sting like a bee. They saw that Ali even though they weren't looking at that Ali. Ali was no longer the Ali of his reputation." (14)

Rightly or wrongly and for better or worse, Ali was still the champion. And, as champion, he felt obligated to fight on.

INSIDE THE NUMBERS: Norton out-landed Ali in 10 of 15 rounds, including 31-7 in round five and 34-15 in round eight. Norton landed 45% of his total punches, the fifth highest percentage by an Ali opponent in the 47 fights tracked by CompuBox. Norton's 94 landed jabs were the fourth highest by an Ali opponent. Norton landed 56% of his power punches, third highest by an Ali opponent. Norton threw just 18 punches in round one and just 26 in the fifteenth -- rounds he'd probably would have loved to have back. Norton out-landed Ali in total punches in each of their three fights, amassing a 716-545 edge in connects. Surprisingly, in their three fights, Norton had a 256-248 edge in landed jabs, hitting on 34% of them to just 22% for Ali, who landed 29% of his jabs in 47 fights tracked by CompuBox. Ali's opponents landed 24% of their jabs.

Date:	September 28, 1976					City: Bronx, NY				Venue: Yankee Stadium					
Opponent:	Ken Norton														
Result:	Ali by unanimous decision -- Retains World Heavyweight Title														

Referee:	Arthur Mercante Sr.															
Round	1	2	3	4	5	6	7	8	9	10	11	12	13	14	15	Total
Ali	X			X			X		X	X	X	E	X		X	8 (1E)
Norton		X	X		X	X		X				E		X		6 (1E)

Judge:	Harold Lederman															
Round	1	2	3	4	5	6	7	8	9	10	11	12	13	14	15	Total
Ali	X						X		X	X	X		X	X	X	8
Norton		X	X	X	X	X		X				X				7

Judge:	Barney Smith															
Round	1	2	3	4	5	6	7	8	9	10	11	12	13	14	15	Total
Ali	X		X				X		X		X		X	X	X	8
Norton		X		X	X	X		X		X		X				7

MUHAMMAD ALI UD 15 KEN NORTON

09/28/76 - NEW YORK

Total Punches Landed / Thrown															
	1	2	3	4	5	6	7	8	9	10	11	12	13	14	15
ALI	15/41	13/32	15/47	10/36	7/13	4/17	17/66	15/45	9/44	11/54	22/74	14/48	24/78	13/59	10/55
	36.6%	40.6%	31.9%	27.8%	53.8%	23.5%	25.8%	33.3%	20.5%	20.4%	29.7%	29.2%	30.8%	22%	18.2%
NORTON	9/18	26/50	12/38	16/33	31/79	23/64	16/31	34/59	5/11	14/30	24/43	23/46	22/51	20/56	11/26
	50%	52%	31.6%	48.5%	39.2%	35.9%	51.6%	57.6%	45.5%	46.7%	55.8%	50%	43.1%	35.7%	42.3%

Jab Landed / Thrown															
	1	2	3	4	5	6	7	8	9	10	11	12	13	14	15
ALI	3/11	7/17	8/29	2/11	2/2	2/10	5/26	4/17	4/36	6/33	8/34	5/19	4/28	4/29	7/43
	27.3%	41.2%	27.6%	18.2%	100%	20%	19.2%	23.5%	11.1%	18.2%	23.5%	26.3%	14.3%	13.8%	16.3%
NORTON	4/10	10/25	5/26	5/18	3/16	7/26	7/19	5/17	2/7	4/16	17/27	6/18	10/25	9/32	0/7
	40%	40%	19.2%	27.8%	18.8%	26.9%	36.8%	29.4%	28.6%	25%	63%	33.3%	40%	28.1%	0%

Power Punches Landed / Thrown															
	1	2	3	4	5	6	7	8	9	10	11	12	13	14	15
ALI	12/30	6/15	7/18	8/25	5/11	2/7	12/40	11/28	5/8	5/21	14/40	9/29	20/50	9/30	3/12
	40%	40%	38.9%	32%	45.5%	28.6%	30%	39.3%	62.5%	23.8%	35%	31%	40%	30%	25%
NORTON	5/8	16/25	7/12	11/15	28/63	16/38	9/12	29/42	3/4	10/14	7/16	17/28	12/26	11/24	11/19
	62.5%	64%	58.3%	73.3%	44.4%	42.1%	75%	69%	75%	71.4%	43.8%	60.7%	46.2%	45.8%	57.9%

Final Punch Stat Report			
Total	Total Punches	Total Jabs	Power Punches
ALI	199/709	71/345	128/364
	28.1%	20.6%	35.2%
NORTON	286/635	94/289	192/346
	45 %	32.5 %	55.5 %

30.

MAY 16, 1977 - CAPITOL CENTER, LANDOVER, MD
MUHAMMAD ALI W 15 ALFREDO EVANGELISTA

Ali's brutal Bicentennial schedule merited a long rest, and at first it was to be a retirement. His commitment to stepping away, at least at the time, was robust enough to prompt THE RING's editor-in-chief, Nat Loubet, to grant Ali 60 days to ponder his decision before officially withdrawing recognition. (1)

"The last time Ali called it quits he returned to the ring wars some seven months after his retirement," Loubet wrote. "Is he sincere in his announced retirement? Or is this a ploy to push promoters into offering a larger purse than Ali might get if he did not scare the 'angels' into the possible loss of a good boxing meal ticket?"

Loubet's decision to wait turned out to be a wise one. When the money from the Norton fight began running low -- an issue compounded by a recent divorce (2) -- Ali, following a month of public vacillating, decided to remain champion. The total time off: Seven-and-a-half months.

Following the hard fight with Norton, Ali dipped deep into the heavyweight pool and chose 22-year-old Alfredo Evangelista, a shaggy-haired Spain-based Uruguayan who was coming off an eight-round decision loss to unrated Italian speedster Lorenzo Zanon before his adopted home fans a little more than three months earlier. The defeat originally toppled Evangelista from the top 10 in the WBA and WBC ratings, which is where Evangelista needed to be in order to qualify for a title shot. Once Ali had finalized his choice of opponent, however, the sanctioning bodies -- dubbed "The Alphabet Boys" by its critics -- shuffled their ratings in order to accommodate Ali as well as their need to collect their percentage of both fighters' purses. (3) The WBA slotted the man Ali dubbed "The Spanish Bull" seventh while the WBC deemed him 10th best. (4)

The Zanon loss dropped Evangelista's record to 14-1-1 with 11 knockouts, with the best victories coming against Giuseppe Ros in his sixth pro fight (W 8), Jose Manuel Urtain in his eighth (KO 5), Lucien Rodriguez in his ninth (KO 4) and Rudi Lubbers in his 13th (KO 3). The loss to Zanon, combined with his anonymity among American boxing fans, led to Evangelista being a 10-to-1 betting underdog, the seventh double-digit underdog Ali had faced in the nine fights of his second title reign. Only Frazier in the Thrilla (6-to-5) and Norton in the rubber match (2-to-1) were viewed as legitimate challengers to Ali's crown. (5)

Ali, who worked off 20 pounds in six weeks (6), scaled a respectable 221 1/4 while Evangelista's considerable baby fat made his 209 1/2 look 20 pounds more. As the fight began, a totally relaxed Ali glided about the ring while throwing in a shuffle while Evangelista drew laughter when he dropped his arms, stuck his chin out and mocked Ali's hands-down mobility.

"The kid's got a sense of humor and is apparently not necessarily awed," noted an amused Howard Cosell. Late in the first Ali backed to the ropes, wiggled his hips and covered up but Evangelista, like Lyle and Young, refused to take the bait.

Boxing's version of "Dance Fever" ended with Ali throwing just 26 punches to Evangelista's 14, but, thanks to a couple of late body shots, he challenger actually led Ali 5-3 in total connects and 4-1 in landed power shots.

Evangelista, the first Spanish resident to challenge for the heavyweight title since Paolino Uzcudun lost to Primo Carnera in 1933, tried to increase the pressure in round two by attacking Ali's body with vicious-looking hooks, but the still-playful Ali reacted with a faux wobble, then a series of jabs that helped spark chants of "Ali, Ali, Ali!" The pace remained slow (30 punches for Ali, 29 for Evangelista), but Ali did better as he landed 11 punches to the challenger's seven.

Ali continued to play with Evangelista in rounds three through five while the challenger tried to use his work rate and industrious body punching to draw a more serious response from the champion. It didn't work; Ali stood in front of Evangelista with hands at his waist, faked a bolo punch and threw in plenty of "Rope-a-Dope" as Evangelista blasted away. In those rounds Evangelista averaged 59.7 punches per round to Ali's 41.3 and out-landed him 42-39 overall and 38-15 power, but the challenger's connects lacked the steam to convince Ali to shift into a more serious mode.

While Ali intensified his attack in the sixth, it was done of his own volition rather than anything Evangelista did. Whatever the reason, the results showed as Ali ascended to 19 of 52 (including 10 of 27 jabs) while Evangelista descended to 7 of 23. But the seventh saw a role-reversal as Evangelista produced his best numbers of the fight (19 of 81 overall, 18 of 60 power) while Ali's activity was almost nonexistent (0 of 3 overall, including zero power shot attempts). If ever a round was ceded by default, round seven of Ali-Evangelista was it, and the crowd "rewarded" the champ by showering him with boos.

The lack of sustained action left Cosell in a despairing state. He filled time by recalling Ali's better moments such as the "Thrilla" to illustrate how much the great man had slipped since. Cosell viewed the event as a circus-like spectacle, and the audience's negative feedback proved that this circus was not delivering the promised entertainment value. Ali did just enough to win enough rounds to get the job done, but given the high standard he set in his prime as well as in the "Rumble" and the "Thrilla," it depressed Cosell to see Ali going through the motions against a determined but clearly inferior opponent.

Both men's performances came in waves; Ali shined in the ninth (17-2 overall, 12-0 jabs) and won the 10th (10-5), 11th (11-8), 13th (13-6) and 14th (13-7) while Evangelista found his final high-water mark in the 12th when he out-threw Ali 73-36 and out-landed the champ 14-7. But while Evangelista's effort throughout appeared earnest and a genuine reflection of his overall skill, Ali's ups and downs were more a product of willful acceleration and deceleration. Sensing Ali wasn't giving the paying customers his full value, they spewed their displeasure even as Evangelista pounded away with combinations.

As the 15th round droned on, it was obvious Ali wouldn't -- or couldn't -- raise the bar and give his audience, at the very least, a pleasing finish. The punches that once had cut through the air with blinding speed and connected with snap and precision were slower, fuzzier and wide of the mark. The legs looked lively enough as they carried him away from potential danger but everything else about his game was sub-par. An overwhelming pall of dissatisfaction enveloped the arena.

"We're counting down until the end of this inglorious affair," Cosell intoned in the closing moments of the fight as the crowd's level of indignation intensified. After the final bell, Evangelista's corner congratulated their man for lasting the distance, something most observers didn't expect given he had never fought past round eight until now. Ali, surrounded by his retinue, leaned over the top rope and registered no particular emotion. For him, it was just another day at the office.

The final stats saw Ali with a small but perceptible lead in overall connects (164-141) with Ali leading big in jabs (99-23) and Evangelista dominating in power connects (118-65). Neither was accurate (Ali led 29%-25% overall while Evangelista prevailed 29%-27% power), but the only outstanding part of Ali's game was the jab, which landed at a 31% rate.

Unlike Ali's first appearance in Landover when he was fortunate to get past Jimmy Young, there was no controversy about this decision. Referee Harry Cecchini, who was working his first championship fight after 35 years in the game, saw Ali up 71-65 while judges Terry Moore and Ray Klingmeyer each turned in 72-64 scorecards. Similarly, the round-by-round stat breakdowns had Ali ahead 9-5-1 overall (including six of the final seven rounds) and 11-2-2 in jabs while the Spain-based challenger dominated the power connects breakdown 11-4.

"Ali surprised me," Evangelista said through an interpreter. "I didn't think he'd go 15 rounds. I thought he'd get tired. I asked him 'why do you run so much?' I wanted him to fight, but he wouldn't do it. I was never hurt. He hit me hard, but never hurt me." (7)

He also felt his effort validated the title opportunity that was granted to him through jurisdictional maneuvering.

"I'm very happy," he said. "I proved to the American audience I am a good fighter and worthy of fighting Muhammad Ali." (8)

"I'm so thankful for the fight that man put up," Ali told Cosell. "You all know now, he is no bum. No heavyweight, not even that 22-year-old boy, can dance 15 rounds like I did. So I'm not what I used to be. To show you I'm a legend, the greatest fighter in the history of the world, an old man, 35, fat as you say, still, I can out-dance any heavyweight in the history of boxing. That shows you that I'm in a class of my own."

INSIDE THE NUMBERS: Yet another dismal statistical performance by Ali, who averaged 37.4 punch attempts and 10.9 connects per round. Ali landed zero punches in round seven, three in round one and just seven in the twelfth. Ali landed just 65 power punches, his lowest total in a 15-round fight.

Date:	May 16, 1977			City: Landover, MD				Venue: Capitol Center								
Opponent:	Alfredo Evangelista															
Result:	Ali by unanimous decision -- Retains World Heavyweight Title															

Referee:	Harry Cecchini															
Round	1	2	3	4	5	6	7	8	9	10	11	12	13	14	15	Total
Ali																71
Evangelista																65

Judge:	Terry Moore															
Round	1	2	3	4	5	6	7	8	9	10	11	12	13	14	15	Total
Ali																72
Evangelista																64

Judge:	Ray Klingmeyer															
Round	1	2	3	4	5	6	7	8	9	10	11	12	13	14	15	Total
Ali	5	5	5	4	5	5	4	5	5	5	5	4	5	5	5	72
Evangelista	4	4	5	5	4	4	5	4	4	4	4	5	4	4	4	64

MUHAMMAD ALI UD 15 ALFREDO EVANGELISTA
05/16/77 - LANDOVER, MD

Total Punches Landed / Thrown	1	2	3	4	5	6	7	8	9	10	11	12	13	14	15
ALI	3/26	11/30	10/34	17/44	12/46	19/52	0/3	11/45	17/43	10/36	11/47	7/36	13/47	13/38	10/34
	11.5%	36.7%	29.4%	38.6%	26.1%	36.5%	0%	24.4%	39.5%	27.8%	23.4%	19.4%	27.7%	34.2%	29.4%
EVANGELISTA	5/14	7/29	16/59	14/69	12/51	7/23	19/81	13/42	2/19	5/16	8/27	14/73	6/21	7/29	6/19
	35.7%	24.1%	27.1%	20.3%	23.5%	30.4%	23.5%	31%	10.5%	31.3%	29.6%	19.2%	28.6%	24.1%	31.6%

Jab Landed / Thrown	1	2	3	4	5	6	7	8	9	10	11	12	13	14	15
ALI	2/14	7/20	8/23	9/26	7/28	10/27	0/3	3/19	12/27	8/24	4/19	2/9	7/30	11/30	9/23
	14.3%	35%	34.8%	34.6%	25%	37%	0%	15.8%	44.4%	33.3%	21.1%	22.2%	23.3%	36.7%	39.1%
EVANGELISTA	1/5	1/10	2/21	1/18	1/19	0/6	1/21	4/14	0/3	2/6	4/14	2/16	1/4	1/6	2/7
	20%	10%	9.5%	5.6%	5.3%	0%	4.8%	28.6%	0%	33.3%	28.6%	12.5%	25%	16.7%	28.6%

Power Punches Landed / Thrown	1	2	3	4	5	6	7	8	9	10	11	12	13	14	15
ALI	1/12	4/10	2/11	8/18	5/18	9/25	0/0	8/26	5/16	2/12	7/28	5/27	6/17	2/8	1/11
	8.3%	40%	18.2%	44.4%	27.8%	36%	0%	30.8%	31.3%	16.7%	25%	18.5%	35.3%	25%	9.1%
EVANGELISTA	4/9	6/19	14/38	13/51	11/32	7/17	18/60	9/28	2/16	3/10	4/13	12/57	5/17	6/23	4/12
	44.4%	31.6%	36.8%	25.5%	34.4%	41.2%	30%	32.1%	12.5%	30%	30.8%	21.1%	29.4%	26.1%	33.3%

Final Punch Stat Report	Total Punches	Total Jabs	Power Punches
ALI	164/561	99/322	65/239
	29.2%	30.7%	27.2%
EVANGELISTA	141/572	23/170	118/402
	24.7%	13.5%	29.4%

31.

Entering this, his 19th title defense overall and the 10th of his second reign, Muhammad Ali had faced and beaten some of boxing history's most fearsome punchers. Archie Moore, Sonny Liston, Joe Frazier and George Foreman belong on anyone's list of greatest knockout artists as they scored 266 of them in 392 fights. Ali also faced Cleveland Williams (58 KOs in 92 fights), George Chuvalo (64 KOs in 93 fights), and Mac Foster (30 KOs in 36 fights, all wins by KO) as well as Bob Foster (a terror at light heavyweight but not so much at heavyweight), Floyd Patterson (an overlooked hitter who regained his title with a single left hook that left his opponent twitching), Ron Lyle (of which Cosell said he could do nothing else but punch), Ken Norton (who had a full assortment of single-shot bombs), "The Bellflower Belter" Jerry Quarry, Henry Cooper (owner of " 'Enry's 'Ammer") and even LaMar Clark (who scored 42 KOs in 43 wins according to Boxrec, albeit against soft competition). Given this lineup, it's a miracle Ali had been floored just four times officially and hadn't been driven to the deck by a genuine punch since the first Frazier fight in 1971.

So, when Ali committed to fight Earnie Shavers following the Alfredo Evangelista fight, he authorized a match that pitted one of the sport's most durable chins against the man many still say is the most destructive shot-for-shot power-puncher boxing has ever produced. Shavers certainly looked the part: His squat bowling ball physique bulged with muscles and the combination of his shaven skull and neatly trimmed goatee was intimidation personified. His record was even scarier: Of his 54 wins, 52 were by knockout, including 21 in the first round. Although his left hook was more than capable of finishing any fight, his right cross was the true crippler.

But Shavers also had two major shortcomings: His chin and his stamina.

Of his five defeats, three were by knockout. After dominating Ron Stander for the first two rounds of their May 1970 fight, the hometown hero thrilled the Omaha crowd by hammering the tiring Shavers in rounds three and four before the final punch in the fifth caused the semi-conscious Shavers to pitch forward and land on his face. Then, after rolling off 33 straight wins, the last of which was a first-round knockout of ex-champ Jimmy Ellis that vaulted Shavers to world prominence, Quarry crushed him in 141 seconds in December 1973 at Madison Square Garden. Finally, in September 1975, Shavers dropped Lyle in round two in front of Lyle's home fans in Denver but Lyle cleared the cobwebs, went toe-to-toe with Shavers and left him face-first on the mat in round six.

As for his stamina, Shavers' enormous power rendered that moot most of the time but during those rare occasions in which he was taken into the later rounds he either sputtered to the finish line in victory or squandered hard-earned leads in defeat. Two fights after losing to Quarry, Shavers led journeyman Bob Stallings at the halfway mark but by the ninth he was running on fumes. A ninth-round knockdown by Stallings helped him win a six rounds to four decision on all three scorecards, which, given Stallings' 21-24 record coming in, was one of 1974's most shocking upsets. Just 22 days later Shavers faced Jimmy Young, who he had stopped in three rounds 21 months earlier. Shavers seemingly had the fight won in the fourth when he floored Young with a vicious left hook but Young arose and battered Shavers for the remainder of the 10-rounder. Most ringsiders believed Young had done enough to win, as did referee Harry Cecchini, who scored the bout 46-45 for Young. But Cecchini was overruled by judges Larry Barrett (47-44 Shavers) and especially Tom Kelly, whose 47-47 card resulted in a draw.

The stamina gap between the two was breathtaking: In 60 pro fights, Shavers had fought past round six just seven times while Ali, a 56-fight veteran, had gone 10 or more rounds 26 times, including the full 15 rounds in four of his last five. Shavers, no spring chicken at 32, was keenly aware of this dynamic, so much so that it dominated his pre-fight thinking. Who could blame him? After all, only one previous fight, the Lyle loss, had been scheduled for as many as 12 rounds and now he was confronted with the prospect of having to last 15.

"It had been ingrained in me since day one in training that I shouldn't punch myself out, that I should take it easy early on," Shavers wrote in his autobiography. "My handlers figured that Ali would try to draw me in, then sit back and absorb my punches until I burned myself out." (1)

To prevent that, Shavers sparred 215 rounds during a training camp that was two weeks longer than normal. He spent the first 10 days chopping wood, lifting weights and rowing at a private lake. Shavers' quick-burning metabolism inspired fears of coming in the fight too light. His solution: Ice cream -- and lots of it. (2) Still, he scaled 211 1/4, just 2 1/4 pounds heavier than his most recent fight, a second round knockout over Howard Smith. Ali, for his part, scaled 225.

While the questions about his endurance bothered Shavers, he was immune to Ali's pre-fight bluster. That's because he and Ali already knew each other and were friends.

"When the press wasn't around Ali would carry on a normal, civil conversation with me," he wrote. "Once the media was present, Ali would go instantly into his act." (3)

That act included dubbing Shavers "The Acorn" for his bald pate.

"From acorns grow mighty oaks," Shavers countered. (4)

Ali continued the "Acorn" shtick during referee Johnny LoBianco's final instructions as he rubbed Shavers' head, then LoBianco's balding skull, with his right glove. Once the fight began, however, all joking was put to the side.

Following a feel-out first round that was controlled by Ali's jab (29 of 50 attempted punches to just 26 total punches for the conserving challenger), Shavers proved in round two that the hype surrounding his heavy right hand was completely justified. The first one drove Ali back into the neutral corner pad, caused him to grab Shavers and look into the crowd with hyperbolically widened mouth and eyes. The second one, however, nearly knocked the heavyweight crown off Ali's head.

With a minute remaining in the round Shavers came over the top of an Ali jab and nailed him with a right to the temple. The blow sent a shock wave through Ali's nervous system, causing the champ's legs to do a stutter-step and his right arm to instinctively reach for the top rope. As the crowd numbering 14,613 roared in surprise, Ali's fertile mind conjured a way to neutralize the crisis: Make a funny face and beckon Shavers in with his right glove. Shavers, who should have known better given his friendship with Ali, hesitated, which bought Ali just enough time to regain his equilibrium.

"My instincts told me I had the champ reeling, but I let Ali con me into thinking otherwise," Shavers wrote. "If, at that crucial moment, I had taken the fight to him, the title could have changed hands right there. But Ali's recuperative powers were extraordinary, and he recovered quickly. His antics bought him the time he needed to clear his head. I remember Ali being so cunning in the second round when he was hurt. I didn't want to go in for the kill and get killed instead. If only I had not held back in that second round, and instead had thrown everything I had, I might have won the title right then. But I didn't and what turned out to be my biggest window of opportunity was slammed shut." (5)

As it was, Shavers, who shook Ali again near the end of the round with yet another right, out-landed Ali 20-7 overall and 17-3 power, connecting on an impressive 52% of his power punches to Ali's 13%. But while Shavers won the skirmish, the resourceful Ali won that war of survival.

Ali further cleared his head by keeping his distance in the third by alternating between dancing and covering up on the ropes while Shavers stalked and landed frequent but relatively light blows to conserve his energy. Although Shavers out-landed Ali 14-6 overall and 10-1 in power shots, all three judges awarded the round to Ali.

In light of Ali's controversial decision victories over Young and Norton, NBC, which aired the Ali-Shavers fight in prime time, experimented with semi-open scoring. Between each round, the network flashed a graphic detailing the judges' scores for the round as well as a running total. In theory, only the audience at home could see the scores but a smart trainer like Angelo Dundee knew how to bend a situation in his favor. Dundee, knowing monitors were in each dressing room, asked Baltimore matchmaker Eddie Hrica to watch the broadcast and relay the results via hand signals to Dundee. Unfortunately for Shavers, his team didn't possess the same nimbleness of thought. (6)

The gimmick also exposed the illogical scoring patterns that heavily favored Ali during this period in this career. In addition to the curious scoring in round three, the fourth round saw Shavers out-throw Ali 63-26, out-land him 22-1 overall, 9-0 jabs and 13-1 power, achieve percentage gaps of 35%-4% overall and 42%-7% power and land the single hardest shot of the round, a massive right hand in the closing moments. While judges Tony Castellano and Eva Shain (the first female to judge a world heavyweight title fight) rightly saw Shavers the winner, referee Johnny LoBianco awarded the round to Ali.

There were other examples:

* In the seventh, Shavers prevailed 15-9 in total connects and 44-30 in attempted punches, but Ali got the nod from LoBianco and Castellano while Shain favored Shavers.

* In round eight, a round that saw Shavers out-throw Ali 79-17 overall and out-land him 17-3 overall and 12-3 power, it was Shain's turn to stretch the bounds of credulity when she scored for Ali while the other two saw Shavers the winner.

* In round nine, Shavers again threw more (65-22), landed more (13-4) and landed twice as many power punches (8-4), but Lobianco saw it even while Castellano and Shain awarded the round to Ali.

* The 10th, 11th and 12th were close numerically (Ali led 24-22, 23-17 and 22-20) but all three officials gave Ali those rounds.

Thanks to Hrica, Dundee knew that Ali was ahead eight rounds to four on the cards of Shain and Castellano and 8-3-1 on LoBianco's, which meant all Ali needed to do to retain the title was keep his feet. But had CompuBox existed in 1977, the round-by-round breakdowns might have prompted the broadcasters to question the scorecards, for Shavers led Ali seven rounds to five in terms of overall connects and had a lead in the raw numbers. But again, in this era of boxing, a challenger had to nearly decapitate a champion in order to win a decision on points.

Shavers still had that punch, however, and going into the final nine minutes it was Ali's gas tank that was nearing empty, not Shavers'.

In the final minute of the 13th Shavers drove Ali to the corner pad with a right, after which he landed a right-left-right to the chin that had Ali holding on. After LoBianco broke them up, Shavers connected with yet another right to the button that snapped Ali's head, and, a few seconds later, another right to the jaw. Shavers out-threw Ali 70-29 overall and out-landed him

20-12 overall and 19-5 power. This time, all three judges awarded the round to Shavers, only the third time that the challenger swept a round compared to Ali's six.

The 14th featured the best two-way action of the fight thus far as Shavers tore after Ali and Ali furiously fended him off. At one point Ali fell to the canvas near his own corner but LoBianco correctly called the fall a slip. From there the pair swapped power shots at a pace that belied the late stage of the fight. Although Ali out-landed Shavers 27-24 overall, Shavers, the effective aggressor, threw more (81-60) and connected with more power punches (23-21). Shavers won the session on all three scorecards, the first round Shavers won despite being out-landed.

"The 13th was Shavers' best round to that point," wrote Pat Putnam. "The 14th was even better. Rocked by hard right hands, Ali survived, but the legs that had carried him through 56 professional fights were beginning to fail. At the end of 14th round, the champion had to dip into his reserve of strength just to get back to his corner. Wearily he slumped on his stool, his eyes glazed by fatigue. When the bell for the 15th round rang, Ali could barely stand." (7)

Situations such as force the greatest ones to summon that extra supply of adrenaline, courage and professional pride that gives them the extra fuel they need to push through. It pulled Ali off the canvas against Banks, Cooper and Frazier, it helped him endure the pounding in Kinshasa as well as the agony of Manila and he hoped it would get him through the Shavers surge.

At first, it looked as if Shavers would break through. He started the 15th strong as he bulled Ali to the corner and rocked him with a right to the jaw, hammered him with an overhand right along the ropes and sent him tottering backward with a glancing right to the chin and a heavy right to the ribs. Trapped in his own corner, Ali tried to fight his way out with a shoeshine combination but the blows were too light and too inaccurate to stave off Shavers. Shavers was hitting Ali with telling regularity and each landed blow visibly moved the champion, who was growing older by the second.

Freed from his psychological chains, Shavers went all out for the kill as he cut loose with wild, power-packed blows that mostly missed the mark. As the fight entered its final minute Shavers and Ali fought not just against each other but against their preconceived levels of endurance. Racked with pain and exhaustion they pushed past the physical barriers and propelled themselves to a level of violence rarely seen in any round, much less the final round of a heavyweight championship contest. Even so, as the clock wound down below 30 seconds, Shavers looked like the easy winner.

Then, with stunning swiftness, Ali turned the round. A split-second after Shavers missed with a right, Ali connected with a right to the temple that stopped the challenger in his tracks. As the crowd rose as one, Ali blasted Shavers with a combination highlighted by a right uppercut to the jaw, then another right to the head that caught Shavers as he was retaliating.

With the clock nearing the 10-second mark, Ali landed a heavy right to the temple that scrambled Shavers' wires and threatened to turn out his lights. A hook-right to the jaw propelled his increasingly limp body to the ropes, which saved him from slumping to the floor. Shavers stumbled forward behind a protective shell, and it was everything he could do to stay upright as Ali, showing more energy than he had in years, continued to pursue the kill. In the waning moments, Ali punctuated an extraordinary round with a six-punch bouquet that Shavers barely survived.

At the bell, Ali snappily turned toward his corner while Shavers, his upper body tilting with exhaustion, trudged to his. Numerically, the damage inflicted by both men was astonishing: Ali went 40 of 90 overall -- both highs for the fight -- and connected on 34 of his 72 power shots while Shavers went 29 of 81 overall and 26 of 61 power. The pair attempted 171 punches overall and 133 power shots, numbers suited more for lightweights than a pair of tired thirty-something heavyweights. So much for Shavers stamina issues on this night: He threw 70 punches in round 13, 81 in the 14th and 81 again in the final round.

Ali's heroic surge rightfully earned him the final round on all scorecards but the reaction to their aggregate scoring was decidedly negative. Shain's card of 9-6 for Ali triggered loud boos while Castellano's cinching 9-6 score only added to the volume. Referee LoBianco completed the sweep as he saw it 9-5-1. The unofficial Associated Press scorecard had Ali leading 10-5 while the United Press International writer had it 8-6-1 for Ali.

The statistics, however, indicated that Shavers had out-landed Ali 266-208 overall, out-threw him 878-709 and connected at a higher percentage (30%-29% overall and 37%-34% power). The round-by-round breakdowns had Shavers up 8-7 overall, Ali ahead 10-4-1 in jabs and Shavers up 12-3 in power shots.

"It's hard to win a decision against Ali," Shavers said. "I knew I had to knock him out. Looking back at it, if I had to change anything I would put more pressure on him sooner." (8)

"I'm tired," Ali said in the post-fight press conference, his voice barely above a whisper. "I hurt all over. This man Earnie Shavers is a great fighter. He reminds me of Joe Frazier with the pressure he puts on. Somebody once told me that I bring out the best in every man I face. Everybody gets up to fight me. Everybody has their best night when they face me.

"It's time to say goodbye," he concluded. "I feel in my bones this would be a good time to go out." (9)

It would have been. But Ali, a fighter to the end, would not -- or perhaps could not -- walk away.

INSIDE THE NUMBERS: Shavers, bogged by stamina issues throughout his career, fought the fight of his life vs. Ali, throwing 878 punches (58.5 per round- hvt. avg.: 44.7), the third highest total by an Ali opponent in 47 fights tracked by CompuBox. Ali threw 90 punches in round fifteen (landed 40), his highest total since round eight in Manila, when he threw 85 against Smokin' Joe and landed 41.

Date:	September 29, 1977					City: New York, NY				Venue: Madison Square Garden							
Opponent:	Earnie Shavers																
Result:	Ali by unanimous decision -- Retains World Heavyweight Title																
Referee:	**Johnny LoBianco**																
	Round	1	2	3	4	5	6	7	8	9	10	11	12	13	14	15	Total
	Ali	X		X	X	X		X		E	X	X	X			X	9 (1E)
	Shavers		X				X		X	E				X	X		5 (1E)
Judge:	**Eva Shain**																
	Round	1	2	3	4	5	6	7	8	9	10	11	12	13	14	15	Total
	Ali	X		X		X			X	X	X	X	X			X	9
	Shavers		X		X		X	X						X	X		6
Judge:	**Tony Castellano**																
	Round	1	2	3	4	5	6	7	8	9	10	11	12	13	14	15	Total
	Ali	X		X		X		X		X	X	X	X			X	9
	Shavers		X		X		X		X					X	X		6

MUHAMMAD ALI UD 15 EARNIE SHAVERS
09/29/77 - NEW YORK

Total Punches Landed / Thrown

	1	2	3	4	5	6	7	8	9	10	11	12	13	14	15
ALI	8/50	7/46	6/44	1/26	18/65	4/17	9/30	3/17	4/22	24/78	23/70	22/65	12/29	27/60	40/90
	16%	15.2%	13.6%	3.8%	27.7%	23.5%	30%	17.6%	18.2%	30.8%	32.9%	33.8%	41.4%	45%	44.4%
SHAVERS	4/26	20/46	14/46	22/63	14/32	15/68	15/44	17/79	13/65	22/59	17/57	20/61	20/70	24/81	29/81
	15.4%	43.5%	30.4%	34.9%	43.8%	22.1%	34.1%	21.5%	20%	37.3%	29.8%	32.8%	28.6%	29.6%	35.8%

Jab Landed / Thrown

	1	2	3	4	5	6	7	8	9	10	11	12	13	14	15
ALI	4/29	4/22	5/28	0/12	15/50	2/8	2/11	0/3	0/5	7/39	13/40	9/32	7/19	6/20	6/18
	13.8%	18.2%	17.9%	0%	30%	25%	18.2%	0%	0%	17.9%	32.5%	28.1%	36.8%	30%	33.3%
SHAVERS	2/15	3/13	4/19	9/32	2/11	2/23	4/20	5/26	5/26	6/25	5/24	5/23	1/22	1/16	3/20
	13.3%	23.1%	21.1%	28.1%	18.2%	8.7%	20%	19.2%	19.2%	24%	20.8%	21.7%	4.5%	6.3%	15%

Power Punches Landed / Thrown

	1	2	3	4	5	6	7	8	9	10	11	12	13	14	15
ALI	4/21	3/24	1/16	1/14	3/15	2/9	7/19	3/14	4/17	17/39	10/30	13/33	5/10	21/40	34/72
	19%	12.5%	6.3%	7.1%	20%	22.2%	36.8%	21.4%	23.5%	43.6%	33.3%	39.4%	50%	52.5%	47.2%
SHAVERS	2/11	17/33	10/27	13/31	12/21	13/45	11/24	12/53	8/39	16/34	12/33	15/38	19/48	23/65	26/61
	18.2%	51.5%	37%	41.9%	57.1%	28.9%	45.8%	22.6%	20.5%	47.1%	36.4%	39.5%	39.6%	35.4%	42.6%

Final Punch Stat Report

Total	Total Punches	Total Jabs	Power Punches
ALI	208/709	80/336	128/373
	29.3%	23.8%	34.3%
SHAVERS	266/878	57/315	209/563
	30.3%	18.1%	37.1%

32.

FEBRUARY 15, 1978 - LAS VEGAS HILTON, LAS VEGAS, NV
LEON SPINKS W 15 MUHAMMAD ALI I

The day after the Shavers fight, a press conference was held at Madison Square Garden. Shortly before it began, MSG matchmaker Teddy Brenner approached Ali and had a brief but blunt chat.

"I took him aside and said, 'champ, why don't you announce your retirement?' " Brenner told author Thomas Hauser. "He asked, 'what for?' And I told him, 'because sooner or later, some kid that couldn't carry your bucket is going to beat you. You're going to be beaten by guys that have no business being in the ring with you. It's just a matter of time. If you take a big piece of iron and put it down on the center of the floor and let a drop of water hit it every 10 seconds, eventually you'll get a hole in the center of that piece of iron, and that's what's happening to you. You're getting hit; you're gonna get hurt. You've proven everything that a great champion can possibly prove. You don't need this. Get out!' "

Brenner backed up his words at the press conference by stating that he would never allow Ali to fight at the Garden again. (1) Brenner was as good as his word. Not only that, he was right about the state of Ali's career. But no one ever suspected that the "kid" who would beat him would be Ali's very next challenger -- Leon Spinks.

On paper, the pairing was absurd. On one side stood Ali, a living legend in his chosen sport who also used his notoriety to expand his influence into the worlds of politics and religion. That fusion of physical prowess, off-the-charts charisma and social impact resulted in Ali becoming the most famous person walking the earth. On the other side stood Spinks, a novice pro who was less than two years removed from *his* greatest accomplishment to date, winning a gold medal at the 1976 Summer Olympics in Montreal. But Olympic gold was the only point of similarity between Spinks and Ali, who, as Cassius Clay, acquired his prize in 1960.

The statistical gulfs were staggering. Ali was making the 11th defense of his second reign (and 20th overall) while Spinks was about to log his eighth professional *fight*. Ali, a 17 year pro with 498 rounds under his belt, had logged nearly as many rounds in his last two fights -- 30 -- than the 31 rounds Spinks had in his entire pro career to this point. Spinks' situation was similar to that faced by 1956 Olympic gold medalist Pete Rademacher, whose hustle and ingenuity resulted in his challenging then-heavyweight champion Floyd Patterson in his pro debut. But while Rademacher was fighting an accomplished champion and a future Hall of Famer, Spinks was tackling a bona fide icon.

From Ali's standpoint, the Spinks fight was the definition of a low-risk fight. Not only was Spinks infinitely less experienced as a pro, he had also struggled against his two best opponents in Scott LeDoux (a debatable D 10) and Alfio Righetti (W 10), the victory that ostensibly earned Spinks his date with destiny. Also, Spinks had earned sufficient name recognition from the gold medal drive that was heavily chronicled by ABC as well as from coverage of his pro bouts from CBS, which would also air Ali-Spinks. Additionally, Spinks' crude and wild-swinging ways seemed a perfect fit for Ali's counters and his high-energy style appeared profoundly unsuited to the 15-round championship distance, a road Ali had completed 12 times. Finally, Ali needed a breather after his demanding rubber match with Ken Norton and his unexpected 15-round war with Earnie Shavers less than five months earlier. For these reasons, Team Ali saw the Spinks fight as a win-win-win-win-win-win. The odds-makers agreed, but the relatively narrow 10-to-1 price given the gulfs also acknowledged the dramatic erosion Ali had shown against Young, Norton and Shavers.

If the WBC had its way, it would have been Ali-Norton IV instead of Ali-Spinks I. That's because Norton was the sanctioning body's number one contender and thus, Ali was obligated to fight him. Ali, however, wanted an easier fight following the struggle against Shavers and he knew the power of his name and his status as undisputed heavyweight champion carried weight with the public, the press and boxing historians.

With both sides at loggerheads, a compromise was struck: The WBC would permit the Spinks fight to proceed on the condition that the winner had until March 17, 1978 to sign for a Norton fight with the promoter of his choice, then actually fight Norton by July 7. If neither man heeded this edict, a purse bid for the fight would be staged on April 7. (2) With that, Ali versus Spinks received the WBC's blessing.

Spinks and his team ignored the legion of naysayers and proceeded to give themselves the best chance of victory. For the first time in his life Spinks holed himself away at a training camp in the Catskills. (3) Though he once managed to escape to a billiards room in South Carolina, Spinks mostly stuck with the program and whipped himself into tremendous condition. Conversely, the unconcerned Ali went through the motions at his facility in Deer Lake, Pa., but still managed to work off 17 1/2 pounds in four weeks. (4) He called the gap-toothed Spinks "The Beaver" and "The Vampire," but like his fellow Marine Norton, the fun-loving Spinks shrugged off Ali's barbs and launched a few of his own verbal bombs.

The weights and physiques reflected each man's pre-fight preparation as Spinks scaled a hard and ready 197 1/4 while the 224 1/4-pound Ali, despite being three-quarters of a pound lighter than for the Shavers fight, appeared thicker and softer than usual.

With the strains of "Semper Fidelis" blaring over the PA system, Spinks entered the ring and soaked up the atmosphere by smiling at the fans and waving his arms in the air. Meanwhile, a somber Ali entered to "Pomp and Circumstance" and indulged in none of his usual pre-fight antics. He simply walked to Spinks' corner and shook hands with everyone before returning to his work station. At Ali's request, ring announcer Chuck Hull introduced the champion as being from Louisville, a clear nod to his roots.

Ali opened the fight by getting on his toes and flicking jabs that fell far short of the target while Spinks pursued behind a hyperactive bob-and-weave. Within seconds Ali backed into the ropes and employed the "Rope-a-Dope" that famously ensnared George Foreman a little more than three years earlier. Ali's intent was crystal-clear: He wanted the hyped-up Spinks to burn off his nervous energy, after which he would pick apart his exhausted quarry en route to a mid-rounds knockout.

Spinks eagerly took the bait by hammering Ali with hooks and crosses to all available legal targets. But the challenger also intentionally hit Ali's arms and shoulders, a tactic advocated by assistant trainer and onetime middleweight contender George Benton, who believed that would sap the power from Ali's blows in the later rounds. At one point Spinks unloaded 22 unanswered punches before Ali pinned Spinks' arms and spun away from the ropes.

Following a few more seconds of dancing, Ali returned to the ropes and Spinks responded with a torrent of uppercuts that smashed through the guard. The buoyant challenger even found time to look over Ali's shoulder and flash a huge grin. Spinks was feeling great about himself, for despite taking an Ali right to the jaw with 35 seconds left, he had won the first round overwhelmingly by landing 28 of his 54 punches (52%) as well as a stratospheric 68% of his power shots (26 of 38). Conversely, Ali threw 22 punches and landed six.

Ali refused to sit on his stool between rounds and he continued to clown away the early rounds. Spinks, on the other hand, continued to apply his ambitious industriousness. Ali threw just nine punches in round two and landed none of them while Spinks connected on 18 of his 67 punches. He even out-jabbed the great Ali 7-0 during those three minutes, something unimaginable during Ali's best years.

Though it was early, Spinks' energetic attack and Ali's casual attitude threatened to flip the numbers argument. Before the fight, Ali's vast gaps in experience created lopsided figures in his favor but now, the most important numerals seemed to be 36 and 24 -- their respective ages.

Rounds three through seven featured more of the same and by round's end Spinks had built enormous statistical leads of 205-65 in total punches and 168-26 in landed power shots, which included a 55-0 bulge in body connects. Yes, Ali had some moments of effectiveness but had he not been Muhammad Ali, the most magnetic figure of his era, he probably would have lost every round on the scorecards. The good news was that, unlike the fights with Young, Norton and Shavers, Spinks *was* getting proper credit from two of the judges: Lou Tabat and Harold Buck had Spinks up 69-64 while Art Lurie had it 67-66 for the challenger. Despite the great start by Spinks, 15 rounds is still a long time and between rounds seven and eight Spinks started to show the first signs of fatigue.

"It's all right," chief second Angelo Dundee told Ali. "He's starting to stand up, this kid. That's his style, you'll nail him." Dundee knew that Spinks had learned the bob-and-weave at Joe Frazier's gym in Philadelphia, a tactic that was to be used specifically for this fight. Dundee correctly reasoned that Spinks, once tired, would revert to old habits and reassume the stand-up style that would render him vulnerable to Ali's attack.

As if on cue, Spinks began the eighth with a more straight-up style and Ali exploited it by stabbing the challenger's face with jabs and one-twos. At one point, Spinks dropped his gloves and dared Ali to stand his ground but the champion continued to move. Although Ali lost the eighth statistically (27-14 overall, 14-11 jabs, 13-3 power), he won the round on all scorecards because he was far more effective in comparison to previous rounds. Whatever the reason, Ali was finally starting the close the gap.

Spinks returned to the bob-and-weave in the ninth, and the move paid instant dividends as he backed Ali to the ropes and unleashed a 17-punch outburst. Ali slapped on a clinch to stop the surge, after which he danced around the challenger, though with increasing sluggishness. Spinks piled up the numbers (27-16 overall, 21-10 power) when Ali inevitably returned to the ropes and was nailed by a late one-two. Despite Spinks' apparent control, Buck and Lurie gave the round to Ali while Tabat saw it for Spinks.

Dundee, ever the master motivator, projected confidence between rounds nine and 10.

"He's ready...he's ready," Dundee urged. "Let's go to work. Bury him. The left hook will take him out."

For a change, Ali responded. After spending some time along the ropes Ali suddenly spun Spinks into the ropes and unleashed his hardest and fastest flurries of the fight. Now it was Spinks who was trapped and being forced to defend himself, and, for the first time in the fight, he appeared overwhelmed. At round's end Ali had thrown 95 punches and landed 46, his highest totals by far to this point, while Spinks plummeted to fight-lows of 36 attempted punches and 14 connects. This time, Ali swept the cards -- and rightly so.

While Spinks had mounted a wonderful challenge thus far, it now appeared the youngster had finally hit the wall. Rounds 11 through 15, known by many as "the championship rounds," were also viewed as "Ali's Alley." Spinks may have engaged in 15-round sparring sessions at the Catskills but while that might have boosted his confidence coming into the ring, it couldn't have prepared him fully for what he was about to experience. Was he up to this challenge?

Thanks to a spirited exchange in the final minute, Spinks actually out-landed Ali 27-21 overall and 19-11 power in the 11th but in the 12th Ali appeared to finally hit his stride by going 24 of 77 overall to Spinks' 18 of 51. On many scorecards -- including the official ones -- Ali was quickly closing the gap and making up for his early laziness.

Spinks' lead trainer Sam Soloman felt that his charge needed an extra boost to get him through the final three rounds. There was no other way to explain what a CBS camera captured between rounds 12 and 13 when he had Spinks drink from a mysterious bottle.

"You're doing it baby! You're doing it!" Soloman told Spinks. "But I want you to keep that left hand going!" Then he told Spinks to "spit it (water) out while I give you some juice." Spinks then drank from the bottle.

Up until a few years ago, water was the only liquid a fighter could legally ingest during a fight, but the word "juice" confirmed Spinks was drinking something other than that.

Whatever it was, it helped Spinks in rounds 13 and 14 as he out-landed Ali 53-21 in total connects, 21-12 in jabs and 32-9 in power shots. With one round remaining, the sports world was forced to confront this reality: Leon Spinks could be just one round away from springing an upset of epic proportions.

Just as he had in the homestretch of "The Thrilla in Manila," Ali summoned the contents of his auxiliary gas tank and proceeded to empty it in a desperate attempt to save his championship. Spinks, who was now on the doorstep of achieving his life's dream at an impossibly early stage of his professional development, responded with his own inspirational resurgence. The result was one of the most drama-filled and action-packed 180 seconds in heavyweight championship history.

Ali fired one-twos with a strength and conviction previously unseen in the fight while Spinks' blows were cutting and extraordinarily accurate. The crowd inside the Hilton Hotel in Las Vegas roared at the spectacle that unfolded before them. As the round wore on, Ali broke away and sprinted ahead. A big right briefly knocked Spinks off balance but the challenger fired back with his own two-fisted assault. Ali spun off the ropes and rained one-twos on Spinks but a right-left followed by two hard lefts to the face forced Ali to back off. Ali was trying his hardest to knock Spinks out but the flurries that had stopped numerous opponents in his youth no longer had their sense-separating snap. Thus, Spinks absorbed every blow and came back with even more. A left-right, two uppercuts and a final left-right to the jaw by Spinks ended what would be declared THE RING's 1978 Round of the Year.

Spinks' final surge enabled him to nose ahead of Ali 48-47 in total connects. But Ali never before had thrown and landed as many power punches in a single round -- 91 and 44 respectively -- and it was clear he dearly wanted to walk out of the ring with his championship intact. Spinks, however, landed more total punches on Ali than any other opponent ever had, or ever would.

The statistics suggested a resounding Spinks win. He out-threw Ali 943-774, out-landed him 419-254 overall and 312-145 power and nearly out-jabbed him (109 for Ali, 107 for Spinks). Spinks was also the markedly more accurate fighter as he landed 44% of his total punches to Ali's 33%, 31% of his jabs to Ali's 26%, and 52% of his hooks, crosses and uppercuts to Ali's 42%. Then again, Ali had been out-landed by Young, Shavers and Norton and the judges denied them victory because they believed the challengers had not sufficiently "taken" the title from the champion. Would they dare deny Spinks now?

Incredibly, the decision was split, and ring announcer Hull maximized every bit of drama as he rendered the verdict. Tabat saw the fight 145-140 for Spinks. Cheers. Lurie viewed it 143-142 for Ali. Boos. Then, Buck's card: 144-141 for the winner...and *new* champion.

The word "new" electrified the Spinks contingent, who then lifted their man onto their shoulders. Ali, ever the sportsman, made his way through the throng to congratulate his conqueror.

"Naturally you want to go out with the title," Ali told Bob Halloran. "It was a close fight. He was the most aggressive, so I imagine he won. For whatever reason he took it and you can't take it from him. I did the best I could. He proved all the reporters wrong. They said he didn't have a chance, but I knew he was a good fighter and that's why I fought him. It's just another experience in life."

When he was asked whether this would be his last fight, Ali said no.

"I would like to do something that's never been done before: To be the only man to win the title a third time," Ali said. "It would be a good fight and I'm sure the public would want it. But I have to decide if I want it."

Spinks, though triumphant, was respectful and realistic.

"I trained hard and I tried hard (because) I knew it would be a hard fight," he said at the post-fight press conference. "I had to really suffer and dedicate myself to training. I had a big opportunity to beat my man Ali. Me and Ali both knew what our job was. We knew what to do."

When asked whether he would give Ali a rematch, he said, "I'm going to give him another shot." But when asked whether he would bypass top contender Norton to give Ali an immediate rematch -- which would go against the document demanded by the WBC and signed by both Ali and Spinks as a condition for the organization's blessing -- he said, "I haven't decided yet."

That decision would have to wait. At least for now, Leon Spinks was now the undisputed heavyweight champion of the world. Still just 24, Spinks shook up the world with an upset that virtually no one saw coming. As Spinks celebrated his triumph, Ali, who had pulled off the same feat nearly 14 years earlier in Miami Beach, was forced to confront his new reality the same way Liston had to all those years ago.

> *INSIDETHE NUMBERS: Ali was valiant in defeat, landing 44 of 91 power shots in round fifteen -- highs in both categories for the 47 fights tracked by CompuBox. Ali threw 105 punches in round fifteen, his second highest total (the 113 he fired in round 11 against Mac Foster is number one). Spinks landed 419 punches, the most ever by an Ali opponent in the study. As a point of comparison, Frazier landed 378 in his first fight with Ali and 354 in his third. Ali and Spinks combined to land an average of 45 punches per round, 33% higher than the heavyweight norm.*

Date:	February 15, 1978				City: Las Vegas, NV				Venue: Hilton Hotel							
Opponent:	Leon Spinks															
Result:	Spinks by split decision -- Lost World Heavyweight Title															
Judge:	Lou Tabat															
	Round	1	2	3	4	5	6	7	8	9	10	11	12	13	14	15	Total
	Ali	9	9	9	9	9	10	9	10	9	10	10	10	9	9	9	140
	Spinks	10	10	10	10	10	9	10	9	10	9	9	9	10	10	10	145
Judge:	Harold Buck															
	Round	1	2	3	4	5	6	7	8	9	10	11	12	13	14	15	Total
	Ali	9	9	9	10	9	9	9	10	10	10	10	10	9	9	9	141
	Spinks	10	10	10	9	10	10	10	9	9	9	9	9	10	10	10	144
Judge:	Art Lurie															
	Round	1	2	3	4	5	6	7	8	9	10	11	12	13	14	15	Total
	Ali	9	9	9	10	10	9	10	10	10	10	10	10	9	9	9	143
	Spinks	10	10	10	9	9	10	9	9	9	9	9	9	10	10	10	142

LEON SPINKS SD 15 MUHAMMAD ALI
02/15/78 - Las Vegas

Total Punches Landed / Thrown															
	1	2	3	4	5	6	7	8	9	10	11	12	13	14	15
SPINKS	28/54	18/67	39/90	29/67	26/58	29/58	36/72	27/49	27/63	14/36	27/62	18/51	22/51	31/70	48/95
	51.9%	26.9%	43.3%	43.3%	44.8%	50%	50%	55.1%	42.9%	38.9%	43.5%	35.3%	43.1%	44.3%	50.5%
ALI	6/22	0/9	10/35	12/48	9/51	10/36	18/55	14/54	16/53	46/95	21/54	24/77	6/29	15/51	47/105
	27.3%	0%	28.6%	25%	17.6%	27.8%	32.7%	25.9%	30.2%	48.4%	38.9%	31.2%	20.7%	29.4%	44.8%

Jab Landed / Thrown															
	1	2	3	4	5	6	7	8	9	10	11	12	13	14	15
SPINKS	2/16	7/37	3/15	4/20	8/22	4/17	9/25	14/27	6/17	6/14	8/33	8/25	12/31	9/25	7/20
	12.5%	18.9%	20%	20%	36.4%	23.5%	36%	51.9%	35.3%	42.9%	24.2%	32%	38.7%	36%	35%
ALI	3/13	0/6	6/28	4/24	6/34	8/30	12/35	11/46	6/26	14/36	10/32	14/50	6/25	6/29	3/14
	23.1%	0%	21.4%	16.7%	17.6%	26.7%	34.3%	23.9%	23.1%	38.9%	31.3%	28%	24%	20.7%	21.4%

Power Punches Landed / Thrown															
	1	2	3	4	5	6	7	8	9	10	11	12	13	14	15
SPINKS	26/38	11/30	36/75	25/47	18/36	25/41	27/47	13/22	21/46	8/22	19/29	10/26	10/20	22/45	41/75
	68.4%	36.7%	48%	53.2%	50%	61%	57.4%	59.1%	45.7%	36.4%	65.5%	38.5%	50%	48.9%	54.7%
ALI	3/9	0/3	4/7	8/24	3/17	2/6	6/20	3/8	10/27	32/59	11/22	10/27	0/4	9/22	44/91
	33.3%	0%	57.1%	33.3%	17.6%	33.3%	30%	37.5%	37%	54.2%	50%	37%	0%	40.9%	48.4%

Final Punch Stat Report			
	Total Punches	Total Jabs	Power Punches
SPINKS	419/943	107/344	312/599
	44.4%	31.1%	52.1%
ALI	254/774	109/428	145/346
	32.8%	25.5%	41.9%

33.

On March 18, 1978 -- 31 days after shocking the world with his split decision victory over Muhammad Ali -- Leon Spinks made his decision. Instead of facing number-one challenger Ken Norton as he was mandated to do, Spinks decided to give Ali a rematch the following September. The WBC responded by voting 15-2 to strip Spinks of the title and retroactively awarding it to Norton, who won a 15-round decision over Jimmy Young in a title eliminator the previous November to become the body's mandatory challenger.

"We've been kicked around for such a long time," said WBC president Jose Sulaiman. "There will be no more delays, no further meetings, no more requests. The law is the law. These people must abide by the law. I would love Spinks to accept the commitments he's made." (1)

Although Spinks no longer had the honor of being undisputed champion, the move was financially sound. In a story written by the New York Times' Michael Katz on March 1, 1978, the original deal between CBS and Top Rank called for CBS to have exclusive rights to televise Spinks' first three title defenses against anyone not named Muhammad Ali. The total budget allocated for purses for each of those three bouts would be $1.5 million. Ronald "Butch" Lewis, a vice president for Top Rank who also was promoting Spinks, met with Norton's team in Las Vegas and made the following offer: Spinks would get a $1 million base purse plus $300,000 in training expenses while Norton would get the remaining $200,000.

"It's all we can afford because of our agreement with CBS," Lewis said.

"It's like kicking Kenny in the butt," responded public relations man Bobby Goodman, who was working closely with the Norton camp. Norton himself was "insulted," but called their bluff by accepting the offer via telegram shortly thereafter. Sixteen days later, however, Spinks made public his choice to fight Ali. (2)

CBS then was given rights of first refusal for the rematch. CBS refused because it felt it couldn't afford Top Rank's $7 million price tag, a development that then opened the bidding to NBC and ABC. While an NBC spokesman said his network was "interested," ABC leaped at the chance and secured the rights to Spinks-Ali II in May. The purses: $3.75 million for Spinks, $3.25 million for Ali.

The fight was pushed back to September because the Nevada State Athletic Commission suspended Spinks for 90 days in March for not telling state officials he had sustained a rib injury before the first Ali fight. Spinks aggravated the cartilage during the bout, which resulted in time off to recover. Meanwhile, the WBC staged an elimination bout March 25 between Earnie Shavers and undefeated Larry Holmes, which Holmes won on points to earn a crack at Norton's WBC title on June 9. Holmes went on to dethrone Norton by razor-thin split decision in one of the decade's best fights. As was the case for Spinks with Ali, Norton prospered financially as he reportedly made $3 million to Holmes' $500,000.

Arum tried to stage the fight in Bophuthatswana, a South African homeland for the Tswana people, and Mauritius, an island in the Indian Ocean, but thanks to protests from civil rights groups led by the Rev. Jesse Jackson and human rights groups in Africa, Spinks-Ali II ended up landing in New Orleans, specifically the Louisiana Superdome. (3)

Ali, determined to squeeze out one last great effort and become the first three-time heavyweight titlist, began training shortly after the rematch was signed in April. Preparing with a zeal not seen in years, the combination of hard work in the gym and dietary discipline transformed the soft physique he displayed in Las Vegas to a considerably tighter and toned body in New Orleans.

"I've never suffered like I'm forcing myself to suffer now," Ali told Pat Putnam of Sports Illustrated. "I've worked this hard for fights before, but never for this long. All the time, I'm in pain. I hurt all over. I hate it, but I know this is my last fight, and it's the last time I'll ever have to do it. I don't want to lose and spend the rest of my life looking back and saying, 'Damn, I should have trained harder.' " (4)

When Ali stepped on the scale, his 221 pounds, though only three-and-a-quarter pounds lighter than before fight one, appeared noticeably trimmer and better distributed. Interestingly, the weigh-in for the main event took place the day before the fight while the weigh-ins for the other three title fights occurred the day of the event. (5)

Ali's laser-like focus stood in stark contrast to Spinks, who spent more time handling legal problems that working out in the gym. According to a United Press International report, Spinks was arrested April 21 when police found cocaine in Spinks' hat band and marijuana in his jacket pocket during a pre-dawn stop at a restaurant parking lot. (6) A St. Louis grand jury refused to hand down an indictment on those charges, but on June 23, the day Spinks began driving from North Carolina to Michigan to begin training for the Ali rematch, he was arrested for the second time in two days and the fifth time that year for a traffic violation for driving 45 mph in a 20 mph zone, according to an Associated Press report. (7) Spinks' repeated violations of the law turned him into the butt of jokes on the late-night talk shows and confirmed suspicions that Spinks had become a "too much, too soon" poster child. Spinks scaled 201, three-and-three-quarters pounds heavier than was the case in February.

Spinks' out-of-the-ring problems had a profound effect on conventional wisdom entering the rematch. A pre-fight poll among RING staffers and boxing notables Joe Louis, Gene Tunney,

Jersey Joe Walcott, Floyd Patterson, Lou Nova, Ken Norton, Larry Holmes, Ernie Terrell and Ron Lyle. Five of the six boxing writers picked Ali while the fighters were mixed. Louis, Tunney and Patterson gave non-committal answers while the rest strongly picked Ali. (8)

Spinks-Ali II was one of four title fights on a card billed as "The Carnival of Champions," which, for old-timers, revived memories of the most recent Carnival of Champions held at New York City's Polo Grounds in September 1937. That card also featured four world title fights as Harry Jeffra dethroned bantamweight king Sixto Escobar on points, Lou Ambers kept his lightweight title by decision over Pedro Montanez, world welterweight champion Barney Ross decisioned challenger Ceferino Garcia and Fred Apostoli stopped middleweight titlist Marcel Thil in 10 rounds. But while the attendance at the Polo Grounds was 32,600, the Spinks-Ali rematch drew 63,350, an indoor record for boxing that stood for more than 38 years.

One other such "Carnival," staged over three days at the Olympic Club in New Orleans in 1892, culminated with James J. Corbett's conquest of longtime heavyweight champion John L. Sullivan. This "Carnival" promised to be just as historic, if not more so.

The first three title fights in New Orleans saw WBA bantamweight champion Jorge Lujan outpoint Albert Davila, Danny Lopez score an off-the-floor second-round knockout of Juan Malvarez to keep his WBC featherweight belt and Mike Rossman upset longtime WBA light heavyweight champion Victor Galindez by 13th round TKO. The atmosphere inside the Superdome was supercharged as the main event neared, as was the U.S. public, for the ABC telecast was watched by 73.3 million households, second only to the final episode of "Roots" for the largest TV audience in American history to that point. (9)

Following a 12-minute, 43 second ABC feature that detailed the life and times of Ali, the stage was set for the rematch. After Joe Frazier sang the national anthem, the contrasts were further illuminated. As both awaited the final instructions from referee Lucien Joubert, a smiling Spinks waved to ringsiders while a serious Ali looked at no one except Spinks.

Ali said before the fight that there would be no "Rope-a-Dope" and that he'd be dancing for 15 rounds. (10) He was as good as his word. Yes, the legs didn't have the spring of old but the fact he remained in constant motion was impressive nonetheless. Whenever Spinks moved in close, Ali immediately pulled him into a clinch. But while Spinks out-landed Ali 10-4 in overall punches thanks to some well-timed rights that accounted for more of his eight landed power shots, Ali's eye-catching movement and strategic command allowed him to win the first round on the scorecards of referee Joubert and judge Herman Dutrieux while the other judge, Ernest Cojoe, voted for Spinks.

The second round resembled the first in terms of strategy: Ali dancing, jabbing and clinching, Spinks charging and winging. When Spinks pushed him to the ropes early in the session, Ali acted as if the strands were electrified as he instantly grabbed Spinks and spun out to ring center. This time there would be no free shots along the ropes; if Spinks was to beat Ali, he would have to beat him at ring center and do so while Ali was on the move. Even the best opponents had problems reaching Ali when he was in dancing mode, but for the first time in years Ali was able to sustain it. Though Ali and Spinks landed nine punches each, Ali's superior output (35 to 26), easier-to-see connects and ring generalship allowed him to sweep the judges' cards.

Another contrast between the pair was their corners. While Dundee did whatever talking was needed to Ali, an army of people besides chief second Sam Soloman and assistant George Benton shouted advice. An impromptu compromise was struck; each person who wanted to speak to Leon would take his turn, then give way to the next person before the next round. A fed-up Benton left the corner following the fifth round, the only one Spinks would sweep on the scorecards, and only because Ali was penalized for holding behind Spinks' head.

"(Spinks) wasn't listening to a damn thing I was telling him," Benton said. "They (the rest of the corner) really didn't know what they were doing." (11)

Through six rounds the fight remained close numerically as each had landed 57 punches overall while Ali led on two cards (4-1-1 by Joubert and 4-2 by Dutrieux) and 3-3 on the third (Cojoe). Starting in the seventh, however, Ali began to put distance between himself and Spinks on the scorecards as his punch-and-clinch tactics thoroughly foiled Spinks' attempts to bully the older man and the sense of drama built with the crowd that cheered Ali's every move. Ali swept rounds seven through 11 on the scorecards but statistically the fight remained within Spinks' grasp as Ali led just 109-103 in overall connects through 11. But any doubt about the outcome was snuffed out in rounds 12 and 13 when Ali produced a fight-high 60 punches and 22 connects in the 12th (including 10 landed jabs) and out-landed Spinks 13-7 while nearly doubling the champion's output in the 13th (53-28).

The 14th and 15th was overwhelmed by thoughts of what was about to happen rather than the relatively even action that was taking place in the ring. Howard Cosell, so deeply connected to Ali's career through all the years, was moved to recite Bob Dylan's lyrics to "Forever Young" halfway through the 14th.

"May your hands always be busy, may your feet always be swift, may you have a strong foundation, when the winds of changes shift," he said. "And every time the winds of changes have shifted in the life of Muhammad Ali, he has found a way to come back, to triumph. That's the mark of the man."

During the 15th, the euphoric crowd broke into chants of "Ali, Ali, Ali" while those seated in the first few rows pressed toward ringside so that they could rush the ring.

When the final bell sounded, all knew that Ali had done enough to make the history he and everyone watching wanted to see. The judges agreed as Joubert and Cojoe scored 10-4-1 and

Dutrieux saw it 11-4. The stats also saw Ali a winner, albeit more narrowly (167-144 overall and 68-30 jabs while the more aggressive Spinks led 114-99 in power shots).

Had it not been for the history Ali was seeking, this rematch would have been characterized a slow and dull affair as Ali averaged 44.5 punches per round to Spinks' 33, both below the 44.7 heavyweight average. But Ali's late-round surge enabled him to win the round-by-round breakdown 7-4-4 overall and 10-2-3 jabs but trail 9-4-2 in power connects. No matter; Ali was the unquestioned ring master and his reward was immortality.

"Against Spinks the second time, my plan was simple: Jab, jab and throw the right hand," Ali told Hauser years later. "If he got in close, tie him up. No 'Rope-a-Dope', fight the whole time in the center of the ring. And throw lots of punches at the end of each round. Closing a round right impresses the judges, and I wanted to give Spinks something to remember between rounds." (12)

Not only did Ali give Spinks plenty to remember, he did the same for the entire world.

INSIDE THE NUMBERS: The rematch was more about what Spinks didn't do -- and that was throw his hands. Spinks landed just 144 of 495 total punches (33 attempts and 9.6 connects per round, 29.1% accuracy) after landing 419 punches in the first fight (27.9 per round and the most ever by an Ali opponent in the 47 Ali fights tracked by CompuBox) and throwing 943 (62.9 per round). Ali, who featured more movement and quickness in the rematch, needed to land just 167 of 667 after landing 254 of 774 in the first fight. Spinks never threw more than 41 punches in any round of the rematch.

Date:	September 15, 1978				City: New Orleans, LA			Venue: Superdome								
Opponent:	Leon Spinks															
Result:	Ali by unanimous decision -- Regains WBA Heavyweight Title															

Referee:	Lucien Joubert															
	Round	1	2	3	4	5	6	7	8	9	10	11	12	13	14	15	Total
	Ali	X	X	X	X			X	X	X	X	X	X	E			10 (1E)
	Spinks					X	X							E	X	X	4 (1E)

Judge:	Ernest Cojoe															
	Round	1	2	3	4	5	6	7	8	9	10	11	12	13	14	15	Total
	Ali		X	X			X	X	X	X	X	X	X		X	E	10 (1E)
	Spinks	X			X	X								X		E	4 (1E)

Judge:	Herman Dutrieux															
	Round	1	2	3	4	5	6	7	8	9	10	11	12	13	14	15	Total
	Ali	X	X	X			X	X	X	X	X	X		X		X	11
	Spinks				X	X							X		X		4

MUHAMMAD ALI UD 15 LEON SPINKS
09/15/78 - NEW ORLEANS

Total Punches Landed / Thrown															
	1	2	3	4	5	6	7	8	9	10	11	12	13	14	15
ALI	4/25	9/35	13/42	7/37	14/48	10/47	9/50	10/39	12/51	13/47	8/43	22/60	13/53	11/40	12/50
	16%	25.7%	31%	18.9%	29.2%	21.3%	18%	25.6%	23.5%	27.7%	18.6%	36.7%	24.5%	27.5%	24%
SPINKS	10/29	9/26	6/32	8/30	13/39	11/30	8/30	10/35	13/41	7/27	8/36	12/41	7/28	11/35	11/36
	34.5%	34.6%	18.8%	26.7%	33.3%	36.7%	26.7%	28.6%	31.7%	25.9%	22.2%	29.3%	25%	31.4%	30.6%

Jab Landed / Thrown															
	1	2	3	4	5	6	7	8	9	10	11	12	13	14	15
ALI	0/9	5/17	4/21	2/20	4/25	3/27	3/28	2/21	7/27	8/31	2/22	10/30	8/42	4/23	6/30
	0%	29.4%	19%	10%	16%	11.1%	10.7%	9.5%	25.9%	25.8%	9.1%	33.3%	19%	17.4%	20%
SPINKS	2/11	3/14	1/14	2/9	3/10	3/10	1/8	3/15	1/15	0/11	2/9	2/12	3/11	3/16	1/10
	18.2%	21.4%	7.1%	22.2%	30%	30%	12.5%	20%	6.7%	0%	22.2%	16.7%	27.3%	18.8%	10%

Power Punches Landed / Thrown															
	1	2	3	4	5	6	7	8	9	10	11	12	13	14	15
ALI	4/16	4/18	9/21	5/17	10/23	7/20	6/22	8/18	5/24	5/16	6/21	12/30	5/11	7/17	6/20
	25%	22.2%	42.9%	29.4%	43.5%	35%	27.3%	44.4%	20.8%	31.3%	28.6%	40%	45.5%	41.2%	30%
SPINKS	8/18	6/12	5/18	6/21	10/29	8/20	7/22	7/20	12/26	7/16	6/27	10/29	4/17	8/19	10/26
	44.4%	50%	27.8%	28.6%	34.5%	40%	31.8%	35%	46.2%	43.8%	22.2%	34.5%	23.5%	42.1%	38.5%

Final Punch Stat Report			
	Total Punches	Total Jabs	Power Punches
ALI	167/667	68/373	99/294
	25%	18.2%	33.7%
SPINKS	144/495	30/175	114/320
	29.1%	17.1%	35.6%

34.

OCTOBER 2, 1980 - CAESARS PALACE, LAS VEGAS, NV
LARRY HOLMES KO 10 MUHAMMAD ALI

If a Hollywood screenwriter had been guiding Muhammad Ali's career, the final scene likely would have been the triumphant aftermath of the Leon Spinks rematch. There would have been no need for embellishment because the reality was so perfect: Ali, moments after being declared the first man ever to win a piece of the heavyweight championship of the world three times, hoisted on the shoulders of his supporters and blowing kisses to the 63,350 spectators inside the Louisiana Superdome. Ali had earned that beautiful ending, for not only was he a ring immortal, he was arguably the most significant global sporting figure history had ever known.

But Ali would not have that Hollywood ending. After beating Spinks, Ali held on to the WBA title until officially relinquishing it on June 26, 1979 via a letter to Mike Mortimer, chairman of the WBA championship committee. (1) According to promoter Bob Arum, Ali clung to the belt until the last possible minute and had to be paid handsomely before releasing his grip.

"We knew Muhammad Ali was going to retire but as long as he delayed I couldn't make definite plans," he said. "Ali wanted a million dollars. I agreed to give him $300,000. So that did it and we set up the (John) Tate-(Gerrie) Coetzee fight (for the vacant belt). (2)

Ali tried to keep himself busy by fighting exhibitions, speaking with world leaders such as U.S. President Jimmy Carter, China's Deng Xiaoping and the Soviet Union's Leonid Brezhnev as well as other sundry activities and endeavors. Soon, however, he began to once again feel the urge to compete, the need to command attention, and the necessity to make enough money to maintain the lifestyle to which he had grown accustomed.

In February 1980 he told the Associated Press he was 75 percent sure he would return to boxing, and his initial target was Tate, who won the WBA belt by outpointing Coetzee before 81,000 of Coetzee's countrymen in South Africa the previous October. An agreement in principle was struck between Ali's manager Herbert Muhammad and Top Rank President Bob Arum in which a Tate-Ali fight would take place in late June, with Ali making $12 million and Tate $7 million. The sites under consideration included New Orleans and Taiwan. (3)

Although no contract had yet been signed, all Tate had to do to secure a fight with Ali was to get past Mike Weaver on March 31. For 14 rounds and two minutes Tate was on track, building an enormous lead on points. But Weaver, who said he had silently recited the 23rd Psalm between the 14th and 15th rounds, produced the miracle he sought by landing a mammoth hook to the jaw that left Tate unconscious and the Ali-Tate matchup dead.

With Tate out of the picture, many believed Ali's focus would shift to Weaver. Indeed it did, but because Ali was no longer rated by the WBA, its president, Rodrigo Sanchez, imposed conditions. First, Ali would need to either fight at least one warm-up fight (if not two) or engage in an extended sparring session against a viable opponent (Marty Monroe had been mentioned). Second, Ali would need to undergo a complete physical. That plan was scuttled after Ali suffered a cut inside his mouth while sparring with Jeff Sims. (4)

With Weaver no longer a viable option, the rumors continued to fly. One of those involved Bill Sargent, a promoter of rock concerts and Broadway shows. He reportedly scheduled a five-week series of Monday night fights and concerts between August 11 and September 8, 1980 in which Ali would fight Bernardo Mercado in Rio de Janeiro on the first date and WBC titlist Larry Holmes in Las Vegas on the final one while acts such as the Rolling Stones and The Eagles would comprise the musical portion of the program. That venture, ambitious as it was, never came to pass. (5)

In the end, Ali signed to fight Holmes, who won the WBC championship (which had once been Ali's) three months before Ali-Spinks II with a magnificent split-decision victory over defending titlist Ken Norton. Since then Holmes had established himself as boxing's best big man by registering seven defenses, all by knockout, to advance his record to 35-0 with 26 knockouts. It was the longest knockout string by a heavyweight champion since Joe Louis completed his *third* seven-fight streak in September 1946. If Holmes somehow stopped the rock-chinned Ali, Holmes would tie Tommy Burns for the all-time record.

Despite his accomplishments, the 30-year-old Holmes still had an army of critics that saw "The Easton Assassin" as an attempted clone of "The Greatest." Yes, many elements of Holmes' style mirrored Ali's and, in one case, it was even better. While Ali's jab was a flashy flick, Holmes' was a ramrod. Holmes may have owned the greatest jab of all time, even better than those utilized by Sonny Liston and Joe Louis. But outside the ring Holmes was blunt while Ali was playful, and the younger man's attempts at emulating Ali's persona came off as stiff and unnatural because they *were* stiff and unnatural.

"Holmes, still wanting to be 'somebody' and still smarting from the public's failure to embrace him, overcompensated," wrote RING editor-in-chief Bert Randolph Sugar. "He began to sound like a cross between Ali and Don King, prodding Ken Norton here, calling himself, like Ali, 'The People's Champ,' there. He even resorted to some known Ali stratagems, like hollering out to his crown of loyalists, 'who's the champ?', and having the sycophants holler back, in unison, 'Larry Holmes!' It was great theatre, but it wasn't Larry Holmes. When Ali walked, there was always a crowd in his wake. Now Holmes was one of those, walking in his shadow. You can't take on the attributes of a god without being burned and Ali was a god to his followers. They never forgave Holmes for being 'like' Ali." (6)

Now, Holmes was about to have a chance to beat Ali and finally gain the public acceptance for which he thirsted.

"I'm going to end the saga of Muhammad Ali once and for all and finally get the recognition I deserve," Holmes said. "I'm tired of being in this man's shadow while I do all the fighting and all he does is talk, talk, talk. I will shut Muhammad Ali up once and for all." (7)

First, however, a date and site needed to be locked down.

On April 28, 1980 it was announced that Holmes-Ali would take place July 11 at the 165,000-seat Maracana Stadium in Rio de Janeiro, with Ali set to make $8 million and Holmes $4 million. The fight was to be co-promoted by Don King and Murad Muhammad, a former security guard for Ali who now was leading a promotional company called Prime Sports.

However, the July 11 date and site was scuttled for two reasons. First, Prime Sports was unable to complete the necessary financial arrangements. Second, organizers realized the impracticality of hosting a boxing match inside such a cavernous structure.

Ali, for his part, wasn't worried.

"The fight may not be in Rio but it'll be held somewhere," he said. "It's not for me to worry about. That's for the promoters and managers to work out and they'll do it because they're all out to make money. I'm just training for Holmes." (8)

Two months later, a new date and venue was finalized: October 2 at Caesars Palace in Las Vegas. While Ali was still slated to make $8 million, Holmes made out much better. Not only was he guaranteed $6 million, the defending champ would be fighting at Caesars for the ninth time in his last 12 fights. (9)

Had it been anyone but Ali, Holmes would have been an overwhelming favorite. If Fighter A was a well-conditioned, highly skilled champion at the peak of his physical powers and if Fighter B was a 38-year-old former titlist coming off a two-year layoff, Fighter B would have been rated a long shot -- at best. This very scenario had played out several times throughout heavyweight championship history, with Fighter B coming up woefully short each time.

For example, the 35-year-old James J. Jeffries emerged from a nearly six-year retirement to challenge Jack Johnson in a fight thick with racial hostility but the 32-year-old Johnson taunted and toyed with the rugged "Boilermaker" before ending the fight with three 15th-round knockdowns. Forty years later, a 36-year-old Louis challenged his successor, the 29-year-old Ezzard Charles, following a 27-month layoff. While sentiment ran deep for "The Brown Bomber," Charles' youth and immense ring skill plainly demonstrated what Father Time had taken from Louis. Louis lost a lopsided 15-round decision.

Like Johnson-Jeffries and Charles-Louis, Holmes-Ali would match the man who embodied "the man who beat the man" title lineage against the man who won and held a title in his stead and, if the latter won, he would restore the direct line of succession. If those two previous fights were an indicator, Ali would be fighting two foes on October 2 -- Holmes and History.

Still, Ali's supporters had reason to believe his story would turn out differently. First, Ali had employed Holmes as a sparring partner during the mid-1970s, which meant Ali knew Holmes' flaws. Second, would Holmes, who admired Ali as a youth and had worked for him as a young adult, continue to put Ali on a pedestal by seeing him as his hero and his former boss instead of an opponent seeking to take his heavyweight championship? Finally, for all of his gifts as a boxer, Ali had a special brand of magic that fortified his already massive self-belief and negatively affected his opponents' confidence. Yes, Holmes had all the advantages in skill, talent and chronology, but would he be able to handle boxing's high priest of psychological warfare?

Ali made sure those story lines would drive the narrative in the fight's final days.

"They said I couldn't beat Sonny Liston but I knocked him out and won the title," Ali defiantly declared in a preview story written by United Press International Executive Sports Editor Joe Carnicelli. "They said I couldn't beat Joe Frazier but I stopped him in the 'Thrilla in Manila.' They said George Foreman was the baddest, meanest heavyweight who ever lived and that I had no chance but I knocked him out in eight rounds. Now they're telling me I'm too old, I haven't fought enough, I'm out of shape, I don't have the reflexes, that Larry Holmes is too quick and too strong for me. People don't realize that I'm the greatest of all time -- the greatest of all time! I'll prove it to them when I knock out Larry Holmes." (10)

More than most fights of its type, deeply-held sentiment more than held its own against cold, hard reality. In a poll conducted by THE RING in its October 1980 issue, the 40 respondents not named Holmes and Ali picked Holmes by a surprisingly slim 22-16-2 margin. The fence-sitters were RING editor-in-chief Bert Randolph Sugar, who said Ali would give Holmes "a helluva fight" and would take the fight to a decision, and Sylvester Stallone, who said "my friendship with both fighters makes it difficult for me to make a pick." (11)

Others who picked Ali to win included matchmaker Don Chargin, ring announcer Jimmy Lennon Sr., referee Marty Denkin, and a quintet of fighters and former fighters -- Carmen Basilio, Emile Griffith, Buster Mathis Sr., Vito Antuofermo and Floyd Patterson. (12)

Another indicator of Ali's gift for persuasion: The odds opened with Holmes as a remarkably slim 11-to-9 favorite. (13)

Though Ali's physique looked flabby during most of training -- he began camp weighing an unsightly 254 1/2 -- by fight week it appeared he had not only melted off pounds but also years. The September 29, 1980 cover of Sports Illustrated showed an astonishingly trim Ali, his hair free of gray flecks and his taut face scrunched into a playful sneer. Reports would surface later that Ali had used thyroid medicine and other drugs to rapidly lose weight.

"He's no Liston. He's no Frazier. He's only Larry Holmes, and he's nothing," read the cover's pullout quote. "I can see it now. Pop! Pop! Bam! Holmes is down. Eight...nine...ten! For the world-record setting, never-to-be broken fourth time, Muhammad Ali is the heavyweight champion of the world!"

For the hundreds of millions -- if not billions -- who loved Ali, the SI cover was a most welcome sight. Perhaps he *could* shock the world one more time. That belief was further stoked at the weigh-in where Ali scaled 217 1/2, his lightest since "The Rumble in the Jungle" nearly six years earlier.

"This was the first miracle," Ali declared, saying that the second would come inside the ring situated in the outdoor parking lot of Caesars Palace.

Ali did his best to unnerve Holmes by spewing invective -- "I'm your master. I'm your teacher" -- and lunging at him while being held back by his team. Holmes, having seen all of this before, remained stone-faced and intensely focused. Better yet for Holmes, he scaled a sleek 211 1/2 pounds, nearly three pounds lighter than he weighed during his most recent defense against Scott LeDoux nearly four months earlier.

The tension was thick as the two men stood in their corners and awaited the opening bell.

Once that bell sounded, however, the brutal truth was revealed: Ali's beautiful and improbably youthful exterior was a mirage that obscured the decay wrought by age and 20 years of punishment inside the professional ring. Conversely, Holmes was as primed as he ever would be. His legs had spring while Ali's didn't. His jab slammed home while Ali's pawed. Holmes' right connected with a flushness and frequency that would have been frightful against anyone, much less an icon like Ali.

In round one, Holmes threw 63 punches and landed 28 (44%), landed 12 of his 36 jabs (33%) and 16 of his 27 power shots (59%) while Ali could only muster 12 punches, landing three. The second round was worse for Ali as he landed just one of his 16 punches -- a jab -- while whiffing on all of his four power shot attempts. Holmes, on the other hand, mostly worked behind his jab -- 11 of 41 (27%) -- and was selective but accurate with his hooks, crosses and uppercuts (6 of 12, 50%).

The hope that had energized the scene before round one gradually ebbed as Holmes continued to methodically pick apart the fistic corpse that was Ali. Round after round the gulf between the two grew: Holmes out-landed Ali 25-1 in the third, 33-4 in the fourth, 38-3 in the fifth and 35-11 in the sixth. Holmes' jab was particularly withering as he landed 14, 26, 28 and 23 in those rounds. Worse yet, the accuracy with which he struck Ali was sickening -- 43%, 61%, 64% and 55% overall, 33%, 58%, 60% and 51% in jabs and 73%, 78%, 83% and 63% in power shots. Ali was a human punching bag forced to absorb an inhuman amount of punishment. Had it been any other fighter but Ali, ringside officials and corner people alike would have given serious thought to stopping the contest.

But because it *was* Ali, the fight was not stopped.

Finally, in the seventh round, Ali exhibited a shadow of his former self as he got on his toes and flicked the jab. The sleepy, depressed crowd perked up, hopeful that the ghost of Ali had finally been stirred. But even then, Ali was unable to produce his entire arsenal. That's because while Ali had his best round by far – landing 15 of 50 -- every single punch was a jab. Unfortunately for Ali, Holmes was still Holmes, and Holmes still worked Ali over to the tune of 27 of 48 overall (56%), 19 of 31 jabs (61%) and 8 of 17 power (47%).

In terms of competitive effort, the seventh was Ali's last. Now, with eight long rounds to go, Ali shifted into survival mode. He covered up as best as he could while Holmes accelerated his assault. Holmes upped his work rate from 48 punches in the seventh to 67 in the eighth without sacrificing any of his accuracy.

Then came the ninth. The awful ninth.

Two particular blows by Holmes vividly illustrated just how far Ali had slipped as a fighter. A vicious uppercut to the face caused Ali to turn away in pain and a follow-up right to the kidney which, according to longtime friend Lloyd Wells, made Ali scream.

By round's end it was patently obvious that Ali not only would be beaten, he appeared likely to get knocked out for the first time in his professional career. The stats for round nine were jarring: Holmes out-threw Ali 93-17, out-landed him 47-2 overall, 16-2 jabs and 31-0 in power shots while also creating percentage gulfs of 51%-12% overall, 36%-15% jabs and 63%-0% power.

Even then, Ali was given one last chance to turn things around.

"I wanted to stop it at the end of the ninth round," referee Richard Greene said in the post-fight news conference. "Angelo said, 'give him another round' " (14)

The beat -- and the beating -- went on. Holmes threw 92 punches to Ali's three and out-landed him 54-0 overall, 38-0 jabs and 16-0 power. Holmes landed 59% of his total punches, 55% of his jabs and 70% of his hooks, crosses and uppercuts. To Sylvester Stallone, watching this round was "like watching an autopsy on a man who's still alive."

Holmes was a man in deep conflict with himself as he administered this historic assault.

273

"Ali was not going to quit," Holmes wrote in his autobiography "Against the Odds." "He was there to take a beating, a beating I was not eager to deliver. The dilemma for me was how to bring an end to this fight without doing permanent damage to the man. Somehow I had to convince Greene, the referee, that he needed to step in and call this fight off.

"I began fighting in bursts to show Ali he was defenseless against me, then stepping back so I didn't do too much damage," he continued. "What's the formula of aggression that would show the referee enough is enough? It's tough to find exactly how many punches it takes to make a referee step in. A couple of times I thought he would and I stepped back to let him, but Ali tried to keep things going. It went on and on like that -- it seemed forever. Damn you, Ali." (15)

If it had been Ali's choice, he would have continued no matter what. Drew "Bundini" Brown, Ali's longtime cheerleader/witch doctor, felt the same way.

Angelo Dundee, on the other hand, had reached his breaking point.

"Bundini kept hollering to me to 'let it go' but Angelo told me, 'I am the chief second! I stop the fight!' " Greene said. (16)

And with that, this most public slaughter was ended.

The final numbers were horrifying: Holmes landed 340 punches to Ali's 42, 205 jabs to Ali's 36 and 135 power connects to Ali's six. Holmes had averaged 65.1 punches per round, including 92.5 in the final two rounds, while Ali averaged a mere 19.8, including 10 in the final two rounds. In fact, Holmes threw nearly as many punches in the last six minutes (185) as Ali did in the entire fight (198). The percentage gulfs were huge -- 52%-21% overall, 46%-23% jabs and 65%-15% power -- but the action in the ring seemed even more lopsided than that.

"Ali was particularly pathetic," wrote KO magazine's managing editor Steve Farhood. "He was the stone-handed juggler smiling weakly as he bends over to pick up the rubber balls he has dropped. He was the myopic artist no longer able to draw a straight line, much less paint a masterpiece. He was an old man, naked and aging, embarrassing himself on the stage where he was once so magnificent. The only reason they didn't laugh is because they remembered when." (17)

"The fight?" Sugar asked in his post-fight report. "There was no fight. It was futile left jab that never jabbed. A cocked right that never uncocked. A mysterious battle plan that never went into battle. And a legend that died." (18)

"I told him I loved him and respected him and I meant it," Holmes said in the post-fight story produced by the UPI's Carnicelli. "Now people all over the world will know me as a champion. I fought the best heavyweight in the world. A hell of an athlete and a hell of a man and I beat him.

Ali was a great champion but we all come and we all go and I'm sure Larry Holmes won't be around forever. I fought like a champion and I did what I had to do to win. He was one of the great fighters of all time and now I hope by beating him I can get the recognition I deserve." (19)

Ali's wretched state was further illustrated by the fact he didn't attend the post-fight news conference. The former champ had always made it a point to make himself available to the media, but this time his handlers persuaded Ali to skip the session and go directly to his hotel suite.

"Before leaving the ring however, Ali, who had goaded Holmes during the early rounds of the fight with comments like, 'fight, sucker, fight,' walked over to (Holmes) and told him he was 'a good fighter' who 'deserved to win,' " wrote the UPI's Milton Richman. (20)

In retrospect, Ali thinking he could beat Holmes was foolish. But it's a testament to Ali's magic that millions of others were so willing to be fools with him.

INSIDE THE NUMBERS: Even in his darkest hour, Ali managed to land 11 jabs in round six and 15 jabs in round seven. Those 26 landed jabs accounted for 62% of his landed punches in this fateful fight. Holmes' 340 landed punches (over ten rounds) ranks fourth for high totals among Ali fights counted. Holmes' 52.2% connect percentage ranks third. Holmes' 444 jabs thrown (a sign of mercy as opposed to power shots?) ranks first among Ali foes, as does his 205 landed jabs -- 96 more than the second-rated fight (Norton III) -- as does his 46.2% connect percentage with the jab. Holmes landed 65.2% of his power punches, also number one for opponents among fights counted. Ali's 42 landed punches was his second lowest total among fights counted, second only to the 4 punches he needed to do away with Liston in their rematch. Ali landed 6 power punches -- that's right, 6 -- for the entire 10 rounds against Holmes.

Date:	October 2, 1980					City: Las Vegas, NV				Venue: Caesars Palace						

Opponent: Larry Holmes

Result: Holmes by TKO after the 10th round (corner retirement) -- For Holmes' WBC Heavyweight Title

Judge: Chuck Minker

Round	1	2	3	4	5	6	7	8	9	10	11	12	13	14	15	Total
Ali	9	9	9	9	9	9	9	9	9	9						90
Holmes	10	10	10	10	10	10	10	10	10	10						100

Judge: Duane Ford

Round	1	2	3	4	5	6	7	8	9	10	11	12	13	14	15	Total
Ali	9	9	9	9	9	9	9	9	8	9						89
Holmes	10	10	10	10	10	10	10	10	10	10						100

Judge: Richard Steele

Round	1	2	3	4	5	6	7	8	9	10	11	12	13	14	15	Total
Ali	9	9	9	9	9	9	9	9	9	9						90
Holmes	10	10	10	10	10	10	10	10	10	10						100

LARRY HOLMES KO 10 MUHAMMAD ALI

10/02/80 - LAS VEGAS

Total Punches Landed / Thrown															
	1	2	3	4	5	6	7	8	9	10	11	12	13	14	15
HOLMES	28/63	17/53	25/58	33/54	38/59	35/64	27/48	36/67	47/93	54/92	-/-	-/-	-/-	-/-	-/-
	44.4%	32.1%	43.1%	61.1%	64.4%	54.7%	56.3%	53.7%	50.5%	58.7%	-	-	-	-	-
ALI	3/12	1/16	1/12	4/22	3/14	11/27	15/50	2/25	2/17	0/3	-/-	-/-	-/-	-/-	-/-
	25%	6.3%	8.3%	18.2%	21.4%	40.7%	30%	8%	11.8%	0%	-	-	-	-	-

Jab Landed / Thrown															
	1	2	3	4	5	6	7	8	9	10	11	12	13	14	15
HOLMES	12/36	11/41	14/43	26/45	28/47	23/45	19/31	18/43	16/44	38/69	-/-	-/-	-/-	-/-	-/-
	33.3%	26.8%	32.6%	57.8%	59.6%	51.1%	61.3%	41.9%	36.4%	55.1%	-	-	-	-	-
ALI	1/6	1/12	0/6	2/14	3/11	11/25	15/50	1/18	2/13	0/2	-/-	-/-	-/-	-/-	-/-
	16.7%	8.3%	0%	14.3%	27.3%	44%	30%	5.6%	15.4%	0%	-	-	-	-	-

Power Punches Landed / Thrown															
	1	2	3	4	5	6	7	8	9	10	11	12	13	14	15
HOLMES	16/27	6/12	11/15	7/9	10/12	12/19	8/17	18/24	31/49	16/23	-/-	-/-	-/-	-/-	-/-
	59.3%	50%	73.3%	77.8%	83.3%	63.2%	47.1%	75%	63.3%	69.6%	-	-	-	-	-
ALI	2/6	0/4	1/6	2/8	0/3	0/2	0/0	1/7	0/4	0/1	-/-	-/-	-/-	-/-	-/-
	33.3%	0%	16.7%	25%	0%	0%	0%	14.3%	0%	0%	-	-	-	-	-

Final Punch Stat Report			
	Total Punches (Body Landed)	Total Jabs (Body Landed)	Power Punches (Body Landed)
HOLMES	340 (0)/651	205 (0)/444	135 (0)/207
	52.2%	46.2%	65.2%
ALI	42 (0)/198	36 (0)/157	6 (0)/41
	21.2%	22.9%	14.6%

35.

The bludgeoning Ali received from Holmes should have resulted in the end of his career, and when he surrendered his boxing license to the Nevada State Athletic Commission in late December and promised not to pursue reinstatement it certainly looked as if that was the case. But in the fall of 1981 rumors of yet another Ali comeback began to stir.

Ali's immense pride, the asset that fueled his greatest triumphs, couldn't stomach the thought that a TKO loss while sitting on the stool would be the final scene of what had been a theatrical boxing career.

The overarching issue -- one that should have been disqualifying -- was Ali's health, which was in clear decline. Not only was Ali's speech slurred and gravelly, his movement and general coordination had decayed and, without the aid of the Thyrolar that helped him shed more than 30 pounds in less than two months before the Holmes fight, his physique had the thickness and softness expected of someone five weeks short of 40. To combat those concerns, Ali underwent a battery of tests at New York University in October 1981 with pathologist Dr. Harry Demopoulos heading the 30-doctor team that was involved in the studies.

"There's absolutely no evidence that Muhammad has sustained any injury to any vital organ -- brain, liver, kidneys, heart, lungs -- nervous system, or muscle or bone systems," Dr. Demopoulos said in William Nack's Sports Illustrated story. "His blood tests indicate he has the vessels of a young man."

He also said Ali's slurring was circumstantial rather than innate.

"If the slurring were due to permanent damage, it would be there all the time," he said, adding that fatigue and stress were the most common triggers. In retrospect, all of it was wishful thinking. But Ali was such a charismatic and financial force that some were still willing to move mountains for him. (1)

James Cornelius, described in press releases as a "Los Angeles-based entrepreneur," was the man charged with finding those mountains that were willing to be moved. He tried convincing U.S. commissions that Ali was still fit to fight, but none gave their consent. Cornelius persisted, and eventually he found a place willing to stage an Ali fight. Now operating under the umbrella of Sports Internationale Ltd., Cornelius put together a fight between Ali and onetime title challenger Trevor Berbick that was to be staged December 11, 1981 on Paradise Island in the

Bahamas. (2) While the exotic locale stacked up well with other Ali fight sites, everything else connected with the venture was anything but paradise.

First, there was the opponent. Berbick, a 27-year-old Jamaican fighting out of Canada, was rated fourth by the WBA and sported a 19-2-1 record that included 17 knockouts. Standing 6-foot-2 and scaling a solid 218 pounds, the Canadian and Commonwealth heavyweight titlist used his broad shoulders to burrow inside and clubbing blows that crushed inferior opponents and wore down the better ones. Berbick vaulted to world prominence with a stunning ninth-round KO of former WBA titlist John Tate on the Roberto Duran-Sugar Ray Leonard I "Brawl in Montreal" card in June 1980, and since then he had gone 4-1 with four early-round knockouts, the most recent of which was a two-rounder against Conroy Nelson in July. The lone defeat in that stretch came against WBC champion Larry Holmes, who was looking to break Tommy Burns' all-time record of eight consecutive knockouts in heavyweight title fights. Not only did Berbick's legs stand up to Holmes' bombs for 15 rounds, he stood up to Holmes himself by spewing taunts throughout the early rounds before "The Easton Assassin" pulled away in the "championship rounds." While Ali historically had done well against aggressors, Berbick's persistent smash-mouth style was not what Ali needed at this stage of his life.

Recognizing his depleted state, Ali set a modest goal for himself.

"I've just got to win six rounds on the cards of the three officials; so I'll have to fight for six rounds," Ali told the Associated Press the day before the fight. (3) It was just another illustration of how far Ali had declined physically and in terms of his own expectations. Just three years earlier in New Orleans, a 36-year-old Ali made good on his promise to dance for nearly all 15 rounds in regaining the title from Leon Spinks. Now, he just wanted to get by.

So did the promotion, which was beset with numerous financial and organizational problems. The venue bore a regal name -- Queen Elizabeth Sports Centre -- but in reality it was a converted baseball stadium that was still under construction. The fight card started late because organizers couldn't find the key that unlocked the front gate of the stadium. Only two pairs of gloves were available for the five-fight undercard, forcing each corner to unlace the gloves after each bout so that the next pair of fighters could use them. While Ali, Berbick and Thomas Hearns (who fought Ernie Singletary) had their own locker rooms, the other nine fighters were jammed into the remaining dressing room. A borrowed cowbell was used to start and end each round. (4)

The main event almost didn't happen because Berbick had received only $100,000 of his $350,000 guarantee and said he wouldn't fight until he was paid the full amount. At 5:40 p.m., just hours before stepping into the ring, Berbick got his money thanks to SelecTV, the pay-cable channel airing the card. (5)

"For a fight of this magnitude, this tops it all," Eddie Futch, who guided Pete McIntyre to a 10-round decision win over Mike Fisher, told the New York Times' George Vescey. "The promoters just didn't understand the details. They didn't anticipate the expenses. Their money ran out before the details could be taken care of." (6)

Despite the chaos, the event was blessed by a comfortable moonlit night and, thanks to ticket prices being slashed from $50 to $5, a decent turnout of 8,000. (7)

A somber Ali, scaling a pudgy 236 1/4, trudged toward the ring and once there, he and his corner awaited Berbick's arrival. The onetime "Ali Circus" appeared flat emotionally, for they knew Ali had shown woeful energy throughout the 11-week training cycle. According to Nack, Ali, wearing a rubber corset, walked more than he ran during roadwork, shadowboxed listlessly, then climbed into a waiting limousine that took him back to his hotel. (8) Ali and his retinue knew full well that the string that Ali had played the past few years was frayed and nearing disintegration. For a man who had mastered the 15-round distance, 10 rounds now seemed an eternity.

The more energetic Berbick bounded into the squared circle four minutes later and as he danced around the ring a stony Ali ignored him instead of launching into his usual pre-fight antics. Referee Zach Clayton, who counted Foreman out the night Ali regained the title, delivered the final instructions. Ali, looking bored at times, said nothing as he shadowboxed while Berbick refused to look Ali in the eyes.

The fight's opening seconds yielded an encouraging sign for Ali fans because in walking out of the corner, firing three soft jabs and landing with an overhand right, he already showed more life than he had in most of the Holmes bout. Yes, his punches were slow and lacked snap and his legs shuffled rather than danced, but he began most of the skirmishes and connected more often. Even before the end of round one, blow-by-blow commentator Don Dunphy declared the first "a very good round" for Ali, and he was right. Even a late flurry of body shots from Berbick couldn't negate Ali's good work in the first three minutes, which saw Ali throw 66 punches to Berbick's 41 and out-land him 16-12 overall as well as 7-2 in jabs. If Ali could do this five more times, he would do enough to earn the decision and make a good case for the fight he wanted next -- a crack at Mike Weaver's WBA title. (9)

It wasn't to be. The first was the only instance in which Ali out-landed Berbick, and the effort required to keep the rugged Jamaican at bay had already cut into his gas tank more than it should have. If fighting three minutes against an opponent that largely ceded the round taxed his energy supply, what would happen once the younger bull revved up his attack?

In round two, Berbick's steady pressure forced Ali to retreat more quickly than he wanted and his rights to the ribs during clinches inflicted damage that registered on Ali's face. As the crowd chanted Ali's name, Berbick gestured with his gloves as if to say "why are you cheering him? *I'm* from your part of the world." Then, to punctuate his point, he fired a hook toward Ali's head and blasted more rights to the ribs as Ali clinched. While he couldn't duplicate his success in

280

round one, Ali still fought with conviction but it was evident to all that conviction alone wasn't going to be enough.

"Ali's reflexes are gone," Dunphy declared as round two began its final minute. "He knows what to do but he can't do it." Then, ever the hopeful soul, Dunphy added, "at least he can't up to now." His right hands, once crisp and stinging, lacked speed and were occasionally delivered with an awkward downward chop. Ali's activity -- and the overwhelming sentiment -- may have won his the second round as he threw 68 punches to Berbick's 51, but more objective eyes saw Berbick's more frequent (22 to 15) and heavier connects.

Ali may have even won the third as he threw more punches (56 to 48) and jabbed better than anyone could have hoped (11 of 43, 26%). For his part, Berbick out-landed Ali 22-16 overall and landed 19 of his 38 power shots (50%) to Ali's 5 of 13 (39%).

Based on the expectations game, Ali fared much better in the first nine minutes against Berbick than at any time during the Holmes fight, and, at least for an instant, thoughts about a potential Ali-Weaver fight danced in some heads.

"Sure, Ali could never dethrone Holmes, but he might have a chance against Weaver, who was out-boxed by Tate for nearly the entire fight before a miraculous hook flattened Tate with 45 seconds left in the final round," they might have said to themselves. *"Maybe Ali was right about blaming the weight loss and the prescription drugs concealing his true ability in the Holmes fight. Even at 39 Ali owns a far better chin than Tate does and he's still a bit quicker on his feet than the cement-footed Weaver. If Ali gets himself into prime shape, if everything falls into place during the fight and if he stays away from that big left hook he might shock the world one more time."*

Logan Hobson, who would later develop CompuBox with partner Bob Canobbio, was then a reporter for United Press International as well as a devoted Ali fan. As he sat ringside he was optimistic that Ali still had enough in reserve to wring out another victory.

"The fight was competitive enough where I was hoping he was going to do it," he said in a July 2017 phone interview. "He was doing so much better than he did against Larry Holmes. But then he got tired and he just couldn't (keep going). He was missing the fastball and he was not getting there in time. Berbick had said before the fight that if Ali was hurt he would let up on him. He said he wouldn't step it up on Ali like Holmes did."

Berbick might have believed his words, but when he got the chance to dominate inside the ring he took it with both hands. Quite literally.

Nearly a minute into round four, Berbick showed what 27 could do and Ali showed what 39 wouldn't allow him to do. Berbick drove Ali toward the ropes with a series of heavy body shots, then maintained the pressure as Ali desperately tried to fend him off with clinches and the

"Rope-a-Dope." The crowd tried to spark Ali with "Ali, bomaye" chants but even the ghosts of Kinshasa couldn't regenerate the Ali of old. Instead, they got an old Ali.

Round four was a wipeout for Berbick as he landed 38 of 68 punches to Ali's 9 of 51 as well as 33 of 59 power shots to Ali's 5 of 21. Only Berbick's fatigue in the final minute saved Ali from oblivion, but another benefit of being 27 was that all he needed to revive himself was the 60-second rest period. Ali, on the other hand, required more time than the sport of boxing could grant him.

Rounds five, six and seven delivered a sobering and punishing message to Ali while allowing Berbick to separate himself on the scorecards and the statistics. In those rounds Berbick out-landed Ali 95-36 overall and 82-10 power, with the seventh -- especially the final minute -- being the worst by far. In that round Berbick out-threw Ali 89-28 overall (including 72-9 power) and out-landed him 41-8 overall and 39-1 power.

Berbick's dominance was such that he occasionally barked at the old champion.

"At one point I heard Berbick say, 'c'mon old man, show me your speed.' I was livid...*livid!*" Hobson remembered. "The Brooklyn was coming out in me. Ali wasn't punching and Berbick was taunting him. I don't remember if Ali started punching him at that point, but Berbick was asserting his dominance and playing with Ali's mind. How sad is that: Somebody playing with *Ali's* mind. I thought, 'knock it off, show some respect.' I wanted to climb into the ring and backhand him. How *dare* he try to play with Ali's mind? Ali was the master of that game and here was Berbick talking to Ali. That made it even more insulting to me. It upset me more that he had the psychological balls to do that."

As Berbick pounded away, Ali dug into those bag of tricks by widening his eyes and opening his mouth in mock duress. The ploy had convinced the likes of Frazier, Shavers and Spinks to throttle down their attacks but Berbick did what they should have done: Hit Ali even more. Berbick, whose contempt was now replaced by compassion, yelled at Clayton to stop the fight but the onetime Harlem Globetrotter held firm and allowed the battering to continue.

Most other boxers, even those at their zenith, wouldn't have survived those nine minutes but while Ali's physical abilities were long gone his competitive drive, his resourcefulness and his toughness remained in prime form. But in boxing, landed punches are the ultimate currency.

As Ali sat on his stool between rounds, his inner being was hard at work. Just as he had in the "Thrilla in Manila" and before the final rounds against Norton (twice) and Shavers, Ali sought out his emergency energy supply, broke the glass and waited for the adrenaline rush to kick in. It saved him in all four bouts and he had every reason to believe it would help him again.

As the bell sounded for round eight Ali broke out the old butterfly float and a facsimile of the bee-like sting. The crowd that had sat through Ali's mid-rounds crisis suddenly perked up as their hero tried to turn back the clock. Berbick did his best to bull Ali and while he got in some heavy blows Ali shook them off and got back on the bicycle. But as the round wore on, so did Ali. Berbick's body blasts and hurtful hooks broke the spell that had ensnared so many others. If Ali had any doubts before they were erased now: The jig was up, and the "Ali Mystique" was no more.

Berbick's late rally overcame Ali's early surge as he out-landed the legend 22-17 despite being out-thrown 59-56 and forged a huge 18-6 lead in landed power shots. Berbick further separated himself in the ninth as he upped his work rate to 70 punches to Ali's 41 and out-landed him 23-11 overall, including 20-0 in power shots.

"Win, lose or draw, I hope he doesn't fight again," Dunphy said between rounds nine and 10.

"I pray he never fights again," added referee Davey Pearl, who, along with Randy Shields, served as Dunphy's color commentator.

The 548th round of Ali's 21-year professional career started as the first against Tunney Hunsaker had -- on his toes, using the jab and firing right hands over the top. But while Hunsaker couldn't touch the whippet-quick teen-age gold medalist, Berbick feasted on the geriatric shell that remained. In the final 90 seconds Berbick climbed all over Ali and attempted to put him away, but Ali, though imprisoned by age, excess weight and physical deterioration, still had enough savvy and toughness to make it to the final bell. If nothing else, Ali could be proud that he earned the privilege of ending this fight on his feet instead of on his stool.

The punishment Berbick dished out was extraordinary. He threw 100 punches and landed 45, including 36 of 86 power shots. The shadow of Ali, 9 of 60 overall and 3 of 22 power, paled in comparison.

Berbick's second-half surge allowed him to pull away on the scorecards. Alonzo Butler submitted the kindest card at 97-94 while colleagues Jay Edson and Clyde Gray delivered harsher news by seeing Berbick the 99-94 winner.

The statistics backed up the judges while also delivering a brutally honest assessment. Berbick led 279-129 in total connects and pounded out an enormous 236-45 gap in landed power shots. Ali absorbed 43% of Berbick's total punches and 45% of his power shots while landing just 24% and 26% respectively.

A press conference was conducted at a makeshift pressroom on the second floor of a Holiday Inn undergoing renovation at Paradise Island at 10:30 a.m. the day after the fight. It was here that Ali, who arrived 30 minutes late, finally admitted the obvious -- his boxing career had come to an end.

"Father Time has caught up with me," Ali said. "I'm finished. I've got to face the facts. For the first time, I feel that I'm 40 years old. I know it's the end. I'm not crazy. After Holmes I had excuses: I was too light, I didn't breathe right. No excuses this time, but at least I didn't go down. No pictures of me on the floor, no pictures of me falling through the ropes, no broken teeth, no blood. I'm happy I'm still pretty. I came out all right for an old man. We all lose sometimes. We all grow old." (10)

Indeed we do.

The Berbick fight was Ali's first loss in 16 appearances outside the United States. He won thrice in London (KO 5, KO 6 versus Henry Cooper, KO 3 Brian London), four times elsewhere in Europe (KO 12 Karl Mildenberger, KO 7 Juergen Blin, KO 11 Al "Blue Lewis, KO 5 Richard Dunn), four times in Asia (W 15 Mac Foster, W 12 Rudi Lubbers, W 15 Joe Bugner II, KO 14 Joe Frazier III), three times elsewhere in North America (W 15, W 12 George Chuvalo II, KO 5 Jean-Pierre Coopman) and once in Africa (KO 8 George Foreman) before losing to Berbick in the Bahamas. If ever a fighter personified the concept of a "world champion," it was Muhammad Ali.

"Because of me," Ali said, "the whole world watches boxing now." (11)

The assembled media had either followed Ali from the very beginning or jumped on the bus sometime during its 61 stops. Thanks to the extraordinary access he had granted them, they not only knew Ali as a legendary athlete but also as a human being who experienced the full range of emotions and shared most of them with them. The connection was deep, heartfelt and beyond debate. Now, the whirlwind that was known as "The Ali Circus" was about to fold up its tents and ride into the sunset, once and forever. That realization hit hard and the emotions enveloping the room were raw and real. Even hard-bitten veterans Bob Waters, Dick Young, Dave Anderson and Ed Schuyler were moved by the occasion.

Steve Farhood, elected into the International Boxing Hall of Fame in 2017, was also in the room, a room that stirred feelings of unworthiness.

"To put it in perspective, I'm 24 years old," Farhood said during a June 2017 phone interview. "As excited as I was (to be there), I felt like I didn't belong because I looked around me and I saw all these writers like Michael Katz, Eddie Schuyler, Dick Young, all these writers who I had grown up reading. They had been around the world with Ali, and I kind of felt like I didn't deserve what I was getting, which was, of course, would turn out to be a memory of a lifetime.

"Everybody knew that this was really it," he continued. "I don't know if that was the feeling after the Holmes fight -- probably it was, he took such a beating in that fight everybody figured there wouldn't be any more -- but this time everybody knew there would be no more. If you couldn't beat Trevor Berbick there was really no point in going on. The press conference was actually on my floor where I was staying. I had a buddy with me and we went there and it was similar to waiting for a funeral to begin. Everybody was really quiet. Berbick was there first and he was speaking and nobody wanted to hear what he had to say. This was about Ali. It was awkward because this guy just won the fight and he might as well have been a kid filling the soda machine.

"Of course Ali finally walks in, a little bit late, and one of the first things I remember hearing was Ed Schuyler, this great old tough reporter from the AP who had been around the world with Ali in places he probably never even heard of before he went there, and he just looked at Ali and said, 'thanks, champ, for a helluva ride.' It was an emotional moment for the hard-core guys, and they didn't cry in their beer too often. That was, to me, the official ending of it all. When we left there that day, you knew it would never be the same because of what he brought to a fight from a writer's perspective was unique and was never going to be matched. The overriding theme of it, being a young kid, was, 'this is something I'm never going to forget, this is something I probably don't deserve to be at, and this is the end of the greatest athlete in the history of the world.' "

Hobson, who was also in the room, agreed with Farhood's description of the experience.

"You have the wake and then the funeral, but this fight was like the headstone dedication," he said. "This was like putting the period at the end of the sentence. Ali seemed fine with it and I didn't remember feeling sad for him. Berbick was gracious and Schuyler set the tone. It wasn't as horribly sad as you think it would be. In retrospect, all of us had done our mourning after the Holmes fight. That fight was like watching a mugging. He was brutalized in that fight and he wouldn't quit. Here, there was no reason for him to quit and there was no time in which I felt like yelling, 'stop the fight.' "

During the final years of Ali's career it had been feared that once he lost the title and faded from the scene that he would take the sport of boxing with him. The same fears had been expressed when giants like John L. Sullivan, Jack Dempsey, Joe Louis and Rocky Marciano had left the scene and each time boxing produced a new focal point. Such would also be the case with Ali, and just as it had been with the others, the fears of boxing's impending extinction proved unfounded. However, the post-Ali era was especially blessed because the sport would be fueled not just by one fighter, but several.

"Ali hadn't been a constant presence in the last couple of years, and it had been a while since the Holmes fight," Farhood observed. "And don't forget: I was coming to the Bahamas off Leonard-Hearns. The baton had been passed to the non-heavyweights at that point. We had Hearns and we had Leonard and we had Duran and Hagler -- the Four Kings -- and it was a great time. I don't know that we necessarily knew at that point, as Ali was retiring, that it was going to be as great a period as it was, but in fact, the era was in very good hands and didn't need Ali at that point. Ali had carried boxing in America, almost-singlehandedly, in the 1970s but the early 1980s was a great time. Boxing was on TV like crazy and we had the big closed-circuit fights. It was not that sad a time for boxing fans -- it was sad in one sense because it was the end of Ali -- but it wasn't that sad in terms of 'will the sport flourish?' The sport was flourishing at that exact point."

One measure of a fighter's worth is whether he left the sport in better shape than it was when he first arrived. When Cassius Marcellus Clay broke into the professional boxing scene following his triumph in the 1960 Rome Olympics, the sport was hurtling toward the abyss. Thanks to the gold medalist's savant-like skills in terms of self-marketing he revived his sport in a way few others had and the results spoke for themselves. Now, as the nearly 40-year-old Ali announced his departure from "The Sweet Science," it was evident he had set the stage for another Golden Era whose star power wasn't isolated to only the heavyweights. Inspired by Ali, a plethora of stars spanning dozens of pounds built on the foundation Ali assembled. They spoke for themselves, they fought for themselves and the fans who paid to see them, and they fought for the sport that gave them a chance to build new lives.

Thanks to the rise of pay-cable outlets and pay-per-view platforms, the purses these fighters generated dwarfed those generated by Ali and they, too, became household names worldwide. Though no longer able to contribute, Ali surely must have surveyed the scene, took it all in and exhaled in satisfaction.

The Ali Era was over. Let the New Era begin.

INSIDE THE NUMBERS: In his Last Hurrah, Ali, approaching his 40th birthday, landed an average of 8.4 jabs per round, 3.1 more per round than the heavyweight average. Also, 65% of his landed punches versus Berbick were jabs, with the CompuBox average being 28%. Ali landed just 51 power punches in his losses to Berbick and Holmes. He landed 68 power shots in rounds thirteen and fourteen alone versus Frazier in Manila, his last great performance. Ali went through hell in his final professional round as Berbick, showing no mercy, threw 100 punches in round ten (86 of which were power punches), the most by an Ali opponent among fights counted. But Ali displayed his trademark courage in surviving that round as well as announcing his permanent exit from the sport as an in-ring participant.

Date: December 11, 1981   City: Nassau, Bahamas   Venue: Queen Elizabeth Sports Centre
Opponent: Trevor Berbick
Result: Berbick by unanimous decision

Judge:	Alonzo Butler																
	Round	1	2	3	4	5	6	7	8	9	10	11	12	13	14	15	Total
	Ali																94
	Berbick																97

Judge:	Jay Edson																
	Round	1	2	3	4	5	6	7	8	9	10	11	12	13	14	15	Total
	Ali																94
	Berbick																99

Judge:	Clyde Gray																
	Round	1	2	3	4	5	6	7	8	9	10	11	12	13	14	15	Total
	Ali																94
	Berbick																99

287

TREVOR BERBICK UD 10 MUHAMMAD ALI
12/11/81 - BAHAMAS

Total Punches Landed / Thrown										
	1	2	3	4	5	6	7	8	9	10
BERBICK	12/41	22/51	22/48	38/68	31/71	23/53	41/89	22/56	23/70	45/100
	29.3%	43.1%	45.8%	55.9%	43.7%	43.4%	46.1%	39.3%	32.9%	45%
ALI	16/66	15/68	16/56	9/51	19/53	9/60	8/28	17/59	11/41	9/60
	24.2%	22.1%	28.6%	17.6%	35.8%	15%	28.6%	28.8%	26.8%	15%

Jab Landed / Thrown										
	1	2	3	4	5	6	7	8	9	10
BERBICK	2/16	4/12	3/10	5/9	4/11	7/14	2/17	4/6	3/16	9/14
	12.5%	33.3%	30%	55.6%	36.4%	50%	11.8%	66.7%	18.8%	64.3%
ALI	7/40	8/45	11/43	4/30	11/30	8/43	7/19	11/47	11/34	6/38
	17.5%	17.8%	25.6%	13.3%	36.7%	18.6%	36.8%	23.4%	32.4%	15.8%

Power Punches Landed / Thrown										
	1	2	3	4	5	6	7	8	9	10
BERBICK	10/25	18/39	19/38	33/59	27/60	16/39	39/72	18/50	20/54	36/86
	40%	46.2%	50%	55.9%	45%	41%	54.2%	36%	37%	41.9%
ALI	9/26	7/23	5/13	5/21	8/23	1/17	1/9	6/12	0/7	3/22
	34.6%	30.4%	38.5%	23.8%	34.8%	5.9%	11.1%	50%	0%	13.6%

Final Punch Stat Report			
	Total Punches (Body Landed)	Total Jabs (Body Landed)	Power Punches (Body Landed)
BERBICK	279 (0)/647	43 (0)/125	236 (0)/522
	43.1%	34.4%	45.2%
ALI	129 (0)/542	84 (0)/369	45 (0)/173
	23.8%	22.8%	26%

CAREER SUMMARY

Muhammad Ali is rightly considered one of the greatest boxers ever to walk the earth, not just because of the otherworldly talent he showed during his best years but also because of the toughness he demonstrated during his declining years and his gift for self-promotion that lifted his sport from potential extinction. Outside the ring, the combination of time, circumstance and a change in majority attitude fueled a sea change in terms of how Ali was perceived. In the mid- to late-1960s he was a highly polarizing figure but by the mid-1970s he was largely viewed as a sporting icon whose fan base transcended race, gender, religion and nationality.

But as great as he was to watch inside the ring and to listen to beyond the ropes, Ali was hardly the greatest in terms of statistics. In his 47 career fights, Ali rated a minus-1.7 on CompuBox's plus-minus scale that compares the fighter's overall connect percentage with that of his opponents. Ali's terrible final nine fights had a lot to do with that but even if Ali had retired after the "Thrilla in Manila" as Dr. Ferdie Pacheco recommended, his plus-minus rating would have been a puny plus-0.4 (34.9% for Ali, 34.5% for his opponents) and he still would have been underwater in power-punch accuracy (39.3% for Ali, 41.7% for his opponents).

A piece of irony: CompuBox conducted a study of 12 heavyweight champions and in terms of plus-minus rating and in a points system based on their placement in 10 statistical categories, Ali was dead last. Guess who was first? Joe Frazier. Adding insult to injury for Ali and his fans, Frazier's lead over the second-place fighter, Sonny Liston, was seven points (88 to 81). Worse yet for Ali, his was the only plus-minus rating in the study that was in negative territory. The only other fighter whose rating was similar to Ali's was Evander Holyfield, who rated a plus-one because he, like Ali, fought on far too long.

So why did Frazier score so highly in these studies? Here's why: Most fans remember "Smokin' Joe" for his five fights with Ali and George Foreman, fights in which Frazier went 1-4 and appeared easy to hit. That certainly was the case against Foreman, who nearly quadrupled Frazier's connects in their bouts (a combined 32.9 versus 9.3) and landed a far higher percentage of power punches in those bouts (51%-38%) but, as detailed in this book, Frazier got more than his pound of flesh against Ali and he performed even better against the 10 other fighters he faced in his statistical profile -- Jimmy Ellis (twice), Oscar Bonavena (twice), Jerry Quarry, (twice) Joe Bugner, Ron Stander, Terry Daniels, Bob Foster, Manuel Ramos, Buster Mathis Sr. and George Chuvalo. In these fights, Frazier's bob-and-weave defense effectively blunted their attacks while Frazier's searing body barrage and monstrous hooks connected with almost superhuman frequency. Frazier's performance in these fights further illustrate just how tough and skilled Ali had to be to win their series.

The main source for Ali's statistical woes lies in his defense, which proved quite leaky once his opponents got close enough to access it. Of the 474 CompuBox-tracked rounds, opponents landed 50% or more of their power punches 119 times, which translates to 25.1% of the time. The "Young Clay" yielded only three such rounds while the "Prime Ali" surrendered 25 (including 11 to Chuvalo and six to Mildenberger), but once his legs lost the strength and spring to carry him away from punches his technical deficiencies forced him to employ other options such as "the Rope-a-Dope" or the short-lived "Mirage," which was merely the "Rope-a-Dope" at ring center. Those options led to 91 more rounds of tasting 50% or more of his opponents' hooks, crosses and uppercuts. Exacerbating the problem was the sheer numbers of rounds the older Ali had to fight due to his decreasing punching power (two KOs in his last 10 fights and none in his final seven); the Young and Prime Ali fought just 119 CompuBox-tracked rounds while the "Comeback Years" and "Past Prime" versions logged 355. The increased exposure to potential punishment led to a numbers game that Ali was destined to lose.

Even as Ali struggled with virtually every other part of his game, the one asset that remained above average was his jab. The typical heavyweight throws 20.4 jabs, lands 5.3 of them and connects at a 26% rate but in the 47 CompuBox-tracked fights Ali threw 26.9, landed 7.9 and boasted 29.4% accuracy. Even the Past Prime Ali was very close to the historical norms as he threw 23, landed 5.3 and recorded 23% accuracy.

Another incredible stat: The jab accounted for 47% of Ali's connects in the 47-tracked fights, far above the 28% overall CompuBox average. Also: Ali landed 40% or more of his jabs in 10 fights. As a point of comparison, only one fighter on the current CompuBox categorical leaders list has landed 30% or more of his jabs -- Gennady Golovkin at 33.5%.

A double-digit connect round for jabs is a relatively rare feat but Ali either reached or exceeded that threshold in 151 of the 474 CompuBox-tracked rounds -- or 31.9% of the time. He out-jabbed his opponents in 36 of the 47 fights and of the 11 fights in which he was out-jabbed, only six occurred in the first three phases of his career (Liston II, Mildenberger, Bob Foster, Norton I, Lyle and Bugner II). To further emphasize how great a jabber Ali was, he recorded at least 20 jab connects in a round 22 times and 30 or more landed jabs in a round four times. Perhaps the most illustrative example of Ali's jabbing prowess can be found in the following statistic: Ali put together not one, but two, streaks of double-digit jab connects totaling more than 15 rounds -- 23 (from round eight of Patterson I through all 15 rounds of Chuvalo I) and 17 (the final five rounds versus Mac Foster through all 12 rounds of the Chuvalo rematch).

From time to time, however, the opponents managed to turn the tables on Ali, for they recorded double-digit jab connect rounds 35 times. The first man to turn the trick was Henry Cooper, who landed 14 jabs on Ali in round two of their first fight and did it again in round five of the rematch when he landed 10. Only 11 other fighters were able to land 10 or more jabs on Ali in a single round -- Liston (once), Mildenberger (twice), Folley (twice), Mac Foster (once), Al "Blue" Lewis (once), Bob Foster (three times), Bugner (once in their first fight), Norton (six times in fight one, once in fight two, three times in fight three), Dunn (once), Spinks (once in fight one) and Holmes (all 10 rounds). Only Holmes managed to top 20 jab connects in a round against Ali -- he did it four times -- and in the sickening 10th he landed 38, the most ever landed against Ali in a single round.

In total, Ali out-landed his opponents 7,953-7,010 overall and 3,749-1,892 jabs but was out-done 5,118-4,204 in power shots. The Young Clay out-landed all six opponents overall while the Prime Ali earned a 7-2-1 split in 10 fights. The "Comeback Years" Ali came out ahead 15-6 in 21 fights while the Past Prime version was out-landed in seven of 10 fights.

Other interesting stats from Ali's career include:

* Ali threw 100 or more punches in a round six times -- 113 in round 11 against Mac Foster, 108 in round nine versus Mac Foster, 107 in round 10 against Al "Blue" Lewis, 105 in round nine in the second George Chuvalo fight, 105 in round 12 of the Chuvalo rematch and 105 in round 15 of the first Leon Spinks bout -- while his opponents reached that milestone just once. That took place in the final round of Ali's career when Trevor Berbick threw exactly 100 punches in round 10.

* Ali topped 50 total connects in a round three times (57 in round seven against Al "Blue Lewis, 54 in round nine in the George Chuvalo rematch and 50 in the final round of "The Thrilla in Manila") and logged 40 total connects three more times (47 in round 11 of fight three against Joe Frazier, 47 in round nine in the first George Chuvalo fight, and 47 in round 15 of the first Leon Spinks fight.

* Ali exceeded 40 power connects in a round just once in the 47 fights studied as he landed 44 in the final round of the first Spinks fight. He landed 35 or more power shots five more times (39 in rounds eight and 11 of the "Thrilla", 36 in round 13 of Frazier III and in round three of the first Spinks bout, and 35 in round six against Al "Blue" Lewis).

* Ali landed 50% or more of his jabs in a given round an astonishing 39 times, including 28 occasions in which he landed double-digit jabs to achieve it. The top performance in this regard was when he landed 37 of 56 jabs (66.1%) in the seventh round against Al "Blue" Lewis.

* On the negative side, Ali failed to land a single punch in a given round seven times. He went 0 of 12 in round one in the first Patterson bout, 0 of 9 in round 2 of the first Leon Spinks fight, 0 of 7 in round four versus Ron Lyle, 0 of 5 in round one against Jimmy Young and 0 of 3 in round 1 versus Lyle, in round seven against Alfredo Evangelista, and in round 10 against Larry Holmes.

* Ali's most defining punch was his jab, but on 25 occasions he failed to land a jab in a given round. On four occasions he went 0 of 19 (round eight of the second Frazier fight, round one versus Karl Mildenberger, round five in the rematch against Floyd Patterson and round seven

291

versus Jimmy Young), and on two occasions he did not even *attempt* a jab (round five against Bob Foster, Round 1 versus Chuck Wepner). Ali not throwing a jab is as rare as Jorge Paez sporting a conventional hairstyle or George Foreman sticking and moving. Like a jab-free Ali round, those two things actually happened as well.

*Ali failed to land a power punch in a given round just four times. He went 0 of 10 in round two against Buster Mathis Sr., 0 of 9 in round two of the second Ken Norton fight, 0 of 7 in round nine of the Trevor Berbick bout and 0 of 6 in round three against Jimmy Ellis.

* Ali connected on 60% or more of his total punches 10 times, and on eight of those occasions he landed more than 10 punches in doing so. His best performance in this regard was the famous 14th round assault versus Frazier in the "Thrilla" as he went an astonishing 50 of 74 (67.6%), and other notable performances include his 47 of 74 (63.5%) surge in round nine of the first George Chuvalo fight, his 57 of 90 (63.3%) outburst in round seven versus Al "Blue" Lewis, his 47 of 76 explosion in round 11 of the "Thrilla," and his 26 of 42 (61.9%) symphony in round three against Cleveland Williams. Other double-digit connect performances in this regard occurred when he went 18 of 29 (62.1%) in round one of fight one versus Joe Bugner, 13 of 20 (65%) in round eight of the first Bugner match, and 15 of 25 (60%) in round 11 against Al "Blue" Lewis." For the record, Ali's highest total accuracy in a given round was when he went 7 of 9 (77.8%) in round seven of the second Jerry Quarry fight.

In writing and researching this book, Ali proved to be as fascinating a figure statistically as he was in every other aspect of his life. It is extremely rare for an athlete to become among the greatest of all time in his field, but Ali stands alone in that he predicted that perch for himself even before he did anything to deserve that label, then proceeded to make good on it. When Ali died in June 2016, the tributes poured in from every corner of the globe and those making the tributes encompassed every possible strata of human existence. In a world that has grown so divisive, Muhammad Ali was that rarest of commodities -- a uniting force. That, as much as anything else, should represent a big share of his legacy.

APPENDIX

ADDITIONAL ALI SCORECARDS

Date:	October 29, 1960			City: Louisville, KY						Venue: Freedom Hall						
Opponent:	Tunney Hunsaker															
Result:	Clay by unanimous decision															

Referee:	Paul Matchuny															
	Round	1	2	3	4	5	6	7	8	9	10	11	12	13	14	15	Total
	Clay	5	5	5	5	5	5										30
	Hunsaker																19

Judge:	Sidney Baer															
	Round	1	2	3	4	5	6	7	8	9	10	11	12	13	14	15	Total
	Clay	5	5	5	5	5	5										30
	Hunsaker	4	4	4	4	4	4										24

Judge:	Walter Beck															
	Round	1	2	3	4	5	6	7	8	9	10	11	12	13	14	15	Total
	Clay	5	5	5	5	5	5										30
	Hunsaker																23

Date:	February 21, 1961			City: Miami Beach, FL			Venue: Miami Beach Auditorium									
Opponent:	Donnie Fleeman															
Result:	Clay by TKO after 6th round (corner retirement)															

Referee:	Bill Regan															
	Round	1	2	3	4	5	6	7	8	9	10	11	12	13	14	15	Total
	Clay	10	10	10	10	10	10										60
	Fleeman																49

Judge:	Stuart Winston															
	Round	1	2	3	4	5	6	7	8	9	10	11	12	13	14	15	Total
	Clay	10	10	10	10	10	10										60
	Fleeman																52

Judge:	Barry Pearlman															
	Round	1	2	3	4	5	6	7	8	9	10	11	12	13	14	15	Total
	Clay	10	10	10	10	10	10										60
	Fleeman																50

Date: June 26, 1961 City: Las Vegas, NV Venue: Las Vegas Convention Center
Opponent: Duke Sabedong
Result: Clay by unanimous decision

Referee: Harold Krause

Round	1	2	3	4	5	6	7	8	9	10	11	12	13	14	15	Total
Clay	5	5	5	5	5	5	5	5	5	5						50
Sabedong																34

Judge: John Romero

Round	1	2	3	4	5	6	7	8	9	10	11	12	13	14	15	Total
Clay	5	5	5	5	5	5	5	5	5	5						50
Sabedong																38

Judge: Dick Kanellis

Round	1	2	3	4	5	6	7	8	9	10	11	12	13	14	15	Total
Clay																49
Sabedong																43

Date: November 29, 1961 City: Louisville, KY Venue: Freedom Hall
Opponent: Willie Besmanoff
Result: Clay by TKO at 1:55 of the 7th round

Referee: Don Asbury

Round	1	2	3	4	5	6	7	8	9	10	11	12	13	14	15	Total
Clay	10	10	10	10	10	10										60
Besmanoff	9	9	9	9	9	9										54

Judge: Tom Nuckles

Round	1	2	3	4	5	6	7	8	9	10	11	12	13	14	15	Total
Clay	10	10	10	10	10	10										60
Besmanoff	9	9	9	9	9	9										54

Judge: Walter Beck

Round	1	2	3	4	5	6	7	8	9	10	11	12	13	14	15	Total
Clay	10	10	10	10	10	10										60
Besmanoff	9	9	9	9	9	9										54

Date: February 28, 1962 City: Miami Beach, FL Venue: Miami Beach Convention Center
Opponent: Don Warner
Result: Clay by TKO at 0:34 of the 4th round

Referee: Cy Gottfried

Round	1	2	3	4	5	6	7	8	9	10	11	12	13	14	15	Total
Clay	10	10	10													30
Warner	9	9	9													27

Judge: Bunny Lovett

Round	1	2	3	4	5	6	7	8	9	10	11	12	13	14	15	Total
Clay	10	10	10													30
Warner	9	9	10													28

Judge: Unknown

Round	1	2	3	4	5	6	7	8	9	10	11	12	13	14	15	Total
Clay	10	10	10													30
Warner	9	9	9													27

Date:	May 19, 1962				City: New York, NY			Venue: St. Nicholas Arena									
Opponent:	Billy Daniels																	
Result:	Clay by TKO at 2:21 of the 7th round																	

Referee:	Mark Conn															
	Round	1	2	3	4	5	6	7	8	9	10	11	12	13	14	15	Total
	Clay																5
	Daniels																1

Judge:	Leo Birnbaum															
	Round	1	2	3	4	5	6	7	8	9	10	11	12	13	14	15	Total
	Clay																4
	Daniels																2

Judge:	Artie Aidala															
	Round	1	2	3	4	5	6	7	8	9	10	11	12	13	14	15	Total
	Clay																4
	Daniels																2

COMPARISON REPORT

MUHAMMAD ALI - 47 FIGHTS

TOTAL PUNCHES			
ALI	CATEGORY	47 OPPONENTS	HEAVYWEIGHT AVG.
50.1	AVERAGE THROWN/RD	42.1	44.7
16.8	AVERAGE LANDED/RD	14.8	15.2
33.5%	PERCENTAGE	35.2%	34%

JAB			
ALI	CATEGORY	47 OPPONENTS	HEAVYWEIGHT AVG.
26.9	AVERAGE THROWN/RD	16.8	20.4
7.9	AVERAGE LANDED/RD	4	5.2
29.4%	PERCENTAGE	23.8%	25.5%

POWER			
ALI	CATEGORY	47 OPPONENTS	HEAVYWEIGHT AVG.
23.3	AVERAGE THROWN/RD	25.3	24.3
8.9	AVERAGE LANDED/RD	10.8	9.9
38.2%	PERCENTAGE	42.7%	40.7%

REPORT NOTES
Ali landed nearly 8 jabs per round, while opponents landed 42.7% of their power punches. Opponents landed 10.8 power punches per round to 8.9 for Ali.

COMPARISON REPORT

MUHAMMAD ALI - THE YOUNG ALI - JOHNSON THRU COOPER I

TOTAL PUNCHES			
ALI	CATEGORY	6 OPPONENTS	HEAVYWEIGHT AVG.
64.8	AVERAGE THROWN/RD	38	44.7
18.9	AVERAGE LANDED/RD	12.3	15.1
29.2%	PERCENTAGE	32.4%	33.8%
8.3% (1)	BODY LANDED RATIO	38.3% (1)	31.4% (OVERALL)

JAB			
ALI	CATEGORY	6 OPPONENTS	HEAVYWEIGHT AVG.
30.2	AVERAGE THROWN/RD	10.4	20.5
6.4	AVERAGE LANDED/RD	2.9	5.2
21.2%	PERCENTAGE	27.9%	25.4%

POWER			
ALI	CATEGORY	6 OPPONENTS	HEAVYWEIGHT AVG.
34.6	AVERAGE THROWN/RD	27.6	24.2
12.5	AVERAGE LANDED/RD	9.4	9.9
36.1%	PERCENTAGE	34.1%	40.9%

REPORT NOTES

Surprisingly, the young Ali had a -3.2 plus/minus rating. Why? Because he landed just 21.2% of his jabs. He increased that percentage by 12.2% in his prime. The young Ali threw 20 more punches per round than the heavyweight avg., but landed just 29.2%. He landed 36.6% of his total punches in his prime. Opponents landed 34.1% of their power punches vs. the young Ali.

COMPARISON REPORT

MUHAMMAD ALI - THE PRIME YEARS - LISTON I THRU FOLLEY

TOTAL PUNCHES			
ALI	CATEGORY	10 OPPONENTS	HEAVYWEIGHT AVG.
51.6	AVERAGE THROWN/RD	34.8	44.7
18.9	AVERAGE LANDED/RD	11.7	15.2
36.6%	PERCENTAGE	33.6%	34%

JAB			
ALI	CATEGORY	10 OPPONENTS	HEAVYWEIGHT AVG.
31.8	AVERAGE THROWN/RD	17.5	20.4
10.5	AVERAGE LANDED/RD	4.2	5.2
33%	PERCENTAGE	24%	25.5%

POWER			
ALI	CATEGORY	10 OPPONENTS	HEAVYWEIGHT AVG.
19.8	AVERAGE THROWN/RD	17.4	24.3
8.4	AVERAGE LANDED/RD	7.5	9.9
42.4%	PERCENTAGE	43.1%	40.7%

REPORT NOTES

Ali's plus/minus during his prime years was +3- his highest rating of the four phases of his career outlined in this book. He outlanded opponents 18.9-11.7 in total punches and 10.5-4.2 in jabs- doubling the hvt. avg. for jabs landed per round. Ali's movement & speed prevented opponents from throwing, as they averaged just 34.8 punches thrown per round, 10 fewer than the hvt. avg.

COMPARISON REPORT

MUHAMMAD ALI - THE COMEBACK YEARS - QUARRY I THRU FRAZIER III

TOTAL PUNCHES			
ALI	CATEGORY	21 OPPONENTS	HEAVYWEIGHT AVG.
50.6	AVERAGE THROWN/RD	40.7	44.7
18	AVERAGE LANDED/RD	14.3	15.2
35.6%	PERCENTAGE	35.1%	34%

JAB			
ALI	CATEGORY	21 OPPONENTS	HEAVYWEIGHT AVG.
26.7	AVERAGE THROWN/RD	15.1	20.4
8.6	AVERAGE LANDED/RD	3.3	5.2
32.2%	PERCENTAGE	21.9%	25.5%

POWER			
ALI	CATEGORY	21 OPPONENTS	HEAVYWEIGHT AVG.
24	AVERAGE THROWN/RD	25.6	24.3
9.4	AVERAGE LANDED/RD	11	9.9
39.2%	PERCENTAGE	43%	40.7%

REPORT NOTES

Ali's plus/minus in the Comeback Years was +.5 He landed 8.6 jabs per round (he landed 10.5 in Prime Years). Opponents landed 43% of their power punches (Ali landed 39.2%) and outlanded Ali 11 -9.4 in power punches per round.

COMPARISON REPORT

MUHAMMAD ALI - PAST PRIME- (COOPMAN THRU BERBICK)

TOTAL PUNCHES			
ALI	CATEGORY	10 OPPONENTS	HEAVYWEIGHT AVG.
43.4	AVERAGE THROWN/RD	51	44.7
12.3	AVERAGE LANDED/RD	18.6	15.2
28.3%	PERCENTAGE	36.5%	34%

JAB			
ALI	CATEGORY	10 OPPONENTS	HEAVYWEIGHT AVG.
23	AVERAGE THROWN/RD	21.7	20.4
5.3	AVERAGE LANDED/RD	5.5	5.2
23%	PERCENTAGE	25.3%	25.5%

POWER			
ALI	CATEGORY	10 OPPONENTS	HEAVYWEIGHT AVG.
20.4	AVERAGE THROWN/RD	29.4	24.3
6.9	AVERAGE LANDED/RD	13	9.9
33.8%	PERCENTAGE	44.2%	40.7%

REPORT NOTES
Ali's plus/minus in his last 10 fights (post Frazier III) was -8.2 Opponents landed 36.5% of their total punches and 18.6 per round, to 28.3% and 12.3 per round for Ali. Opponents landed 44.2% of their power punches (13 per round) to 6.9 per round for Ali. Ali's 5.3 landed jabs per round was half his total from his Prime Years.

HEAD TO HEAD COMPARISON REPORT
MUHAMMAD ALI VS. JOE FRAZIER
MUHAMMAD ALI VS. JOE FRAZIER - THREE FIGHT COMPARISON

MUHAMMAD ALI	CATEGORY	JOE FRAZIER	HEAVYWEIGHT AVG.
	TOTAL PUNCHES		
61.7	AVERAGE THROWN/RD	41.7	44.7
23.3	AVERAGE LANDED/RD	22	15.2
37.8%	PERCENTAGE	52.8%	34%

MUHAMMAD ALI	CATEGORY	JOE FRAZIER	HEAVYWEIGHT AVG.
	JABS		
22	AVERAGE THROWN/RD	3.1	20.4
6.1	AVERAGE LANDED/RD	0.9	5.2
27.7%	PERCENTAGE	29%	25.5%

MUHAMMAD ALI	CATEGORY	JOE FRAZIER	HEAVYWEIGHT AVG.
	POWER		
39.7	AVERAGE THROWN/RD	38.6	24.3
17.2	AVERAGE LANDED/RD	21.2	9.9
43.3%	PERCENTAGE	54.9%	40.7%

REPORT NOTES

Ali threw 20 more punches per round in their three fights, but landed just 1.3 more per round, as Frazier landed an incredible 52.8% of his total punches (only Floyd Mayweather & Gennady Golovkin currently land 40% or more of their total punches.) Frazier landed 54.9% of his power punches vs. Ali- 14.2% higher than the heavyweight avg. Jab? I don't need no stinking jab: 21.2 of Frazier's 22 landed punches (96.4) were power punches. (CompuBox avg.: 72%-12.1 of 16.8)

HEAD TO HEAD COMPARISON REPORT
MUHAMMAD ALI VS. KEN NORTON
ALI VS. NORTON - THREE FIGHT COMPARISON

TOTAL PUNCHES			
MUHAMMAD ALI	CATEGORY	KEN NORTON	HEAVYWEIGHT AVG.
50.8	AVERAGE THROWN/RD	42.7	44.7
14	AVERAGE LANDED/RD	18.4	15.2
27.6%	PERCENTAGE	43.1%	34%

JABS			
MUHAMMAD ALI	CATEGORY	KEN NORTON	HEAVYWEIGHT AVG.
28.5	AVERAGE THROWN/RD	19.1	20.4
6.4	AVERAGE LANDED/RD	6.6	5.2
22.5%	PERCENTAGE	34.6%	25.5%

POWER			
MUHAMMAD ALI	CATEGORY	KEN NORTON	HEAVYWEIGHT AVG.
22.3	AVERAGE THROWN/RD	23.7	24.3
7.6	AVERAGE LANDED/RD	11.8	9.9
34.1%	PERCENTAGE	49.8%	40.7%

REPORT NOTES

Breaking down the trilogy, Norton was the more efficient fighter, landing 18.4 of 42.7 punches per round (43.1%) to 14 of 50.8 for Ali (27.6%- Ali landed 33.5% in 47 fights tracked by CompuBox). They landed similar amount of jabs, with Norton landing 12.1% higher. Norton also landed 49.8% of his power punches (11.8 per round) to 34.1% for Ali (34.1%).

CATEGORICAL POINTS LEADERS - NOTABLE
HEAVYWEIGHT CHAMPS

FIGHTER (#FIGHTS)	+/-	TOTAL LND/RD	TOTAL THR/RD	TOTAL CONN %	JABS LND/RD	POWER LND/RD	POWER CONN %	OTC%	OPC%	OPP LND/RD	TOTAL PTS
COMPUBOX CATEGORIES											
JOE FRAZIER(18)	+19.8	24.9	50.3	49.5%	2.5	22.4	53.6%	29.7%	38.5%	17.6	88
SONNY LISTON(10)	+8.6	22.1	61.5	35.9%	9.5	12.6	45.7%	27.3%	32.3%	10.4	81
ROCKY MARCIANO(8)	+12.5	18	48.7	37%	1.3	16.8	39.6%	24.5%	33.1%	10.1	76
LENNOX LEWIS(24)	+10.7	21.2	44.9	47.2%	10.9	10.3	56%	36.5%	40.4%	11.3	75
LARRY HOLMES(27)	+7.1	18	47.7	37.7%	9.8	8.2	49.7%	29.6%	36.6%	12.8	66
JOE LOUIS(13)	+11.6	16.4	42.7	38.4%	6	10.4	46%	26.8%	38%	11	65
MIKE TYSON(26)	+12.8	16	35.1	45.6%	2.9	13.1	55.3%	32.8%	38.5%	11.3	64
JACK DEMPSEY(6)	+12.5	15.6	37	42.2%	1	14.6	45.3%	29.7%	35.4%	8.6	63
GEORGE FOREMAN(18)	+4.2	22.1	47.8	46.2%	10.7	11.4	47.9%	42%	46.9%	19.8	59
WLADIMIR KLITSCHKO(15)	+10	13.9	42.1	33%	8.3	5.6	38.1%	23%	26.4%	5.7	58
EVANDER HOLYFIELD(28)	+1	16.9	40.2	42%	4.8	12.1	48.6%	41%	45.6%	18.7	44
MUHAMMAD ALI(47)	-1.7	16.8	50.1	33.5%	7.9	8.9	38.2%	34.2%	41.8%	14.4	41
CompuBox Avg.		16.8	55.5	30.3%	4.7	12.1	37.3%	30.3%	37.3%	16.8	

REPORT NOTES

Ali ranked dead last in plus minus at -1.7. Ali's 50.1 punches thrown per round ranked #3. Ali landed 33.5% of his total punches, right around the heavyweight avg., but 16% lower than his arch rival Frazier. Ali landed 7.9 jabs per round, 2.7 more per round than the hvt. avg. Ali's 8.9 landed power punches per round is around the hvt. avg. but 13.5 fewer per round than #1 Frazier. Ali opponents landed 41.8% of their power punches, only Holyfield & Foreman were hit with a higher percentage of power punches. OTC= opponents total connect pct. OPC= opponents power connect pct. Points Distribution: 12 former champs on the list. 12 points awarded for leader in each category; 11 points for #2; 10 points for #3, etc....

PLUS/MINUS (TOTAL PUNCHES)

FIGHTER	PLUS/MINUS
JOE FRAZIER(18)	+19.8
MIKE TYSON(26)	+12.8
JACK DEMPSEY(6)	+12.5
ROCKY MARCIANO(8)	+12.5
JOE LOUIS(13)	+11.6
LENNOX LEWIS(24)	+10.7
WLADIMIR KLITSCHKO(15)	+10
SONNY LISTON(10)	+8.6
LARRY HOLMES(27)	+7.1
GEORGE FOREMAN(18)	+4.2
EVANDER HOLYFIELD(28)	+1
MUHAMMAD ALI(47)	-1.7

TOTAL PUNCHES LANDED PER ROUND

FIGHTER	TOTAL LND/RD
JOE FRAZIER	24.9
GEORGE FOREMAN	22.1
SONNY LISTON	22.1
LENNOX LEWIS	21.2
LARRY HOLMES	18
ROCKY MARCIANO	18
EVANDER HOLYFIELD	16.9
MUHAMMAD ALI	16.8
JOE LOUIS	16.4
MIKE TYSON	16
JACK DEMPSEY	15.6
WLADIMIR KLITSCHKO	13.9
OVERALL COMPUBOX AVG. LANDED	
16.8	
HEAVYWEIGHT	
15.1	

TOTAL PUNCHES THROWN PER ROUND	
FIGHTER	TOT.THR/RD
SONNY LISTON	61.5
JOE FRAZIER	50.3
MUHAMMAD ALI	50.1
ROCKY MARCIANO	48.7
GEORGE FOREMAN	47.8
LARRY HOLMES	47.7
LENNOX LEWIS	44.9
JOE LOUIS	42.7
WLADIMIR KLITSCHKO	42.1
EVANDER HOLYFIELD	40.2
JACK DEMPSEY	37
MIKE TYSON	35.1
OVERALL COMPUBOX AVG. THROWN	
55.5	
HEAVYWEIGHT	
44.7	

TOTAL CONNECT PCT.	
FIGHTER	TOTAL CONN %
JOE FRAZIER	49.5%
LENNOX LEWIS	47.2%
GEORGE FOREMAN	46.2%
MIKE TYSON	45.6%
JACK DEMPSEY	42.2%
EVANDER HOLYFIELD	42%
JOE LOUIS	38.4%
LARRY HOLMES	37.7%
ROCKY MARCIANO	37%
SONNY LISTON	35.9%
MUHAMMAD ALI	33.5%
WLADIMIR KLITSCHKO	33%
OVERALL COMPUBOX AVG. PERCENTAGE	
30.3%	
HEAVYWEIGHT	
33.8%	

305

JABS LANDED PER ROUND	
FIGHTER	JABS LND/RD
LENNOX LEWIS	10.9
GEORGE FOREMAN	10.7
LARRY HOLMES	9.8
SONNY LISTON	9.5
WLADIMIR KLITSCHKO	8.3
MUHAMMAD ALI	7.9
JOE LOUIS	6
EVANDER HOLYFIELD	4.8
MIKE TYSON	2.9
JOE FRAZIER	2.5
ROCKY MARCIANO	1.3
JACK DEMPSEY	1
OVERALL COMPUBOX AVG. LANDED	
4.7	
HEAVYWEIGHT	
5.2	

POWER LANDED PER ROUND	
FIGHTER	POWER LND/RD
JOE FRAZIER	22.4
ROCKY MARCIANO	16.8
JACK DEMPSEY	14.6
MIKE TYSON	13.1
SONNY LISTON	12.6
EVANDER HOLYFIELD	12.1
GEORGE FOREMAN	11.4
JOE LOUIS	10.4
LENNOX LEWIS	10.3
MUHAMMAD ALI	8.9
LARRY HOLMES	8.2
WLADIMIR KLITSCHKO	5.6
OVERALL COMPUBOX AVG. LANDED	
12.1	
HEAVYWEIGHT	
9.9	

306

POWER CONNECT PCT.	
FIGHTER	POW.CONN.PCT
JOE FRAZIER	49.5%
LENNOX LEWIS	47.2%
GEORGE FOREMAN	46.2%
MIKE TYSON	45.6%
JACK DEMPSEY	42.2%
EVANDER HOLYFIELD	42%
JOE LOUIS	38.4%
LARRY HOLMES	37.7%
ROCKY MARCIANO	37%
SONNY LISTON	35.9%
MUHAMMAD ALI	33.5%
WLADIMIR KLITSCHKO	33%
OVERALL COMPUBOX AVG. PERCENTAGE	
37.3%	
HEAVYWEIGHT	
40.9%	

OPPONENTS TOTAL CONN. PCT.	
FIGHTER	OPP. TOT. CONN. PCT.
WLADIMIR KLITSCHKO	23%
ROCKY MARCIANO	24.5%
JOE LOUIS	26.8%
SONNY LISTON	27.3%
LARRY HOLMES	29.6%
JOE FRAZIER	29.7%
JACK DEMPSEY	29.7%
MIKE TYSON	32.8%
MUHAMMAD ALI	34.2%
LENNOX LEWIS	36.5%
EVANDER HOLYFIELD	41%
GEORGE FOREMAN	42%
OVERALL COMPUBOX AVG. PERCENTAGE	
30.3%	
HEAVYWEIGHT	
33.8%	

OPPONENTS POWER PUNCH CONN. PCT	
FIGHTER	OPP. POW. CONN. PCT.
WLADIMIR KLITSCHKO	26.4%
SONNY LISTON	32.3%
ROCKY MARCIANO	33.1%
JACK DEMPSEY	35.4%
LARRY HOLMES	36.6%
JOE LOUIS	38%
JOE FRAZIER	38.5%
MIKE TYSON	38.5%
LENNOX LEWIS	40.4%
MUHAMMAD ALI	41.8%
EVANDER HOLYFIELD	45.6%
GEORGE FOREMAN	46.9%
OVERALL COMPUBOX AVG. PERCENTAGE	
37.3%	
HEAVYWEIGHT	
40.9%	

OPPONENTS TOTAL PUNCHES LANDED PER RD	
FIGHTER	OPP. LAND. PER RND
WLADIMIR KLITSCHKO	5.7
JACK DEMPSEY	8.6
ROCKY MARCIANO	10.1
SONNY LISTON	10.4
JOE LOUIS	11
LENNOX LEWIS	11.3
MIKE TYSON	11.3
LARRY HOLMES	12.8
MUHAMMAD ALI	14.4
JOE FRAZIER	17.6
EVANDER HOLYFIELD	18.7
GEORGE FOREMAN	19.8
OVERALL COMPUBOX AVG. PERCENTAGE	
16.8	
HEAVYWEIGHT	
15.1	

MUHAMMAD ALI'S BEST STATISTICAL PERFORMANCES
(ALL PHASES)

Most Total Punches Thrown in a Fight

1,132 -- vs. Mac Foster
1,038 -- vs. George Chuvalo I
917 -- vs. Joe Frazier III
893 -- vs. Joe Frazier I
854 -- vs. Floyd Patterson I
774 -- vs. Leon Spinks I
770 -- vs. Buster Mathis Sr.
762 -- vs. Doug Jones
750 -- vs. George Chuvalo II
737 -- vs. Ernie Terrell

Most Total Punches Landed in a Fight

474 -- vs. George Chuvalo I
443 -- vs. Joe Frazier III
380 -- vs. Mac Foster
353 -- vs. Al "Blue" Lewis
341 -- vs. George Chuvalo II
330 -- vs. Joe Frazier I
293 -- vs. Ernie Terrell
276 -- vs. Chuck Wepner
254 -- vs. Leon Spinks I
210 -- vs. Floyd Patterson I

Best Total Connect Percentage in a Fight

55.8% -- vs. Cleveland Williams
48.31% -- vs. Joe Frazier III
48.29% -- vs. Al "Blue" Lewis
47.4% -- vs. George Foreman
46.9% -- vs. Joe Bugner I
46.8% -- vs. Joe Bugner II

MUHAMMAD ALI'S BEST STATISTICAL PERFORMANCES
(ALL PHASES)

46.7% -- vs. Brian London
45.7% -- vs. George Chuvalo I
45.4% -- vs. George Chuvalo II
45.2% -- vs. Chuck Wepner

Most Jabs Thrown in a Fight

716 -- vs. Mac Foster
632 -- vs. George Chuvalo I
625 -- vs. Floyd Patterson I
474 -- vs. Buster Mathis Sr.
445 -- vs. George Chuvalo II
440 -- vs. Joe Frazier I
428 -- vs. Leon Spinks I
416 -- vs. Ken Norton I
412 -- vs. Karl Mildenberger
401 -- vs. Jimmy Ellis

Most Jabs Landed in a Fight

274 -- vs. George Chuvalo I
239 -- vs. Mac Foster
212 -- vs. George Chuvalo II
170 -- vs. Al "Blue" Lewis
142 -- vs. Chuck Wepner
140 -- vs. Floyd Patterson I
135 -- vs. Joe Frazier I
131 -- vs. Jimmy Ellis
110 -- vs. Buster Mathis Sr.
109 -- vs. Ernie Terrell
109 -- vs. Leon Spinks I

MUHAMMAD ALI'S BEST STATISTICAL PERFORMANCES
(ALL PHASES)

Best Jab Connect Percentage in a Fight

50.2% -- vs. Cleveland Williams
47.7% -- vs. George Chuvalo II
46.1% -- vs. Al "Blue" Lewis
46% -- vs. Brian London
45.98% -- vs. Joe Bugner II
44.3% -- vs. Henry Cooper II
43.5% -- vs. George Chuvalo I
40.8% -- vs. Chuck Wepner
40.4% -- vs. George Foreman
39.7% -- vs. Sonny Liston I

Most Power Punches Thrown in a Fight

712 -- vs. Joe Frazier III
462 -- vs. Joe Frazier II
453 -- vs. Joe Frazier I
447 -- vs. Ernie Terrell
416 -- vs. Mac Foster
406 -- vs. George Chuvalo I
374 -- vs. Doug Jones
373 -- vs. Earnie Shavers
372 -- vs. Joe Bugner II
364 -- vs. Ken Norton III

Most Power Punches Landed in a Fight

365 -- vs. Joe Frazier III
200 -- vs. George Chuvalo I
195 -- vs. Joe Frazier I
184 -- vs. Ernie Terrell
183 -- vs. Al "Blue" Lewis
145 -- vs. Leon Spinks I

MUHAMMAD ALI'S BEST STATISTICAL PERFORMANCES
(ALL PHASES)

144 -- vs. Joe Frazier II
141 -- vs. Mac Foster
137 -- vs. Doug Jones
134 -- vs. Chuck Wepner

Best Power Connect Percentage in a Fight

61.9% -- vs. Cleveland Williams
58.1% -- vs. George Foreman
57.1% -- vs. Sonny Liston I
51.5% -- vs. Sonny Banks
51.3% -- vs. Joe Frazier III
51.1% -- vs. Chuck Wepner
50.8% -- vs. Richard Dunn
50.6% -- vs. Al "Blue" Lewis
50.4% -- vs. Jean-Pierre Coopman
49.1% -- vs. George Chuvalo I

Most Total Punches Landed in a Round

57 -- vs. Al "Blue" Lewis (round 7)
54 -- vs. George Chuvalo II (round 9)
50 -- vs. Joe Frazier III (round 14)
47 -- vs. Joe Frazier III (round 11)
47 -- vs. George Chuvalo I (round 9)
47 -- vs. Leon Spinks I (round 15)
46 -- vs. Joe Frazier III (round 7)
46 -- vs. Leon Spinks I (round 10)
46 -- vs. Al "Blue" Lewis (round 6)
45 -- vs. George Chuvalo II (round 12)

Most Jabs Landed in a Round

37 -- vs. Al "Blue" Lewis (round 7)

MUHAMMAD ALI'S BEST STATISTICAL PERFORMANCES
(ALL PHASES)

36 -- vs. George Chuvalo I (round 9)
33 -- vs. George Chuvalo II (round 9)
31 -- vs. Al "Blue" Lewis (round 2)
25 -- vs. Joe Frazier III (round 7)
24 -- vs. Mac Foster (round 9)
24 -- vs. Mac Foster (round 13)
23 -- vs. George Chuvalo II (round 8)
22 -- vs. George Chuvalo I (round 8)
22 -- vs. Cleveland Williams (round 2)
22 -- vs. Al "Blue" Lewis (round 5)
22 -- vs. Mac Foster (round 8)

Most Power Punches Landed in a Round

44 -- vs. Leon Spinks (round 15)
39 -- vs. Joe Frazier III (round 8)
39 -- vs. Joe Frazier III (round 11)
36 -- vs. Joe Frazier III (round 13)
36 -- vs. Leon Spinks I (round 3)
35 -- vs. Al "Blue" Lewis (round 6)
34 -- vs. Sonny Banks (round 3)
34 -- vs. Doug Jones (round 10)
34 -- vs. Earnie Shavers (round 15)
32 -- vs. Joe Frazier III (round 14)
32 -- vs. Leon Spinks I (round 10)

ALI OPPONENTS' BEST STATISTICAL PERFORMANCES
(ALL PHASES)

Most Total Punches Thrown in a Fight

1,021 -- Chuck Wepner
943 -- Leon Spinks I
878 -- Earnie Shavers
752 -- Jimmy Young
704 -- Mac Foster
674 -- Joe Frazier III
670 -- George Chuvalo I
651 -- Larry Holmes
647 -- Trevor Berbick
635 -- Ken Norton III

Most Total Punches Landed in a Fight

419 -- Leon Spinks I
378 -- Joe Frazier I
354 -- Joe Frazier III
340 -- Larry Holmes
335 -- George Chuvalo I
286 -- Ken Norton III
285 -- Mac Foster
279 -- Trevor Berbick
266 -- Earnie Shavers
233 -- Ken Norton I

Best Total Connect Percentage in a Fight

59.9% -- Joe Frazier I
52.5% -- Joe Frazier III
52.2% -- Larry Holmes
50% -- George Chuvalo I
45% -- Ken Norton III
44.4% -- Leon Spinks I

ALI OPPONENTS' BEST STATISTICAL PERFORMANCES
(ALL PHASES)

43.6% -- Alex Miteff
43.1% -- Trevor Berbick
43% -- Ken Norton I
42.4% -- Joe Frazier II

Most Jabs Thrown in a Fight

444 -- Larry Holmes
443 -- Jimmy Young
422 -- Karl Mildenberger
355 -- Ron Lyle
344 -- Leon Spinks I
333 -- Chuck Wepner
315 -- Earnie Shavers
309 -- Al "Blue" Lewis
289 -- Ken Norton III
284 -- Jimmy Ellis

Most Jabs Landed in a Fight

205 -- Larry Holmes
109 -- Ken Norton I
107 -- Leon Spinks I
94 -- Ken Norton III
92 -- Karl Mildenberger
69 -- Bob Foster
68 -- Al "Blue" Lewis
65 -- Jimmy Young
63 -- Jimmy Ellis
63 -- Joe Bugner II

Best Jab Connect Percentage in a Fight

46.2% -- Larry Holmes

ALI OPPONENTS' BEST STATISTICAL PERFORMANCES
(ALL PHASES)

41% -- Ken Norton I
37.1% -- Bob Foster
36.2% -- Joe Frazier III
35.6% -- Henry Cooper I
34.4% -- Trevor Berbick
32.5% -- Ken Norton III
31.52% -- Mac Foster
31.48% -- Henry Cooper II
31.1% -- Leon Spinks I

Most Power Punches Thrown in a Fight

688 -- Chuck Wepner
627 -- Joe Frazier III
599 -- Leon Spinks I
578 -- Joe Frazier I
563 -- Earnie Shavers
546 -- George Chuvalo I
522 -- Trevor Berbick
520 -- Mac Foster
402 -- Oscar Bonavena
402 -- Alfredo Evangelista

Most Power Punches Landed in a Fight

365 -- Joe Frazier I
337 -- Joe Frazier III
312 -- Leon Spinks I
303 -- George Chuvalo I
236 -- Trevor Berbick
227 -- Mac Foster
209 -- Earnie Shavers
200 -- Chuck Wepner

ALI OPPONENTS' BEST STATISTICAL PERFORMANCES
(ALL PHASES)

192 -- Ken Norton III
167 -- Joe Frazier II

Best Power Connect Percentage in a Fight

65.2% -- Larry Holmes
63% -- Joe Frazier I
55.495% -- George Chuvalo I
55.491% -- Ken Norton III
53.7% -- Joe Frazier III
52.3% -- Joe Bugner
52.1% -- Leon Spinks I
52% -- Mac Foster
51% -- Chuck Wepner
50.8% -- Jimmy Young

Most Total Punches Landed in a Round

54 -- Larry Holmes (round 10)
48 -- Leon Spinks I (round 15)
47 -- Larry Holmes (round 9)
46 -- Joe Frazier I (round 13)
46 -- Mac Foster (round 2)
45 -- Trevor Berbick (round 10)
41 -- Trevor Berbick (round 7)
40 -- George Chuvalo I (round 2)
39 -- Joe Frazier III (round 8)
39 -- Leon Spinks I (round 3)

Most Jabs Landed in a Round

38 -- Larry Holmes (round 10)
28 -- Larry Holmes (round 5)
26 -- Larry Holmes (round 4)

ALI OPPONENTS' BEST STATISTICAL PERFORMANCES
(ALL PHASES)

23 -- Larry Holmes (round 6)
19 -- Larry Holmes (round 7)
18 -- Larry Holmes (round 8)
17 -- Ken Norton III (round 11)
17 -- Ken Norton I (round 2)
17 -- Bob Foster (round 4)
16 -- Larry Holmes (round 9)
16 -- Bob Foster (round 2)

Most Power Punches Landed in a Round

45 -- Joe Frazier I (round 13)
41 -- Leon Spinks I (round 15)
39 -- Trevor Berbick (round 7)
38 -- Joe Frazier III (round 8)
38 -- George Chuvalo I (round 2)
37 -- Mac Foster (round 7)
36 -- Leon Spinks I (round 3)
36 -- Trevor Berbick (round 10)
35 -- Joe Frazier I (round 11)
33 -- Joe Frazier III (round 10)
33 -- Trevor Berbick (round 4)

NOTES

Alonzo Johnson

(1) "Under Southern Skies," by Tom Ephrem, THE RING, April 1961, p. 49

(2) THE RING, June 1960, p. 53

(3) Boxrec.com Encyclopedia

(4) THE RING's 1985 Record Book and Boxing Encyclopedia, edited by Herbert G. Goldman, THE RING Publishing Corporation, p. 936

(5) "Rome, Italy Special: Three U.S. Boxers Get Raw Deals," by Nat Fleischer, THE RING, November 1960, p. 10

(6) THE RING's 1985 Record Book and Boxing Encyclopedia, edited by Herbert G. Goldman, THE RING Publishing Corporation, p. 933-36

(7) "Rome, Italy Special: Three U.S. Boxers Get Raw Deals," by Nat Fleischer, THE RING, November 1960, p. 11

(8) Ibid, p. 47

(9) "Glove Action," THE RING, January 1961, p. 41

(10) "Cassius Clay – Sparring Partner!," International Boxing, October 1975, p. 25

(11) "Bonus Boy of Boxing," by Lew Eskin, THE RING, October 1961, p. 17

(12) "Under Southern Skies," by Tom Ephrem, THE RING, May 1961, p. 63

(13) Boxrec Encyclopedia

(14) Ibid

(15) "Louisville, Ky. Boxing News," by Joe Martin, THE RING, July 1961, p. 66

Alex Miteff

(1) "World Ratings," by Nat Fleischer, THE RING, June 1961, p. 12

(2) "Louisville, Ky. Boxing News," by Joe Martin, THE RING, January 1962, p. 61

(3) "Muhammad Ali: His Life and Times," by Thomas Hauser, Simon and Schuster Paperbacks, 1991, p. 43

(4) "Louisville, Ky. Boxing News," by Joe Martin, THE RING, January 1962, p. 61

(5) "Wild Bulls, Discarded Foreigners, and Brash Champions: U.S. Empire and the Cultural Constructions of Argentine Boxers," by Daniel Fridman and David Sheinin, p. 63

Sonny Banks
(1) "Seen and Heard," by Jersey Jones, THE RING, April 1962, p. 51

(2) "Cassius Clay Says: 'I'm Tired of Fighting Unrated Bums,' " THE RING, February 1962, p. 54

(3) "A Man With a Problem," by Nat Loubet, THE RING, May 1962, p. 23

(4) "World Ratings," THE RING, March 1962, p. 18

(5) https://www.youtube.com/watch?v=LjhHW69ZS20&spfreload=10

(6) "After Being Decked in First Clay Knocks Out Banks in Fourth Round," by The Associated Press, reprinted in the Eugene Register Guard, February 11, 1962, Page 1B

(7) https://www.youtube.com/watch?v=LjhHW69ZS20&spfreload=10

(8) "I'm Unbeatable," by Cassius Clay (as told to Nat Loubet), THE RING, February 1963, p. 7

Archie Moore
(1) "Cassius Clay Knocks Out George Logan," by United Press International, published in The News Dispatch, Jeannette, Pa., April 24, 1962, p. 6

(2) "Unbeaten Clay stops Lavorante in 5th," by John Hall, Los Angeles Times, July 21, 1962

(3) "Shadow Box," by George Plimpton, Berkeley Publishing Corporation, 1971, p. 68

(4) Ibid, p. 68-69

(5) "Archie Moore, 84, Master of the Ring, Dies," by Gerald Eskenazi, The New York Times, December 10, 1998

(6) "Murderer's Row: In Search of Boxing's Greatest Outcasts," by Springs Toledo, Tora Book Publishing, 2017, p. 5-6

(7) "Archie Moore, 84, Master of the Ring, Dies," by Gerald Eskenazi, The New York Times, December 10, 1998

(8) "Muhammad Ali: His Life and Times," by Thomas Hauser, Simon and Schuster Paperbacks, 1991, p. 31-35

(9) "The Passing Parade: Highlights of World-Wide Ring Activity During 1962, by Jersey Jones, THE RING, February 1963, p. 25

(10) "Floors Arch in the Fourth: Cassius Becomes Boxing's Prince," by Bob Myers, Associated Press, published in the Ocala Star-Banner, November 16, 1962, p. 10

(11) THE RING, February 1963, p. 14

(12) "Floors Arch in the Fourth: Cassius Becomes Boxing's Prince," by Bob Myers, Associated Press, published in the Ocala Star-Banner, November 16, 1962, p. 10

Doug Jones
(1) "World Ratings," THE RING, April 1963, p. 16

(2) "Around the Tri-States," by Johnny Bizzarro, The RING, April 1963, p. 52

(3) " 'Champ of Prophecy' Cassius Clay KOs Charlie Powell in 3rd Round," by United Press International, published in the Rome News Tribune, January 25, 1963, p. 9

(4) Ibid.

(5) "New York Results of the Month," by Jersey Jones, THE RING, March 1963, p. 52

(6) "I Don't Fight With My Mouth," by Doug Jones (as told to Dan Daniel), THE RING, March 1963, p. 7

(7) "On This Day: Cassius Clay Survives Huge Scare Against Doug Jones," by Matt Christie, www.boxingnewsonline.net, March 13, 2017

(8) "Clay Gains Decision Over Jones," The Associated Press, published in the Spartanburg Herald, March 14, 1963, p. 29

(9) Ibid

(10) "Fight of the Year," by Nat Loubet, THE RING, February 1964, p. 6

(11) "Muhammad Ali: His Life and Times," by Thomas Hauser, Simon and Schuster Paperbacks, 1991, p. 53

(12) "Clay Definitely Won, Rematch Called For," by Nat Loubet, THE RING, May 1963, p. 10

(13) Ibid, p. 11

Henry Cooper I
(1) "World Ratings," THE RING, May 1963, p. 26

(2) https://www.youtube.com/watch?v=7VlLW6DMxZk&spfreload=10

(3) Ibid

(4) http://boxrec.com/media/index.php?title=Fight:22877

(5) " 'E Said 'E Would and 'E Did," by Huston Horn, Sports Illustrated, July 1, 1963

(6) Ibid

(7) United Press International report, March 26, 1963

(8) "Muhammad Ali: His Life and Times," by Thomas Hauser, Simon and Schuster Paperbacks, 1991, p. 54

(9) "Did Ripped Glove in 1963 Save Ali's Future?," by Ron Olver, THE RING, November 1975, p. 30, 35

(10) " 'E Said 'E Would and 'E Did," by Huston Horn, Sports Illustrated, July 1, 1963

(11) https://www.youtube.com/watch?v=7VlLW6DMxZk&spfreload=10

(12) "Fighter of the Year: THE RING Picks Clay Most Valuable for 1963," by Dan Daniel, THE RING, February 1964, p. 50

Sonny Liston I
(1) "Liston Power Marvel: Fleischer Sees Sonny Among All-Time Greats," by Nat Fleischer, THE RING, September 1963, p. 11

(2) "Liston Poses Problems: Heavyweight Contender's Unpleasant Past and Reported Managerial Connections Throw Up Barriers," by Ted Carroll, THE RING, January 1960, p. 24

(3) "How Good Is Liston?," by Ted Carroll, THE RING, October 1963, p. 17

(4) Ibid, p. 17

(5) Ibid, p. 16

(6) "I'm Unbeatable," by Cassius Clay (as told to Nat Loubet), THE RING, February 1963, p. 43

(7) "I Fought Them Both," by Roy Harris (as told to Jersey Jones), THE RING, August 1962, p. 7

(8) "Liston Power Marvel" by Nat Fleischer, THE RING, September 1963, p. 9.; "The Fight That Never Was," THE RING, June 1964, p. 46

(9) "Muhammad Ali: His Life and Times," by Thomas Hauser, Simon and Schuster Paperbacks, 1991, p. 70

(10) Ibid, p.71

(11) "The Greatest Fights Ever: Clay-Liston I," NBC, 1989

(12) " 'Clay Showed Desire to Retire In 1st Liston Fight,' Says Felix," by Barney Felix, THE RING, January 1966, p. 6-7

(13) " 'I Am the Greatest!' Boxing World Stunned: Clay's Victory Greatest Upset Seen Yet in Heavy Division," by Nat Loubet, THE RING, April 1964, p. 7

(14) "It's Clay All the Way," THE RING, March 1971, p. 64

(15) "Muhammad Ali: His Life and Times," by Thomas Hauser, Simon and Schuster Paperbacks, 1991, p. 79

Sonny Liston II
(1) "The Unwanted," by Arthur Daley, New York Times, May 11, 1965, p. 46

(2) "Nat Fleischer Speaks Out," by Nat Fleischer, THE RING, December 1964, p. 5

(3) Clay-Liston Fight Set Despite Barriers," by Dan Daniel, THE RING, November 1964, p. 22

(4) "Nat Fleischer Speaks Out," by Nat Fleischer, THE RING, December 1964, p. 5

(5) "Odd Cast of Characters," by Robert Lipsyte, The New York Times, March 29, 1964

(6) "What is The Real Clay Story," by Dan Daniel, THE RING, March 1965, p. 8

(7) "Clay Faces a Liston Bent on Revenge," by Dan Daniel, THE RING, December 1964, p. 42

(8) "Clay-Liston Set to Go Despite Barriers," by Dan Daniel, THE RING, November 1964, p. 43

(9) "Postponements Rarely Beneficial," by Al Buck, THE RING, March 1965, p. 35

(10) "Where Do Our Heavies Stand Now?", by Dan Daniel, THE RING, February 1965

(11) "Liston is Dropped from RING ratings," by George Girsch, THE RING, December 1965, p. 13

(12) "What I Saw, What I Did, At Lewiston," by Nat Fleischer, THE RING, August 1965, p. 9

(13) Ibid, p. 9.

(14) "Walcott Tells All," by Ed Brennan, THE RING, September 1965, p. 62

(15) "Nat Fleischer Speaks Out," by Nat Fleischer, THE RING, July 1965, p. 5

(16) "Clay Pulled Corkscrew," by Nat Fleischer, THE RING, September 1965, p. 9

Floyd Patterson I
(1) "Clay Coached and Helped Me – Floyd Patterson," by Nat Fleischer, THE RING, April 1965, p. 9

(2) "I Goofed: Patterson," by Dan Daniel, THE RING, June 1964, p. 15, 46

(3) Sports Illustrated, October 14, 1965; "Muhammad Ali: His Life and Times," by Thomas Hauser, Simon and Schuster Paperbacks, 1991, p. 139

(4) "Rabbit Hunting," by Gilbert Rogin, Sports Illustrated, November 22, 1965

(5) "Clay by Knockout Say Experts in RING Poll," THE RING, December 1965, p. 10-11, 38, 40, 44

(6) "Rabbit Hunting," by Gilbert Rogin, Sports Illustrated, November 22, 1965

(7) "Clay Masterful But Merciless," by Nat Fleischer, THE RING, February 1966, p. 8

(8) "Champion as Long as He Wants," by Gilbert Rogin, Sports Illustrated, November 29, 1965

(9) "Did Clay Forfeit KO Victory in Round Six," by Al Buck, THE RING, February 1966, p. 12

(10)   Ibid, p. 33

George Chuvalo I

(1) "Muhammad Ali: His Life and Times," by Thomas Hauser, Simon and Schuster Paperbacks, 1991, p. 213-214

(2) "Bouts With Granite-Chinned Chuvalo Were Ali's Canadian Legacy," by Bill Beacon, The Canadian Press, June 4, 2016

(3) "Patterson, Chuvalo Set for Encore?," by Nat Fleischer, THE RING, April 1965, p. 7

(4) "Chuvalo: A Fighter's Life," by George Chuvalo and Murray Greig, HarperCollins Publishers Ltd., 2013, p. 178

(5) "Chuvalo, Losing to Clay, Finds Name of the Game Still is Boxing," by Nat Fleischer, THE RING, June 1966, p. 8-10.

(6) "Chuvalo: A Fighter's Life," by George Chuvalo and Murray Greig, HarperCollins Publishers Ltd., 2013, p. b178

Henry Cooper II

(1) "Muhammad Ali: His Life and Times," by Thomas Hauser, Simon and Schuster Paperbacks, 1991, p. 143

Brian London

(1) "Facing Ali: The Opposition Weighs In," by Stephen Brunt, The Lyons Press, 2002, p. 69-71

(2) Ibid, p. 70

(3) Ibid, p. 74

(4) https://www.youtube.com/watch?v=K7SRR7R322k&spfreload=10

(5) Ibid

(6) "Facing Ali: The Opposition Weighs In," by Stephen Brunt, The Lyons Press, 2002, p. 77

(7) "On This Day: Muhammad Ali Annihilated Brian London," by Thomas Georgiou, www.boxingnewsonline.net, August 6, 2016

(8) "Clay-London Hoax Proves Flop from Every Angle," by Nat Fleischer, THE RING, October, 1966, p.7

(9) "On This Day: Muhammad Ali Annihilated Brian London," by Thomas Georgiou, www.boxingnewsonline.net, August 6, 2016

Karl Mildenberger

(1) "Muhammad Ali: His Life and Times," by Thomas Hauser, Simon and Schuster Paperbacks, 1991, p. 154

(2) "A Muslim Ministers to a Southpaw," by Martin Kane, Sports Illustrated, September 19, 1966

(3) "Mildenberger Outpoints Machen; Accavallo Wins," by Jack A. Tree, THE RING, May 1966, p. 21

(4) "Mildenberger Ideal Athlete, Clean Fighter, Model Hubby, First Southpaw Challenger," by Jack A. Tree, THE RING, October 1966, p. 45

(5) "Clay Stops Mildenberger in 12th," Associated Press, published in the Sarasota Herald-Tribune, September 11, 1966, p. 1D

(6) "Fight of the Year," by Nat Loubet, THE RING, March 1967, p. 9

(7) "Clay Stops Mildenberger in 12th," Associated Press, published in the Sarasota Herald-Tribune, September 11, 1966, p. 6D

Cleveland Williams

(1) "Still the Biggest Passing Day," by Judy Battista, New York Times, September 27, 2011

(2) "Was This Muhammad Ali at His Greatest?," by Matt Christie, Boxingnewsonline.com, November 14, 2016

(3) "Where Do Our Heavies Stand Now?" by Dan Daniel, THE RING, February 1965, p. 6

(4) "Army? Terrell? Where is Clay Headed," by Dan Daniel, THE RING, March 1966, p. 8

(5) "Where Do Our Heavies Stand Now?" by Dan Daniel, THE RING, February 1965, p. 6

(6) "Great KOs," by Jimmy Jacobs, THE RING, October 1980, p. 90

(7) "Clay Showed Sock as Well as Science," by Nat Fleischer, THE RING, February 1967, p. 38

(8) Ibid, p. 38

(9) Ibid, p. 38

(10) "Dempsey's Startling New Opinion of Cassius: Clay's Early KO over Cat Prompts Jack to Shift Tack," by Al Buck, THE RING, February 1967, p. 38

(11) "Clay Showed Sock as Well as Science," by Nat Fleischer, THE RING, February 1967, p. 38

(12) "Tracking the Cat," by Mark Seal, Scene Magazine, a supplement of the Dallas Morning News, reprinted in the January 1980 issue of THE RING, p. 50

(13) "No Fighter of the Year: Clay's Fine 1966 Record Discounted by Refusal to Accept Army Draft," by Dan Daniel, THE RING, March 1967, p. 6, 58

(14) "Ring Readers Back Bypass of Clay for 1966 Citation," by Dan Daniel, THE RING, April 1967, p. 28

(15) "Louis Clobber Me? He Must Be Joking – Clay," by Nat Fleischer, THE RING, May 1967, p. 34

(16) "Belated Justice," by Michael Rosenthal, THE RING, March 2017, p. 54

Ernie Terrell
(1) "Muhammad Ali: His Life and Times," by Thomas Hauser, Simon and Schuster Paperbacks, 1991, p. 162

(2) "Nat Fleischer Speaks Out," by Nat Fleischer, THE RING, June 1964, p. 5; "Eleven Days in March" by Dan Daniel, THE RING, June 1964, p. 21

(3) The New York Times, August 30, 1964; "Nat Fleischer Speaks Out," by Nat Fleischer, THE RING, December 1964, p. 5

(4) "Nat Fleischer Speaks Out," by Nat Fleischer, THE RING, December 1965, p. 5

(5) "New York Decries Barring of Terrell," by Dan Daniel, THE RING, April 1966, p. 7-8

(6) "Terrell's Fortunes Took Upswing With Okay from FBI to Box Jones in Texas," by Dan Daniel, THE RING, July 1966, p. 8

(7) "Clay-Johnson Parallels Warn Cassius Beware," by Al Buck, THE RING, June 1966, p. 38

(8) "Black Muslims in No Hurry to Let Clay Fight Terrell," by Dan Daniel, THE RING, September 1966, p. 6

(9) Ibid., p. 38; "Nat Fleischer Speaks Out," by Nat Fleischer, THE RING, June 1966, p. 5

(10) "Muhammad Ali: His Life and Times," by Thomas Hauser, Simon and Schuster Paperbacks, 1991, p. 163

(11) "Few Able Challengers Left for Muhammad Ali," The Associated Press, published in the St. Joseph (Mo.) News-Press, February 7, 1967, p. 2B

(12) Ibid

Zora Folley

(1) " 'Phantom' Chop Stops Folley," by Robert Lipsyte, New York Times, published in the Nashua (N.H.) Telegraph, March 23, 1967, p. 12

(2) "World Ratings," by Nat Fleischer, THE RING, May 1967, p. 16

(3) " 'Phantom' Chop Stops Folley," by Robert Lipsyte, New York Times, published in the Nashua (N.H.) Telegraph, March 23, 1967, p. 12

(4) "Nat Fleischer Speaks Out," by Nat Fleischer, THE RING, June 1967, p. 5

(5) "Clay Knocks Out Folley in Seventh," Associated Press, published in Spartanburg Herald, March 23, 1967, p. 33

(6) Ibid

(7) Boxrec Encyclopedia

(8) "Clay Situation Unchanged, Quarry Stirs Up Heavies," by Dan Daniel, THE RING, June 1969, p. 10

(9) "As I See It," by Nat Loubet, THE RING, January 1977, p. 5

(10) "THE RING Withdraws Recognition of Clay as Heavy King," by Dan Daniel, THE RING, May-June 1970, p. 8

(11) "Frazier Is Now Undisputed Champion," by Nat Fleischer, THE RING, May-June 1970, p. 36

(12) "Ring Camera Clicks," THE RING, March 1970, p. 35; "Muhammad Ali's Broadway Debut Wowed a Lifelong Fan," by Joe Dziemianowicz, www.nydailynews.com, June 6, 2016

(13) "Muhammad Ali: His Life and Times," by Thomas Hauser, Simon and Schuster Paperbacks, 1991, p. 197

(14) Ibid, p. 208-09

(15) "Clay Wins Court Fight," The Associated Press, published in the Tuscaloosa News, September 15, 1970, p. 7

(16) "Muhammad Ali: His Life and Times," by Thomas Hauser, Simon and Schuster Paperbacks, 1991, p. 209

Jerry Quarry I

(1) "Here Comes Foreman: Contest Against Quarry Would Be a Natural," by Dan Daniel, THE RING, November 1970, p. 36

(2) "Muhammad Ali: His Life and Times," by Thomas Hauser, Simon and Schuster Paperbacks, 1991, p. 211

(3) "Ali Finishes Quarry in 3; Stage Set for Frazier Fight," by Ed Schuyler Jr., Associated Press, published in the Owosso (Mich.) Argus-Press, October 27, 1970, p. 14

(4) "Clay Guilty in Draft Case; Gets Five Years in Prison," by Martin Waldron, The New York Times, June 20, 1967, p. 1A

(5) "Now It's Frazier vs. Clay: Atlanta's Nine Minutes Set Up Precedent Which Boxing is Not Eager to See Repeated," by Nat Loubet, THE RING, January 1971, p. 10

(6) "Ali Finishes Quarry in 3; Stage Set for Frazier Fight," by Ed Schuyler Jr., Associated Press, published in the Owosso (Mich.) Argus-Press, October 27, 1970, p. 14

(7) https://www.youtube.com/watch?v=r10xqe2GEu8&spfreload=10

(8) "Ali Finishes Quarry in 3; Stage Set for Frazier Fight," by Ed Schuyler Jr., Associated Press, published in the Owosso (Mich.) Argus-Press, October 27, 1970, p. 14

Oscar Bonavena

(1) "Pan Am Games Legacy 1959: It's Not Exactly Peace and Harmony," by Earl Gustkey, Los Angeles Times, August 6, 1987

(2) "Bonavena Carries Power, Strength Through 7 Wins," by Dan Daniel, THE RING, February 1965, p. 22

(3) Ibid, p. 22

(4) "Three Knockdowns Give Ali Win," by The Associated Press, published in the Observer-Reporter (Washington, Pa.), December 8, 1970, p. B-8

(5) https://www.youtube.com/watch?v=WIV7jx_3S_0&spfreload=10

(6) "Clay Takes 15 Rounds," by The Associated Press, published in the Florence Times-Tri Cities Daily, p. 9

(7) "Nat Fleischer Speaks Out," by Nat Fleischer, THE RING, April 1971, p. 5

(8) "Clay Takes 15 Rounds," by The Associated Press, published in the Florence Times-Tri Cities Daily, p. 10

(9) https://www.youtube.com/watch?v=WIV7jx_3S_0&spfreload=10

(10) "Clay Takes 15 Rounds," by The Associated Press, published in the Florence Times-Tri Cities Daily, p. 10

Joe Frazier I
(1) "Frazier 'Disgrace' Says Clay, After Outbrawling Oscar," by Archie Pirolli, THE RING, March 1969, p. 24-25

(2) "Charles, Patterson Too Quiet; Liston Too Involved; Then Came Brash Mr. Clay," by Ted Carroll, THE RING, February 1970, p. 21

(3) "The Chatter Box," by John Ort, THE RING, January 1970, p. 36

(4) "Loser and Still Champion," by Budd Schulberg, Doubleday, 1972, p. 162

(5) "The Battle of the Undefeated Giants," by Thomas Thompson, LIFE, March 5, 1971, p. 47-48

(6) "Nat Fleischer Speaks Out," by Nat Fleischer, THE RING, May 1971, p. 5

(7) "Frazier Outpoints Ali and Keeps Title," by Dave Anderson, New York Times, March 9, 1971, p. 1A

(8) "The Biggest Fight Of 'Em All: Celebrities Galore, Funkiest of Fashions, 'Twas Truly a Night to Remember," THE RING, June 1971, p. 18-21

(9) "Some Staff Predictions on the Big Fight," by Ralph Graves, LIFE, March 5, 1971, p. 3

(10) "Up and Down Old Broadway," by Sam Taub, THE RING, June 1971, p. 35

(11) "Frazier Says Blows to Body Won," by Deane McGowen, New York Times, March 9, 1971, p. 29

(12) "Clay Legend is Dead," By George Girsch, THE RING, June 1971, p. 38

(13) Ibid, THE RING, June 1971, p. 13

(14) "Frazier Says Blows to Body Won," by Deane McGowen, New York Times, March 9, 1971, p. 29

(15) "Frazier Outpoints Ali and Keeps Title," by Dave Anderson, New York Times, March 9, 1971, p. 1A

(16) Ibid, p. 1A

(17) Ibid, p. 29

Ali's Odyssey: The Long Road Back

(1) World Ratings, THE RING, May 1971, p. 18

(2) Associated Press archives,
https://www.youtube.com/watch?v=pKrdzTz1ON0&spfreload=10

(3) "Muhammad Ali Wins Supreme Court Decision, Overturning His Conviction for Draft Evasion," by Phil Pepe, New York Daily News; reposted June 3, 2016 on www.nydailynews.com

(4) "Muhammad Ali: His Life and Times," by Thomas Hauser, Simon and Schuster Paperbacks, 1991, p. 238-39

(5) "Muhammad Ali Wins Supreme Court Decision, Overturning His Conviction for Draft Evasion," by Phil Pepe, New York Daily News; reposted June 3, 2016 on www.nydailynews.com

Jimmy Ellis

(6) Ibid, p. 240

(7) Boxrec.com Encyclopedia

(8) "Muhammad Ali Unleashes Power to KO Elllis in 12," The Associated Press, published in The Spokesman Review, July 27, 1971, p. 16

Juergen Blin

(9) "Facing Ali: The Opposition Weighs In," by Stephen Brunt, The Lyons Press, 2002, p. 133

(10) Ibid, p. 133

(11) Ibid, p. 132

(12) Ibid, p. 136

Mac Foster

(13) "Muhammad Ali Unanimous Winner in Japanese Fight," by Leslie Nakashima, United Press International Asia Sports Editor, published in the The (Lexington, N.C.) Dispatch, April 1, 1972, p. 11

(14) "Progress Award," by John Ort, THE RING, March 1970, p. 12

(15) "Muhammad Ali Unanimous Winner in Japanese Fight," by Leslie Nakashima, United Press International Asia Sports Editor, published in the The (Lexington, N.C.) Dispatch, April 1, 1972, p. 11

George Chuvalo II

(16) "Chuvalo: A Fighter's Life," by George Chuvalo and Murray Greig, HarperCollins Publishers Ltd., 2013, p. 259

(17) Boxrec Encyclopedia

(18) "Chuvalo: A Fighter's Life," by George Chuvalo and Murray Greig, HarperCollins Publishers Ltd., 2013, p. 262

Jerry Quarry II
(19) "Ali, Foster Get Wins Over Jerry and Mike Quarry," Natchez News Leader, July 2, 1972, Page 1-B

(20) Ibid

Al "Blue Lewis"
(21) "It Takes a Determined Referee to Cool Ali's Ring Behavior," by Lew Eskin, Boxing Illustrated, March 1975, p. 39

(22) Ibid, p. 39

Floyd Patterson II
(23) Boxrec Encyclopedia

Bob Foster
(24) "Ali KO Master of Foster; Frazier and Foreman Now May Run Into Legal Snags," by Dan Daniel, THE RING, February 1973, p. 9.

Joe Bugner I
(25) "Muhammad Ali: His Life and Times," by Thomas Hauser, Simon and Schuster Paperbacks, 1991, p. 481

(26) "Joe Bugner: My Story," by Joe Bugner with Stuart Mullins, New Holland Publishers, 2013, p. 84

Ken Norton I
(27) "In The Corner," by Dave Anderson, William Morrow and Company, Inc., 1991, p. 234

(28) Ibid, p. 235

(29) "Muhammad Ali: His Life and Times," by Thomas Hauser, Simon and Schuster Paperbacks, 1991, p. 251

(30) "Jaw Buster Norton's Side Opposes Delay If Foreman is Ready to Defend His Title," by John Greensmith, THE RING, July 1973, p. 60

(31) "Norton Whips Ali...But What Really Happened?," International Boxing, August 1973, p. 36

(32) "Jaw Buster Norton's Side Opposes Delay If Foreman is Ready to Defend His Title," by John Greensmith, THE RING, July 1973, p. 60

(33) Ibid, p. 60

(34) Ibid, p. 60

(35) Ibid, p. 6

(36) Ibid, p. 60

(37) "World Ratings," by Nat Loubet, THE RING, July 1973, p. 20

(38) "Putting Heavy Jigsaw Puzzle Pieces Together Problem for Promoters," by Nat Loubet, THE RING, June 1973, p. 8

Ken Norton II
(39) "Going the Distance," by Ken Norton with Marshall Terrill and Mike Fitzgerald, Sports Publishing Inc., 2000, p. 71

(40) Ibid, p. 71

(41) "Norton Confident, Sees Ali Tough," by Ken Norton, THE RING, September 1973, p. 35

(42) "Ali Predicts He'll Triumph in 12 or Less," by Muhammad Ali, THE RING, September 1973, p. 7, 36

(43) "Norton Best Foe," The Associated Press, published in The Evening News (Newburgh, N.Y.), September 11, 1973, Page 5B

Rudi Lubbers
(44) "A Retrospective Look at Muhammad Ali: The 'Once and Future Champion' in Words and Pictures," by Dave Anderson, THE RING, October 1979, p. 30.

(45) "Ali Whips Lubbers for 12, Reserving Right for Joe," by Frank Hastings, THE RING, January 1974, p. 8-9

Joe Frazier II
(46) "Muhammad Ali: His Life and Times," by Thomas Hauser, Simon and Schuster Paperbacks, 1991, p. 254-55

(47) "Court Orders May Stop Foreman From Defending Title in This Country," by Dan Daniel, THE RING, January 1974, p. 6

(48) "In The Corner," by Dave Anderson, William Morrow and Company, Inc., 1991, p. 242

(49) "Ali A Phoney With Punch and Tongue, Says Frazier," by Joe Frazier, THE RING, February 1974, p. 9

(50) "Ali Says His Condition is Amazing, Victory Sure," by Muhammad Ali, THE RING, February 1974, p. 32

(51) "Ali's Hand Treatments Stir a Mystery in Camp," by Gerald Eskenazi, New York Times, January 20, 1974, Section 5, p. 1

(52) Ibid

(53) "World Ratings," by Nat Loubet, THE RING, February 1974, p. 20

(54) "Ali Beats Frazier on Decision Here," by Dave Anderson, New York Times, January 29, 1974

(55) "Court Orders May Stop Foreman From Defending Title in This Country," by Dan Daniel, THE RING, January 1974, p. 7

(56) "In The Corner," by Dave Anderson, William Morrow and Company, Inc., 1991, p. 243

George Foreman
(1) "Muhammad Ali: His Life and Times," by Thomas Hauser, Simon and Schuster Paperbacks, 1991, p. 263-64

(2) Ibid, p. 264

(3) "Muhammad Ali: His Life and Times," by Thomas Hauser, Simon and Schuster Paperbacks, 1991, p. 260

(4) Ibid, p. 260

(5) "By George: The Autobiography of George Foreman," by George Foreman and Joel Engel, Villard Books, 1995, p. 98-99

(6) Ibid, p. 101

(7) "Muhammad Ali: His Life and Times," by Thomas Hauser, Simon and Schuster Paperbacks, 1991, p. 266

(8) "Revisiting 'The Rumble in the Jungle,' " by Josh Peter, USA Today, October 29, 2014, published on the Louisville Courier-Journal website

(9) "Muhammad Ali: His Life and Times," by Thomas Hauser, Simon and Schuster Paperbacks, 1991, p. 264

(10) "No Ali-Foreman Bout Until Late-October," by Thomas A. Johnson, New York Times, September 18, 1974

(11) "Muhammad Ali: His Life and Times," by Thomas Hauser, Simon and Schuster Paperbacks, 1991, p. 273

(12) "Ali Outfought, Outlasted and Outwitted Foreman in a Classic Upset," by Nat Loubet, THE RING, January 1975, p. 6

(13) Ibid, p. 8

(14) "Shadow Box," by George Plimpton, Berkeley Publishing Corporation, 1971, p. 303 (paperback version)

(15) "Muhammad Ali: His Life and Times," by Thomas Hauser, Simon and Schuster Paperbacks, 1991, p. 277

(16) "Greatest Fights Ever: The Rumble in the Jungle," NBC, aired in April 1990

(17) Ibid

(18) "Muhammad Ali: His Life and Times," by Thomas Hauser, Simon and Schuster Paperbacks, 1991, p. 277

(19) "Greatest Fights Ever: The Rumble in the Jungle," NBC, aired in April 1990

(20) "Facing Ali: The Opposition Weighs In," by Stephen Brunt, The Lyons Press, 2002, p. 188-89

Chuck Wepner
(1) Ali's Slashing Fists Couldn't Reach Wepner's Fighting Heart!," International Boxing, August 1975, p. 36

(2) Ibid, p. 36

(3) "The Chuck Wepner Miracle: Wepner's Story of Fight to Get Chance at Title One of Boxing's Wild Dramas," by Dan Daniel, THE RING, April 1975, p. 50

(4) "Ali Title, City's Pride on Line," By Al Abrams, Pittsburgh Post-Gazette, March 24, 1975, p. 16

(5) "Chuck Wepner Calls the Day He Lost to Muhammad Ali the Greatest of His Life," by Sam Gardner, Foxsports.com, June 4, 2016

(6) "Ali's Slashing Fists Couldn't Reach Wepner's Fighting Heart!," International Boxing, August 1975, p. 35

(7) "Chuck Wepner Calls the Day He Lost to Muhammad Ali the Greatest of His Life," by Sam Gardner, Foxsports.com, June 4, 2016

(8) Ibid

(9) Ibid

(10) "Winner's Fall in 9th Ruled Knockdown," by Dave Anderson, New York Times, March 25, 1975

(11) "Muhammad Ali: His Life and Times," by Thomas Hauser, Simon and Schuster Paperbacks, 1991, p. 299-300

(12) "Editorial: Shooting Fish in a Barrel," International Boxing, August 1975, p. 39

(13) "Chuck Wepner Movie Starring Liev Schreiber Sparks Interest in Boxer," by Neil Best, Newsday.com, May 6, 2017

Ron Lyle
(1) "Ali Finds Out Nobody Laughs at an Unfunny Clown," by Randy Gordon, International Boxing, October 1975, p. 35

(2) "Lyle, Imprisoned for 7 1/2 Years, Is Not Bitter as Ring Heights Beckon Him," by Mike Hayes, THE RING, February 1973, p. 17

(3) Ibid, p. 18

(4) "Ali Finds Out Nobody Laughs at an Unfunny Clown," by Randy Gordon, International Boxing, October 1975, p. 34-35

(5) Ibid, p. 37

(6) "Ali Knocks Out Lyle in 11, Rope-a-Dope No, Mirage," by Nat Loubet, THE RING, August 1975, p. 9

(7) "Ali Finds Out Nobody Laughs at an Unfunny Clown," by Randy Gordon, International Boxing, October 1975, p. 37

Joe Bugner II

(1) Boxrec Encyclopedia

(2) "Ali-Bugner Battle No. 2," by Nat Loubet, THE RING, September 1975, p. 6

(3) "Press and Fans Criticize Bugner for Kuala Fight, Mrs. Joe Talks Emigration," by Ron Olver, THE RING, October 1975, p. 68-69

Joe Frazier III

(1) "Muhammad Ali: His Life and Times," by Thomas Hauser, Simon and Schuster Paperbacks, 1991, p. 313

(2) Ibid, p. 314

(3) "Superfight III: How Ali and Frazier Stack Up in 20 Different Categories," Big Book of Boxing, November 1975, p. 25-26

(4) "Muhammad Ali: His Life and Times," by Thomas Hauser, Simon and Schuster Paperbacks, 1991, p. 321

(5) "Ali's Victory Over Frazier in 1, One of All Time Greats," by Nat Loubet, THE RING, December 1975, p. 35

(6) "Muhammad Ali: His Life and Times," by Thomas Hauser, Simon and Schuster Paperbacks, 1991, p. 324

(7) "A Chastened, Sore Ali Praises His Rival," Associated Press, published in the New York Times, October 1, 1975

(8) "Fight of the Year," by George Girsch," THE RING, March 1975, p. 10

(9) "Special Section: The 100 Greatest Title Fight of All-Time," by Steve Farhood, THE RING, Holiday 1996, p. 28

(10) "Muhammad Ali: Fighter of the Year," by Dan Daniel, THE RING, March 1975, p. 8

(11) "Joe Frazier Statue to be Unveiled in Philadelphia," BoxingScene.com, September 1, 2015

Past-Prime Ali Bridge

(1) "Readers Writes," Boxing Illustrated, October 1977, p. 64

(2) "Joe Bugner: My Story," by Joe Bugner with Stuart Mullins, New Holland Publishers, 2013, p. 90

Jean-Pierre Coopman

(1) "Muhammad Ali: His Life and Times," by Thomas Hauser, Simon and Schuster Paperbacks, 1991, p. 329-30

(2) Ibid, p. 331

(3) Ibid, p. 331

(4) "Ali and the Pussy Cat," by Mario Rivera Martino, THE RING, May 1976, p. 6

(5) Nat Fleischer's RING Record Book and Boxing Encyclopedia, 1979 edition, THE RING Book Shop, p. 119

(6) "One-Nighter in San Juan," by Mark Kram, Sports Illustrated, March 1, 1976

(7) Facing Ali: The Opposition Weighs In," by Stephen Brunt, The Lyons Press, 2002, p. 256

(8) Ibid, p. 257

(9) Ibid, p. 257

Jimmy Young

(1) "Muhammad Ali: His Life and Times," by Thomas Hauser, Simon and Schuster Paperbacks, 1991, p. 336

(2) Ibid, p. 337-38

(3) "Norton vs. Young: The Heavyweight Showdown," by Greg Nolan, Boxing Illustrated, October 1977, p. 19

(4) Ibid, p. 19

(5)https://www.youtube.com/watch?v=oYF5UNSn7yw&spfreload=10

(6) "Muhammad Ali vs. Jimmy Young; Covered from Ringside," by Nat Loubet, THE RING, July 1976, p. 6

(7) "Clay's Sparring Jousts Enthrall Virginia Fans," by Jack Levinson, THE RING, May 1972, p. 58

(8) Boxrec Encyclopedia

(9) "Young 'Ducks' Away From Title," United Press International, published in the Deseret News, May 1, 1976, p. 6A

(10) "Young Thinks He Won Bout," United Press International, published in the Leader-Post, May 1, 1976, p. 37

(11) "Ali Retains Title with Left Jab," Associated Press, published in the Leader-Post, May 1, 1976, p. 37

(12) "Young Thinks He Won Bout," United Press International, published in the Leader-Post, May 1, 1976, p. 37

(13) "Our Exclusive Investigation Reveals Muhammad Ali Lost to Jimmy Young," by Peter King, World Boxing, September 1976, p. 36

(14) "Muhammad Ali vs. Jimmy Young; Covered from Ringside," by Nat Loubet, July 1976, p. 7

(15) "Young 'Ducks' Away From Title," United Press International, published in the Deseret News, May 1, 1976, p. 6A

(16) Ibid

(17) Ibid

Richard Dunn
(1) "Ali Blitz Flattens Dunn Five Times for KO in 5th," by Jack A. Tree, THE RING, August 1976, p. 12

(2) "For Fighting Muhammad Ali I Got 52,000 Pounds, Says Richard Dunn But David Haye Will Get Millions Against Useless Lumps – and Good Luck to Him," by Patrick Collins, The Daily Mail Online, November 16, 2009

Ken Norton III
(1) "Norton vs. Young: The Heavyweight Showdown," by Greg Nolan, Boxing Illustrated, October 1977, p. 18-19

(2) Ibid, p. 19

(3) Ibid, p. 19

(4) Nat Fleischer's RING Record Book and Boxing Encyclopedia, 1979 edition, THE RING Book Shop, p. 119

(5) "Welcome to the Big Time," by Earnie Shavers with Mike Fitzgerald and Marshall Terrill, Sports Publishing LLC, 2002, p. 111-12

(6) "Ali-Norton III Remembered Through Schuyler's Eyes," by Lee Groves, BoxingScene.com, June 5, 2010

(7) "Boxing Returns to Yankee Stadium," Associated Press, June 2, 2010

(8) "Ali-Norton III Remembered Through Schuyler's Eyes," by Lee Groves, BoxingScene.com, June 5, 2010

(9) "Ken Norton's Own Story: My Secret Weapon Will Destroy Ali," by Ken Norton, International Boxing, April 1978, p. 36

(10) "Judges' 'Rally' Decisive," by Dick Young, published in The St. Petersburg Independent, September 30, 1976, p. 4-C

(11) "Ali-Norton III Remembered Through Schuyler's Eyes," by Lee Groves, BoxingScene.com, June 5, 2010

(12) "Roundup of 1976: Once Again Ali Dominates Boxing Interest Through Action, Inaction and Controversy," by Nat Loubet, THE RING, March 1977, p. 16

(13) "Muhammad Ali: His Life and Times," by Thomas Hauser, Simon and Schuster Paperbacks, 1991, p. 340

(14) "Ali-Norton III Remembered Through Schuyler's Eyes," by Lee Groves, BoxingScene.com, June 5, 2010

Alfredo Evangelista
(1) "As I See It," by Nat Loubet, THE RING, January 1977, p. 5

(2) "Muhammad Ali: His Life and Times," by Thomas Hauser, Simon and Schuster Paperbacks, 1991, p. 342

(3) "Ali 'Punches Enough' to Defeat Evangelista," by Ed Schuyler Jr., published in the Schenectady Gazette, May 17, 1977, p. 28

(4) "As I See It," by Nat Loubet, THE RING, July 1977, p. 5

(5) Nat Fleischer's RING Record Book and Boxing Encyclopedia, 1979 edition, THE RING Book Shop, p. 119

(6) "Ali (Ho-Hum) Beats Evangelista in 15," United Press International, published in Nashua Telegraph, May 17, 1977, p. 20

(7) Ibid

(8) Ibid

Earnie Shavers

(1) "Welcome to the Big Time," by Earnie Shavers with Mike Fitzgerald and Marshall Terrill, Sports Publishing LLC, 2002, p. 125

(2) Ibid, p. 119

(3) Ibid, p. 120

(4) Ibid, p. 120

(5) Ibid, p. 125

(6) "Once More to the Well," by Pat Putnam, Sports Illustrated, October 10, 1977

(7) Ibid

(8) "Ali Decision Winner Over Shavers," combination of Associated Press and United Press International reports, St. Petersburg Times, September 30, 1977, Page 1C

(9) "Ali Beats Shavers on Decision," by Dave Anderson, New York Times, September 30, 1977, p. 1

Leon Spinks I

(1) "Muhammad Ali: His Life and Times," by Thomas Hauser, Simon and Schuster Paperbacks, 1991, p. 348-49

(2) "Ken Norton: Champion on a Cardboard Throne," by Gary Morgenstein, International Boxing, August 1978, p. 32

(3) Ibid, p. 351

(4) "He's the Greatest, I'm the Best," by Pat Putnam, Sports Illustrated, February 27, 1978

Leon Spinks II

(1) "Ken Norton: Champion on a Cardboard Throne," by Gary Morgenstein, International Boxing, August 1978, p. 33

(2) "Spinks-Ali Return Likely, Norton 'Insulted' by Offer," by Michael Katz, New York Times, March 1, 1978

(3) "Ali-Spinks Rematch Sails to a New Port," by Michael Katz, The New York Times, March 10, 1978

(4) "Muhammad Ali: His Life and Times," by Thomas Hauser, Simon and Schuster Paperbacks, 1991, p. 356

(5) "Ali Champ Third Time, Rossman Stops Galindez, In Carnival of Champions," by Nat Loubet, THE RING, December 1978, p. 8

(6) "Spinks Free on Bond in Drug Case," United Press International, April 22, 1978

(7) Sports News Briefs, New York Times, June 23, 1978

(8) "The Experts Predict: The Ring Staff and Others Who Should Know Make Their Predictions," THE RING, September 1978, p. 11

(9) "At Ringside," by Robert J. Thornton, International Boxing, February 1979, p. 10

(10) "I've Solved the 'Spinks Riddle,' " by Muhammad Ali, THE RING, September 1978, p. 6

(11) "At Ringside," by Robert J. Thornton, International Boxing, February 1979, p. 6; "The Master," by Tom Junod, Sports Illustrated, November 2, 1992

(12) "Muhammad Ali: His Life and Times," by Thomas Hauser, Simon and Schuster Paperbacks, 1991, p. 359

Larry Holmes
(1) "Ali to Retire Once Again," by United Press International, June 27, 1979

(2) "Reluctant Ali Was Paid $300,000 to Announce His Retirement," by The Associated Press, July 16, 1979

(3) "Ali's Return Set for June," Big Book of Boxing, July 1980, p. 29

(4) Ibid, p. 60

(5) "Ali Update," KO Magazine, October 1980, p. 21

(6) "What's Next for Holmes," by Bert Randolph Sugar, THE RING, December 1979, p. 15

(7) "Logic Favors Holmes, History on Ali's Side," by Joe Carnicelli, United Press International, Nov. 27-28, 1980

(8) "Ali's Fight in Brazil Called Off," by Joe Carnicelli, United Press International, published in the Ottawa Journal, May 13, 1980, p. 17

(9) "Ali-Holmes Bout Set for Caesars Palace," Associated Press, published in the Ocala Star Banner, July 18, 1980, p. 2C

(10) ""Logic Favors Holmes, History on Ali's Side," by Joe Carnicelli, United Press International, Nov. 27-28, 1980

(11) "Ali-Holmes Pick 'Em: The Experts Try Their Hand at Selecting a Winner, THE RING, October 1980, p. 28-29

(12) "At Ringside," by Robert J. Thornton, International Boxing, February 1981, p. 8

(13) "Logic Favors Holmes, History on Ali's Side," by Joe Carnicelli, United Press International, Nov. 27-28, 1980

(14) Fight story by Milton Richman, United Press International, October 2, 1980 (wire copy provided by Joe Carnicelli)

(15) "Larry Holmes: Against the Odds," by Larry Holmes with Phil Berger, St. Martins Press, 1998, p. 166

(16) Fight story by Milton Richman, United Press International, October 2, 1980 (wire copy provided by Joe Carnicelli)

(17) "Amen," by Steve Farhood, KO magazine, February 1981, p. 57

(18) "Holmes-Ali: 'The Last Hurrah,' The Night 'The Greatest' Was Anything But," by Bert Randolph Sugar, THE RING, December 1980, p. 21

(19) Fight story by Joe Carnicelli, United Press International Executive Sports Editor, October 2, 1980

(20) Fight story by Milton Richman, United Press International, October 2, 1980 (wire copy provided by Joe Carnicelli)

Trevor Berbick
(1) "Not With a Bang, But a Whisper," by William Nack, Sports Illustrated, December 21, 1981

(2) "Berbick Defeats Ali on Decision," by George Vescey, New York Times, December 12, 1981

(3) "Ali Wants Weaver Title Bout," Associated Press, published in the Wilmington Morning Star, December 9, 1981, p. 1D

(4) "Muhammad Ali: His Life and Times," by Thomas Hauser, Simon and Schuster Paperbacks, 1991, p. 429

(5) "Berbick Defeats Ali on Decision," by George Vescey, New York Times, December 12, 1981

(6) Ibid

(7) "Berbick Pounds Out Decision Over Ali," by Michael Farber, Montreal Gazette, December 11, 1981, p. 15

(8) "Not With a Bang, But a Whisper," by William Nack, Sports Illustrated, December 21, 1981

(9) "Ali Wants Weaver Title Bout," Associated Press, published in the Wilmington Morning Star, December 9, 1981, p. 1D

(10) "Muhammad Ali: His Life and Times," by Thomas Hauser, Simon and Schuster Paperbacks, 1991, p. 430

(11) "The Curtain Closes on a Great Act: Ali's Traumas in the Bahamas," by Dave Anderson, THE RING, February 1982, p. 37

27460196R00204

Printed in Poland
by Amazon Fulfillment
Poland Sp. z o.o., Wrocław